A HANDBOOK OF

JAPANESE USAGE

A HANDBOOK OF JAPANESE USAGE

Francis G. Drohan

CHARLES E. TUTTLE COMPANY
Rutland, Vermont & Tokyo, Japan

Published by Charles E. Tuttle Company, Inc.
of Rutland, Vermont & Tokyo, Japan
with editorial offices
at 2-6 Suido 1-chome, Bunkyo-ku, Tokyo 112

Library of Congress Catalog Card No. 91-077203
International Standard Book No. 0-8048-1610-7

First edition, 1992
Second printing, 1993

Printed in Japan

CONTENTS

INTRODUCTION

The usual two-year Japanese course does not take the student beyond the basics. From that level to the point where one has a good command of the language, there is a wide gap that up to now has not been covered by a suitable study aid. This handbook sets out to fill that gap.

In European languages, the chief stumbling block for beginners is morphology—the changes in word endings for number, person, gender, and even case. Morphology is not a problem in Japanese, but everyone who has studied the language knows the difficulty of mastering those words that perform a role within a sentence rather than express meaning. Called "function words," they are the greatest hurdle to proficiency in Japanese. This book is a guide to these function words, as well as to other words and expressions not fully explained in regular dictionaries.

In the following pages, a variety of charts present the essentials of Japanese grammar. Chart 1 shows the whole scheme of Japanese grammar, with its ten parts of speech. Charts 2 and 3 reveal how all the words commonly classified as personal and demonstrative pronouns, adjectival nouns and adverbs, coalesce into a rational *ko-sa-a-do* system. Charts 4 through 8 give the conjugations of the three regular verb forms; Chart 9 conjugates the verbs *kuru* and *suru;* Chart 10 conjugates adjectives and adjectival nouns; Charts 11 and 12 conjugate auxiliary verbs, a separate part of speech in Japanese.

In the main body of this handbook, entries are arranged in alphabetical order, with examples in *romaji* as well as in Japanese script. All the examples were culled from purely Japanese sources; in many cases the translation given is not the most evident one, but the one that best matches the original. For the *romaji,* the Hepburn system of romanization is used.

At the back of the handbook is a series of appendixes dealing with *kanji, kana,* numbers and counters, punctuation marks, as well as a list of common onomatopoeic expressions and the grammar that governs their use.

I. PARTS OF SPEECH

Following is an explanation of the terms used in the chart.

- 単語 *tango* WORDS are divided into:
- 自立語 *jiritsu-go* INDEPENDENT WORDS and
- 付属語 *fuzoku-go* DEPENDENT WORDS. Independent words are either
- 活用語 *katsuyō-go* CONJUGATED WORDS or
- 無活用語 *mukatsuyō-go* NON-CONJUGATED WORDS. Of the conjugated words,
- 述語となるもの *jutsu-go to naru mono* some become PREDICATES, namely:
- 用言 *yōgen* VERBALS, i. e.,
- 動詞 *dōshi* VERBS,
- 形容詞 *keiyōshi* ADJECTIVES, and
- 形容動詞 *keiyōdōshi* ADJECTIVAL NOUNS.

- 主語となるもの *shugo to naru mono* Some become SUBJECTS, namely:
- 体言 *taigen* NOMINALS, i. e.,
- 名詞 *meishi* NOUNS and
- 代名詞 *daimeishi* PRONOUNS.

- 修飾するもの *shūshoku suru mono* Some are MODIFIERS. Those that modify verbals are
- 副詞 *fukushi* ADVERBS. Those that modify nominals are
- 連体詞 *rentaishi* ADNOUNS. Independent, non-conjugated words are
- 接続詞 *setsuzokushi* CONJUNCTIONS and
- 感動詞 *kandōshi* INTERJECTIONS. Dependent, conjugated words are
- 助動詞 *jodōshi* AUXILIARY VERBS; dependent, non-conjugated words are
- 助詞 *joshi* PARTICLES.

The Japanese count nouns and pronouns as one part of speech, and auxiliary verbs as a distinct part of speech, giving ten in all.

Chart 1. Parts of Speech
品詞体系表

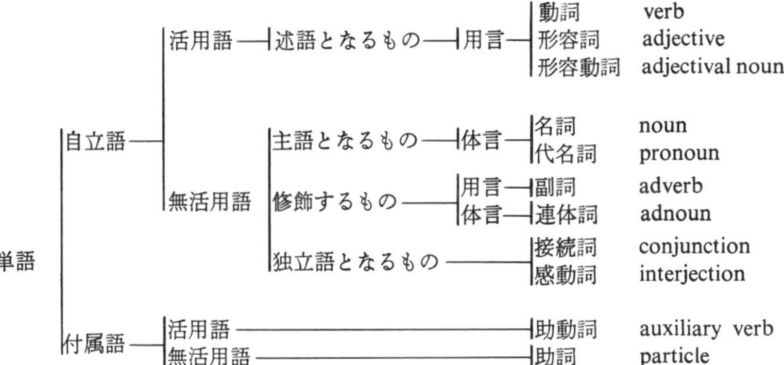

II. THE KO-SO-A-DO SYSTEM

Terms used in the conjugation charts are as follows:

From left, downwards:

自称 (*jishō*), 対称 (*taishō*) and 他称 (*tashō*) correspond with our 1st, 2nd and 3rd persons.

近称 (*kinshō*), 中称 (*chūshō*) and 遠称 (*enshō*) denote the degrees of proximity: proximal, mesial and distal. English has only two such degrees, 'this', 'that', 'here', 'there', etc.

不定称 (*futeishō*), the indeterminate, serves as an interrogative on its own, and an indeterminate when combined with the particles *ka, mo* and *demo*.

Across, left to right on top:

人代名詞 (*jin-daimeishi*) are the personal pronouns.

指示代名詞 (*shiji-daimeishi*) are the demonstratives; they are divided into:

事物 (*jibutsu*), those that denote objects (as an exception, → *kore*[1] 4).

場所 (*basho*), those that denote location. For *koko-ra, soko-ra* etc., → *-ra* 3.

方角 (*hōgaku*), those that denote direction.

To the right, in the *kōgo* frame:

連体詞 (*rentaishi*) are 'adnouns', and express relationship.

形容動詞 (*keiyōdōshi*) are adjectival nouns, treated under the heading *keiyō-dōshi*.

副詞 (*fukushi*) are adverbs, and, as in English, describe circumstances of actions.

Many words in the *bungo* frame have carried over into modern Japanese: *izure ni se yo, kanata konata sagashi-mawaru, ware-nagara,* etc. This is the reason for their inclusion.

Chart 2. The Kōgo ko-so-a-do System

口　語

		人代名詞	指示代名詞			連体詞	形容動詞	副詞
			事物	場所	方角	関係	状態	
自称		おれ　ぼく　わたし　わたくし						
対称		きさま　おまえ　きみ　あなた						
他称	近称	こいつ　このかた	これら　これ	ここら　ここ	こちら　こっち	この	こんな	こう
	中称	そいつ　そのかた	それら　それ	そこら　そこ	そちら　そっち	その	そんな	そう
	遠称	かれ　あいつ　あのかた	あれら　あれ	あそこら　あすこ　あそこ	あちら　あっち	あの	あんな	ああ
不定称		だれ　どいつ　どなた　どのかた	なに　どれ	どこら　どこ	どちら　どっち	どの	どんな	どう

Chart 3. The Bungo ko•so•a•do System

文　語

		人代名詞	指示代名詞		
自称		あ・あれ　わ・われ　おのれ　予　それがし　みづから	事物	場所	方角
対称		な　なれ　なんぢ　そち　そこ　そなた			
他称	近称	こ　これ	こ　これ	ここ	こち　こなた
	中称	そ　それ	そ　それ	そこ	そち　そなた
	遠称	か　かれ　あ　あれ	かれ　あれ	あそこ　あしこ　かしこ	あち　あなた　かなた
不定称		た　たれ　それがし　なにがし	いづ　いづれ	いづこ　いづく　いづら	いづち　いづかた

III. CONJUGATIONS

Terms used in the conjugation charts are as follows:

- 基本形 *kihonkei* the dictionary form (not an infinitive).
- 語幹 *gokan* the stem, or invariable part, of conjugables.
- 未然形 *mizenkei* is followed by such auxiliaries as *-nai* and *-u*.
- 連用形 *ren'yōkei* is followed by such auxiliaries as *-masu* and *-ta*.
- 終止形 *shūshikei* the final form (same as the dictionary form).
- 連体形 *rentaikei* is followed by nominals, and the nominalizer *no*.
- 仮定形 *kateikei* the conditional (is followed by *-ba*).
- 命令形 *meireikei* the imperative (in the *godan* chart, is not necessarily followed by *ro* or *yo*).

Chart 4. Go-dan Conjugation

五段活用表

基本形	書く	貸す	打つ	死ぬ
語幹	書	貸	打	死
未然形	書か＋ない	貸さ＋ない	打た＋ない	死な＋ない
	書こ＋う	貸そ＋う	打と＋う	死の＋う
連用形	書き＋ます	貸し＋ます	打ち＋ます	死に＋ます
	書い＋た	貸し＋た	打っ＋た	死ん＋だ
終止形	書く	貸す	打つ	死ぬ
連体形	書く＋とき	貸す＋とき	打つ＋とき	死ぬ＋とき
仮定形	書け＋ば	貸せ＋ば	打て＋ば	死ね＋ば
命令形	書け	貸せ	打て	死ね
基本形	飛ぶ	飲む	乗る	買う
語幹	飛	飲	乗	買
未然形	飛ば＋ない	飲ま＋ない	乗ら＋ない	買わ＋ない
	飛ぼ＋う	飲も＋う	乗ろ＋う	買お＋う
連用形	飛び＋ます	飲み＋ます	乗り＋ます	買い＋ます
	飛ん＋だ	飲ん＋だ	乗っ＋た	買っ＋た
終止形	飛ぶ	飲む	乗る	買う
連体形	飛ぶ＋とき	飲む＋とき	乗る＋とき	買う＋とき
仮定形	飛べ＋ば	飲め＋ば	乗れ＋ば	買え＋ば
命令形	飛べ	飲め	乗れ	買え

The *go-dan* conjugation is so named because it uses all five vowels; for example, *kakanai, kakimasu, kaku, kakeba,* and *kakō to suru.*

Chart 5. Go-dan Verbs Ending in -iru

Although the following verbs, because they end with *-iru,* appear to be *kami-ichidan* verbs, they are in fact *go-dan* verbs. Thus, the verb *chiru* (be scattered) conjugates as follows: *chiranai, chirō to suru, chirimasu*, and *chitte* (not *chinai*, *chiyo to suru, chimasu,* and *chite*).

1. HIGH-FREQUENCY VERBS					
散る	*chiru*	be scattered	切る	*kiru*	cut
入る	*hairu*	enter	参る	*mairu*	go, come, visit
走る	*hashiru*	run	交じる	*majiru*	mingle
要る	*iru*	be necessary	握る	*nigiru*	grasp
限る	*kagiru*	restrict	知る	*shiru*	get to know
2. LESS COMMON VERBS					
契る	*chigiru*	pledge	捩る	*nejiru*	twist
弄る	*ijiru*	fiddle with	罵る	*nonoshiru*	abuse verbally
入る	*iru*	go in	陥る	*ochi-iru*	fall, sink
かじる	*kajiru*	gnaw	誹る	*soshiru*	slander
みなぎる	*minagiru*	overflow	過る	*yogiru*	pass by, drop in
3. LOW-FREQUENCY VERBS					
脂ぎる	*aburagiru*	be greasy	滅入る	*me-iru*	feel gloomy
愚痴る	*guchiru*	grumble	もぎる	*mogiru*	wrench
簸る	*hiru*	winnow	もじる	*mojiru*	parody, twist
放る	*hiru*	release	詰る	*najiru*	rebuke
穿る	*hojiru*	pick, dig out	にじる	*nijiru*	edge forward
いびる	*ibiru*	torment, roast	せびる	*sebiru*	pester for
熱る	*ikiru*	become sultry	すじる	*sujiru*	wriggle
煎る	*iru*	boil down	たぎる	*tagiru*	seethe
かしる	*kashiru*	curse	魂消る	*tama-giru*	be frightened
霧る	*kiru*	become misty	迸る	*tobashiru*	gush
軋る	*kishiru*	creak	とちる	*tochiru*	muff lines
こじる	*kojiru*	gouge, wrench	野次る	*yajiru*	jeer at
くじる	*kujiru*	gouge, scoop	捩る	*yojiru*	twist, distort.

Chart 6. Go-dan Verbs Ending in -eru

Although the following verbs, because they end with *-eru*, appear to be *shimo-ichidan* verbs, they are in fact *go-dan* verbs. Thus, the verb *heru* (decrease) conjugates as follows: *heranai, herō to suru, herimasu,* and *hette* (not *henai, heyō to suru, hemasu,* and *hete*).

1. HIGH-FREQUENCY VERBS

耽る	*fukeru*	be absorbed in	喋る	*shaberu*	chatter
減る	*heru*	decrease	茂る	*shigeru*	grow thick
帰る	*kaeru*	return	湿る	*shimeru*	become damp
蹴る	*keru*	kick	滑る	*suberu*	slip, slide
練る	*neru*	knead	照る	*teru*	shine

2. LESS COMMON VERBS

焦る	*aseru*	fret	孵る	*kaeru*	be hatched
嘲る	*azakeru*	ridicule	覆る	*kutsugaeru*	be overturned
伏せる	*fuseru*	hide, lie in ambush	錬る	*neru*	temper
捻る	*hineru*	twist	煉る	*neru*	refine
翻る	*hirugaeru*	turn over; wave	甦る	*yomigaeru*	rise from the dead
返る	*kaeru*	return			

3. LOW-FREQUENCY VERBS

だべる	*daberu*	chatter	滑る	*numeru*	be slippery
彫る	*eru*	carve	阿る	*omoneru*	flatter
選る	*eru*	choose	競る	*seru*	compete
える	*eru*	ridicule	弄る	*seseru*	pick, play with
侍る	*haberu*	attend on	湿気る	*shikeru*	become damp
へる	*heru*	humble oneself	そべる	*soberu*	lie sprawled
熱る	*hoderu*	feel hot	たける	*takeru*	shout, rage
反る	*kaeru*	turn over	猛る	*takeru*	act violently
陰る	*kageru*	become cloudy	つめる	*tsumeru*	pinch
かける	*kakeru*	soar	つねる	*tsuneru*	pinch
くねる	*kuneru*	be crooked	うねる	*uneru*	undulate
減る	*meru(heru)*	decrease	うせる	*useru*	root with nose
倒る	*nomeru*	fall forward			

Note the *shimo ichidan* homonyms: (経る *henai, heyō to suru, hemasu, hete*) 経る *heru* pass through; 代える *kaeru* interchange; 替える *kaeru* change; 換える *kaeru* change; 占める *shimeru* occupy; 閉める *shimeru* shut; 絞める *shimeru* strangle, wring; 総べる *suberu* rule, control.

Chart 7. Kami-ichidan Conjugation

上一段活用表

基本形	射る	着る	過ぎる	落ちる
語幹	射	着	過ぎ	落ち
未然形	射＋ない	着＋ない	過ぎ＋ない	落ち＋ない
	射＋よう	着＋よう	過ぎ＋よう	落ち＋よう
連用形	射＋ます	着＋ます	過ぎ＋ます	落ち＋ます
	射＋た	着＋た	過ぎ＋た	落ち＋た
終止形	射る	着る	過ぎる	落ちる
連体形	射る＋とき	着る＋とき	過ぎる＋とき	落ちる＋とき
仮定形	射れ＋ば	着れ＋ば	過ぎれ＋ば	落ちれ＋ば
命令形	射＋ろ	着＋ろ	過ぎ＋ろ	落ち＋ろ
基本形	似る	伸びる	見る	降りる
語幹	似	伸び	見	降り
未然形	似＋ない	伸び＋ない	見＋ない	降り＋ない
	似＋よう	伸び＋よう	見＋よう	降り＋よう
連用形	似＋ます	伸び＋ます	見＋ます	降り＋ます
	似＋た	伸び＋た	見＋た	降り＋た
終止形	似る	伸びる	見る	降りる
連体形	似る＋とき	伸びる＋とき	見る＋とき	降りる＋とき
仮定形	似れ＋ば	伸びれ＋ば	見れ＋ば	降りれ＋ば
命令形	似＋ろ	伸び＋ろ	見＋ろ	降り＋ろ

A common term for *kami-ichidan* and *shimo-ichidan* verbs is "vowel-stem" verbs; *go-dan* verbs are commonly called "consonant stem" verbs. The *kami-ichidan* conjugation is based on the *i* line, and the *shimo-ichidan* conjugation is based on the *e* line. The imperative of these two conjugations adds *ro* or *yo*; *go-dan* verbs usually do not add them.

Many *go-dan* verbs also end in *-iru* or *-eru*, and care must be taken not to confuse them with *kami-ichidan* or *shimo-ichidan* verbs.

Chart 8. Shimo-ichidan Conjugation

下一段活用表

基本形	植える	受ける	載せる	捨てる
語幹	植え	受け	載せ	捨て
未然形	植え＋ない	受け＋ない	載せ＋ない	捨て＋ない
	植え＋よう	受け＋よう	載せ＋よう	捨て＋よう
連用形	植え＋ます	受け＋ます	載せ＋ます	捨て＋ます
	植え＋た	受け＋た	載せ＋た	捨て＋た
終止形	植える	受ける	載せる	捨てる
連体形	植える＋とき	受ける＋とき	載せる＋とき	捨てる＋とき
仮定形	植えれ＋ば	受けれ＋ば	載せれ＋ば	捨てれ＋ば
命令形	植え＋ろ	受け＋ろ	載せ＋ろ	捨て＋ろ

基本形	出る	寝る	述べる	暮れる
語幹	出	寝	述べ	暮れ
未然形	出＋ない	寝＋ない	述べ＋ない	暮れ＋ない
	出＋よう	寝＋よう	述べ＋よう	暮れ＋よう
連用形	出＋ます	寝＋ます	述べ＋ます	暮れ＋ます
	出＋た	寝＋た	述べ＋た	暮れ＋た
終止形	出る	寝る	述べる	暮れる
連体形	出る＋とき	寝る＋とき	述べる＋とき	暮れる＋とき
返定形	出れ＋ば	寝れ＋ば	述べれ＋ば	暮れれ＋ば
命令形	出＋ろ	寝＋ろ	述べ＋ろ	暮れ＋ろ

Chart 9. Kuru, Suru Conjugation

来る，する活用表

基本形	来る	する
語幹	来	す
未然形	来＋ない（こ＋ない）	し＋ない
	来＋よう（こ＋よう）	し＋よう
連用形	来＋ます（き＋ます）	し＋ます
	来＋た（き＋た）	し＋た
終止形	来る	する
連体形	来る＋とき	する＋とき
仮定形	来れ＋ば	すれ＋ば
命令形	来＋い（こ＋い）	し＋ろ，せ＋よ

While some verbs like *gozaru* are classified as "defective", *kuru* and *suru* are referred to as "irregular" verbs.

Besides *shi* + *nai* and *shi* + *yō*, most reference books also include *se* + *nu*, *sa* + *reru*, and *sa* + *seru* in the *mizenkei* category. Also, *suru* follows the *ichidan* conjugations in adding *ro* and *yo* in the imperative, giving *shi* + *ro* and *se* + *yo*.

Chart 10. Adjective and Adjectival Noun Conjugation

形容詞，形容動詞の活用表

基本形	よい	美しい	確かだ	元気だ
語幹	よ	美し	確か	元気
未然形	よかろ＋う	美かろ＋う	確かだろ＋う	元気だろ＋う
連用形	よかっ＋た	美しかっ＋た	確かだっ＋た	元気だっ＋た
	よく＋なる	美しく＋なる	確かに＋なる	元気に＋なる
			確かで＋ある	元気で＋ある
終止形	よい	美しい	確かだ	元気だ
連体形	よい＋とき	美しい＋とき	確かな＋とき	元気な＋とき
仮定形	よけれ＋ば	美しけれ＋ば	確かなら＋ば	元気なら＋ば

Adjectives are conjugated like verbs, except for the fact that in modern Japanese they have lost the imperative form. Adjectival nouns also have no imperative form.

Chart 11. Auxiliary Verb Conjugation A
助 動 詞 活 用 表 A

基本形	せる	させる	れる	られる	れる	られる	ない	たい	らしい
主要意味	尊敬 使役	尊敬 使役	受身	受身	尊敬 自発 可能	尊敬 自発 可能	打消	希望	推量
型	動詞型						形容詞型		
未然形	せ	させ	れ	られ	れ	られ	なかろ	たかろ	—
連用形	せ	させ	れ	られ	れ	られ	なく なかっ	たく たかっ	らしく らしかっ
終止形	せる	させる	れる	られる	れる	られる	ない	たい	らしい
連体形	せる	させる	れる	られる	れる	られる	ない	たい	らしい
仮定形	せれ	させれ	れれ	られれ	れれ	られれ	なけれ	たけれ	らしけれ
命令形	せよ しろ	させよ させろ	れよ れろ	られよ られろ	—	—	—	—	—

使役 (*shieki*) factitive　尊敬 (*sonkei*) respect　受身 (*ukemi*) passive
可能 (*kanō*) possibility　自発 (*jihatsu*) spontaneity　打消 (*uchikeshi*) negative
希望 (*kibō*) desire　推量 (*suiryō*) conjecture　型 (*kata*) type

Note: Auxiliary verbs are considered a distinct part of speech. The remainder will be found in chart 12. Also, while *-rareru, -reru, -saseru, -seru* are conjugated like verbs, the remaining three on this chart are conjugated like adjectives.

Chart 12. Auxiliary Verb Conjugation B
助動詞活用表 B

基本形	そうだ[1]	そうだ[2]	ようだ	だ	ます	です	た (だ)	ぬ (ん)
主要意味	様態	伝聞	比況	断定	丁寧	丁寧	過去完了	打消
型	形容動詞型				特別活用型			
未然形	そうだろ	—	ようだろ	だろ	ましょ ませ	でしょ	たろ	—
連用形	そうに そうで そうだっ	そうで	ように ようで ようだっ	で だっ	まし	でし	—	ず
終止形	そうだ	そうだ	ようだ	だ	ます	です	た	ぬ (ん)
仮定形	そうなら	—	ようなら	なら	ますれ	—	たら	ね
命令形	—	—	—	—	ませ まし	—	—	—

様態 (*yōtai*) evidential 伝聞 (*denbun*) report 比況 (*hikyō*) comparison
断定 (*dantei*) assertion 丁寧 (*teinei*) politeness 過去完了 (*kako-kanryō*) completion

-sō da[1], *-sō da*[2], *-yō da* and *da* are conjugated like adjectival nouns, while *-masu, desu, -ta* and *-nu* belong to a special type of conjugation.

-sō da[1] (evidential) follows Base 2 (雨が降りそうだ。It looks like rain.)
-sō da[2] (report) follows Base 3 (雨が降るそうだ。They say it will rain.)

A HANDBOOK OF

JAPANESE USAGE

A

ā[1] ああ　副詞　adverb

指示語句、他称、遠称。状態を表す *Shiji-goku, tashō, enshō; jōtai wo arawasu.* Demonstrative phrase, 3rd. person, distal; denotes state:

- ああいう風にしてください。 *Ā iu fū ni shite kudasai.* Do it like that.
- ああ忙しくては身体に悪い。 *Ā isogashikute wa karada ni warui.* You'll ruin your health hustling like that.
- ああまで有名とは知らなかった。 *Ā made yūmei to wa shiranakatta.* I didn't know he was so famous.

ā[2] ああ　感動詞　interjection

1. 肯定・承知の声 *Kōtei・shōchi no koe* Expression of assent or agreement:

- 雨が降っているのか。 *Ame ga futte iru no ka?* Is it raining?
  ああ、降っている。 *Ā, futte iru.* Yes, it is.
- 雨が降っていないのか。 *Ame ga futte inai no ka?* Isn't it raining?
  ああ、降っていない。 *Ā, futte inai.* No, it isn't.

2. 驚き・悲しみ・喜び・嘆きの声 *Odoroki・kanashimi・yorokobi・nageki no koe* Expression of surprise, sorrow, joy, lament:

- ああ、驚いた。 *Ā, odoroita!* What a surprise!
- ああ、そうですか。 *Ā, sō desu ka?* Oh, is that so?
- ああ、楽しかった。 *Ā, tanoshikatta!* How delightful it was!
- ああ、母が生きていたらなあ。 *Ā, haha ga ikite itara nā!* Ah, if only Mother were alive!

NOTE. There are two interjections, both written with a short *a:*

1. 呼びかけの声 *yobi-kake no koe* vocative:
   - あ、沖くん、ちょっと。 *A, Oki-kun, chotto.* I say, Oki (come here a moment).
2. 驚きの声 *odoroki no koe* expression of surprise:
   - あっ、財布を落とした。 *A', saifu wo otoshita!* Oh dear, I've lost my purse!

achira あちら　代名詞　pronoun

指示代名詞、他称、遠称。方角を示す *Shiji-daimeishi, tashō, enshō; hōgaku wo shimesu* Demonstrative pronoun, 3rd. person, distal; denotes direction:

- あちらに見えるのは浅間山です。 *Achira ni mieru no wa Asama-yama desu.* What you see over there is Mt. Asama.
- こちらよりあちらの方が上質です。 *Kochira yori achira no hō ga jōshitsu desu.* The ones over there are of better quality than these.
- あちら様は校長先生ですか。 *Achira-sama wa kōchō sensei desu ka?* Is that person over there the principal?

NOTE. As a noun, *achira* refers to foreign countries, especially those in the West:

- あちらでは今何が流行しているのか。 *Achira de wa ima nani ga ryūkō shite iru no ka?* What is in fashion abroad now?

-agari 上がり　接尾語　suffix

A. 動詞の連用形に付いて、文字どおりの意味を表す *Dōshi no ren'yō-kei ni tsuite, moji-doori no imi wo arawasu* With Base 2 of verbs, expresses literal meaning:

- 立ち上がり *tachi-agari* rising; 飛び上がり *tobi-agari* jumping up.

B. 名詞に付く *Meishi ni tsuku* Is added to nouns.

1. 動作や状態がもう終わったことを示す *Dōsa ya jōtai ga mō owatta koto wo shimesu* Denotes that the action or state has already ended:

- 雨上がりの道 *ame-agari no michi* road after rain; 病み上がりの人 *yami-agari no hito* a convalescent; 湯上がりタオル *yu-agari taoru* bath towel.

2. かつての職業や境遇を表す *Katsute no shokugyō ya kyōgū wo arawasu* Denotes former occupation or status:

- 学生上がりの力士 *gakusei-agari no rikishi* student turned wrestler; 軍人上がり *gunjin-agari* ex-soldier; 役人上がり *yakunin-agari* retired civil servant.

agaru 上がる　敬語として　as a respect verb

1. 謙譲を表す *Kenjō wo arawasu* Expresses deference:

- ご相談に上がってもいいでしょうか。 *Go-sōdan ni agatte mo ii deshō ka?* May I drop in to discuss the matter? (= *ukagau*)

2. 尊敬を表す *Sonkei wo arawasu* Expresses respect:

- 昼食はなにを上がりますか。 *Chūshoku wa nani wo agarimasu ka?* What will you have for lunch? (= *meshi-agaru*)

-agaru 上がる 接尾語 suffix verb

1. 下から上へ移る *Shita kara ue e utsuru* Rise, ascend:
   - 起きあがる *oki-agaru* rise to one's feet; 飛び上がる *tobi-agaru* leap to one's feet.
2. すっかり…する *Sukkari. . . suru* Do . . . thoroughly:
   - 出来上がる *deki-agaru* be completed; 仕上がる *shi-agaru* be finished.
3. 行き着くところまで行っている *Yuki-tsuku tokoro made itte iru* Be gone as far as it can go:
   - 震え上がる *furue-agaru* shudder; 煮上がる *ni-agaru* boil up, seethe.

-age 上げ・揚げ 接尾語 suffix

- 油揚げ *abura-age* fried bean curd; 賃上げ *chin-age* wage raise; 引き上げ *hiki-age* raise; act of raising; repatriation; 肩上げ・腰上げ *kata-age* • *koshiage* tuck taken in at shoulder or waist; 繰り上げ *kuri-age* putting forward (in time); 棟上げ *mune-age* framework-raising ceremony; 値上げ *ne-age* price increase; お手上げ *ote-age* giving up in despair; 売り上げ *uri-age* sales.

-ageru 上げる 接尾語 suffix verb

A. 特定の動詞の連用形に付く *Tokutei no dōshi no ren'yōkei ni tsuku* Is added to Base 2 of certain verbs.

1. 丁寧を表す *Teinei wo arawasu* Expresses politeness:
   - 厚くお礼を申し上げます。 *Atsuku o-rei wo mōshi-agemasu.* Please accept my sincere gratitude.
   - もう一杯差し上げましょうか。 *Mō ippai sashi-agemashō ka?* May I pour you another drink?
2. すっかり…する *Sukkari . . . suru* Do . . . thoroughly:
   - 洗い上げる *arai-ageru* wash thoroughly; 書き上げる *kaki-ageru* finish writing; 縛り上げる *shibari-ageru* tie up.

B. 動詞の連用形+「て」に付いて、謙譲を表す *Dōshi no ren'yōkei + "-te" ni tsuite, kenjō wo arawasu* With Base 2 of verb + *-te,* expresses deference:

- テレビをつけて上げましょうか。 *Terebi wo tsukete agemashō ka?* Shall I turn on the TV for you?
- 心配して上げているわ、兄さんのこと。 *Shinpai shite agete iru wa, niisan no koto!* I am worried for you (my brother)!

aida 間 形式名詞として as a formal noun

一続きの時間・空間を示す *Hito-tsuzuki no jikan • kūkan wo shimesu* Denotes a continuum of time or space:

• ラジオを聞いている間に眠ってしまった。 *Rajio wo kiite iru aida ni nemutte shimatta.* I fell asleep while listening to the radio.

NOTES.

1. In the epistolary style *(sōrō-bun), aida* expressed cause, but in modern Japanese it usually corresponds with the English conjunction "while".
2. With *aida,* the subject of the main clause need not be the same as that of the subordinate clause:
   • そこにいる間は，好天だった。 *Soko ni iru aida wa, kōten datta.* The weather was fine while we were there.
   • そうしている間に病気になった。 *Sō shite iru aida ni, byōki ni natta.* Meanwhile, he fell ill.
3. The verb preceding *aida* may be in the present tense, even when the main verb is in the past:
   • 彼女が何かを作っている間、二郎はおもちゃをいじっていた。*Kanojo ga nani ka wo tsukutte iru aida, Jirō wa omocha wo ijitte ita.* Jirō fiddled with the toys while she prepared something (to eat).
4. The verb preceding *aida* is usually in the progressive form:
   • 私が生きている間はそんなことは許さない。 *Watashi ga ikite iru aida wa, sonna koto wa yurusanai!* You won't do that while I'm alive!
5. The addition of *ni* to *aida* restricts the duration:
   • 赤ちゃんが眠っている間，手紙を書いた。 *Akachan ga nemutte iru aida, tegami wo kaita.* While (All the time) the baby was asleep, she wrote letters.
   • 赤ちゃんが眠っている間に、手紙を書いた。 *Akachan ga nemutte iru aida ni, tegami wo kaita.* While the baby was asleep, she wrote (managed to write) a letter.

→ *kan, ma*

amari 余り　名詞 noun

Base 2 of the verb *amaru* is basically a noun, but is used also as an adverb and an adjectival noun.

1. 一定の数・量以上にあること・もの *Ittei no kazu • ryō ijō ni aru koto • mono* Being above, or what is above, a certain quantity:

• 弁当の余りをごみ箱に入れなさい。 *Bentō no amari wo gomi-bako ni irenasai.* Put the remainders from your lunches in the garbage can.

2. ある数を別の数で割ったとき，割り切れないでできた数 *Aru kazu wo betsu no kazu de watta toki, wari-kirenaide dekita kazu* Remainder (mathematical):

• 二十五を四で割ると、余りは一。 *Nijūgo wo yon de waru to, amari wa ichi.* Four into twenty-five leaves one.

3. 普通の程度を越えて甚だしいこと *Futsū no teido wo koete hanahadashii koto* Being excessive:

- 余りの暑さに卒倒した。 *Amari no atsusa ni sottō shita.* He fainted from the unbearable heat.

4. 程度の甚だしいことの結果 *Teido no hanahadashii koto no kekka* Result of excess:

- 悲しみのあまり、病気になった。 *Kanashimi no amari, byōki ni natta.* Grief made her ill.
- 嬉しさのあまり、小躍りした。 *Ureshisa no amari, ko-odori shita.* She danced for joy.

5. 打ち消しを伴って、副詞的に;「それほど」 *Uchikeshi wo tomonatte, fukushi-teki ni; sore hodo* With a negative, adverbially; = to that extent:

- あまり知らない人だ。 *Amari shiranai hito da.* He is a comparative stranger.
- あまり心配しないでください。 *Amari shinpai shinaide kudasai.* Don't worry too much (over it).

6. 肯定の言い方を伴って,副詞的に;「ひじょうに」 *Kōtei no ii-kata wo tomonatte, fukushi-teki ni; hijō ni* With a positive expression, adverbially; = very:

- それはあまりにも酷い。 *Sore wa amari ni mo hidoi.* That's going too far.
- あまりに気の毒だ。 *Amari ni ki no doku da.* What a pity! (I really feel sorry for him.)

-amari 余り 接尾語 suffix

その数量よりいくらか多い *Sono sūryō yori ikura ka ooi* Somewhat more than . . . :

- 四十歳余りの人 *yonjissai-amari no hito* a person over forty; 千円余りする。*Sen'en-amari suru.* It costs ¥1000 odd; 一時間余り待たされた。*Ichijikan-amari matasareta.* I was kept waiting for more than one hour.

anata あなた 代名詞 pronoun

1. (古語「彼方」) 指示代名詞、他称、遠称。方角を示す (*kogo* 彼方) *Shiji daimeishi, tashō, enshō; hōgaku wo shimesu* (written 彼方 in classical Japanese) Demonstrative pronoun, 3rd. person, distal; denotes direction:

- 海の彼方に *umi no anata ni* beyond the sea; 百年彼方の話なり。*Momo-tose anata no hanashi nari.* It's something that happened long, long ago.

2. (現代語「貴方」) 人代名詞、対称 (*gendai-go* 貴方) *Jin-daimei-shi, taishō* (written 貴方 in modern Japanese) Personal pronoun, 2nd. person:

- 次はあなたの番です。 *Tsugi wa anata no ban desu.* It's your turn next.
- あなた任せの態度はだめです。 *Anata-makase no taido wa dame desu.* You mustn't leave the responsibility to others.

NOTE. It is interesting to compare the present-day usage of this pronoun with its original meaning. Also, the student must be careful not to equate it with the English "you"; it may not be used so freely, and not at all toward superiors.

anna da あんなだ 形容動詞 adjectival noun

他称、遠称。状態を表す *Tashō, enshō; jōtai wo arawasu* 3rd. person, distal; expresses state:

- 私もあんな成績を取りたい。 *Watashi mo anna seiseki wo toritai.* I, too, should like to obtain such results.
- あんなに働いては無理だ。 *Anna ni hataraite wa muri da.* Working like that is too much for you.
- どうしてあんなかなのか分からない。 *Dōshite anna na no ka wakaranai.* Why it should be like that, I don't know.

NOTE. The group of words *anna, donna, konna, sonna* is found classified as both adjectival noun and adnoun. *Anna da* is the full, final form (Base 3).

ano[1] あの 連体詞 adnoun

他称、遠称。関係を表す *Tashō, enshō; kankei wo arawasu* 3rd. person, distal; denotes relationship:

- これよりあの方がいい。 *Kore yori ano hō ga ii.* The one over there is better than this.
- あの頃は良かったなあ。 *Ano koro wa yokatta nā!* Those were the days!

ano[2] あの

代名詞「あ」に、格助詞「の」 *Daimeishi "a" ni, kaku-joshi "no"* The pronoun *a* + the case particle *no*.

1. 呼びかけの声 *Yobi-kake no koe* A vocative:

- あの、落とし物です。 *Ano, otoshi-mono desu.* Excuse me, but you've dropped something.

2. ためらいなどを表す *Tamerai nado wo arawasu* Expresses a sense of hesitancy:

- あの、私にはよく分かりません。 *Ano, watashi ni wa yoku wakari-masen.* H'm, I don't quite understand.

are あれ 代名詞 pronoun

人代名詞、他称、遠称。人・物・時間・場所を指す *Jin-daimeishi, tashō, enshō; hito, mono, jikan, basho wo sasu* Personal pronoun, 3rd. person, distal; refers to persons, things, time, and place. *Are* was formerly a first-person pronoun, synonymous with *ware:*

- あれは弟と妹だ。 *Are wa otōto to imōto da.* Those are my brother and sister.
- あれは博物館だ。 *Are wa hakubutsukan da.* That over there is a museum.
- あれ以来会っていない。 *Are irai atte inai.* I haven't met him since.

NOTE. Another use of *are* is to refer to something in a vague way, or to something one is loath to express:

- あれで哲学者だ。 *Are de tetsugaku-sha da.* He is a philosopher, in a sense.
- 頼んでおいたあれはどうなった? *Tanonde oita are wa dō natta?* What has become of that matter I spoke to you about?

HOMONYM. 荒れ *are* roughness: 肌荒れ *hada-are* roughness of skin; 荒れ野 *are-no* wilderness; 荒れ模様 *are-moyō* signs of a coming storm.

There is also the interjection *are*, as in: あれ、不思議だな。*Are, fushigi da na!* What! That's strange.

aru[1] ある 動詞 verb

Aru is an irregular verb in that its negative form is the adjective *nai,* q. v. It derives from the *bungo* verb *ari*, which conjugates as follows: 1. *ara* 2. *ari* 3. *ari* 4. *aru* 5. *are* 6. *are*. It is now written mostly in *kana*, but the two ideographs 有る and 在る will be found in many compounds:

- 有り余る *ari-amaru* be in excess; 有り高 *ari-daka* amount in hand; 有様・有り様 *ari-sama* state; 在処・在り処 *ari-ka* whereabouts; 在り来たりの *ari-kitari no* ordinary.

aru ~ iru

For animate things (and self-propelling vehicles), *iru* is usually used to express location. However, *aru* is used to express what would be location in English, in the following contexts: status, conditions, surroundings, and standpoint.

- 会社で高い地位にある。 *Kaisha de takai chii ni aru.* He ranks high in the company.

• 私は苦しい立場にある。 *Watashi wa kurushii tachiba ni aru.* I am in a fix.

aru² ある　補助動詞として　as a supplementary verb
他動詞の連用形 ＋「て」を受けて、動作結果の状態を表す *Tadōshi no ren'yōkei + "-te" wo ukete, dōsa-kekka no jōtai wo arawasu* Following Base 2 of transitive verbs + *-te,* denotes state resulting from action:

• 窓は閉めてある。 *Mado wa shimete aru.* The windows have been closed (and remain so).
• 壁に額が掛けてある。 *Kabe ni gaku ga kakete aru.* There is a picture hanging on the wall. (Lit., A picture has been hung on the wall.)

NOTE. Not all transitive verbs allow this construction:

• 靴はもう履いている。 *Kutsu wa mō haite iru.* He has his boots on already.

NOTE. The case particle *wo* will be found after what in English is the grammatical subject:

• 間違いを直してありますか。 *Machigai wo naoshite arimasu ka?* Have the errors been corrected?

HOMONYM. 或、 now written ある; e.g., ある日、ある人、etc. It is an adnoun.

aruiwa¹ あるいは　接続詞　conjunction
「または」に等しい *"Mata wa" ni hitoshii* Equivalent to *mata wa* (either/or):

• あるいは赤くあるいは白い。 *Aruiwa akaku aruiwa shiroi.* Some are red, others white.
• 凧はあるいは高くあるいは低く飛んでいた。 *Tako wa aruiwa takaku aruiwa hikuku tonde ita.* The kites were flying, now high, now low.
• 英語あるいは数学を専攻したい。 *Eigo aruiwa sūgaku wo senkō shitai.* I want to specialize in either English or math.

NOTE. The English alternative conjunction is translated in various ways:

• 一両日　*ichi-ryōiitsu* one or two days.
• 三月か四月（か）に見えるでしょう。 *San-gatsu ka shi-gatsu (ka) ni mieru deshō.* He will be here in March or April.
• 黒または青色のインクで書くこと。 *Kuro mata wa ao-iro no inku de kaku koto.* Write in either black or blue ink.
• 数学もしくは論理学を選択すること。 *Sūgaku moshikuwa ronrigaku wo sentaku suru koto.* There is a choice of either math or logic.
• 電車で来たのですか、それともバスでですか。 *Densha de kita no desu ka, soretomo basu de desu ka?* Did they come by train or by bus?

- 十人乃至十五人の人数が要るでしょう。 *Jūnin naishi jūgonin no ninzū ga iru deshō*. It will take ten or fifteen (people) to do it.

aruiwa[2] あるいは 副詞 adverb
「ひょっとしたら」に等しい *"Hyotto shitara" ni hitoshii* Means possibly:

- あるいはそうかも知れない。 *Aruiwa sō ka mo shirenai*. Perhaps that's true.
- もう正午なのに彼はやって来ない。あるいは病気かも知れない。 *Mō shōgo na noni kare wa yatte konai. Aruiwa byōki ka mo shirenai.* It's already noon, but he hasn't come yet; maybe he is ill.

-aruku 歩く 接尾語 suffix verb
動詞の連用形に付いて、「あちこち回って...する」 *Dōshi no ren'yōkei ni tsuite, "achi-kochi mawatte . . . suru"* With Base 2 of verbs, = "go around (not necessarily on foot) doing . . . ":

- 売り歩く *uri-aruku* peddle; 持ち歩く *mochi-aruku* carry around; 飲み歩く *nomi-aruku* go around drinking; 渡り歩く *watari-aruku* wander about.

asa-na See *na*[3].

asoko (asuko) あそこ(あすこ) 代名詞 pronoun
他称、遠称。場所を示す *Tashō, enshō; basho wo shimesu* 3rd. person, distal; denotes place:

- 売店はあそこです。 *Baiten wa asoko desu*. The kiosk is over there.
- あそこは一度行ってみたいな。 *Asoko wa ichi-do itte mitai na*. I should like to go there sometime.
- あそこまで歩きましょう。 *Asoko made arukimashō*. Let's walk over.

→ *doko, koko, soko.*

-atari 当たり 接尾語 suffix
1. 食べ物や暑さのために身体を壊すこと *Tabemono ya atsusa no tame ni karada wo kowasu koto* Being affected by food poisoning or heatstroke:

- 食当たり[食中り] *shoku-atari* food poisoning; 暑気当たり[暑気中り] *shoki-atari* heatstroke.

2. その量を基準と考えて *Sono ryō wo kijun to kangaete* In proportion to:

- 一人当たり五千円をもらった。 *Hitori-atari gosen'en wo moratta.* They got ¥5,000 apiece.

• 反当たり収穫はどのくらいですか。 *Tan-atari shūkaku wa dono kurai desu ka?* How much is the yield per acre?

atashi あたし
Familiar form for *watashi,* most frequently used by women and older men.

atchi あっち
Intensified form of *achi,* which is the contraction of *achira.*

-ate[1] 当て 接尾語 suffix
1. 等量配分を示す *Tōryō haibun wo shimesu* Denotes equal distribution:
• 一人当て一万円を払った。 *Hitori-ate ichiman'en wo haratta.* He paid them ¥10,000 each. → *-atari*
2. 保護するもの *Hogo suru mono* A protector:
• 腹当て *hara-ate* stomach-wrapper; breastplate; 頬当て *hoo-ate* visor; 肩当て *kata-ate* shoulder-pad; 腰当て *koshi-ate* bustle; 胸当て *mune-ate* breastplate; chest protector; bib; 尻当て *shiri-ate* seat lining; 脛当て *sune-ate* greaves; shin guards.

-ate[2] 宛て 接尾語 suffix
1. Same as *-atari:*
• 一人宛て二千円 *hitori-ate nisen'en* ¥2,000 each.
2. 目指す *Mezasu* Addressed to:
• 田中さん宛ての手紙があります。 *Tanakasan-ate no tegami ga arimasu.* There is a letter for Mr. Tanaka.

ato 後
形式名詞として *Keishiki meishi to shite* As a formal noun:
• 皆が帰った後、鍵を掛けた。 *Minna ga kaetta ato, kagi wo kaketa.* When they had all gone home I locked up.

-ta ato ～ -te kara
The former stresses the time element, the latter plays it down:
• 御飯を食べた後、テレビを見た。 *Gohan wo tabeta ato, terebi wo mita.* This sentence tells WHEN we watched TV.
• 御飯を食べてから、テレビを見た。 *Gohan wo tabete kara, terebi wo mita.* This tells WHAT we did after our meal.

NOTE. *-te nochi* is equivalent to *-ta ato.*

ato ～ nochi ～ ushiro あと（後）～ のち（後）～ うしろ（後ろ）

ato, antonym = *saki, mae:* covers both time and place, and in the context of time, usually implies "reckoning from now"; it has many other connotations.

nochi, antonym = *mae*: refers only to time, and usually implies "reckoning from then".

ushiro, anotonym = *mae:* refers only to place.

-au 合う 接尾語 suffix verb

動詞の連用形に付いて、「互いに...する」 *Dōshi no ren'yōkei ni tsuite, "tagai ni . . . suru"* With Base 2 of verbs, = "do reciprocally":

- 愛し合う *aishi-au* love each other, love one another; 話し合う *hanashi-au* consult with; 語り合う *katari-au* converse with; 褒め合う *homeau* compliment each other; 嚙み合う *kami-au* bite each other, mesh (of gears).

-awaseru 合わせる 接尾語 suffix verb

動詞の連用形に付いて、「偶然にそうなる」 *Dōshi no ren'yōkei ni tsuite, "gūzen ni sō naru"* With Base 2 of verbs, = "happen to . . ."

- 有り合わせる *ari-awaseru* happen to be there, happen to have; 居合わせる *i-awaseru* happen to be present; 来合わせる *ki-awaseru* happen to come on the scene; 持ち合わせる *mochi-awaseru* happen to have; 乗り合わせる *nori-awaseru* happen to be on the same conveyance; 通り合わせる *toori-awaseru* happen to pass by.

NOTE. Some of the above are used mostly in the Base 2 form, as nouns:

- 有り合わせの金 *ari-awase no kane* money in hand.

NOTE. 見合わせる *mi-awaseru* is an exception; it can mean: 1. see each other; 2. compare; 3. postpone.

B

-ba[1] ば 接続助詞 conjunctive particle

活用語の仮定形につく *Katsuyō-go no kateikei ni tsuku* Is added to Base 5 of conjugables.

In classical Japanese it was added to Bases 1 and 5, giving:

- 急がば回れ。 *Isogaba maware.* The more haste, the less speed.
- 風波やまねばおなじところにあり。 *Kaza-nami yamaneba onaji tokoro ni ari.* Because the storm had not abated, we were in the same place. *(Tosa Nikki)*

1. 仮定条件を表す *Katei-jōken wo arawasu* Expresses open condition:

- 雨が降れば行かない。 *Ame ga fureba ikanai.* If it rains I'm not going.

2. 恒常条件を表す *Kōjō-jōken wo arawasu* Denotes a foregone conclusion:

- 一に二を足せば、三になる。 *Ichi ni ni wo taseba, san ni naru.* Add two to one and you get three.

3. 並列を表す *Heiretsu wo arawasu* Denotes listing:

- 池もあれば、森もある。 *Ike mo areba, mori mo aru.* There are both lakes and woods.
- 親もなければ、妻もない。 *Oya mo nakereba, tsuma mo nai.* He has neither parents nor wife.

4. 順態仮定条件を表す *Juntai katei-jōken wo arawasu* Expresses what is, in effect, a temporal clause under the guise of a condition:

- 聞いてみれば、その通りだった。 *Kiite mireba, sono toori datta.* I asked, and found it was true. (When I asked, I found it was true.)
- 窓から覗けば、降るような星空だった。 *Mado kara nozokeba, furu yō na hoshi-zora datta.* I looked out of the window and saw a star-studded sky. (When I looked out of the window, there was a star-studded sky.)

NOTE. Some idiomatic uses:

1. 「…ば…ほど〜」の形で、「…すると、なお一層〜」 *". . . -ba . . . hodo 〜" no katachi de, ". . . suru to, nao issō〜"* In. . . *-ba hodo* form, = "the more. . . the more〜":

- 延ばせば延ばすほど、するのが嫌になる。 *Nobaseba nobasu hodo, suru no ga iya ni naru.* The longer you put it off, the harder it will be to do it.

2. 「…ばいいのですが」の形で、願望を表す *". . . -ba ii no desu ga" no katachi de, ganbō wo arawasu* In . . . *-ba ii no desu ga* form, expresses a wish:

- 明日友達が来ればいいのですが。 *Asu tomodachi ga kureba ii no desu ga.* I hope my friends come tomorrow.

3. 疑問詞＋「…ばいいのか」の形で、手段・方法を表す *Gimonshi + ". . . -ba ii no ka" no katachi de, shudan hōhō wo arawasu* In interrogative + . . . *-ba ii no ka?* form, denotes the manner of doing . . . :

- どうして調べればいいのか分からない。 *Dō shite shirabereba ii no ka wakaranai.* I don't know how to look it up.

4. 「…ばいいのに」の形で、願望を表す *". . . -ba ii no ni" no katachi de, ganbō wo arawasu* In . . . *-ba ii no ni* form, expresses a (forlorn) wish:

- 母が居ればいいのに。 *Haha ga ireba ii no ni!* If only mother were here!
- そんなことをしなければ良かったのに。 *Sonna koto wo shinakereba yokatta no ni!* You oughtn't to have done that!

5. 「…なければならない［いけない・だめ］」の形で、義務を表す "... *nakereba naranai* [*ikenai* • *dame*]" *no katachi de, gimu wo arawasu* In . . . *nakereba naranai* [*ikenai/dame*] forms, expresses obligation:
   - もう帰らなければならない。 *Mō kaeranakereba naranai.* I must go home now.
   - 宿題をしなければいけない。 *Shukudai wo shinakereba ikenai.* You must do your homeowrk.
   - もっと早く起きなければだめですよ。 *Motto hayaku okinakereba dame desu yo.* You will have to get up earlier.

   NOTE. Sometimes the *naranai, ikenai,* or *dame* is elided:
   - 今薬を飲まなければ。 *Ima kusuri wo nomanakereba.* I must take my medicine now.

   NOTE: *-nakereba* also is sometimes contracted to *-kerya, -kya.*

-ba[2] 場 接尾語 suffix

劇の一場面 *Geki no ichi-bamen* Scene in a drama: → *-maku,* act
- 第二幕第三場 *Dai ni-maku dai sanba.* Act 2, Scene 3.

-bai 倍 助数詞 *josūshi* counter

同じ数・量を二回か二回以上加える *Onaji kazu • ryō wo ni-kai ka ni-kai ijō kuwaeru* Denotes factor of multiplication:
- 人数は一年で倍になった。 *Ninzū wa ichi-nen de bai ni natta.* The number (of persons) doubled in one year.
- 弟の倍の体重がある。 *Otōto no bai no taijū ga aru.* He is twice as heavy as his younger brother.
- 物価は去年の一倍半になっている。 *Bukka wa kyonen no ichibai-han ni natte iru,* Prices are one and a half times higher than last year.
- 百倍の顕微鏡で見た。 *Hyaku-bai no kenbikyō de mita.* I saw it with a microscope of 100 magnifications.

bakari ばかり 副助詞 adverbial particle

体言・副詞・助詞・用言の連体形に付く *Taigen • fukushi • foshi • yōgen no rentaikei ni tsuku* Is added to nominals, adverbs, particles, and to Base 4 of verbals.

1. 明白でない量・状態・程度を表す *Meihaku de nai ryō • jōtai • teido wo arawasu* Denotes indeterminate amount, state or degree:

- 二時間ばかり待っていた。 *Ni-jikan bakari matte ita.* I waited for about two hours.

2. 「ただそれだけ」と限定する意を表す *"Tada sore dake" to gentei suru i wo arawasu* Expresses a sense of restriction:

- 毎日雨ばかり降る。 *Mai-nichi ame bakari furu.* It does nothing but rain, day in, day out.
- ただ泣くばかりだった。 *Tada naku bakari datta.* She did nothing but cry.
- 背が高いばかりで、あまり体力がない。 *Se ga takai bakari de, amari tairyoku ga nai.* He is all height, with no great strength.
- きれいなばかりで、役には立たない。 *Kirei na bakari de, yaku ni wa tatanai.* It is merely pretty, serving no purpose.
- 毎日家にばかりいた。 *Mai-nichi ie ni bakari ita.* He stayed indoors all the time.

3. 過去の助動詞「た」に付いて、「完了して間もない」意を表す *Kako no jodōshi "-ta" ni tsuite, "kanryō shite ma mo nai" i wo arawasu* After the past auxiliary *-ta,* denotes that the action has just been completed:

- 今十時を打ったばかりだ。 *Ima jūji wo utta bakari da.* The clock has just struck ten.
- 焼いたばかりのパンを買ってきた。 *Yaita bakari no pan wo katte kita.* I went and bought some newly-baked bread (→ *-tate*)

4. 動詞の終止形に付いて、「まだしないが、今にもしそう」なことを表す *Dōshi no shūshikei ni tsuite, "mada shinai ga, ima ni mo shisō" na koto wo arawasu* With Base 3 of verbs, indicates that the action is likely to take place at any moment:

- 飯は炊くばかりになっている。 *Meshi wa taku bakari ni natte iru.* The rice is set for cooking.
- 駅に入るばかりのところで、止まってしまった。 *Eki ni hairu bakari no tokoro de, tomatte shimatta.* The train stopped just as it was about to enter the station.

NOTES. Some idiomatic uses:

1. 「とばかり」の形で、「まるで…と言うように」 *"to bakari" no katachi de, "marude. . . to iu yō ni"* In *to bakari* form, = "as if to say. . .:

- 待っていたとばかり、今度は夏子をさらっていった。 *Matte ita to bakari, kondo wa Natsuko wo saratte itta.* Now he snatched Natsuko away as if this was the chance he had been waiting for.

2. 「…ばかりに」の形で、「それだけが原因だ」 *". . . bakari ni" no katachi de, "sore dake ga gen'in da"* In . . . *bakari ni* form, "for the simple reason that. . .":

- 引き受けたばかりに酷い目にあった。 *Hiki-uketa bakari ni, hidoi me*

ni atta. I got into terrible trouble just for having taken it on.

- ちょっと油断したばかりに事故を起こした。 *Chotto yudan shita bakari ni, jiko wo okoshita.* A slight distraction on his part led to an accident.

3.「否定形 + ばかりか」の形で、「...だけでなく、かえって」て*"hiteikei + bakari ka" no katachi de, ". . . dake de naku, kaette"* In the negative + *bakari ka* form, = "far from . . . , on the contrary":

- 反省しないばかりか、悪口を言い返した。 *Hansei shinai bakari ka, warukuchi wo ii-kaeshita.* Far from showing compunction, he went so far as to answer back.

NOTE. This is one of the particles that may come between a verb and its auxiliary:

- 働いてばかりいると、人間はだめになる。 *Hataraite bakari iru to, ningen wa dame ni naru.* Working non-stop will cripple a person.

NOTE. Other particles that share this property are: *dake, de mo, gurai, made, nado, nan ka, nante, sae,* but not *koso, nomi, shika* or *sura.*

NOTE. *bakkari* is an emphatic form, while *bakashi* and *bakkashi* are colloquial.

HOMONYM. *-bakari (hakari)* of various forms of weighing scales: ばね秤 *bane-bakari,* spring scales; 皿秤 *sara-bakari* a balance.

-bamu ばむ　接尾語　suffix verb

色々な語に付いて、動詞を作り、「そのさまを帯びる」 *Iro-iro na go ni tsuite, dōshi wo tsukuri, "sono sama wo obiru"* Added to various parts of speech, verbalizes them, and adds the meaning: "(gradually) take on the appearance of. . . ":

- いくらか気色ばんで話した。 *Ikura ka keshiki-bande hanashita.* His face showed a slight indignation as he spoke.
- 銀杏が黄ばみ、あたりはすっかり秋めいていた。 *Ichō ga ki-bami, atari wa sukkari akimeita.* The ginkgo trees were turning yellow, and all around were signs of fall.

→ *-biru, -gumu, -meku, -ramu*

-ban 番　助数詞　counter

順序・等級などを表す *Junjo・tōkyū nado wo arawasu* Denotes such things as order and classification:

- クラスで二番です。 *Kurasu de ni-ban desu.* He is second in his class.

-banashi[1] 話　接尾語　suffix

- 昔話 *mukashi-banashi* old tale; 笑い話 *warai-banashi* joke.

-banashi[2] 放し　接尾語　suffix

- 野放し *no-banashi* leaving free; 手放し *te-banashi* openly, (手話 *shu-wa* sign language); → *-ppanashi*

-bara 腹　接尾語　suffix

Besides its literal meaning of "belly", it also has the connotation of 本心 *honshin* true intention, and 心中 *shin-chū* bottom of one's heart.

- 後腹 *ato-bara* afterpains; ビール腹 *bīru-bara* beer belly; 追い腹 *oi-bara* following one's master in death; → *-hara, -ppara*

-bari 張り　接尾語　suffix

1. 張ってあること *Hatte aru koto* Covering, being covered:

- ガラス張り *garasu-bari* glazing, glazed; 銀張り *gin-bari* silver plating; 板張り *ita-bari* boarding, fulling; 紙張り *kami-bari* papering, papered; 皮張り *kawa-bari* leather-covered; 金張り *kin-bari* gold plating; 絹張り *kinu-bari* silk finish; 切り張り *kiri-bari* patching; 目張り *me-bari* sealing with paper; 千枚張り *senmai-bari* many-layered.

2. 意志力 *Ishi-ryoku* Will-power:

- 踏ん張り *fun-bari* holding out; 頑張り *gan-bari* tenacity; 息張り *iki-bari* straining; 一点張り *itten-bari* persistence; 欲張り *yoku-bari* avarice, grasping person.

3. 人名に付いて、その人に似ていることを示す *Jinmei ni tsuite, sono hito ni nite iru koto wo shimesu* With a person's name, means: "in the style of. . . "

- 竜之介張りの小説 *Ryūnosuke-bari no shōsetsu* novel in the Ryūnosuke style.

→ *-hari, -ppari*

-baru 張る　接尾語　suffix verb

体言に付いて、動詞を作り、「そのものらしく振る舞う」 *Taigen ni tsuite, dōshi wo tsukuri, "sono mono-rashiku furumau"* Added to nominals, verbalizes them, and adds the meaning: "act like. . . ":

- 踏ん張る *fun-baru* hold out; 頑張る *gan-baru* (from 我に張る *ga ni haru*) persist; 儀式張る *gishiki-baru* be formal; 頬張る *hō-baru* cram one's mouth; 威張る *i-baru* put on airs; 角張る *kaku-baru* • *kado-baru* be angular, be rigid; 格式張る *kakushiki-baru* stand on ceremony; 嵩張る *kasa-baru* be bulky; 気張る *kibaru* exert oneself; 強ばる *kowa-baru* become stiff.

- 四角張った話をした。 *Shikaku-batta hanashi wo shita.* He amde a formal sort of speech.
- そんなに欲張るな。 *Sonna ni yoku-baru na!* Don't be so greedy!

-beki See next entry.

-beshi べし 助動詞（雅） *jodōshi* (*ga*) auxiliary verb (classic style) The conjugation is as follows: 1. *beku*/*bekara* 2. *beku*/*bekari* 3. *beshi* 4. *beki*/*bekaru* 5. *bekere* 6. —.

ラ変以外の動詞の終止形に付く *"Ra-hen" igai no dōshi no shūshikei ni tsuku* Is added to Base 3 of all verbs except those of *"ra-hen"*.

1. 当然を表す *Tōzen wo arawasu* Denotes what is reasonable or expected:

- 責任を負うべきだ。 *Sekinin wo ou-beki da.* He should accept the responsibilities.

2. 義務を表す *Gimu wo arawasu* Denotes obligation:

- 言うべきことをはっきり言え。 *Iu-beki koto wo hakkiri ie.* Say clearly what you have to say.

3. 唯一の可能性を表す *Yuiitsu no kanōsei wo arawasu* Denotes the only possibility:

- 打つべき手をすべて打った。 *Utsu-beki te wo subete utta.* I left no stone unturned.

NOTE. *"Ra-hen"*, short for ラ行変格活用 *(ra-gyō henkaku katsuyō)*, comprised only four verbs in *bungo*, and of these, only two have carried over into modern Japanese: *ari* and *ori*, Base 3 of *"ra-hen"* is *-ri*, while that of the regular *ra* column is *-ru*, giving 作るべし (Base 3 of *tsukuru*), but 有るべし (Base 4 of *ari*).

NOTE. Strictly speaking, a *bungo auxiliary* should be attached only to a *bungo* verb form, hence: ...すべし、not . . . するべし、which has come into use. Examples of the carry-over from *bungo*:

- なるべく早くお帰りください。 *Naru-beku hayaku o-kaeri kudasai.* Please come back as soon as possible.
- 注意すべきところはここです。 *Chūi su-beki tokoro wa koko desu.* This is where you have to be careful.
- 芝生に入るべからず。 *Shibafu ni hairu-bekarazu.* Keep off the grass.
- 安息日を聖日とすべきことを覚ゆべし。 *Ansoku-jitsu wo seijitsu to subeki koto wo oboyu-beshi.* Remember to keep holy the sabbath day. (Exod. 20, 8)

NOTE. *oboyu* was the old form of modern *oboeru.*

-biru びる 接尾語 suffix verb

名詞・形容詞の語幹に付いて、動詞を作り、「らしくなる」 *Meishi・keiyōshi no gokan ni tsuite, dōshi wo tsukuri, "-rashiku naru"* Added to nouns and to stem of adjectives, verbalizes them, and adds the meaning: "take on the appearance of. . .":

- 古びて黄色になる。 *Furu-bite ki-iro ni naru.* It yellows with age.
- 田舎びた *inaka-bita* countrified; 雅びた *miya-bita* refined; 幼びた *osana-bita* looking childish; 大人びたムード *otona-bita mūdo* an air of maturity. → ***-bamu, -meku, -ramu***

-bon 本 接尾語 suffix

The ideograph 本 is read *-bon* in many compounds dealing with books:

- 文庫本 *bunko-bon* paperback; 複製本 *fukusei-bon* facsimile; 戯作本 *gesaku-bon* light reading; 自筆本 *jihitsu-bon* holograph; 浄瑠璃本 *jōruri-bon jōruri* book; 上製本 *jōsei-bon* de luxe edition; 巻子本 *kansu-bon* scroll; 稽古本 *keiko-bon* script; 稀覯本 *kikō-bon* rare book; 古版本 *kohan-bon* old edition; 滑稽本 *kokkei-bon* humorous book; 蒟蒻本 *konnyaku-bon* hectographed copy; 好色本 *kōshoku-bon* erotic work; 教則本 *kyōsoku-bon* manual; 奈良絵本 *Narae-bon* Nara picture book; 人情本 *ninjō-bon* love story; 流布本 *rufu-bon* popular text; 洒落本 *share-bon* gay-quarters novelette; 袖珍本 *shūchin-bon* pocket-size book; 手沢本 *shutaku-bon* "ex libris"; 単行本 *tankō-bon* independent volume; 通行本 *tsūkō-bon* popular book; 和製本 *wasei-bon* book in Japanese binding; 洋製本 *yōsei-bon* book bound in Western style; 床本 *yuka-bon Gidayū* libretto; ぞっき本 *zokki-bon* remainders. → ***-pon***

bungo 文語

Bungo is a word we tend to use very loosely; in Japanese, the term covers three distinct senses:

1. 文章を書くときに使う語 *bunshō wo kaku toki ni tsukau go* written style;

2. 文語体の文章 *bungo-tai no bunshō* composition in this style;

3. 江戸時代までの古典的なことば *Edo-jidai made no koten-teki na kotoba* classical style in use up to the Edo period.

The following *kokugo* scheme will help to put things in their true light:

hanashi kotoba / spoken language	
	hōgen dialect
	hyōjun-go standard language
	kōgo-bun spoken style

kaki kotoba *written language*	*Nara-jidai no kotoba* Nara-period language *Heian-jidai no kotoba* Heian-period language *Kamakura-jidai no kotoba* Kamakura-period language *Muromachi-jidai no kotoba* Muromachi-period language *Edo-jidai no kotoba* Edo-period language *Meiji-jidai no kotoba* Meiji-period language *Taishō-jidai no kotoba* Taishō-period language *Shōwa/Heisei-jidai no kotoba* Shōwa/Heisei-period language

NOTE. The written languages of the Meiji, Taishō, and Shōwa/Heisei periods use the *nari, keri,* and *sōrō* endings.

NOTE. As will be evident from this chart, three elements come into play:
1. whether we are speaking of the written or spoken language;
2. the historical era to which the piece belongs;
3. the style, especially with reference to the last four eras.

Gendai-go is taken as referring to the language (spoken or written) as used since World War II, → *bungo, gendai-go, kogo, kō-go*

-buri[1] 振り 接尾語 suffix (from 振る *furu* swing)
名詞や動詞の連用形に付く *Meishi ya dōshi no ren'yōkei ni tsuku* Is added to nouns or Base 2 of verbs.

1. 様子・仕方を示す *Yōsu・shikata wo shimesu* Denotes appearance, way of doing:
- 仕事ぶりは真面目だ。 *Shigoto-buri wa majime da.* To judge only from his way of working, he seems reliable.
- 走りっぷりがいい。 *Hashirippuri ga ii.* He has a good stride.
- 古ぶり *inishie-buri* time-honored custom; 万葉ぶり *Manyō-buri* Manyō style; 女ぶり・女っぷり *onna-buri・onnappuri* woman's looks; 男ぶり・男っぷり *otoko-buri・otokoppuri* man's looks, man's reputation; 知らんぷり *shiran-puri* feigned ignorance; 素振り *so-buri* air, manner.

2. 形や嵩 *Kata ya kasa* Build, bulk:
- 大振り *oo-buri* large build; 小振り *ko-buri* small build.

3. それだけの時間が経った意を表す *Sore dake no jikan ga tatta i wo arawasu* Denotes the lapse of that amount of time:
- 三年ぶりで帰国した。 *Sannen-buri de kikoku shita.* He came home after a lapse of three years. (*ni* may replace *de*)
- 久しぶりに便りがあった。 *Hisashi-buri ni tayori ga atta.* We had a letter from him after a long silence.

- 五年ぶりの豊作だ。 *Gonen-buri no hōsaku da.* It is the first good harvest in five years.

4. 振ること *Furu koto* Act of swinging or moving:

- 身振り手振りで話す。 *Mi-buri te-buri de hanasu.* He speaks using gestures.

-buri² 降り 接尾語 suffix (from 降る *furu* precipitate)

雨・雪などの降る様子・程度 *Ame • yuki nado no furu yōsu • teido* Manner or amount of precipitation:

- 土砂降り *dosha-buri* downpour; 吹き降り *fuki-buri* driving rain; 本降り *hon-buri* raining in earnest; 小降り *ko-buri* light rain; 大降り *oo-buri* heavy rain; 横降り *yoko-buri* driving rain (= 横雨 *yoko-ame*).

-buru 振る 接尾語 suffix verb

名詞や形容詞・形容動詞の語幹に付いて、動詞を作り、「それらしい様子」を示す *Meishi ya keiyōshi • keiyōdōshi no gokan ni tsuite, dōshi wo tsukuri, "sorerashii yōsu" wo shimesu* With nouns, and the stem of adjectives and adjectival nouns, forms verbs, and adds the meaning: "pose . . . ":

- 兄貴ぶる *aniki-buru* be patronising; 偉ぶる *era-buru* be conceited; 学者ぶった人 *gakusha-butta hito* pedant.
- 上品ぶっている。 *Jōhin-butte iru.* He is putting on airs.
- 神経が高ぶっている。 *Shinkei ga takabutte iru.* He has the jitters.
- 利口ぶった口をきく。 *Rikō-butta kuchi wo kiku.* He talks as if he knew everything.

C

-cha (-tcha) ちゃ、っちゃ

「ては」の略 *"-te wa" no ryaku* Contraction of *-te wa:*

- 出ちゃだめよ。 *De-cha dame yo!* You mustn't go out!
- 笑っちゃいけない。 *Wara-tcha ikenai.* It's no laughing matter.

-chigaeru 違える 接尾語 suffix verb

動詞の連用形に付いて、「誤る・仕損なう」 *Dōshi no ren'yōkei ni tsuite, "ayamaru • shi-sokonau"* With Base 2 of verbs, adds the meaning: "mismanage", "bungle":

- 履き違える *haki-chigaeru* put on another's shoes by mistake, have a wrong idea of; 言い違える *ii-chigaeru* make a slip of the tongue;

聞き違える *kiki-chigaeru* mis-hear; 首を寝違える *kubi wo ne-chigaeru* get a crick in the neck while sleeping.

-chimau ちまう
「てしまう」の略 *"-te shimau" no ryaku* Contraction of *-te shimau:*
• 食べられちまった。 *Taberare-chimatta.* It has been eaten up.
→ *shimau*

-chō¹ 丁 接尾語 suffix
1. 町より小さく分けた区画 *Machi yori chiisaku waketa kukaku* A further subdivision of machi:
• 青葉町三丁目 *Aoba-chō san-chō-me* place-name
2. 和製本の一枚 *Wasei-bon no ichi-mai* One leaf of Japanese-style binding:
• 乱丁本・落丁本はお取り替え致します。 *Ran-chō-bon • raku-chō-bon wa o-tori-kae itashimasu.* Books with defective binding will be replaced.
3. 豆腐・蒟蒻などを数える語 *Tōfu • konnyaku nado wo kazoeru go* Counter for pieces of *tōfu, konnyaku* and the like:
• 豆腐一丁 *tōfu itchō* one block of *tōfu.*

-chō² 町 接尾語 suffix
1. 市街の区切り *Shigai no kugiri* Division of a city:
• 沼津市大和町 *Numazu-shi Yamato-chō* place-name.
2. 土地の広さの単位 *Tochi no hirosa no tan'i* Unit of square measure: =c. 10,000 sq. m., or 2.451 acres.
3. 距離の単位 *Kyori no tan'i* Unit of long measure: = c. 109 m.

-chō³ 帳 接尾語 suffix
書き込み用に紙を綴じたもの *Kakikomi-yō ni kami wo tojita mono* A number of sheets of writing-paper bound together:
• 日記帳 *nikki-chō* diary (book); 手帳 *te-chō* notebook.
NOTE. 帳 originally meant "curtain", so we get 蚊帳 *kaya* mosquito net.

-chō⁴ 長 接尾語 suffix
1. 団体の責任者 *Dantai no sekinin-sha* Head, leader, chief (*osa*):
• 社長 *sha-chō* company president; 看護婦長 *kangofu-chō* head nurse.
2. 勝ること・ところ *Masaru koto • tokoro* Superiority, merit:

• 一長一短 *itchō-ittan* merits and demerits; 特長 *toku-chō* strong point.

3. 長さ *Nagasa* Length:

• 身長 *shin-chō* stature (cf. 慎重 caution; 伸張 expansion; 新調の newly-made); 全長 *zen-chō* overall length; †船長 *sen-chō* ship's overall length, ship's captain.

4. 大きくなること *Ookiku naru koto* Increase in size:

• 生長 *seichō* growth (of plants); 成長 *seichō* maturation.

5. 長くなること *Nagaku naru koto* Increase in length:

• 延長 *en-chō* extension; 伸長 *shin-chō* elongation.

-chō[5] 挺　　接尾語　suffix

1. 細長いものを数える語 *Hoso-nagai mono wo kazoeru go* Counter for long, thin objects (includes such items as tools, instruments, guns, candles, inkslabs, etc.):

• バイオリン三挺 *baiorin san-chō* three violins; 鋏一挺 *hasami itchō* one pair of scissors.

2. 人力車・かごなどを数える語 *Jinrikisha • kago nado wo kazoeru go* Counter for rickshaws, palanquins, etc.:

• かご二挺 *kago-ni-chō* two palanquins.

Note. 丁 is often substituted.

-chō[6] 朝　　接尾語　suffix

1. 国王の在位する期間 *Koku-ō no zai-i suru kikan* Reign; dynasty:

• 平安朝 *Heian-chō* Heian era; 明朝 *Min-chō* Ming dynasty (read *myō-chō* = tomorrow morning); *Min-chō* is also a kind of typeface.

2. 朝鮮のこと *Chōsen no koto* Concerning (pre-war) Korea:

• 日朝関係 *Nitchō kankei* Japan-Korea relations.

3. 外国に対して、日本のこと *Gaikoku ni taishite, Nihon no koto* Japan, as distinguished from other countries:

• 本朝 *Hon-chō (= waga kuni)* this country; 帰朝 *ki-chō* coming back to Japan.

-chō[7] 庁　　接尾語　suffix

役人が事務を行なう場所 *Yakunin ga jimu wo okonau basho* Government offices:

• 県庁 *ken-chō* prefectural offices; 警視庁 *keishi-chō* Metropolitan Police Board.

→ 省 *shō* department; 局 *kyoku* bureau; 署 *sho* station.

-chō[8] 調　接尾語 suffix

1. 音楽で、音階の種類 *Ongaku de, onkai no shurui* In music, tone, tune, key:

• 長調 *chō-chō* major key; ハ調 *ha-chō* tone C.

2. 詩歌で、音数によるリズム *Shiika de, onsū ni yoru rizumu* In poetry, meter:

• 七五調 *shichi-go-chō* seven-five meter.

-chō[9] 貼　接尾語 suffix

紙に包んだ薬を数える語 *Kami ni tsutsunda kusuri wo kazoeru go* Counter for doses of medicine wrapped in paper:

• 三十貼で、一週間分です。 *Sanjitchō de, isshūkanbun desu.* There are 30 doses, one week's supply.

chū 中　接頭語・自立語・接尾語 *settōgo • jiritsugo • setsubigo* prefix, independent word and suffix

A. As an independent word.

1. 中ほど・普通 *Naka-hodo • futsū* Medium, average:

• 中の品 *chū no shina* average quality goods.

2. 偏らないこと *Katayoranai koto* Being unbiased:

• 中を取る *chū wo toru* steer a middle course.

3. 中国・中学の略 *Chūgoku • chūgaku no ryaku* Contraction of China, Junior High:

• 中ソ関係 *Chū-So kankei Sino-Soviet relations;* 市立中 *shiritsu-chū • ichi-ritsu-chū* Municipal Junior High (*ichi-ritsu,* to avoid confusion with 私立 *shi-ritsu → watakushi*).

B. As a prefix.

1. 真ん中 *Mannaka* Center:

• 中心となって働く *chū-shin to natte hataraku* play a leading role.

2. ものとものとの間 *Mono to mono to no aida* In between:

• 中継放送 *chū-kei hōsō* relay broadcast.

3. 中ほど *Naka-hodo* Halfway:

• 中立を守る *chū-ritsu wo mamoru* remain neutral.

4. 内側 *Uchigawa* The inside:

• 中外（＝内外 *nai-gai*) at home and abroad.

5. (毒が）当たる *(Doku ga) ataru* Be poisoned, become addicted:

• 中毒する *chū-doku suru* be poisoned, become addicted.

NOTE. There are many *jū-bako* words (Appendix A) with the prefix *chū-*:

• 中細の *chū-boso no* medium fine (brush, nib); 中古の *chū-buru/*

chū-ko no second-hand; 中辛の *chū-gara no* medium spiced; 中型・中形の *chū-gata no* middle-sized; 中腰 *chū-goshi* half-sitting posture; 中幅の *chū-haba no* of medium width; 中くらいの *chū-kurai no* of average (height, etc.).

C. As a suffix.

1. 内側 *Uchi-gawa* The inside:
- 空気中の酸素 *kūki-chū no sanso* the oxygen in the air.

2. ある時期の間 *Aru jiki no aida* During a certain period:
- 寒中 *kanchū* (in) the cold season; 暑中 *sho-chū* (in) the hot season.

3. しているうちに *Shite iru uchi ni* In progress:
- 営業中 *eigyō-chū* open for business; 工事中 *kōji-chū* under construction.

4. 真ん中 *Mannaka* The center:
- 南中 *nan-chū* southing; 北中 *hoku-chū* northing.

5. ある範囲の全体 *Aru han'i no zentai* Throughout:
- 午前中 *gozen-chū* (in the) forenoon; 国中 *kuni-jū* all over the country.

NOTE. The addition of *ni* restricts the time period:
- 今週中に出来上がる *Konshū-chū ni deki-agaru.* It will be ready within the week.

6. 予想と事実が一致すること *Yosō to jijitsu ga itchi suru koto* Come true, score:
- 命中・的中する *mei-chū・teki-chū suru* hit the mark, come true; 熱中する *netchū suru* become absorbed in.

D. 中 is the mean in the following series of threes:
- 長・中・短 *chō・chū・tan* long, medium short, as in 中編小説 *chū-hen shōsetsu* novelette.
- 大・中・小 *dai・chū・shō* large, medium, small, as in 中脳 *chū-nō* midbrain.
- 男・中・女 *dan・chū・jo* masc., neuter, fem., as in 中性 *chū-sei* neuter gender.
- 遠・中・近 *en・chū・kin* distant, mid-distance, close, as in 中景 *chū-kei* middle-distance view.
- 北・中・南 *hoku・chū・nan* north, middle, south, as in 中部 *chū-bu* middle section (geog.).
- 上・中・下 *jō・chū・ge* early, middle, late, as in 中旬 *chū-jun* middle ten-day period of a month
- 古・中・近 *ko・chū・kin* early, middle, late, as in 中世 *chū-sei* middle ages.

- 高・中・小 *kō・chū・shō* higher, middle, lower, as in 中等 *chū-tō* middle level.
- 高・中・低 *kō・chū・tei* higher, middle, lower, as in 中学年 *chū-gakunen* middle (school) grades.
- 老・中・青 *rō・chū・sei* old, middle age, young, as in 中年 *chū-nen* middle age.
- 大・中・少 *tai・chū・shō* three grades of military ranks, as in 中佐 *chū-sa* lieutenant colonel
- 強・中・とろ *tsuyo・chū・toro* strong, medium, weak, as in 中火 *chū-bi* medium strength of fire.
- 前・中・後 *zen・chū・kō* first, middle, last, as in 中略 *chū-ryaku* omission (of middle part).

E. The reading of 中 in even high-frequency compounds can be perplexing; here are some examples:

- 家中 1. *ka-chū* inside the house; the whole family; *daimyo's* retainers.
  2. *uchi-jū* all over the house; the whole family.
- 年中 1. *nen-jū* all the year round, always.
  2. *nen-jū, nen-chū* as in 年中行事 *nen-chū (nen-jū) gyōji* regular annual events.
- 日中 1. *nitchū* daytime; during the day (also "Japan-China")
  2. *hi-naka* in 昼日中に *hiru hi-naka ni* in broad daylight.
- 連中 *ren-chū, ren-jū* company, set, troupe (slightly disparaging).
- 最中 1. *sai-chū* (at the) height (of).
  2. *monaka* bean-jam wafer.
- 心中 1. *shin-jū* double [group] suicide.
  2. *shin-chū* heart, true motive.
- 夜中 1. *ya-chū,* nighttime; during the night.
  2. *yo-naka* midnight.
  3. *yo-jū* (hist.) = *yo-dōshi* all night long.

D

-da[1] だ 助動詞 auxiliary verb

The conjugation is as follows: 1. *daro* 2. *datt'* (だっ), *de* 3. *da* 4. *na* 5. *nara* 6. —.

断定・解説を表す *Dantei・kaisetsu wo arawasu* Expresses assertion or explanation. The *-da* corresponds to the copula of Western languages.

1. 体言に付く *Taigen ni tsuku* Is added to nominals:

- 問題の核心はこれだ。 *Mondai no kakushin wa kore da.* This is the heart of the matter.

2. 助詞に付く *Joshi ni tsuku* Is added to particles:

- 大寒は今からだ。 *Daikan wa ima kara da.* The severe cold starts now.

3. 動詞・助動詞・形容詞の終止形には、未然形「だろ」と仮定形「なら」だけが付く *Dōshi • jodōshi • keiyōshi no shūshikei ni wa, mizen-kei "daro" to kateikei "nara" dake ga tsuku* Only Base 1 (*daro*) and Base 5 (*nara*) may be added to the final form of verbs, auxiliaries and adjectives:

- 知っているだろう。 *Shitte iru darō.* He probably knows.
- 面白くないなら止めよう。 *Omoshiroku nai nara yameyō.* If it's boring, let's quit.
- 高いなら買わない。 *Takai nara kawanai.* If it's expensive, I won't buy it.

NOTE. The auxiliaries to which *daro* and *nara* may be attached are: *-reru, -rareru; -seru, saseru; -nai, -tai, -rashii, -nu* and *-ta.*

- 雨に降られるだろう。 *Ame ni furareru darō.* They will probably be caught in the rain.
- 食べたくないなら、食べなくてもいい。 *Tabetaku-nai nara, tabenakute mo ii.* If you don't want to, you don't have to eat it.
- 私が忘れたなら、教えてください。 *Watashi ga wasureta nara, oshiete kudasai.* If I should happen to forget, please tell me.

4. 連体形「な」は、助詞「の」「ので」「のに」に連なる場合だけに用いる *Rentaikei "na" wa, joshi "no", "no de", "no ni" ni tsuranaru baai dake ni mochiiru* Base 4 *na* is used only before the particles *no, no de, no ni:*

- 今病気なのだ。 *Ima byōki na no da.* He is ill just now.
- 休日なので人出が多い。 *Kyūjitsu na no de hito-de ga ooi.* There is a good turn-out because of the holiday.
- 冬なのにずいぶん暖かだ。 *Fuyu na no ni zuibun atataka da.* It is quite warm for winter.

5. 仮定形「なら」は、助動詞「ます」にも付く *Kateikei "nara" wa, jodōshi "-masu" ni mo tsuku* Base 5 *nara* may be added also to the auxiliary verb *-masu:*

- お出でになりますなら、お伴致します。 *Oide ni narimasu nara, o-tomo itashimasu.* If you intend to go, I will go with you.

6. 連用形「で」は、中止法と、「ある」「ない」が続く、という二つの用

法がある *Ren'yōkei "de" wa, chūshi-hō to, "aru", "nai" ga tsuzuku, to iu futatsu no yōhō ga aru* Base 2 *de* has two usages: to mark a pause, and before *aru* and *nai*:

- これが原文で、あれが翻訳だ。 *Kore ga genbun de, are ga hon'yaku da.* This is the original and that is the translation.
- 人間は理性のある動物である。 *Ningen wa risei no aru dōbutsu de aru.* Man is a rational animal.
- 本当でないことも言った。 *Hontō de nai koto mo itta.* He also said things that were not true.

7. 断定の「だ」「です」「である」は、助詞「の」に続く場合、説明・判断の気持ちの加わった言い方になる *Dantei no "da", "desu", "de aru" wa, joshi "no" ni tsuzuku baai, setsumei • handan no kimochi no kuwawatta ii-kata ni naru* When the copulae *da, desu, de aru* follow the particle *no,* they acquire a sense of explanation or personal opinion:

- ちょっと待って、鉛筆を捜しているのだ。 *Chotto matte, enpitsu wo sagashite iru no da.* Wait a moment, please; (you see) I am looking for a pencil.
- 具体的な構想を持っているのですか。 *Gutai-teki na kōsō wo motte iru no desu ka?* (You mean to say that) He has a definite plan?

NOTE. Base 2 *datt'* is followed by *-te, -ta, -tari,* but there is also a *datte* derived from *da* and *tote.* → *datte*

-da² だ

Voiced form of past auxiliary *-ta,* found in verbs ending in *-bu, -gu, -nu:* 選ぶ *eran-da;* 泳ぐ *oyoi-da;* 死ぬ *shinda.*

-dai¹ 大　接尾語　suffix

名詞に付いて、「そのくらいの大きさ」 *Meishi ni tsuite, "sono kurai no ookisa"* With nouns, = about the size of. . . :

- 実物大の *jitsubutsu-dai no* life-size; 鶏卵大の *keiran-dai no* egg-size.

-dai² 代　接尾語　suffix

1. 王位などの期間・順序を数える語 *Ō-i nado no kikan • junjo wo kazoeru go* Counter for period or order of reigns: → *-chō⁶*

- 三代将軍 *san-dai Shōgun* the third Shōgun; 歴代の天皇 *reki-dai no Tennō* successive Emperors.

2. 年齢・時間などを示す *Nenrei • jikan nado wo shimesu* Indicates age or period:

- 十代の少年少女 *jū-dai no shōnen-shōjo* teenagers; 千九百八十年代 *sen-kyūhyaku-hachijū-nen-dai* the 1980's.

-dai[3] 台 接尾語 suffix

1. 小高い、平らなところを示す *Ko-dakai, taira na tokoro wo shimesu* Denotes a slightly raised, flat surface:
   - 見晴らし台 *miharashi-dai* lookout; 物干し台 *monohoshi-dai* drying-platform.
2. 車・機械などを数える語 *Kuruma • kikai nado wo kazoeru go* Counter for vehicles, machines and the like:
   - 車三台 *kuruma san-dai* three automobiles; 旋盤数台 *senban sū-dai* several lathes.
3. 値段・数量などの大体の範囲を示す *Nedan • sūryō nado no daitai no han'i wo shimesu* Denotes a rough estimate of price, quantity, and such:
   - 千円台の品 *sen'en-dai no shina* something costing roughly ¥1000; 四十台の人 *yonjū-dai no hito* a person in his forties.
4. 盛り土の上の建物 *Mori-tsuchi no ue no tatemono* Tower:
   - 気象台 *kishō-dai* weather station; 天文台 *tenmon-dai* observatory; 灯台 *tō-dai* lighthouse.

daimeishi 代名詞 pronoun

人・事物・場所など、その名を言わないで、直接に指して言う言葉 *Hito • jibutsu • basho nado, sono na wo iwanaide, chokusetsu ni sashite iu kotoba* A word that refers to persons, things, places, etc. directly, without using their name.

1. 人称代名詞 *Ninshō daimeishi* (also *jin-daimeishi*) Personal pronoun:
   1. 自称 *ji-shō* 1st. person
      - わたくし、わたし、ぼく、おれ *watakushi, watashi, boku, ore.*
   2. 対称 *tai-shō* 2nd. person
      - あなた、きみ、おまえ *anata, kimi, omae.*
   3. 他称 *ta-shō* 3rd. person
      - このかた、そのかた、あのかた、かれ。 *kono kata, sono kata, ano kata, kare.*
   4. 不定称 *futei-shō* indeterminate
      - どのかた、どなた、だれ *dono kata, donata, dare.*
2. 指示代名詞 *Shiji daimeishi* Demonstrative pronoun:
   - これ、それ、あれ、どれ、なに *kore, sore, are, dore, nani.*
   - ここ、そこ、あそこ（あすこ）、どこ *koko, soko, asoko (asuko), doko.*
   - こちら、こっち、そちら、そっち、あちら、あっち、どちら、どっち *kochira, kotchi, sochira, sotchi, achira, atchi, dochira, dotchi.*

NOTE. The three degrees of proximity, in the case of both personal and demonstrative pronouns, are:

- 近称　*kin-shō* proximal: このかた、これ、ここ、こちら *kono kata, kore, koko, kochira.*
- 中称　*chū-shō* mesial: そのかた、それ、そこ、そちら *sono kata, sore, soko, sochira.*
- 遠称　*en-shō* distal: あのかた、かれ、あれ、あそこ、あちら *ano kata, kare, are, asoko, achira.*

These pronouns form a large part of the paradigm of *ko-so-a-do* words. See Introduction (II).

-daka　高　　接尾語　suffix

1. 金額の高いことを示す　*Kingaku no takai koto wo shimesu* Denotes that the sum is above that quoted (mainly in stock-market quotations):

- 五円高　*goen-daka* up by ¥5.

2. 分量・数量の意を表す　*Bunryō・sūryō no i wo arawasu* Adds the idea of quantity or number:

- 出来高　*deki-daka* yield, output; 生産高　*seisan-daka* output; 売上高 *uriagedaka* sales; 残高　*zan-daka* remainder.

dake　だけ　　副助詞　adverbial particle

体言・用言の連体形・副詞などに付く　*Taigen・yōgen no rentaikei・fukushi nado ni tsuku* Is added to nominals, to Base 4 of verbals, and to adverbs and other parts of speech.

1. 限定を表す　*Gentei wo arawasu* Expresses restriction:

- 一度だけ言っておく。 *Ichido dake itte oku.* I'll tell you once and for all.
- 君だけは分かってほしい。 *Kimi dake wa wakatte hoshii.* I sincerely hope that you, at least, will understand.
- 見ただけで気持ちが悪くなる。 *Mita dake de kimochi ga waruku naru.* The mere sight of it makes me sick.

Note the effect of a change in position of the particle:

- 注射だけで治る。 *Chūsha dake de naoru.* An injection is all he needs.
- 注射でだけ治る。 *Chūsha de dake naoru.* Only an injection will cure him.

2. 最低の限度を表す　*Saitei no gendo wo arawasu* Denotes lowest limit:

- これだけは確かだ。 *Kore dake wa tashika da.* This alone is certain.
- それだけ読めれば充分だ。 *Sore dake yomereba jūbun da.* It is enough if you can read that much.

3. 程度を表す　*Teido wo arawasu* Denotes degree:

- 二つだけ年上だ。 *Futatsu dake toshi-ue da.* He is two years older.

- 歩けるだけ歩きなさい。 *Arukeru dake aruki nasai.* Walk as far as you can.

4. 相当を表す *Sōtō wo arawasu* Denotes correspondence or equivalence:

- 飴を三百円だけ買ってきた。 *Ame wo sanbyaku-en dake katte kita.* He went and bought ¥300 worth of candy.
- 弁当を食べるだけの時間もない。 *Bentō wo taberu dake no jikan mo nai.* There isn't even time to have lunch.

NOTE. Some idiomatic uses.

1. 「…だけのことはある」の形で、相応の意を表す *". . . dake no koto wa aru" no katachi de, sō-ō no i wo arawasu* In *. . . dake no koto wa aru* form, = be worth one's while:

- 勉強しただけのことはあった。 *Benkyō shita dake no koto wa atta.* It was worth his while to have studied.
- さすがに大学を出ただけのことはある。 *Sasuga ni daigaku wo deta dake no koto wa aru.* It was well worth his while to have graduated from university.

2. 「…ば…だけ」の形で、程度を表す *". . . -ba . . . dake" no katachi de, teido wo arawasu* In *. . . ba . . . dake* form, denotes degree:

- 読めば読むだけ面白くなる。 *Yomeba yomu dake omoshiroku naru.* The more you read (it) the more interesting it becomes.

3. 「…だけに」「…だけあって」の形で、相応の意を表す *". . . dake ni", ". . . dake atte" no katachi de, sō-ō no i wo arawasu* In *. . . dake ni* or *. . . dake atte* form, expresses a sense of suitability:

- 末っ子だけにひとしお可愛がられた。 *Suekko dake ni hitoshio kawaigarareta.* She was loved all the more for being the youngest child.
- こんなことがあっただけに、母亡きあとは寂しいだろう。 *Konna koto ga atta dake ni, haha naki ato wa sabishii darō.* Because of these events, life after Mother's death will be all the more lonely.
- 母親がきれいなだけあって、彼女も美人だ。 *Haha-oya ga kirei na dake atte, kanojo mo bijin da.* It is little wonder that she is such a belle, when her mother is so beautiful.

dake and case particles

Ga and *wo* follow, but are often omitted; *ni, e, kara,* etc. may precede or follow, but their position influences the meaning, as in 1 above.

dake ~ shika

1. *dake* is used in both positive and negative contexts, *shika* only in negative.
2. *dake* may modify a whole clause, while *shika* rarely does so.
3. *dake. . . shika* is a frequent combination:

- この湖だけにしかいない魚だ。 *Kono mizuumi dake ni shika inai sakana da.* It is a fish found only in this lake.

NOTE. *dake* is one of the particles that may come between a verb and its auxiliary. → *bakari, -kiri, nomi, shika*

da no だの　副助詞　adverbial particle

助動詞「だ」に、格助詞「の」からなる; 体言・用言の終止形・形容詞の語幹に付く *Jodōshi "-da" ni, kaku-joshi "no" kara naru; taigen • yōgen no shūshikei • keiyōshi no gokan ni tsuku* Composed of the auxiliary *da* and the case particle *no;* added to nominals, to Base 3 of verbals, and to stem of adjectives.

総括的な例や、両極端の例を列挙して、その他にも列挙出来るというゆとりを残す

Sōkatsu-teki na rei ya, ryō-kyokutan no rei wo rekkyo shite, sono hoka ni mo rekkyo dekiru to iu yutori wo nokosu Lists representative examples, or examples of both extremes, to suggest that the listing is not exhaustive:

- 何だのかんだので金が要る。 *Nan da no kan da no de kane ga iru.* I need money for one thing or another.
- お菓子だの果物だの随分食べたね。 *O-kashi da no kudamono da no zuibun tabeta ne.* What with sweets, fruit and so on, you had quite a feast, didn't you?
- 行くだの行かないだの、はっきりしない人だ。 *Iku da no ikanai da no, hakkiri shinai hito da.* He is the kind that can't make up his mind whether to go or not.
- 「出て行け」だの「死ね」だのと辛く当たる。 *"Dete ike!" da no, "Shine!" da no to tsuraku ataru.* He takes it out on him, saying such things as "Get lost!", and "Go to hell!"
- 寂しいだの辛いだのと、不平ばかり言っている。*Sabishii da no tsurai da no to, fuhei bakari itte iru.* She is forever complaining, saying that she is lonely, or having a hard time of it, or something like that.

-dara だら

過去の助動詞「だ」の仮定形 *Kako no jodōshi "-da" no kateikei* Base 5 (conditional) of past auxiliary *-da* (of *eran-da, oyoi-da, shin-da*):

- その本を読んだらどうですか。 *Sono hon wo yondara dō desu ka?* How about reading the book?

-darake だらけ　接尾語　suffix

体言に付いて、形容動詞を作り、「嫌になるほどいっぱいある」という意

味を添える *Taigen ni tsuite, keiyōdōshi wo tsukuri, "iya ni naru hodo ippai aru" to iu imi wo soeru* Added to nominals, makes adjectival nouns of them, giving the idea of a surfeit:

- 教室は埃だらけだった。 *Kyōshitsu wa hokori-darake datta.* The classroom was covered with dust.
- 借金だらけで、首が回らない。 *Shakkin-darake de, kubi ga mawaranai.* I am up to my ears in debt. → *-mamire*

  血だらけの *chi-darake no* gory; 傷だらけの *kizu-darake no* covered with wounds; 間違いだらけの *machigai-darake no* full of errors.

NOTE. Undesirable excess is usually implied, but exceptions will be found, like:

- 花だらけの *hana-darake no* covered in flowers.

dare だれ（誰） 代名詞 pronoun

人代名詞、他称、不定称 *Jin-daimeishi, tashō, futeishō* Personal pronoun, 3rd. person, indeterminate:

- あの人はだれですか。 *Ano hito wa dare desu ka?* Who is that person?
- だれが書いたのでしょうか。 *Dare ga kaita no deshō ka?* Who wrote it, I wonder?
- だれにしましょうか。 *Dare ni shimashō ka?* Who shall I choose?
- だれにもそのことを言うな。 *Dare ni mo sono koto wo iu na.* Don't tell anyone.

NOTE. *donata* is the polite form; *ta* and *tare* are old forms.

dare ka

- だれかいないか。 *Dare ka inai ka?* Is anybody there?
- だれかが来たようだ。 *Dare ka ga kita yō da.* It seems somebody has come.
- だれかに知らせてください。 *Dare ka ni shirasete kudasai.* Please tell somebody.
- だれか（を）呼んでください。 *Dare ka (wo) yonde kudasai.* Please call somebody.
- だれか適当な人を捜している。 *Dare ka tekitō na hito wo sagashite iru.* We are looking for a suitable person.

dare mo

- だれもが知っていることだ。 *Dare mo ga shitte iru koto da.* It is common knowledge.
- だれも来なかった。 *Dare mo konakatta.* Nobody turned up.

dare de mo

- だれでも欠点のない人はない。 *Dare de mo ketten no nai hito wa nai.* Nobody is without his faults. (Nobody is perfect.)

- だれ（に）でもそんなことが出来る。 *Dare (ni) de mo sonna koto ga dekiru.* Anyone can do that.

dare + verb + -de mo, -te mo

- だれが見ても構わない。 *Dare ga mite mo kamawanai.* It doesn't matter who sees it.
- だれが読んでも、僕は絶対に読まない。 *Dare ga yonde mo, boku wa zettai ni yomanai.* No matter who reads it, I certainly won't.

NOTE. There are also the two phrases **dare hitori** and **dare shi mo**:

- だれ一人として喜ばぬものはなかった。 *Dare hitori to shite yorokobanu mono wa nakatta.* Everyone without exception was pleased.
- だれしも同じことだ。 *Dare shi mo onaji koto da.* Everyone is in the same boat.

-dari → *-tari*[1]

-daro だろう 助動詞 auxiliary verb

「だ」の未然形と推量の助動詞「う」からなる。動詞型・形容詞型の活用語の連体形、特殊の助動詞「た」・「ぬ」の連体形に付く。体言やある助詞にも付く。 *"-Da" no mizenkei to, suiryō no jodōshi "-u" kara naru. Dōshi-gata • keiyōshi-gata no katsuyō-go no rentaikei, tokushu no jodōshi "-ta" • "-nu" no rentaikei ni tsuku. Taigen ya aru joshi ni mo tsuku.* Consists of Base 1 of the copula *-da* and the conjectural auxiliary *-u*. Is added to Base 4 of verb-type and adjective-type conjugables, and to Base 4 of the special conjugation auxiliaries *-ta* and *-nu*. Is added also to nominals and to some particles.

1. 推量を表す *Suiryō wo arawasu* Expresses conjecture:

- もうすぐ来るだろう。 *Mō sugu kuru darō.* He should be coming shortly.
- その日を決して忘れないだろう。 *Sono hi wo kesshite wasurenai darō.* I don't think they will ever forget that day.
- 一体、何だろう。 *Ittai, nan darō?* What on earth is it, I wonder?
- 式が始まるのは、九時からだろう。 *Shiki ga hajimaru no wa, ku-ji kara darō.* It will probably be nine o'clock before the ceremony begins.

2. 相手に同意を求める *Aite ni dōi wo motomeru* Asks the other party to agree:

- その説は少しおかしいだろう。 *Sono setsu wa sukoshi okashii darō.* Don't you think that theory a bit odd?

NOTE. *darō* always implies conjecture, and does not correctly translate the definite future of Western languages.

-dasu 出す　接尾語　suffix verb

動詞の連用形に付く *Dōshi no ren'yōkei ni tsuku* Is added to Base 2 of verbs.

1. 中から外へ移す動作を表す *Naka kara soto e utsusu dōsa wo arawasu* Expresses the act of taking out or putting out:

- 袋からお菓子を取り出した。 *Fukuro kara o-kashi wo tori-dashita.* She took some sweets out of the bag.
- 窓から頭を突き出した。 *Mado kara atama wo tsuki-dashita.* I stuck my head out of the window.

2. 動作を始めるという意味を添える *Dōsa wo hajimeru to iu imi wo soeru* Adds the meaning of beginning the action:

- 雨が降り出した。 *Ame ga furi-dashita.* It has begun to rain.
- 急に皆が笑いだした。 *Kyū ni mina ga warai-dashita.* Suddenly they all burst out laughing.
- 詩を作り出すと、寝食を忘れる。 *Shi wo tsukuri-dasu to, shinshoku wo wasureru.* Once he starts composing poems, he forgets to sleep and eat.

NOTE. With verbs like *tsukuru,* the context will have to be the guide as to which of the two meanings is implied:

- もうすぐ新型を作り出す。 *Mō sugu shin-gata wo tsukuri-dasu.* We begin producing the new model very soon.
- 一日百台を作り出す。 *Ichi-nichi hyaku-dai wo tsukuri-dasu.* We turn out a hundred cars a day.

3. 努力して、隠れていたものを明らかにする *Doryoku shite kakurete ita mono wo akiraka ni suru* Brings to light, with some effort:

- 考え出す *kangae-dasu* devise; 聞き出す *kiki-dasu* find out; 見いだす *miidasu* (from old form *miizu*) discover; 思い出す *omoi-dasu* recollect; 探り出す *saguri-dasu* spy out.

NOTE. Cases of both *-dasu* and *-deru* added to the same verb will be met with; the difference is not always a matter of transitive and intransitive:

- 吹き出る *fuki-deru* break out (in sores); 吹き出す *fuki-dasu* burst out (laughing); 食み出る *hami-deru* protrude = 食み出す *hami-dasu;* 抜け出る *nuke-deru* steal out = 抜け出す *nuke-dasu;* 突き出る *tsuki-deru* protrude; 突き出す *tsuki-dasu* thrust out, hand over to the police; 浮き出る *uki-deru* rise to surface, stand out; 浮き出す *uki-dasu* stand out (in relief).

-date[1] 立て　接尾語　suffix

A. 動詞の連用形に付いて、名詞を作り *Dōshi no ren'yōkei ni tsuite, mei-shi wo tsukuri* Is added to Base 2 of verbs, nominalizes them.

1. 「ことさらに…する」という意味を添える *"Kotosara ni . . . suru" to iu imi wo soeru* Adds the idea of doing on purpose:

- 隠し立てをする *kakushi-date wo suru* keep something secret; 庇い立てする *kabai-date suru* shield, stand up for.

2. 「やたらに…する」という意味を添える *"Yatara ni . . . suru" to iu imi wo soeru* Adds the idea of doing to excess, doing at random:

- 咎め立てをする *togame-date wo suru* find fault with; 義理立てをする *giri-date wo suru* do something out of a sense of duty.

B. 名詞に付く。 *Meishi ni tsuku.* Is added to nouns.

1. 車につける牛馬、船につける櫓などを数える語 *Kuruma ni tsukeru gyūba, fune ni tsukeru ro nado wo kazoeru go* Counter for number of oxen or horses set to draw a vehicle, the number of oars to a boat, etc.:

- 四頭だての馬車 *yontō-date no basha* a four-horse carriage; 八挺だての船 *hatchō-date no fune* an eight-oared boat.

2. 映画・演劇などの一回に見せる数 *Eiga • engeki nado no ikkai ni miseru kazu* Number of features showing at one session:

- 三本立て *sanbon-date* triple feature.

3. その準備・設備をすること *Sono junbi • setsubi wo suru koto* Preparing or equipping:

- 陣立て *jin-date* battle array; 献立 *kon-date* menu.

-date[2] 建て 接尾語 suffix

建物の材料・様式・階数などを表す語 *Tatemono no zairyō • yōshiki • kaisū nado wo arawasu go* Word denoting material, architectural style, number of storeys, etc. of buildings:

- 煉瓦建ての *renga-date no* made of brick; 三階建ての *sangai-date no* three-storeyed; 平屋建て *hiraya-date* one-storey house; → *-zukuri*

-datera だてら（立て＋ら）接尾語 suffix (pejorative)

身分を示す名詞に付いて、「その人にふさわしくない」という意を添える *Mibun wo shimesu meishi ni tsuite, "sono hito ni fusawashiku nai" to iu i wo soeru* With nouns indicating status, adds the sense of "unbecoming to such a person":

- 法師だてらに *hōshi-datera ni* monk as he is; 女だてらに *onna-datera ni* woman as she is; 子供だてらに *kodomo-datera ni* out of keeping with his youth.

-dateru 立てる 接尾語 suffix verb

名詞に付いて、「そのような様子にする」 *Meishi ni tsuite, "sono yō na yōsu ni suru"* With nouns, adds the idea of setting up as:

- 荒立てる *ara-dateru* excite, aggravate; 泡立てる *awa-dateru* whip, froth up; 苛立てる *ira-dateru* irritate; 角立てる *kado-dateru* aggravate; 逆立てる *saka-dateru* ruffle; 先立てる *saki-dateru* let go ahead; 騒ぎ立てる *sawagi-tateru* raise an uproar; そば立てる *soba-dateru* prick up one's ears; 役立てる *yaku-dateru* profit by; 用立てる *yō-dateru* lend

-datsu 立つ 接尾語 suffix verb (intransitive form of *-dateru*)
名詞に付いて、「…のようになる」 *Meishi ni tsuite, ". . . no yō ni naru"* With nouns, adds the idea of "become like . . .":

- 節くれ立つ *fushikure-datsu* be knotty or bony; 際だつ *kiwa-datsu* stand out; 水際立った *mizugiwa-datta* fine, brilliant; 怖気だつ *ojike-datsu* be seized with fear; 主立つ *omo-datsu* play a central role; 表立つ *omote-datsu* become public; 殺気立つ *sakki-datsu* become excited; 鳥肌立つ *torihada-datsu* have gooseflesh.

NOTE. This list omits the verbs listed (under the entry *-dateru*) in their transitive form, and also a few verbs in which *-datsu* has the meaning of "set out" (*su-datsu, tabi-datsu, tsure-datsu,* etc.).

datte[1] だって 接続詞 conjunction

1. 理由を述べる語 *Riyū wo noberu go* States the reason why:

- だって、今日は休みだから。 *Datte, kyō wa yasumi da kara.* After all, today is a holiday, you see.

2. 反対の気持を表す *Hantai no kimochi wo arawasu* Expresses a sense of opposition:

- どうして寝ないのか。だって、まだ眠くないんだもの。 *Dōshite nenai no ka? Datte, mada nemuku nain' da mono.* Why don't you go to bed? But I'm not sleepy yet!

datte[2] だって 副助詞 adverbial particle

1. 代表的な例を挙げて、他も同じであることを類推させる *Daihyōteki na rei wo agete, hoka mo onaji de aru koto wo ruisui saseru* Gives a minor example, suggesting that there are weightier ones besides:

- 猿だって木から落ちることもある。 *Saru datte ki kara ochiru koto mo aru.* Even Homer sometimes nods.

2. 強調しながら例を加える *Kyōchō-shinagara rei wo kuwaeru* Emphasizes and furnishes an example:

- 君も損するだろうが、僕だって損する。 *Kimi mo son-suru darō ga, boku datte son-suru.* You may stand to lose, but so do I!

3. 同じようなことを並べて、その他の場合も同じであることを表す

Onaji yō na koto wo narabete, sono hoka no baai mo onaji de aru koto wo arawasu Lists similar examples to suggest that other cases, too, are comparable:

- あの人なら、テニスだって、水泳だって上手だ。 *Ano hito nara, tenisu datte, suiei datte, jōzu da.* He is good all round, tennis, swimming, you name it.

4. 不定称の代名詞を伴って、「それだけではなく、すべてのもの」という意味を表す *Futeishō no daimeishi wo tomonatte, "sore dake de wa naku, subete no mono" to iu imi wo arawasu* With indeterminate pronouns, denotes that not only the case mentioned, but all cases are similar:

- 貧乏人は、どこにだっているよ。 *Binbō-nin wa, doko ni datte iru yo.* The poor you will find everywhere.

5. 数量の語を伴って、「例外なく」という意味を表す *Sūryō no go wo tomonatte, "reigai naku" to iu imi wo arawasu* With quantity words, = without exception:

- 一滴だって飲んでいない。 *Itteki datte nonde inai.* I haven't touched a drop!
- 一日だって欠席したことはない。 *Ichi-nichi datte kesseki shita koto wa nai.* He hasn't missed a single day.

NOTE. Two expressions sounding like this *datte* are found in:

- いくら飲んだって酔わない。 *Ikura nondatte yowanai.* No matter how much he drinks, he doesn't get drunk. (*-tatte*)
- 退学したんだって。 *Taigaku shitan' datte.* I hear he has left school. (→ *-tte*)

de¹ で　接続詞　conjunction

会話で、前の話を受けて、「それで」 *Kaiwa de, mae no hanashi wo ukete, "sore de"* In conversation, leading on from the previous utterance, = Well, in that case:

- で、どうしようと言うのか。 *De, dō shiyō to iu no ka?* Well, then, what do you suggest?
- 皆集まったね。で、何から始めようか。 *Mina atsumatta ne. De, nani kara hajime-yō ka?* We're all here; well then, where shall we begin?

de² で　助動詞　auxiliary verb

指定の助動詞「だ」の連用形 *Shitei no jodōshi "da" no ren'yōkei* Base 2 of informal copula "da":

- 今日は天気で暖かい。 *Kyō wa tenki de, atatakai.* It is fine and warm today.

- 兄は教諭で、弟は技師だ。 *Ani wa kyōyu de, otōto wa gishi da.* The elder brother is a teacher, the younger, an engineer.

de³ で　格助詞　case particle

体言や体言の資格を作る「の」に付いて、動作を行なうさまざまな状況を表す *Taigen ya taigen no shikaku wo tsukuru "no" ni tsuite, dōsa wo okonau sama-zama na jōkyō wo arawasu* Added to nominals and to nominalizing *no*, expresses the various circumstances accompanying actions.

1. 場所を表す *Basho wo arawasu* Expresses the circumstance of place:

- 皆の前で恥をかいた。 *Mina no mae de haji wo kaita.* He disgraced himself in public.
- こんなところで君に会うなんて。 *Konna tokoro de kimi ni au nante!* To think that we should meet in such a place!

2. 時限・所用時間を表す *Jigen • shoyō jikan wo arawasu* Denotes period or time required for an action:

- 一年ぐらいで完成する。 *Ichinen-gurai de kansei suru.* It will be ready in about a year.
- 後一週間で今学期も終わりだ。 *Ato isshūkan de kon-gakki mo owari da.* Another week and this term, too, will be over.

3. 材料を表す *Zairyō wo arawasu* Denotes material of which something is made:

- 籠を竹で編んでいる。 *Kago wo take de ande iru.* They are weaving baskets of bamboo.
- このレンズは合成樹脂で出来ている。 *Kono renzu wa gōsei jushi de dekite iru.* These lenses are made of synthetic resin.

NOTE. As in English, if the raw material is evident in the finished product, use *de;* if it is not, use *kara* (q. v.):

- 酒は米から造る。 *Sake wa kome kara tsukuru.* They make *sake* from rice.

4. 手段・方法・道具を示す *Shudan • hōhō • dōgu wo shimesu* Denotes means, methods, utensils:

- 車で行く *kuruma de iku* go by car; 徒歩で行く *toho de iku* go on foot; 鉛筆で書く *enpitsu de kaku* write in pencil; 日本語で話す *Nihongo de hanasu* speak in Japanese; テレビで見る *terebi de miru* see on TV; 顕微鏡で見る *kenbikyō de miru* see with the aid of a microscope
- 海岸は人でいっぱいだ。 *Kaigan wa hito de ippai da.* The beach is crowded.

5. 原因・理由を表す *Gen'in • riyū wo arawasu* Denotes cause or reason:

- 病気で休んでいる。 *Byōki de yasunde iru.* He is absent through illness.
- 不注意で風をひいた。 *Fu-chūi de kaze wo hiita.* I was careless and caught a cold.
- お元気ですか。はい、おかげさまで。 *O-genki desu ka? Hai, o-kagesama de.* Are you keeping well? Yes, thank you.

6. 動作を行なう団体・人数を示す *Dōsa wo okonau dantai • ninzū wo shimesu* Denotes the group or number of people involved in an action:

- 政府で金を出す。 *Seifu de kane wo dasu.* It is the government that will bear the expense.
- 三人で相談した。 *Sannin de sōdan shita.* The three of them talked it over.

7. 話題・論題を示す *Wadai • rondai wo shimesu* Denotes topic or theme:

- いつも政治のことで議論している。 *Itsu mo seiji no koto de giron shite iru.* They are forever arguing about politics.
- 学制改革で激論した。 *Gakusei kaikaku de gekiron shita.* They had a fierce argument about the reform of the education system.

8. 基準・金額・単位を示す *Kijun • kingaku • tan'i wo shimesu* Denotes standard, sum of money, unit of measurement:

- ダースで売っている。 *Dāsu de utte iru.* They are sold by the dozen.
- 家はいくらで買ったのですか。 *Ie wa ikura de katta no desu ka?* How much did you get the house for?
- 時速八十キロで走った。 *Jisoku hachijikkiro de hashitta.* It ran at a speed of 80 k.p.h.
- 彼だと歩き方で分かった。 *Kare da to aruki-kata de wakatta.* I knew by his gait that it was he.

9. 様態を表す *Yōtai wo arawasu* Denotes mode or aspect:

- 駆け足でやってきた。 *Kake-ashi de yatte kita.* He came running.
- 何食わぬ顔で働いていた。 *Nani-kuwanu kao de hataraite ita.* He was working away as if nothing had happened.
- 熱心な口調で話した。 *Nesshin na kuchō de hanashita.* He spoke in an earnest tone (of voice).

10. 年齢を表す *Nenrei wo arawasu* Denotes age at which something occurs:

- 六十歳で退職するつもりだ。 *Rokujissai de taishoku suru tsumori da.* I intend to retire at sixty.

NOTE. While *de* denotes active location, *ni* denotes static location:

- 奈良で生まれて、大阪に住んでいる。 *Nara de umarete, Oosaka ni sunde iru.* He was born in Nara, and lives in Osaka.

- 学校の前で車に乗った。 *Gakkō no mae de kuruma ni notta.* He got into a car in front of the school.
- 学校の前に車が止まっている。 *Gakkō no mae ni kuruma ga tomatte iru.* There is a car stopped in front of the school.

NOTE. The resultative *-te aru* and both the resultative and the repetitive *-te iru* require the use of *ni* rather than *de:*

- 廊下に並べてある。 *Rōka ni narabete aru.* They are lined up in the corridor.
- 学校に来ている。 *Gakkō ni kite iru.* They have come (here) to school.
- あの店に売っている。 *Ano mise ni utte iru.* They are on sale at that shop. (Also: We sell them to that shop.)

NOTE. Unclassified examples:

- 世に多い話だ。 *Yo ni ooi hanashi da.* It's an everyday affair.
- 悲しみを顔に表した。 *Kanashimi wo kao ni arawashita.* His face showed his sorrow.
- 喜びを字に綴った。 *Yorokobi wo ji ni tsuzutta.* He put in writing the joy he felt.

de⁴ で 接続助詞 conjunctive particle

接続助詞「て」の濁った形 *Setsuzoku-joshi "-te" no nigotta katachi* Voiced form of the conjunctive particle *-te:*

- 読んであげましょうか。 *Yonde agemashō ka?* Shall I read it to you?

de⁵ 出 名詞・接尾語 noun, used also as a suffix

1. ものが出ること *Mono ga deru koto* Coming out or going out:

- 家出 *ie-de* absconding; 門出 *kado-de* departure; 外出 *soto-de (gai-shutsu)* going out; 遠出 *too-de* excursion; 早出 *haya-de* turning up early for work; 遅出 *oso-de* turning up late for work; 日の出 *hi no de* sunrise.

2. 青果物などが市場に出回ること *Seikabutsu nado ga shijō ni de-mawaru koto* Coming on market of vegetables, fruits and so on:

- 今年は葡萄の出が早い。 *Kotoshi wa budō no de ga hayai.* Grapes are on the market early this year.

3. 嵩・分量 *Kasa • bunryō* Bulk, amount:

普通、動詞の連用形＋「出がある」「出がない」の形で *futsū, dōshi no ren'yōkei + "de ga aru", "de ga nai" no katachi de* Usually, in these forms of Base 2 of verbs + *de ga aru* or *de ga nai:*

- 食い出がある *kui-de ga aru* be filling; 飲み出がある *nomi-de ga aru* be satisfying (to the thirst); 使い出がない *tsukai-de ga nai* doesn't go far; 読み出がない *yomi-de ga nai* doesn't take long to read.

4. 出る状態 *Deru jōtai* Manner of coming out or going out:
- お茶の出が悪い *o-cha no de ga warui* the tea is not well drawn; 人の出が少ない *hito no de ga sukunai* the turnout is poor; 水の出が悪い *mizu no de ga warui* there is a poor flow of water.

5. 出身 *Shusshin* Provenance:
- 貴族の出 *kizoku no de* of noble extraction; 九州の出 *Kyūshū no de* native of Kyushu; 名門の出 *meimon no de* highborn; 早稲田出の人 *Waseda-de no hito* Waseda graduate.

6. 突き出た部分 *Tsuki-deta bubun* Projecting part:
- 軒の出は六十センチ。 *Noki no de wa rokujissenchi.* The eaves project 60 cm.

de are であれ　連語 phrase

助動詞「だ」の連用形に、「ある」の命令形 *Dōshi "da" no ren'yōkei ni, "aru" no meireikei* Base 2 of the auxiliary *da* + Base 6 (imperative) of *aru:*
- たとえ先生であれ、悪いことは悪いと言う。 *Tatoe sensei de are, warui koto wa warui to iu.* Even if he is a teacher, I say that what is wrong is wrong.
- 魚であれ、肉であれ、何でも美味しく食べる。 *Sakana de are, niku de are, nan de mo oishiku taberu.* Be it fish or flesh, he eats everything with relish.

NOTE. Similar expressions are:
- 本当にしろ嘘にしろ *hontō ni shiro, uso ni shiro,* whether it be true or false; いずれにせよ *izure ni seyo* in either case; 遅かれ早かれ *osokare hayakare* sooner or later. → *-kare,* old imperative of adjective

de aru である　(from *nite ari . . . de ari . . . de aru*)

「だ」の連用形に、補助動詞「ある」。「だ」の荘重表現 *"Da" no ren'yōkei hi, hojo-dōshi "aru." "Da" no sōchō hyōgen* Base 2 of *da* + supplementary verb *aru.* Formal equivalent of copula *da:*
- 兄弟であることは知らなかった。 *Kyōdai de aru koto wa shiranakatta.* I didn't know they were siblings.
- 今ではそんな若さがなくなったのであろうか。 *Ima de wa sonna wakasa ga nakunatta no de arō ka?* Is it true that such youthful vigor has now deserted me?
- 日本一の川であって、日本海に流れ込む。 *Nippon-ichi no kawa de atte, Nihon-kai ni nagare-komu.* It is the largest river in Japan, and flows into the Sea of Japan.
- 学校の先生であれば、そんなことを言わないはずだ。 *Gakkō no*

sensei de areba, sonna koto wo iwanai hazu da. A schoolteacher oughtn't to say such things.

dekiru 出来る 動詞、上一段 verb, *kami-ichidan (deki-masu)*

「…ことが出来る」の形で、「…する能力がある」 "*. . . Koto ga dekiru" no katachi de, ". . . suru nōryoku ga aru"* In . . . *koto ga dekiru* form, denotes ability:

- 英語を読むことが出来る。 *Eigo wo yomu koto ga dekiru.* He can read English.

NOTE. After an action noun, *suru koto ga* is preferably omitted:

- まだ安心は出来ない。 *Mada anshin wa dekinai.* We still can't feel at ease.
- 事実かどうか保証出来ない。 *Jijitsu ka dō ka hoshō dekinai.* I can't vouch for it.
- だれでも利用できる設備だ。 *Dare de mo riyō dekiru setsubi da.* They are facilities that anyone may use.

NOTE: 出切る *de-kiru, de-kirimasu,* be exhausted:

- もう意見が出切ったようだ。 *Mō iken ga de-kitta yō da.* It looks as if we have run out of ideas.

de mo[1] でも 接続詞 conjunction

1. 上を受けて、それと違ったことを述べるときに使う語 *Ue wo ukete, sore to chigatta koto wo noberu toki ni tsukau go* Introduces something inconsistent with what preceded:

- 参ります。でも、すぐには行かれません。 *Mairimasu. De mo, sugu ni wa ikaremasen.* I intend to go. However, I can't go straight away.

2. 上を受けて、それについて弁護する語 *Ue wo ukete, sore ni tsuite bengo suru go* Following on the previous utterance, offers a vindication:

- 学校をさぼったね。うん、でも、頭が痛かったのだ。 *Gakkō wo sabotta ne. Un, de mo, atama ga itakatta no da.* You played truant, eh! Yes, but (you see) I had a headache.

de mo[2] でも 副助詞 adverbial particle

1. 極端な例を挙げて、他でもそうであることを示す *Kyokutan na rei wo agete, hoka de mo sō de aru koto wo shimesu* Cites an extreme case, to show that the same is true in other cases, too:

- そんなことは馬鹿でも知っている。 *Sonna koto wa baka de mo shitte iru.* Even a fool knows that.
- 子供の足でも、十分あれば行ける。 *Kodomo no ashi demo, jippun areba ikeru.* Even a child could get there on foot in ten minutes.

2.「他にもあるが」という気持ちで、仮に例を挙げる *"Hoka ni mo aru ga" to iu kimochi de, kari ni rei wo ageru* Offers an example, suggesting that there are other possibilities:

- 明日でも来てもらおうか。 *Asu de mo kite moraō ka?* Shall we have you come, say, tomorrow?
- 子供にでも言うように言った。 *Kodomo ni de mo iu yō ni itta.* She said it as if she were speaking to a child.

NOTE. This *de mo* is one of the particles that may come between a verb and its auxiliary. → *-bakari*

de mo[3] でも 接続助詞 conjunctive particle

接続助詞「て」の濁った形+「も」。逆条件を表す *Setsuzoku-joshi "-te" no nigotta katachi + "mo". Gyaku-jōken wo arawasu.* Voiced form of conjunctive particle *-te* + *mo*. Serves as an adversative conjunction:

- いくら読んでも、意味が分からない。 *Ikura yonde mo, imi ga wakaranai.* No matter how much I read it, I don't understand it.
- 転んでも泣かない子だ。 *Koronde mo nakanai ko da.* She is the kind of child that doesn't cry even if she falls.

NOTE. A slang prefix *demo-* is found in such expressions as:

- でも学者 *demo-gakusha* a pedant; でも医者 *demo-isha* a quack. でもキリスト教徒 *demo-Kirisuto kyōto* pseudo-Christian.

de motte でもって probably an overlapping of *de* and *wo motte:*

- それでもって退職した。 *Sore de motte taishoku shita.* He retired for that reason.

denbun 伝聞 名詞 noun

他人から伝え聞くこと *Tanin kara tsutae-kiku koto* Report:

- 雪がよく降るそうだ。 *Yuki ga yoku furu sō da.* They say it snows a lot.

-deru 出る 接尾語 suffix verb

Note that "progress outwards" is not always evident in compounds:

- 申し出る *mōshi-deru* propose, apply for; 名乗り出る *nanori-deru* announce oneself; 願い出る *negai-deru* send in an application; 抜きんでる *nukinderu* excel; 届け出る *todoke-deru* notify; 浮かれ出る *ukare-deru* wander aimlessly.

deshō でしょう 助動詞 auxiliary verb

「です」の未然形「でしょ」に、推量の助動詞「う」。「だろう」の丁寧語で、推量を表す *"Desu" no mizenkei "desho" ni, suiryō no jodōshi "-u." "Darō" no teineigo de, suiryō wo arawasu* Base 1 of *desu* + conjectural auxiliary *-u*. Polite form for *darō*, expresses conjecture:

- きっと明日来るでしょう。 *Kitto asu kuru deshō*. He is sure to come tomorrow.
- あそこは寒いでしょう。 *Asoko wa samui deshō*. It must be cold there.
- もうそろそろ出かけますでしょう。 *Mō sorosoro dekakemasu deshō*. It can't be long now before they leave.

desu です 助動詞 auxiliary verb

The conjugation is as follows: 1. *desho* 2. *deshi* 3. *desu* 4. (*desu*) 5. — 6. —.

丁寧な断定・指定を表す *Teinei na dantei • shitei wo arawasu* Expresses polite assertion or specification.

1.「等しい」「属する」という意味を表す *"Hitoshii", "zoku suru" to iu imi wo arawasu* Denotes equivalence or appurtenance:

- 父は課長です。 *Chichi wa kachō desu*. My father is a section chief.
- じゃが芋はナス科の多年草です。 *Jagaimo wa nasu-ka no tanensō desu*. The potato is a perennial of the eggplant family.

2. ある物事を取り立てて示す *Aru monogoto wo tori-tatete shimesu* Singles something out for specification:

- 試験は昼からです。 *Shiken wa hiru kara desu*. The exam is in the afternoon.
- 買ったのはこれです。 *Katta no wa kore desu*. This is what I bought.

3.「お＋連用形＋です」の形で、動作の主体に対する尊敬を表す *"O + ren'yōkei + desu" no katachi de, dōsa no shutai ni taisuru sonkei wo arawasu* In *o* + Base 2 + *desu* form, expresses respect for the subject of the action:

- 先生がお呼びです。 *Sensei ga o-yobi desu*. The teacher wants to see you.
- どちらへお出掛けですか。 *Dochira e o-dekake desu ka?* Where are you going?

4. 代動詞として用いられる *Dai-dōshi to shite mochiirareru* Serves as a substitute verb:

- 朝御飯にいつもコーヒーだけです。 *Asa-gohan ni itsu mo kōhī dake desu*. I always have only coffee for breakfast.

5. 形容詞に付いて、丁寧を表す *Keiyōshi ni tsuite, teinei wo arawasu* With adjectives, renders the expression polite:

- こちらはまだ寒いです。 *Kochira wa mada samui desu.* It is still cold here.

NOTE. The informal *da* must not be added to Base 3 of adjectives, since this is already the informal ending. It should be added, instead, to adjectival nouns, unless a more polite form is used: *kirei da, kirei desu, kirei de gozaimasu.*

NOTE. *Desu* is added to the same range of particles as *da*, viz.: *bakari, dake, gurai, hodo, kara, made, nado, no, yara.*

desu ne / desu na ですね / ですな

1. 文節の切れ目に付けて勿体を付ける感じを表す *Bunsetsu no kire-me ni tsukete, mottai wo tsukeru kanji wo arawasu* Inserted at junctures in sentence, adds an air of importance:
   - この機械はですね、日本で開発したものです。 *Kono kikai wa desu ne, Nihon de kaihatsu shita mono desu.* This machine, let me tell you, was developed in Japan.
2. 文末に付けて、相手の同意を求める *Bunmatsu ni tsukete, aite no dōi wo motomeru* Added to the end of a sentence, requests the agreement of the other party:
   - 寒いですな。 *Samui desu na.* It is cold, isn't it?
   - これは彼女のですね。 *Kore wa kanojo no desu ne.* This is hers, I suppose.

NOTE. *Desu na* is used by men, especially older men.

de wa¹ では 接続詞 conjunction

「だ」の連用形に、限定助詞「は」。話題を変える意味を表す *"Da" no ren'yōkei ni, gentei-joshi "wa." Wadai wo kaeru imi wo arawasu* Base 2 of *da* + restrictive particle *wa*. Signals change of topic:

- では、これで失礼致します。 *De wa, kore de shitsurei itashimasu.* Well, I'll be off now.

de wa² では 接続助詞 conjunctive particle

格助詞「で」に、限定助詞「は」 *Kaku-joshi "de" ni, gentei-joshi "wa"* Case particle *de* + restrictive particle *wa:*

- 私の考えでは、良い工夫だ。 *Watashi no kangae de wa, yoi kufū da.* To my mind, it's a good idea.
- これとそれとでは、どちらが好きですか。 *Kore to sore to de wa, dochira ga suki desu ka?* Which would you prefer, these ones or those?

-de wa では 接続助詞 conjunctive particle

接続助詞「で」に、限定助詞「は」 *Setsuzoku-joshi "-de" ni, gentei-joshi "wa"* Conjunctive particle *-de* + restrictive particle *wa:*

- 返さないでは気が済まない。 *Kaesanaide wa ki ga sumanai.* I shan't be happy until I have given it back.
- 呼んでは見たが、起きはしない。 *Yonde wa mita ga, oki wa shinai.* I tried calling him, but he hasn't budged.
- そんな本を読んではだめ。 *Sonna hon wo yonde wa dame.* You mustn't read such books.

→ *-te wa*

de wa aru ga ではあるが 連語 phrase

Wa here has its characteristic role of concession:

- 学者ではあるが、良い先生ではない。 *Gakusha de wa aru ga, yoi sensei de wa nai.* It is true that he is a scholar, but he is not a good teacher.

do- ど 接頭語 prefix

名詞・形容詞の上に付いて、意味を強める *Meishi • keiyōshi no ue ni tsuite, imi wo tsuyomeru* Prefixed to nouns and adjectives, strengthens their meaning:

- ど偉い *do-erai* enormous, terrific; どぎつい *do-gitsui* gaudy, loud; ど根性 *do-konjō* doggedness; ど真ん中 *do-mannaka* right in the middle.

do 度 名詞・助数詞 noun, counter

色々なものを計る単位 *Iro-iro na mono wo hakaru tan'i* Unit of measurement;

- 不透明度 *futōmei-do* opacity; 歩度 *ho-do* walking-pace; 緯度 *i-do* latitude; 角度 *kaku-do* angular degree, direction, point of view; 感度 *kan-do* sensitivity; 経度 *kei-do* longitude; 高度 *kō-do* altitude; 硬度 *kō-do* hardness; 光度 *kō-do* luminosity; 強度 *kyō-do* strength, intensity; 民度 *min-do* cultural level; 密度 *mitsu-do* density; 濃度 *nō-do* density; 温度 *on-do* temperature; 精度 *sei-do* precision; 鮮度 *sen-do* freshness; 震度 *shin-do* seismic intensity; 湿度 *shitsu-do* humidity; 透明度 *tōmei-do* transparency.

NOTE. *Do* as a noun is found in such compounds as:

- 度の強いレンズ *do no tsuyoi renzu* "thick" lenses; 何度もやってみる *nando mo yatte miru* make ever so many attempts; 度を過ぎる・

度を越す *do wo sugiru* • *do wo kosu* carry something too far; 得度する *toku-do suru* enter the Buddhist priesthood.

dō どう 副詞 adverb

1. 不定の状態・行動を示す *Futei no jōtai* • *kōdō wo shimesu* Denotes indeterminate state or action:

- どういう意味ですか。 *Dō iu imi desu ka?* What does it mean?
- どうかこうか *dō ka kō ka* somehow or other
- どうもありがとう。 *Dō mo arigatō.* Thanks ever so much.
- どう見ても、音楽家ではない。 *Dō mite mo, ongakka de wa nai.* He is anything but a musician.

2. 相手の気分・意向などについての軽い疑問 *Aite no kibun* • *ikō nado ni tsuite no karui gimon* Mild form of inquiry as to feelings or opinion of the other party:

- 今日はどうですか。 *Kyō wa dō desu ka?* How are you today?/What about today?
- 映画はどうでしたか。 *Eiga wa dō deshita ka?* What did you think of the film?

→ *ā, kō, sō, ikaga.*

dochira どちら 代名詞 pronoun

指示代名詞、不定称。方角を示す *Shiji-daimeishi, futeishō. Hōgaku wo shimesu* Demonstrative pronoun, indeterminate. Indicates direction.

「だれ」「どこ」「どれ」よりも丁寧な言い方 *"Dare", "doko", "dore" yori mo teinei na ii-kata* Is a more polite form for *dare, doko,* and *dore:*

1. どの方角 *dono hōgaku* which direction:

- どちらへ行ったでしょうか。 *Dochira e itta deshō ka?* Which way did they go?

2. どれ・いずれ *dore* • *izure* which (of two or more)?

- 梨と桃とでは、どちらが好きですか。 *Nashi to momo to de wa, dochira ga suki desu ka?* Which do you prefer, pears or peaches?

3. どの場所 *dono basho?* where?:

- どちらにお住まいですか。 *Dochira ni o-sumai desu ka?* Where do you live?

4. どなた *donata?* who?:

- 失礼ですが、どちら様でいらっしゃいますか。 *Shitsurei desu ga, dochira-sama de irasshaimasu ka?* Pardon my asking, but who are you?

NOTE. For *dochira* and particles (*ka, mo, de mo*), see also *dare.*

- どちらかといえば、ここにいたい。 *Dochira ka to ieba, koko ni itai.* Given the choice, I should prefer to stay here.
- どちらも読みやすい。 *Dochira mo yomi-yasui.* They are both (They are all) easy to read.
- どちらにしても、たいした変わりはない。 *Dochira ni shite mo, taishita kawari wa nai.* There's little to choose between them.

NOTE. Both *dochi* and *dotchi* are less standard forms.

doko どこ 代名詞 pronoun
指示代名詞、不定称。場所を示す *Shiji-daimeishi, futeishō. Basho wo shimesu* Demonstrative pronoun, indeterminate. Denotes location.

1. どういうところ *Dō iu tokoro?* What place?:
- ここはどこですか。 *Koko wa doko desu ka?* Where are we now?
- どこのお生まれですか。 *Doko no o-umare desu ka?* Where were you born?

2. どういう点 *Dō iu ten?* What feature?:
- この案のどこがいいのですか。 *Kono an no doko ga ii no desu ka?* What are the merits of this plan?
- お金をもらってどこが悪いのか。 *O-kane wo moratte doko ga warui no ka?* What is wrong with my accepting the money?

NOTE. For *doko* and particles (*ka, mo, de mo*), see also *dare*.
- どこかこの辺に住んでいる。 *Doko ka kono hen ni sunde iru.* He lives somewhere around here.
- どこへ出しても恥ずかしくない。 *Doko e dashite mo hazukashiku nai.* He will do credit to you no matter where he is sent.
- どこでもいいから休みましょう。 *Doko de mo ii kara yasumimashō.* Let's take a rest; anywhere will do.

NOTE. *doko to naku* is considered to be an adverbial phrase:
- どことなく上品なところがある。 *Doko to naku jōhin na tokoro ga aru.* There is something (indefinably) refined about him.

-dokoro どころ (所) 接尾語 suffix
- 居所 *i-dokoro* whereabouts; 聞き所 *kiki-dokoro* beautiful (mus.) passage; 利き所 *kiki-dokoro* key point; 決め所 *kime-dokoro* decisive chance; 泣き所 *naki-dokoro* weak point; 立ち所に *tachi-dokoro ni* at once; よんどころない *yondokoro nai* unavoidable.

NOTE. 当て所 is read *ate-do:* 当て所なくさまよう *ate-do naku samayou* wander aimlessly.

NOTE. There are two characters for *tokoro:* 所 and 処、both with the *on* reading *sho.*

-dokoro de wa nai どころではない　連語　phrase

強く否定する意を表す *Tsuyoku hitei suru i wo arawasu* Expresses a strong sense of negation:

- 忙しくてそれどころじゃない。 *Isogashikute sore-dokoro ja nai.* I am so busy that's out of the question.
- 当時昼寝どころではなかった。 *Tōji hirune-dokoro de wa nakatta.* At the time, I couldn't possibly have taken a nap.
- 事業のために、結婚どころではなかった。 *Jigyō no tame ni, kekkon-dokoro de wa nakatta.* Owing to pressure of business, marriage was out of the question.

-dokoro ka どころか　接続助詞（に準ずるもの） (treated as a) conjunctive particle

体言・用言の終止形・形容動詞の語幹に付いて、前件を否定して、後件を強調する *Taigen・yōgen no shūshikei・keiyō-dōshi no gokan ni tsuite, zenken wo hitei-shite, kōken wo kyōchō suru* Added to nominals, to Base 3 of verbals, and to stem of adjectival nouns, denies the first item and so emphasizes the second:

- フランス語どころか英語も出来ない。 *Furansugo-dokoro ka, Eigo mo dekinai.* He doesn't even know English, let alone French.
- 褒められるどころかあべこべに叱られた。 *Homerareru-dokoro ka, abekobe ni shikarareta.* Far from being praised, on the contrary, I was scolded.
- 旅行は楽しいどころか苦しいだけでした。 *Ryokō wa tanoshii-dokoro ka, kurushii dake deshita.* Far from being pleasant, the trip was a nightmare.
- 独身どころか三人の子供がある。 *Dokushin-dokoro ka, sannin no kodomo ga aru.* Not only is he not a bachelor, he has three children.
- 元気どころか今入院して重体だ。 *Genki-dokoro ka, ima nyūin shite jūtai da.* Far from being in good health, he is now in hospital in a serious condition.

-domo[1] ども（共）　接尾語　suffix

名詞・代名詞に付いて、複数を表す *Meishi・daimeishi ni tsuite, fukusū wo arawasu* Added to nouns and pronouns, (usually) expresses the plural.

1. 他人を指す名詞に付いて、見下す意を表すことが多い *Tanin wo sasu meishi ni tsuite, mi-kudasu i wo arawasu koto ga ooi* With nouns referring to others, often has an air of disdain:

- 家来ども *kerai-domo* one's "men"; 子分ども *kobun-domo* one's followers; 手下ども *teshitadomo* one's "men"; せがれども *segare-domo* one's sons; 野郎ども *yarō-domo* those wretches.

2. 自称の代名詞に付いて、へりくだりの意を表す *Jishō no daimeishi ni tsuite, heri-kudari no i wo arawasu* With lst. person pronouns, has an air of deference:

- 手前ども *temae-domo* I, we (humble); 私ども *wata(ku)shi-domo* I, we (humble).

→ ***-ra, -tachi***

-domo² ども 接続助詞（古） (classical) conjunctive particle

接続助詞「ど」に、係り助詞「も」。用言の已然形に付いて、逆説の条件を表す *Setsuzoku-joshi "-do" ni, kakari-joshi "mo." Yōgen no izenkei ni tsuite, gyakusetsu no jōken wo arawasu* Conjunctive particle *-do* plus correlated particle *mo*. With Base 5 of verbals, expresses adversative condition:

1. 受ける句が確定した条件の場合 *ukeru ku ga kakutei shita jōken no baai* Following a statement of fact:

- 文を書きてやれども、返り事もせず。 *Fumi wo kakite yaredomo, kaeri-goto mo sezu.* He sent a letter, but there was no reply.

2. 受ける句が仮定条件の場合 *Ukeru ku ga katei-jōken no baai* Following a conditional statement:

- 当たらずと言えども遠からず。 *Atarazu to iedomo tookarazu.* It isn't far from the truth.

NOTE. *Keredomo* derives from *kere*, Base 5 of (*bungo*) adjectives, plus this *-domo*.

donata どなた 代名詞 pronoun

人称代名詞、不定称。「だれ」の丁寧な言い方 *Ninshō-daimeishi, futei-shō. "Dare" no teinei na ii-kata* Personal pronoun, indeterminate. Polite form for *dare:*

NOTE. *Donata-sama desu ka?* translated according to situation:

1. to somebody not visible: Who is there?
2. face to face: Who are you?
3. announcing a visitor: What name shall I say?
4. over the phone: Who is speaking, please?

NOTE. For *donata* with particles, see *dare*.

NOTE. In classical Japanese, *donata* used to mean "which" or "which direction."

donna da どんなだ　形容動詞　adjectival noun

程度・状態・数量が不定であることを表す *Teido・jōtai・sūryō ga futei de aru koto wo arawasu* Denotes that the degree, state or amount is indeterminate:

- どんな御用でしょうか。 *Donna go-yō deshō ka?* Can I help you?
- どんなに褒めても褒め足りない。 *Donna ni homete mo home-tarinai.* No praise is too good for him.
- どんなことがあろうとも、計画を捨てない。 *Donna koto ga arō to mo, keikaku wo sutenai.* I will not abandon the plan no matter what.

→ *anna da, konna da, sonna da*

dono どの　連体詞　adnoun

不定称、関係を表す *Futeishō; kankei wo arawasu* Indeterminate; expresses relationship:

- 好きな花はどの花ですか。 *Suki na hana wa dono hana desu ka?* What is your favorite flower?
- どの車を買えばいいか分からない。 *Dono kuruma wo kaeba ii ka wakaranai.* I don't know which kind of car to buy.
- どの点から見ても、このほうがいい。 *Dono ten kara mite mo, kono hō ga ii.* From every point of view, this is the best [better] one.

-doori → *toori*

dore[1] どれ　代名詞　pronoun

不定称、事物を指す *Futeishō; jibutsu wo sasu* Indeterminate; refers to objects:

- どれにしようかなあ。 *Dore ni shiyō ka nā?* Now, which shall I take?
- どれも欲しくない。 *Dore mo hoshiku nai.* I don't want any [either] of them.
- どれもこれも似たり寄ったりだ。 *Dore mo kore mo nitari yottari da.* They are all of a type.

dore[2] どれ　感動詞　interjection

思い立って事をする時に発する語 *Omoitatte koto wo suru toki ni hassuru go* Exclamatory word pronounced as a signal of determination:

- どれ、寝るとしようか。 *Dore! Neru to shiyō ka?* Well, now, shall I go to bed?

dōshi 動詞 verb

The technical language of verbs is as follows.

1. 定義 *Teigi* Definition:

自立語で、それだけで述語になるもの *Jiritsu-go de, sore dake de jutsu-go ni naru mono* Independent words that can of themselves form predicates.

2. 形 *Katachi* Form:

活用をし、口語では、言い切ったとき、ウ段の音で終わる *Katsuyō wo shi, kōgo de wa, ii-kitta toki, "u" dan no oto de owaru* Are conjugated, and in modern Japanese, end in *-u, -ku, -su, -tsu,* etc. as their Base 3 or final form.

3. 意味 *Imi* Meaning:

動作・作用・存在・状態などを表す *Dōsa* · *sayō* · *sonzai* · *jōtai nado wo arawasu* Denote operation, action, existence, state, etc.

4. 活用 *Katsuyō* Conjugation:

1. 五段活用 *Godan katsuyō* Five-step conjugation (uses all five vowels: *kakanai, kaki-masu, kaku, kake-ba, kakō to suru*).
2. 上一段活用 *Kami-ichidan katsuyō* Upper line conjugation (the *-i* line is higher up on the *gojūon* table than the *-e* line).
3. 下一段活用 *Shimo-ichidan katsuyō* Lower line conjugation (the *-e* line).
4. カ行変格活用 *"Ka" gyō henkaku katsuyō* (*ka-hen* for short) The irregular conjugation for the one verb *kuru.*
5. サ行変格活用 *"Sa" gyō henkaku katsuyō* (*sa-hen* for short) The irregular conjugation for the one verb *suru.*

5. 音便 *Onbin* Euphonic changes (occurring with the change from classical Japanese to modern):

1. イ音便 *"I" onbin* From *bungo ka-ki-te* to modern *ka-i-te.*
2. ウ音便 *"U" onbin* From *utsukushiku* to *utsukushū.*
3. 促音便 *Soku-onbin* Bungo *ka-chi-te* becomes *kat-te.*
4. 撥音便 *Hatsu-onbin* Bungo *shi-ni-te* becomes *shi-n-de.*

6. 中止法 *Chūshi-hō* Signalling of a pause in the sentence:

1. 動詞の連用形を使って *Dōshi no ren'yōkei wo tsukatte* Using Base 2:
   - 川に飛び込み、向こう岸へ泳いだ。 *Kawa ni tobi-komi, mukō-gishi e oyoida.* Diving into the river, he swam to the opposite bank.
   - これはコーヒーで、あれはお茶です。 *Kore wa kōhī de, are wa o-cha desu.* This is coffee, and that is tea. (Base 2 of polite copula *desu*).

2. 動詞の連用形に、「て」「で」を使って *Dōshi no ren'yōkei ni, "-te", "-de" wo tsukatte* using Base 2 + *-te, -de:*

• 川に飛び込んで、向こう岸へ泳いだ。 *Kawa ni tobi-konde, mukōgishi e oyoida.* He dived into the river and swam to the opposite bank.

E

e へ　格助詞　case particle
体言または体言の資格を作る「の」に付く *Taigen mata wa taigen no shikaku wo tsukuru "no" ni tsuku* Added to nominals and to nominalizing *no*.

1. 動作・作用の方向を示す *Dōsa・sayō no hōkō wo shimesu* Denotes direction of action:

• 国へ帰りたい。 *Kuni e kaeritai.* I want to go back to my country.

• 花から花へと飛ぶ。 *Hana kara hana e to tobu.* It flies from flower to flower.

2. 動作・作用の帰着点を示す *Dōsa・sayō no kichaku-ten wo shimesu* Denotes destination of action:

• 本を棚へ返した。 *Hon wo tana e kaeshita.* He put the book back on the shelf.

3. 相手・目標を示す *Aite・mokuhyō wo shimesu* Denotes recipient or target of the action:

• 皆さんへよろしく。 *Minasan e yoroshiku.* Best wishes to all. (Here, *ni* would be more usual.)

• 心当たりへ電話で聞いてみた。 *Kokoro-atari e denwa de kiite mita.* inquired by phone at the places he was likely to be.

4.「ところ」を伴って、事件の事態を示す *"Tokoro" wo tomonatte, jiken no jitai wo shimesu* With *tokoro*, denotes circumstances of actions:

• 家を出るところへ、郵便屋さんが来た。 *Ie wo deru tokoro e, yūbin-ya san ga kita.* Just as I was about to leave home, the postman came.

NOTE. In modern Japanese, the distinction in use between *e* and *ni* is not so clear as it was in classical Japanese. Besides, some unexpected uses will be found:

• どっちが先へ死ぬだろう。 *Dotchi ga saki e shinu darō?* Which of (the two of) us will be the first to die? (Sōseki, *Kokoro*)

• どちらへ泊まっていますか。 *Dochira e tomatte imasu ka?* Where are you lodging?

ē ええ　感動詞　interjection
驚き・肯定の返事・ためらいなどを表す *Odoroki・kōtei no henji・*

tamerai nado wo arawasu Expresses surprise, positive reply, hesitation, etc.:

- ええ、そうですか。 *Ē, sō desu ka?* You don't say!
- ええ、すぐに参ります。 *Ē, sugu ni mairimasu.* I'll be there right away!
- ええ、どうしようかね。 *Ē, dō shiyō ka ne?* Let me see, what shall I do?

-eru・-uru 得る 接尾語 suffix verb

The conjugations are as follows: *kōgo* (spoken) → 1. *e* 2. *e* 3. *eru* 4. *eru* 5. *eru* 6. *ero, eyo; bungo* (written) → 1. *e* 2. *e* 3. *u* 4. *uru* 5. *ere* 6. *eyo.* 動詞の連用形に付いて、可能を表す *Dōshi no ren'yōkei ni tsuite, kanō wo arawasu* Added to Base 2 of verbs, expresses the potential:

- 一人でなしえない仕事だ。 *Hitori de nashi-enai shigoto da.* He can't do it on his own.
- 考えうる限り手を尽くす。 *Kangae-uru kagiri te wo tsukusu.* I'll try anything I can think of.
- それは有りうることだ。 *Sore wa ari-uru koto da.* It could very well happen.

NOTE. *-Uru*, Base 4 in *bungo*, has come to be used also as Base 3 in modern Japanese; however, its most frequent use is when it is followed by a formal noun (*koto, tokoro,* etc.). It is also found as an independent verb in many stock phrases:

- 地位をうる *chii wo uru* gain a position; 勝利をうる *shōri wo uru* be victorious.

NOTE. In modern Japanese, a potential form of *go-dan* verbs has evolved:

- 歩ける *arukeru* can walk; 買える *kaeru* can buy; 押せる *oseru* can push.

Modelled on these, a spurious set of forms of *ichi-dan* verbs is coming into use:

- 着れる *kireru* can wear; 見れる *mireru* can see; 寝れる *nereru* can sleep.

Note that the standard forms would be: *kirareru, mirareru, nerareru.* Quite standard, however, are the following three forms: 聞こえる (*kikoeru*), 見える (*mieru*) and 思える (*omoeru*), relics of a Nara era potential:

- 肉眼では見えない。 *Nikugan de wa mienai.* It isn't visible to the naked eye.

- 耳が遠くて聞こえない。 *Mimi ga tookute kikoenai.* He is hard of hearing.
- 雪が降るとは思えない。 *Yuki ga furu to wa omoenai.* A snowfall is unthinkable.

F

-fū 風　接尾語　suffix
そのようであり、その特色や傾向を表す *Sono yō de ari, sono tokushoku ya keikō wo arawasu* Denotes style, characteristic or tendency:
- 絵描き風の人 *ekaki-fū no hito* one looking like an artist; 田舎風の *inaka-fū no* countrified; 唐風の *Kara-fū no* of Chinese style; 昔風の *mukashi-fū no* old-style; 西洋風の *seiyō-fū no* Western style.

-fuku[1] 服　接尾語　suffix
1. 着物のこと *Kimono no koto* Items or style of clothing:
- 衣服 *i-fuku* clothes; 喪服 *mo-fuku* mourning dress; 和服 *wa-fuku* Japanese-style clothes; 洋服 *yō-fuku* Western-style clothes.

2. 薬・茶・たばこなどを飲む回数 *Kusuri・cha・tabako nado wo nomu kaisū* Counter for doses of medicine taken, drinks of tea, smokes, etc.:
- 一日一服を飲むこと。 *Ichi-nichi ippuku wo nomu koto.* To be taken once a day.
- 一服いかがですか。 *Ippuku ikaga desu ka?* Will you have a smoke?

-fuku[2] 幅　接尾語　suffix
掛け軸などを数える語 *Kake-jiku nado wo kazoeru go* Counter for scroll-shaped objects:
- 絵巻物三幅 *emakimono san-puku* three picture-scrolls.

-furi[1] 振り　接尾語　suffix
刀剣を数える語 *Tō-ken wo kazoeru go* Counter for various types of swords:
- 日本刀一振り *Nihon-tō hito-furi* one Japanese sword.

-furi[2] 降り　接尾語　suffix (from 降る *furu* precipitate)
雨・雪などが降ること・降る程度・降り方 *Ame・yuki nado ga furu koto・furu teido・furi-kata* Precipitation, its degree or manner:
- 雨降り *ame-furi* rainfall; 霜降り *shimo-furi* frost, 照り降り *teri-furi* intermittent sunshine and rain; 雪降り *yuki-furi* snowfall.

G

ga[1] が　接続助詞　conjunctive particle

用言・助動詞の終止形に付く *Yōgen / jodōshi no shūshikei ni tsuku* Is added to Base 3 of verbals and auxiliaries.

1. 逆態接続を表す *Gyakutai setsuzoku wo arawasu* Expresses adversative conjunction:

• 貧乏だが、正直だ。 *Binbō da ga, shōjiki da.* He is poor, but he is honest.

2. 並列を表す *Heiretsu wo arawasu* Expresses listing:

• 見に行ったが、なかなか面白い。 *Mi ni itta ga, naka-naka omoshiroi* I went to see it, and found it very interesting.

3.「おう」「よう」を二つ並べて、譲歩の意を表す *"-Ō", "-yō" wo futatsu narabete, jōho no i wo arawasu* With paired tentative forms, expresses concession:

• 勝とうが負けようが、頑張るつもりだ。 *Katō ga makeyō ga, ganbaru tsumori da.* Win or lose, I intend to do my best.

• あの人が行こうが行くまいが、私の知ったことではない。 *Ano hito ga ikō ga ikumai ga, watashi no shitta koto de wa nai.* It's all the same to me whether he goes or not.

4. 体言に付いて、罵る気持ちを表す *Taigen ni tsuite, nonoshiru kimochi wo arawasu* Added to nominals, expresses a sense of contempt:

• この馬鹿者めが。 *Kono bakamono-me ga!* The silly fool!

ga[2] が　格助詞　case particle

主として体言に付く *Shu to shite taigen ni tsuku* Is added chiefly to nominals.

1. 主語であることを示す *Shugo de aru koto wo shimesu* Denotes the grammatical subject:

• 春が来た。 *Haru ga kita.* Spring has come.

• 箱の中に何がありますか。 *Hako no naka ni nani ga arimasu ka?* What's in the box?

• 新しいのが高い。 *Atarashii no ga takai.* The new ones are expensive.

2. 希望・好悪・能力を示す働きをする *Kibō • kō-o • nōryoku wo shimesu hataraki wo suru* Marks the object in expressions of desire, likes and dislikes, ability, etc.:

• お水が飲みたい。 *O-mizu ga nomitai.* I'd like a drink of water.

• お金が要る。 *O-kane ga iru.* I need some money.

- 野球が好きだ。 *Yakyū ga suki da.* They like baseball.
- 二郎は発音が下手だ。 *Jirō wa hatsuon ga heta da.* Jiro is poor at pronunciation.
- 頂上がまだ見えない。 *Chōjō ga mada mienai.* We can't see the summit yet.

NOTE. With the desiderative auxiliary *-tai, ga* expresses a preference, while *wo* expresses the simple desire:

- お茶が飲みたい。 *O-cha ga nomitai.* This sentence expresses a preference for tea, not just any beverage.
- お茶を飲みたい。 *O-cha wo nomitai.* While tea is suggested, another beverage will do.

NOTE. The realization that *ga* is a case particle, while *wa* is an adverbial particle, takes a lot of the mystique out of the *ga* • *wa* muddle. Here are a few hints.

1. When the subject is an interrogative pronoun, always use *ga:*
   - 誰がそう言ったのですか。 *Dare ga sō itta no desu ka?* Who said so?
   - どちらが好きですか。 *Dochira ga suki desu ka?* Which do you prefer?
2. To signal the subject of a subordinate clause, use *ga* or *no:*
   - 彼が立てた物音で、皆が目を覚ました。 *Kare ga tateta mono-oto de, minna ga me wo samashita.* The noise he made woke everybody up.
   - あれは弟が出た学校だ。あれは弟の出た学校だ。 *Are wa otōto ga deta gakkō da. Are wa otōto no deta gakkō da.* That is the school my brother went to.
3. In temporal and conditional clauses, use *ga* only if the subject is different from that of the main clause:
   - 桜が咲く頃日本に帰りたい。 *Sakura ga saku koro Nihon ni kaeritai.* I want to return to Japan in the cherry-blossom season.
   - 兄貴が行くのなら、僕も行く。 *Aniki ga iku no nara, boku mo iku.* If my brother goes, I'm going, too.

     cf. 兄貴は行くのなら、買ってくれるだろう。 *Aniki wa iku no nara, katte kureru darō.* If my brother goes, he will probably buy it for me.

ga[3] が 終助詞のように as a final particle

1. 願望を表す *Ganbō wo arawasu* Expresses a wish:

- うまく行くといいが。 *Umaku iku to ii ga.* I hope all goes well.

2. 不確実を表す *Fu-kakujitsu wo arawasu* Expresses uncertainty:

- そうとも言えないんだが。 *Sō to mo ienai'n da ga.* I shouldn't go so far as to say that.

ga⁴ が 文語の格助詞 classical case particle

Serves as a modifier, corresponding with modern *no;* it is found in stock phrases like:

- 君が代 *Kimi ga yo;* 眠るがごとく *nemuru ga gotoku* as if going to sleep; 鈴が音 *suzu ga ne* the sound of bells; 我が国 *waga kuni* this our land.

-gachi 勝ち 接尾語 suffix

体言・用言の連用形に付いて、「しばしばある」「傾向が強い」という意味を添える *Taigen • yōgen no ren'yōkei ni tsuite, "shiba-shiba aru", "keikō ga tsuyoi" to iu imi wo soeru* Added to nominals and to Base 2 of verbals, adds the idea of frequency or strong tendency in that line:

- 病気勝ち *byōki-gachi* sickly; 曇りがち *kumori-gachi* tend to be cloudy; 黒目がち *kurome-gachi* dark-eyed; 遅れがち *okure-gachi* often late; 留守勝ち *rusu-gachi* often absent; 仕がち *shi-gachi* apt to. . .; 我がちに *ware-gachi ni* scrambling to be first; 忘れがち *wasure-gachi* absent-minded.

NOTE. In 怪我勝ち *kega-gachi* a fluke, *-gachi* has its original meaning of "victory"; its antonym is 怪我負け *kega-make* a chance defeat.

-gaeri[1] 帰り 接尾語 suffix

帰ること・とき *Kaeru koto • toki* Return, or time of return:

- 外国帰り *gaikoku-gaeri* return from abroad; 早帰り *haya-gaeri* early return, morning return; 日帰り *hi-gaeri* one-day trip; 本卦帰り *honke-gaeri* reaching age of 60; 里帰り *sato-gaeri* bride's first visit to her home; 湯帰りの人 *yu-gaeri no hito* person on his way home from bath.

-gaeri[2] 返り 接尾語 suffix

返ること・点 *Kaeru koto • ten* Return, point of return:

- 跳ね返り *hane-kaeri* rebound, tomboy; 見返り *mi-kaeri* collateral, looking back; 先祖返り *senzo-gaeri* atavism; とんぼ返り *tonbo-gaeri* somersault; 寝返り *ne-gaeri* turning over in bed, changing sides.

-gai[1] 蓋 接尾語 suffix

笠や笠の形をしたものを数える語 *Kasa ya kasa no katachi wo shita mono wo kazoeru go* Counter for sedge-hats or other objects of such a shape:

- 笠六蓋 *kasa roku-gai* six sedge-hats.

-gai[2] 外　接尾語　suffix

範囲から出たもの・除け者にすること *Han'i kara deta mono* • *nokemono ni suru koto* Something outside of given sphere; ostracizing:

• 案外 *an-gai* beyond expectation; 号外 *gō-gai* (newspaper) extra; 以外 *i-gai* except (for); 意外 *i-gai* (na/no) unforeseen; 時間外勤務 *jikan-gai kinmu* overtime; 除外 *jo-gai* exclusion; 課外授業 *ka-gai jugyō* extracurricular lessons; 海外 *kai-gai* foreign countries; 戸外 *ko-gai* outdoors; 国外 *koku-gai* overseas; 内外 *nai-gai* at home and abroad; 屋外 *oku-gai* outdoors; 例外 *rei-gai* exception; 論外 *rongai* out of the question; 市外 *shi-gai* suburbs; 体外 *tai-gai* outside the body; 対外 *tai-gai* external, outwards, towards foreign countries; 野外 *ya-gai* open air; 予想外 *yosō-gai* unexpectedness; 在外 *zai-gai* abroad; 存外 *zongai* unexpectedness.

-gai[3] 害　接尾語　suffix

禍・妨げ *Wazawai* • *samatage* Disaster, obstacle:

• 妨害 *bō-gai* obstruction; 迫害 *haku-gai* persecution; 自害 *ji-gai* suicide; 公害 *kō-gai* environmental pollution, public nuisance; 障害 *shō-gai* obstacle; 傷害 *shō-gai* injury; 侵害 *shin-gai* encroachment; 損害 *son-gai* damage; 被害者 *higai-sha* victim; 加害者 *kagai-sha* assailant; 虫害 *chū-gai* damage from insects; 毒害 *doku-gai* damage from poison; 冷害 *reigai* damage from cold; 震害 *shin-gai* damage from earthquakes; 水害 *sui-gai* damage from flooding; 凍害 *tō-gai* damage from frost; 要害 *yō-gai* a fortress.

-gai[4] 街　接尾語　suffix

• 暗黒街 *ankoku-gai* gangland; 地下街 *chika-gai* underground shopping centre; 中心街 *chūshin-gai* city centre; どや街 *doya-gai* flophouse district; 繁華街 *hanka-gai* shopping district, bustling streets; 歓楽街 *kanraku-gai* gay quarters; 市街 *shi-gai* city streets; 商店街 *shōten-gai* shopping district.

gairai-go 外来語　loan words

The great number of loan words in common use in modern Japanese causes problems for the foreigner. The main difficulties are as follows:

1. Words deceptively like English, but borrowed from other languages, such as *koppu* from Dutch, meaning a glass, not a cup.

2. Words whose range of meanings has been curtailed, such as *abekku* a (dating) couple; *biru* a Western-style high-rise.

3. Words contracted after being borrowed, such as *kōporasu* corporate housing; *pasokon* personal computer.
4. Words whose pronunciation has been distorted, such as *fāsuto* for "first"; *kurōzu appu* for the photographic term "close-up", not "close up shop"; *rūzu riifu* for "loose-leaf", not "lose leaf".

-gakari 掛かり 接尾語 suffix
体言に付く *Taigen ni tsuku* Is added to nominals.
1. それだけ必要である *Sore dake hitsuyō de aru* Requiring just that amount:
- 十人がかりの仕事 *jūnin-gakari no shigoto* job for ten (people).

2. 似通った意味 *Ni-kayotta imi* "Savoring of . . . ":
- 芝居がかりの文句 *shibai-gakari no monku* theatrical expression.

3. ...するついでに *...Suru tsuide ni* Combining operations:
- 通りがかりに *toori-gakari ni* in passing.

4. その世話になる *Sono sewa ni naru* Be dependent on:
- 親掛かりの身 *oya-gakari no mi* dependent on one's parents.

NOTE. There are also the 係 of 出納係 *suitō-gakari,* cashier, and the 懸り of 相懸り *ai-gakari,* simultaneous attack, and 神懸り *kami-gakari,* (spiritual) possession.

-gakaru がかる 接尾語 suffix
名詞に付いて、「それに似てくる」という意味を添える *Meishi ni tsuite, "sore ni nite kuru" to iu imi wo soeru* With nouns, adds the meaning of taking on the appearance of . . . :
- 赤みがかった紫色 *akami-gakatta murasaki-iro* reddish purple; 不良がかった *furyō-gakatta* tending towards delinquency; 時代がかった *jidai-gakatta* obsolescent; 神がかってくる *kami-gakatte kuru* turn spooky; 芝居がかった調子 *shibai-gakatta chōshi* air of theatrics; 下がかってくる *shimo-gakatte kuru* drift to indecency.

-gake 掛け 接尾語 suffix
A. 動詞の連用形に付いて、「ついでに」という意味を添える *Dōshi no ren'yōkei ni tsuite, "tsuide ni" to iu imi wo soeru:* With Base 2 of verbs, adds the meaning: "taking the opportunity", "on one's way":
- 行き掛けに *iki- (yuki-) gake ni* on one's way; 学校の帰りがけに *gakkō no kaeri-gake ni* on the way home from school; 通り掛けに訪れる *toori-gake ni otozureru* drop in on one's way.

B. 名詞に付く *Meishi ni tsuku* Is added to nouns.

1. 割合を示す *Wariai wo shimesu* Denotes rate:
  - 定価の八掛けで売る。 *Teika no hachi-gake de uru.* I sell it at a 20% discount.
  - 二つ掛けもある。 *Futatsu-gake mo aru.* It is twice as large (twice as much).
2. 服装を示す *Fukusō wo shimesu* Denotes (manner of) dress:
  - 浴衣がけで *yukata-gake de* in deshabille; たすきがけで *tasuki-gake de* with sleeves tucked up.
3. 座席に座る人数を示す *Zaseki ni suwaru ninzū wo shimesu* Denotes number of persons to a row or seat:
  - 五人掛けにしてください。 *Gonin-gake ni shite kudasai.* Please sit five to a row.
4. 賭けることを示す *Kakeru koto wo shimesu* Denotes the act of betting, risking:
  - 命がけで *inochi-gake de* at the risk of one's life.

-gamashii がましい 接尾語 suffix

動詞の連用形や動作を表す名詞に付いて、形容詞を作り、「...のきらいがある」という意味を添える *Dōshi no ren'yōkei ya dōsa wo arawasu meishi ni tsuite, keiyōshi wo tsukuri, ". . . no kirai ga aru" to iu imi wo soeru* With Base 2 of verbs and with nouns that express action, makes adjectives of them and adds the idea of resemblance (often, to something undesirable):

  - 弁解がましい *benkai-gamashii* apologetic; 晴れがましい *hare-gamashii* ostentatious, embarrassed; 言い訳がましいこと *iiwake-gamashii koto* explanation sounding like an excuse; 冗談がましく *jōdan-gamashiku* jokingly; 未練がましく *miren-gamashiku* with bad grace; 恩着せがましい *onkise-gamashii* patronizing; 押しつけがましい *oshi-tsuke-gamashii* pushing.

-gara 柄 接尾語 suffix

名詞に付いて、その性質・品格・身分・立場などにふさわしい *Meishi ni tsuite, sono seishitsu • hinkaku • mibun • tachiba nado ni fusawashii* Added to nouns, means befitting the nature, dignity, status, position, etc. of:

  - 場所柄もわきまえずに *basho-gara mo wakimaezu ni* oblivious to the occasion; 人柄 *hito-gara* personality; 家柄 *ie-gara* family's standing; 時節柄 *jisetsu-gara* in view of the times; 商売柄 *shōbai-gara* by one's trading instincts.

-garami がらみ (絡み) 接尾語 suffix

A. 名詞に付く *Meishi ni tsuku* Is added to nouns.

1. 「それに関わりがある」 *"Sore ni kakawari ga aru"* Involving . . . :
   - 汚職がらみの事件 *oshoku-garami no jiken* matter involving corruption.
   - 選挙がらみで働く *senkyo-garami de hataraku* work with elections in mind.
2. 「ぐるみ」、「ごと」 *"-Gurumi", "-goto"* Inclusive of . . . :
   - 袋がらみで売る *fukuro-garami de uru* sell in bags; 鞘がらみで打つ *saya-garami de utsu* strike without unsheathing a sword.

B. 数詞に付いて、「およそ」 *Sūshi ni tsuite, "oyoso"* with numerals; = roughly:

- 四十がらみの人が多い。 *Yonjū-garami no hito ga ooi.* Many are in their forties.

-gari がり 接尾語 suffix

- 怖がり *kowagari* coward; 寒がり *samugari* person very sensitive to the cold.

→ *-garu*

-garu がる 接尾語 suffix verb

名詞・形容詞・助動詞「たい」・形容動詞の語幹に付いて、動詞を作り、「そのように感ずる」「そのようなふりをする」意味を添える。 *Meishi, keiyōshi • jodōshi "-tai" • keiyōdōshi no gokan ni tsuite, dōshi wo tsukuri, "sono yō ni kanzuru", "sono yō na furi wo suru" imi wo soeru.* Added to nouns, and to the stem of adjectives, the auxiliary *-tai* and adjectival nouns, verbalizes them and changes the feeling expressed by them from objective to subjective:

- 重宝な *chōhō na* useful → 重宝がる *chōhō-garu* find useful.
- 偉い *erai* admirable → 偉がる *era-garu* fancy oneself
- 不思議な *fushigi na* wonderful → 不思議がる *fushigi-garu* marvel at.
- 欲しい *hoshii* desirable → 欲しがる *hoshi-garu* desire.
- 懐かしい *natsukashii* dear → 懐かしがる *natsukashi-garu* yearn for.
- おかしい *okashii* amusing → おかしがる *okashi-garu* be amused at.
- 残念な *zannen na* regrettable → 残念がる *zannen-garu* feel loss of.

NOTE: *-garu* is not used with first-person subjects. → -tagaru.

-gasane (-kasane) 重ね 接尾語 suffix

重箱・衣服など、重ねたものを数える語 *Jūbako • ifuku nado, kasaneta*

mono wo kazoeru go Counter for layered boxes, layers of clothing and such like:

- 一重ねの訪問着 *hito-kasane no hōmon-gi* a suit of visiting clothes.

NOTE. The ideograph 襲 (also read *osou*) will be found for *-gasane* in the case of items of clothing, mostly *wa-fuku*.

-gashi¹ 貸し 接尾語 suffix

ものを貸すこと *Mono wo kasu koto* The act of lending:

- 賃貸し *chin-gashi* renting, leasing; 日歩貸し *hibu-gashi* daily interest loan; 間貸し *ma-gashi* letting of rooms; 又貸し *mata-gashi* subletting.

-gashi² 菓子 接尾語 suffix

間食用の甘い食べ物 *Kanshoku-yō no amai tabemono* Confectionery:

- 茶菓子 *cha-gashi* light refreshments; 駄菓子 *da-gashi* cheap candy; 和菓子 *wa-gashi* Japanese-style candy; 洋菓子 *yō-gashi* Western-style candy.

-gata¹ 方 接尾語 suffix

1. 仲間・組・所属を表す *Nakama • kumi • shozoku wo arawasu* Denotes allegiance, belonging, attachment:

- 幕府方 *Bakufu-gata* the Bakufu side; 敵方 *teki-gata* the enemy (side).

2. 複数の人の尊敬語 *Fukusū no hito no sonkei-go* Polite plural form:

- あなた方 *anata-gata* you; お客様方 *okyakusama-gata* (you, the) guests.

3. おおよその時刻 *Ooyoso no jikoku* A loosely defined period of time:

- 朝方 *asa-gata* early (in the) morning; 日暮れ方 *higure-gata* (towards) sundown; 夕方 *yūgata* evening.

4. 大体の程度・分量 *Daitai no teido • bunryō* Approximate degree or amount:

- 二割方高い *niwari-gata takai* roughly a fifth more expensive.

-gata² 型 接尾語 suffix

その特徴を持っていること *Sono tokuchō wo motte iru koto* Has the qualities of:

- 指導者型の人 *shidōsha-gata no hito* a born leader; 1990年型の車 1990 *nengata no kuruma* 1990-model car; 血液型 *ketsueki-gata* blood type or group; 大型株 *oo-gata kabu* large-sized stocks.

-gata³ 形　接尾語　suffix

その形のもの *Sono katachi no mono* Shaped like . . . :

• 花形 *hana-gata* floral pattern; 菱形の *hishi-gata no* diamond-shaped; 扇型の *ōgi-gata no* fan-shaped.

NOTE. There is bound to be some overlapping of 型 (read *kei* and *kata*) and 形 (read *kata, kei, gyō, katachi, arawareru*).

-gatai 難い　接尾語　suffix

動詞の連用形に付いて、形容詞を作り、「する・なるのが難しい」 *Dōshi no ren'yōkei ni tsuite, keiyōshi wo tsukuri, "suru • naru no ga muzukashii"* Added to Base 2 of verbs, makes adjectives of them and denotes that something is difficult of attainment:

• 有り難い *ari-gatai* (from その存在が難しい *sono sonzai ga muzukashii*) worth being grateful for; 得難い *e-gatai* difficult to come by, rare; 信じがたい *shinji-gatai* hard to believe; 耐えがたい tae-gatai unbearable.

NOTE. There are also *-nikui* and *-zurai* (づらい); *-gatai* is more literary. Antonyms are 易々 *-ii,* and 易い *-yasui. Ari-gatai* may add the suffixes *-ge, -mi, -sa.*

-ge¹ 気　接尾語　suffix

動詞の連用形・形容詞や形容動詞の語幹・体言に付いて、様子・気分などの意味を表す *Dōshi no ren'yōkei • keiyōshi ya keiyōdōshi no gokan • taigen ni tsuite, yōsu • kibun nado no imi wo arawasu* Added to Base 2 of verbs, the stem of adjectives and adjectival nouns, and to nominals, expresses the idea of semblance or feeling:

• 危なげな *abuna-ge na* unsteady; 有りげな *ari-ge na* likely; 怪しげな *ayashi-ge na* suspicious; 悲し気な *kanashi-ge na* mournful; 物欲しげに *monohoshi-ge ni* wistfully; 惜しげもなく *oshi-ge mo naku* generously; 若気 *waka-ge* youthful ardor; 何気なく言ったこと *nani-ge naku itta koto* a chance remark; 疑わし気に見つめる *utagawashi-ge ni mi-tsumeru* give a person a suspicious look; 急がし気に動く *isogashi-ge ni ugoku* act in a hurried manner.

NOTE. *-ge, -mi, -sa* are synonyms, but there are some slight differences. All three are added to the stem of adjectives and adjectival nouns, but *-ge* is added also to Base 2 of verbs, and *-sa* to stem of the auxiliary *-tai.* For the meanings, see *-mi* and *-sai.*

-ge² 下　接尾語　suffix

• 卑下 *hi-ge* humility, contempt; 上下 *jō-ge* upper and lower, first and second, rise and fall, etc.; 高下 *kō-ge* rank, fluctuation.

gendai-go 現代語

Can mean 1. a living (or modern) language, as opposed to classical language, or 2. in Japan, the language in common use since World War II. → *bungo*.

-gi 着 接尾語 suffix

Can mean 1. clothing, costume, 2. person wearing such clothing, or 3. (ceremony of) putting on (for the first time):

- 雨着 *ama-gi* rain gear; 厚着 *atsu-gi* wearing thick clothes; 烏帽子着 *eboshi-gi* rite marking coming-of-age; 伴纏着 *hanten-gi* (person) wearing a livery coat; 晴着 *hare-gi* one's Sunday best; 袴着 *hakama-gi* rite for boys aged 3 (later, aged 5, 7); 夜着 *yo-gi* bedding, sleeved quilt.

-gimi[1] 君 接尾語 suffix

主に親族名称に付いて、他人を敬って言う言葉 *Omo ni shinzoku-meishō ni tsuite, hito wo uyamatte iu kotoba* Title of respect used mostly towards relatives:

- 父君 *chichi-gimi* (your) father; 母君 *haha-gimi* (your) mother; 姫君 *hime-gimi* Princess; 大君 *oo-gimi* master, lord (read *Oo-kimi,* is His Majesty).

→ *-ue*.

-gimi[2] 気味 接尾語 suffix

名詞や動詞の連用形に付いて、形容動詞を作り、その様子を帯びている状態を表す *Meishi ya dōshi no ren'yōkei ni tsuite, keiyōdōshi wo tsukuri, sono yōsu wo obite iru jōtai wo arawasu* Added to nouns and to Base 2 of verbs, makes adjectival nouns, and expresses the idea of "seeming to . . . .", "tending to . . .":

- 上がり気味 *agari-gimi* on the rise, rather nervous; あせり気味 *aseri-gimi* tending to be impatient; だれ気味 *dare-gimi* flagging; 風邪気味 *kaze-gimi* having a slight cold; こごめ気味 *kogome-gimi* having a stoop; 遅れ気味 *okure-gimi* on the late side; 追われ気味 *oware-gimi* seeming pressed (for time, etc.); 湿り気味 *shimeri-gimi* dampish; 焼け気味で *yake-gimi de* half in desperation.

NOTE. Although this suffix forms adjectival nouns, the compounds are almost invariably followed by Base 3 of the copula (*da, de aru, desu*). → *-gachi, -gakaru*.

-giri 切り　接尾語

1. いろいろな切り方 *Iroiro na kiri-kata* Various ways of cutting:
   - 細切り *koma-giri* cutting fine; 滅多切り *metta-giri* hacking; 撫で切り *nade-giri* mowing down; 大切り *oo-giri* cutting into large pieces; 乱切り *ran-giri* slashing; 薄切り *usu-giri* cutting into thin slices; 輪切り *wa-giri* cutting into round slices.
2. 区切ったもの *Ku-gitta mono* Sections cut:
   - 日切り *hi-giri* fixed date; 区切り *ku-giri* stage (in a course of events) punctuation, pause; 両切り *ryō-giri* cigarette; 千切り (大根) *sen-giri (daikon)* shredded radish; 四つ切り *yotsu-giri* quarto-size (photographic) paper.
3. 剣術の専門語 *Kenjutsu no senmon-go* Terms used in swordsmanship:
   - 胴切り *dō-giri* cutting trunk; 拝み切り *ogami-giri* stroke on forehead; 試し切り *tameshi-giri* test of a new sword.

NOTE. The ideograph 斬 (*zan*) will be found in some compounds (袈裟斬り *kesa-giri* cutting slantwise from shoulder), and 限 (*gen, kagiri*) in the business terms: 先限 *saki-giri* future delivery; 中限 *naka-giri* next month delivery; 当限 *tō-giri* current month delivery.

NOTE. There are also the *-giri* of: 義理 obligation; 青桐 *ao-giri* Phoenix tree; 朝霧 *asa-giri* morning mist; 三つ目錐 *mitsume-giri* three-pointed gimlet.

gisei-go, gitai-go 擬声語・擬態語

Onomatopoeia is dealt with in the Appendix.

-giwa 際　接尾語 suffix

1. 名詞に付いて、「そのすぐそば」という意味を添える *Meishi ni tsuite, "sono sugu soba" to iu imi wo soeru* With nouns, adds the idea of adjacency:
   - 崖際に *gake-giwa ni* at edge of a cliff; 壁際に *kabe-giwa ni* beside wall; 窓際に *mado-giwa ni* at window; 窓際族 *madogiwa-zoku* (useless) employees nearing retirement; 水際に *mizu-giwa ni* at water's edge; 波打ち際に *namiuchi-giwa ni* on foreshore; 死ぬ間際に・死に際に *shinu magiwa ni* • *shini-giwa ni* at point of death; 山際の小屋 *yama-giwa no koya* mountain(-side) hut.
2. 動詞の連用形に付いて,「しようとする時・ところ」*Dōshi no ren'yōkei ni tsuite, "shiyō to suru toki • tokoro"* Added to Base 2 of verbs, means "on the point of"
   - 引き際がきれい *hiki-giwa ga kirei* retire gracefully; 引き際が悪い *hiki-giwa ga warui* cling to one's position; 帰り際に *kaeri-giwa ni*

when about to leave; 終わり際に *owari-giwa ni* at close (of); 日の暮れ際に *hinokure-giwa ni* at close of day; 死に際の言葉 *shini-giwa no kotoba* dying words; 分れ際に *wakare-giwa ni* at moment of parting; 花も散り際になっている。*Hana mo chirigiwa ni natte iru.* The blossoms are about to fall.

go-[1] 御　接頭語　prefix

1. 相手の行為・事物に対して敬意を表す *Aite no kōi • jibutsu ni taishite keii wo arawasu* Expresses respect for actions or belongings of the other party:

- ご家族は皆お元気ですか。 *Go-kazoku wa mina o-genki desu ka?* Are all your family well?

2. 相手に対する自分の行為について謙譲を表す *Aite ni taisuru jibun no kōi ni tsuite kenjō wo arawasu* Expresses deference in regard to one's own actions towards the other party:

- 校舎の方をご案内致しましょう。 *Kōsha no hō wo go-annai itashimashō.* Let me show you round the school (buildings).

3. 大切な事物について敬意を表す *Taisetsu na jibutsu ni tsuite keii wo arawasu* Exprcsses respect for things considered precious:

- 御幣 *go-hei* strips of white paper used in Shintō rituals; 御陵 *go-ryō* mausoleum; 御所 *go-sho* Imperial Palace; 御殿 *go-ten* palace; 御前 *go-zen* Imperial presence (also read *o-mae, on-mae, mi-mae*).

→ *gyo-, mi*[1]*-, o-*[1]

go-[2] 後　接頭語　prefix

時間的に「のち」、空間的に「うしろ」 *Jikan-teki ni "nochi", kūkan-teki ni "ushiro"* In time, "after", in space, "behind":

- 後場 *go-ba* afternoon market; 後漢 *go-Kan* late Han (period); 後家 *go-ke* widow; 後光 *go-kō* halo; 後妻 *go-sai* second wife; 後詰め *go-zume* rearguard.

NOTE. The *go-* readings are far outnumbered by the *kō-* readings. Other readings are:

- 後味 *ato-aji* aftertaste; 後足 *ato-ashi* hind leg; 後腹 *ato-bara* afterpains; 後釜 *ato-gama* successor; 後月 *ato-getsu* previous month; 後金 *ato-kin* payable remainder; 後口 *ato-kuchi* rest, aftertaste; 後先 *ato-saki* (reverse) order, consequences; 後作 *ato-saku* second crop; 後始末 *ato-shimatsu* settlement; 後ほど *nochi-hodo* later on; 後仕手 *nochi-jite* principal actor (Noh); 後々 *nochi-nochi* (in) future; 後目•尻目 *shiri-me* sidelong glance.

NOTE. The ろ of うしろ and the れ of おくれ are now written in:

• 後ろ姿 *ushiro-sugata* back view; 後れ毛 *okure-ge* stray hairs.

go-3 五 ゴ (いつ、いつつ)
• 五月 *go-gatsu, satsuki;* 五人 *go-nin;* 三々五々 *san-san go-go.*

-go 後 接尾語 suffix

時間・空間の語に付いて、「のち」「うしろ」を意味する *Jikan • kūkan no go ni tsuite, "nochi", "ushiro" wo imi suru* With time and place words, means "after" and "behind":
• 午後 *go-go* afternoon; 背後 *hai-go* rear, background; 以後 *i-go* after, since; 終戦後 *shūsen-go* postwar ↔ 戦前 *senzen* prewar.

go-dan katsuyō
The "five-step" conjugation. For more information see Introduction (III).

go-kan 語幹
用言の活用語尾を取り除いた変化しない部分 *Yōgen no katsuyō go-bi wo tori-nozoita henka shinai bubun* Stem of conjugables.

-gokko ごっこ 接尾語 suffix
物真似をして遊ぶこと *Mono-mane wo shite asobu koto* Playing at . . . :
• 鼬ごっこ *itachi-gokko* tit for tat; お店ごっこ *omise-gokko* playing "shop"; 鬼ごっこ *oni-gokko* game of tag; 銀行ごっこ *ginkō-gokko* playing "bank"; 泥棒ごっこ *dorobō-gokko* "cops and robbers".

-gonomi 好み 接尾語 suffix
1. 趣味に基づいたひいき *Shumi ni motozuita hiiki* Preference based on fancy:
• 選り好み *eri • yori-gonomi* picking and choosing; 色好み *iro-gonomi* lewdness; 衣装好み *ishō-gonomi* being particular about dress; 器量好み *kiryō-gonomi* love of fair looks; 物好み *mono-gonomi* being choosy; 渋好み *shibu-gonomi* liking for the *shibui.*
2. その人流に *Sono hito ryū ni* In the style of . . . :
• 玄人好みの *kurōto-gonomi no* in the style of an expert; 利休好みに *Rikyū-gonomi ni* "after" Rikyu (of tea ceremony).

-goro 頃 接尾語 suffix
時間の語に付いて、「その前後」を示す *Jikan no go ni tsuite, "sono zengo" wo shimesu* With time words, denotes approximate time:
• 近頃 *chika-goro* of late; 日頃 *hi-goro* usually, always; 火点し頃

hitomoshi-goro nightfall; 今ごろ *ima-goro* about this time; この頃 *kono-goro* these days; 見頃 *mi-goro* best time for viewing; 身頃 *mi-goro* body of garment; 中頃 *naka-goro* about the middle of; 値頃 *ne-goro* reasonable price; 先頃 *saki-goro* the other day; 食べ頃 *tabe-goro* best time for eating; 手頃な *te-goro na* handy; 年頃 *toshi-goro* marriageable age; 矢頃 *ya-goro* bowshot; 衣頃 *yo-goro* many nights, those nights (*bungo*).

NOTE. *-Goro* may not be used with words indicating loosely defined periods of times, such as *kesa, yūbe,* etc. Particles follow *-goro, ni* being used for emphasis, or when the word after it requires the particle:

- 四月の半ばごろから始まる。 *Shigatsu no nakaba-goro kara hajimaru.* It begins about the middle of April.
- 何時ごろ（に）寝ますか。 *Nanji-goro (ni) nemasu ka?* (At) About what time do you go to bed?
- 三月の終わりごろになると、雪が溶ける。 *Sangatsu no owari-goro ni naru to, yuki ga tokeru.* Towards the end of March the snow melts.

NOTE. Use *-goro* for a point in time, *-gurai* for an amount of time.

- 十日ごろ来るのではないか。 *Tooka-goro kuru no de wa nai ka?* I reckon he will be here about the tenth.
- 十日ぐらいかかるのではないか。 *Tooka-gurai kakaru no de wa nai ka?* It will probably take ten days or so.

-goshi¹ 越し 接尾語 suffix

名詞に付く *Meishi ni tsuku* Is added to nouns.

1. 「それを隔てて」 *"Sore wo hedatete"* Across, through, over:

- 頭越しに *atama-goshi ni* over head of; 襖越しに *fusuma-goshi ni* through sliding door; 葉越しに *ha-goshi ni* through foliage; 垣根越しに *kakine-goshi ni* over fence; 壁越しに *kabe-goshi ni* through wall; 肩越しに *kata-goshi ni* over one's shoulder; 川越しに *kawa-goshi ni* across river; 窓越しに *mado-goshi ni* through window; 眼鏡越しに *megane-goshi ni* over one's spectacles; 月越しの借金 *tsuki-goshi no shakkin* debt outstanding since previous month; 山越しに *yamagoshi ni* beyond mountains; 宵越しの金 *yoi-goshi no kane* money kept overnight.

2. 「その間中続く」 *"Sono aida-jū tsuzuku"* Lasting that length of time:

- 十年越しの交際 *jūnen-goshi no kōsai* a ten-year long association.

→ *-koshi²*

-goshi² 腰 接尾語 suffix

1. 姿勢 *Shisei* Bodily posture:

- 中腰　*chū-goshi* half-sitting posture; 及び腰 *oyobi-goshi* leaning forwards; 受け腰 *uke-goshi* defensive stance; 浮き腰 *uki-goshi* unsteady posture.

2. 何かをする時の意気込み　*Nani ka wo suru toki no iki-gomi* Determination shown:

- 本腰　*hon-goshi* earnestness; 喧嘩腰 *kenka-goshi* defiant attitude; 物腰 *mono-goshi* demeanour; 逃げ腰 *nige-goshi* cold feet; 強腰 *tsuyo-goshi* firm stand; 弱腰 *yowa-goshi* faint-heartedness.

-goto　ごと　接尾語　suffix

名詞に付いて、「それを含めて」 *Meishi ni tsuite, "sore wo fukumete"* With nouns, "inclusive of":

- 家を地所ごと買う　*ie wo jisho-goto kau* buy house and grounds together; 林檎を皮ごと食べる *ringo wo kawa-goto taberu* eat apples skin and all; 橋ごと流される *hashi-goto nagasareru* be swept away together with bridge.

HOMONYMS. 言：独り言 *hitori-goto* soliloquy, 小言 *ko-goto* rebuke; 事：遊び事 *asobi-goto* pastime, 出来事 *deki-goto* event; 琴：竪琴 *tate-goto* harp, 大和琴 *Yamato-goto* Japanese harp.

-goto ni　毎に　接尾語　suffix

名詞または動詞の連体形に付く。 *Meishi mata wa dōshi no rentaikei ni tsuku.* Is added to nouns and to Base 4 of verbs.

1. 「そのたびに」 *Sono tabi ni* Every time . . . :

- 四時間ごとに熱を計る。 *Yojikan-goto ni netsu wo hakaru.* They take temperatures at four-hour intervals.
- 出来上がるごとに配る。 *Dekiagaru-goto ni kubaru.* They give them out according as they are finished.
- 月ごとに　*tsuki-goto ni* month by month; 夜ごとに *yo-goto ni* night after night.

2. 「その一つ一つ」 *"Sono hitotsu-hitotsu"* Severally:

- 家ごとに　*ie-goto ni* from door to door; 一雨ごとに *hitoame-goto ni* with each shower; 会う人ごとに頭を下げる。 *Au hito-goto ni atama wo sageru.* He bows to each person he meets.

gozaru　ござる（御座る）　動詞　verb

The conjugation is as follows: 1. *gozara* 2. *gozari, gozai* 3. *gozaru* 4. *gozaru* 5. *gozare* 6. ——.

A *bungo* verb now used mostly with the *-masu* endings, *gozaru* shares with four other verbs (*irassharu, kudasaru, nasaru, ossharu*) the euphonic change of *-ri* to *i* before *-masu:*

1. 「来る」「行く」の尊敬語　*"Kuru", "iku" no sonkei-go* Exalting alternative for *kuru* and *iku.*

2. 「ある」「居る」の丁寧語　*"Aru", "iru" no teinei-go* Polite alternative for *aru, iru:*

- ここにございます。 *Koko ni gozaimasu.* It is here.

3. 補助動詞「ある」の丁寧語　*Hojo-dōshi "aru" no teinei-go* Polite alternative for the supplementary verb *aru:*

- ここに書いてございます。 *Koko ni kaite gozaimasu.* It is written here.
- 次は終点でございます。 *Tsugi wa shūten de gozaimasu.* The next stop is the last.

NOTE. Adjectives undergo a euphonic change before this verb:

- *hayai → hayō* (early); *utsukushii → utsukushū* (beautiful); *samui → samū* (cold); *omoi → omō* (heavy); *ii → yō* (good).

-gumu　ぐむ　　接尾語　suffix

名詞に付いて、動詞を作り、「その兆しが現われる」 *Meishi ni tsuite, dōshi wo tsukuri, "sono kizashi ga arawareru"* Added to nouns, verbalizes them, and adds the meaning: "show signs of . . .":

- 芽ぐむ　*me-gumu* sprout; 涙ぐむ *namida-gumu* be moved to tears; 角ぐむ *tsuno-gumu* sprout.

→ ***-bamu, -jimiru, -meku.***

gurai　ぐらい（位、くらい）　　副助詞　*fuku-joshi*　　adverbial particle

体言・用言の連体形・副詞・助詞などに付く　*Taigen • yōgen no rentai-kei • fukushi • joshi nado ni tsuku* Is added to nominals, to Base 4 of verbals, to adverbs, particles, etc.

1. 大体の数量・程度を表す　*Daitai no sūryō • teido wo arawasu* Indicates approximate amount or degree:

- 三十分ぐらいかかる。 *Sanjippun gurai kakaru.* It takes about 30 minutes.
- 二千円ぐらいするでしょう。 *Nisen'en gurai suru deshō.* It will cost about ¥2000, I'm sure.

2. 比較の基準を示す　*Hikaku no kijun wo shimesu* Indicates standard of comparison:

- 富士山ぐらい美しい山は少ない。 *Fujisan gurai utsukushii yama wa sukunai.* Few mountains are as beautiful as Mt. Fuji.

- 辛うじて通れるぐらいの狭い道だ。 *Karōjite tooreru gurai no semai michi da.* The road is so narrow that it is only with difficulty that one can get through.

3. 程度の低い限度を表す *Teido no hikui gendo wo arawasu* Denotes that the amount is meager:

- お茶一杯ぐらいくれるだろう。 *O-cha ippai gurai kureru darō.* The least they can do is to give us a cup of tea.

NOTE. *Gurai* is one of the particles that may come between a verb and its auxiliary:

- 見てぐらいくれるかも知れない。 *Mite gurai kureru ka mo shirenai.* He may deign to take a look at it.

→ *kurai.*

-gurumi ぐるみ (包み) 接尾語 suffix
名詞に付いて、「一つにまとめて」という意味を添える *Meishi ni tsuite, "hitotsu ni matomete" to iu imi wo soeru* With nouns, adds the meaning of "inclusive of . . .":

- 家族ぐるみで *kazoku-gurumi de* as a family; 企業ぐるみで *kigyō-gurumi de* throughout the enterprise; 街ぐるみの運動 *machi-gurumi no undō* town-wide campaign; 身ぐるみはがれる *migurumi hagareru* be stripped of all one has.

→ *agete, -goto, nokorazu, -zure.*

-gusa 草・種 接尾語 suffix
名詞に付いて、「材料となるもの」という意味を添える *Meishi ni tsuite, "zairyō to naru mono" to iu imi wo soeru* Added to nouns, adds meaning of "source of", "cause for":

- 語り草 *katari-gusa* topic of the conversation; 質草 *shichi-gusa* pawn pledge; お笑い草・種 *owarai-gusa* amusing topic, laughing-stock.

gyo- 御 接頭語 prefix

- 御物 *gyo-butsu* Imperial property; 御題 *gyo-dai* theme for Imperial poetry contest; 御詠 *gyo-ei* Imperial poem; 御苑 *gyo-en* Imperial gardens; 御宴 *gyo-en* Imperial party; 御意 *gyo-i* Imperial intent, your intent; 御衣 *gyo-i* Imperial garments; 御璽 *gyo-ji* Privy Seal; 御歌 *gyo-ka* Imperial poem; 御感 *gyo-kan* Imperial approval; 御製 *gyo-sei* Imperial poem; 御遊 *gyo-yū* palace concert.

→ *go-*[1], *mi-*[1], *o-*[1], *on-.*

H

hachi- 八　ハチ、ハツ、ハッ、やつ、や、よう

- 八月 *hachi-gatsu* August; 八角 *hakkaku* octogon; 八方 *happō* all directions; 八つ切り *yatsu-giri* cutting into eight parts; 八日 *yō-ka* eight days, the eighth (date); 八千代 *ya-chiyo* forever; 八重 *ya-e* double (blossom); 八百屋 *yaoya* vegetable store; 八百長 *ya-ochō* rigged affairs.

hai はい　感動詞　interjection

1. 名を呼ばれて答える語 *Na wo yobarete kotaeru go* Reply to having one's name called:

- 田中君。はい。 *Tanaka-kun. Hai.* Tanaka. Present. (Here I am.)

2. 相手の言葉を聞いたことを表す *Aite no kotoba wo kiita koto wo arawasu* Signals that one has heard:

- 早く起きなさい。はい。 *Hayaku oki nasai. Hai.* Get up right now! All right!

3. 注意を促す *Chūi wo unagasu* Calls attention:

- はい、話を止めて聞いていなさい。 *Hai, hanashi wo yamete kiite i nasai.* Ahem! Stop talking, and listen, please.

4. 肯定・承諾などの意を表す *Kōtei・shōdaku nado no i wo arawasu* Expresses a sense of affirmation, agreement, etc.:

- 分かりましたか。はい、分かりました。 *Wakarimashita ka? Hai, wakarimashita.* Do you understand? Yes, we do.
- まだ来ないのですか。はい、まだです。 *Mada konai no desu ka? Hai, mada desu.* Hasn't he shown up yet? No, not yet.

5. 自分の発言の終わりに付けて、「間違いありません。」という意味を加える *Jibun no hatsugen no owari ni tsukete, "Machigai arimasen." to iu imi wo kuwaeru* Added to one's own utterance, conveys the idea: "That's for sure.":

- 背の高い人でした。はい。 *Sei no takai hito deshita. Hai.* It was a tall person; I can vouch for that.

6. 馬を進める掛け声 *Uma wo susumeru kake-goe* Word used to urge on a horse:

- はい、はい。 *Hai, hai.* Gee up!

-hai 杯・盃　接尾語　suffix

1. 容器に入った飲食物を数える語 *Yōki ni haitta inshoku-butsu*

wo kazoeru go Counter for containers of food or drink:

- お茶を一杯ください。 *O-cha wo ippai kudasai.* May I have a cup of tea, please?
- お砂糖を二杯頂きます。 *O-satō wo ni-hai itadakimasu.* I'll have two spoons of sugar, if you don't mind. (Count: *ippai, ni-hai, san-bai.*)

2. いか、たこ、などを数える語 *Ika, tako nado wo kazoeru go* Counter for the cephalopods:

- たこ六杯 *tako roppai* six octopuses.

hajime 始め・初め

A practical expedient is to look on 始め as the antonym of 終わり (*owari*)、and 初め as the antonym of 末 (*sue*):

- 始めから終わりまで *hajime kara owari made* from beginning to end; 小説の始めのほう *shōsetsu no hajime no hō;* 四月の初めに *shi-gatsu no hajime ni;* 初めまして。*Hajimemashite.* (greeting used on meeting for first time); 生まれて初めて飛行機に乗った。 *Umarete hajimete hikōki ni notta.* It was my first time on a plane.

-hajimeru 始める 接尾語 suffix verb

動詞の連用形に付いて、「その動作をし出す」という意味を添える *Dōshi no ren'yōkei ni tsuite, "sono dōsa wo shi-dasu" to iu imi wo soeru* With Base 2 of verbs, adds the idea of "begin to . . .":

- 雨が降り始めた。 *Ame ga furi-hajimeta.* It has begun to rain.
- いつから日本語を習い始めましたか。 *Itsu kara Nihongo wo narai-hajimemashita ka?* When did you begin (studying) Japanese?

NOTE. Even when the main verb is an intransitive, it is usual for the "supplementary" verb to be in the transitive form; but see *-dasu.*

-hara 腹 接尾語 suffix

- 赤腹 *aka-hara* brown thrush, dace, newt; 業腹 *gō-hara* resentment; 片腹 *kata-hara* found in *kata-hara-itai* ridiculous; 下腹 *shita-hara* abdomen; 空き腹 *suki-hara* empty stomach; 裏腹 *urahara* contrary.

→ *-bara, -ppara.*

-harai (-barai) 払い 接尾語 suffix

- 足払い *ashi-barai* sweeping one's opponent's legs from under him; 遅払い *chi-harai* delay in paying; 塵払い *chiri-harai* duster, dusting; 未払い *mi-harai* unpaid; お払い *o-harai* payment, junk (*oharai-bako ni naru* get the sack); 支払い *shi-harai* payment; 煤払い *susu-harai* house cleaning; 取り払い *tori-harai* demolition; 露払い *tsuyu-harai* a herald; 厄払い *yaku-harai* exorcism.

NOTE. There is also the religious rite of 祓い exorcism.

→ *-pparai.*

-hari 張り 接尾語 suffix

• 洗い張り *arai-hari* fulling; 傘張り *kasa-hari* covering umbrella ribs with cloth, or the person who does this; 減り張り *meri-hari* modulation; 見張り *mi-hari* (standing) guard; 白張り *shira-hari* starched white garment (worn by court officials); 弓張り *yumi-hari* stretching a bow; 高張り提灯 *taka-hari jōchin* paper lantern (to be held high).

NOTE. This *-hari* serves also as a counter for bows and lanterns:

• 弓二張り *yumi futa-hari* two bows; 二張りの提灯 *futa-hari no chōchin* two (paper) lanterns.

→ *-bari, -ppari.*

-hashira 柱 接尾語 suffix

神仏、遺骨などを数える語 *Shinbutsu, ikotsu nado wo kazoeru go* Counter for (statues of) gods, sets of human remains, etc.:

• 三柱の神 *mi-hashira no kami* three (statues of) gods.

-hateru 果てる 接尾語 suffix verb

動詞の連用形に付いて、「おわる」「すっかり…する」という意味を添える *Dōshi no ren'yōkei ni tsuite, "owaru", "sukkari . . . suru" to iu imi wo soeru* With Base 2 of verbs, adds the meaning of "finish doing", "do . . . to the limit":

• 呆れはてる *akire-hateru* be disgusted with; 荒れ果てる *are-hateru* go to ruin; 消えはてる *kie-hateru* disappear without trace; 困り果てる *komari-hateru* be nonplussed; 朽ち果てる *kuchi-hateru* rot away; 成り果てる *nari-hateru* be reduced to beggary; 絶え果てる *tae-hateru* become extinct; 疲れ果てる *tsukare-hateru* be exhausted; 弱り果てる *yowari-hateru* be worn out, be completely at a loss.

hatsu- 初 接頭語 prefix

A *kun* reading of *hajime,* found in many compounds dealing with first events: (i) stages in child's development; (ii) New Year events; (iii) meteorological events; (iv) for the first time:

• 初商い (ii) *hatsu-akinai* first trading; 初場所 (ii) *hatsu-basho* New Year's Sumo Tournament; 初雛 (i) *hatsu-hina* first dolls' festival;

初便り (iv) *hatsu-dayori* first news, 初氷 (iii) *hatsu-goori* first freeze; 初参り *hatsu-mairi* 初詣で (ii) *hatsu-mōde* first visit (to a shrine or temple); 初耳 (iv) *hatsu-mimi* news to one; 初荷 (ii) *hatsuni* first consignment; 初時雨 (iii) *hatsu-shigure* first winter rain; 初霜 (iii) *hatsu-shimo* first frost; 初節句 (i) *hatsu-zekku* first Boys' or Girls' festival; 初午 (ii) *hatsu-uma* first Horse Day Festival; 初雪 (iii) *hatsu-yuki* first snow; 初夢 (ii) *hatsu-yume* first dream.

→ *hajime, -zome.*

hazu 筈　形式名詞　formal noun

Yu-hazu are the two notches in the bow, to take the string; *ya-hazu* is the notch in the end of the arrow, to fit the string. From these comes the idea of "fitting", "reasonable".

活用語の終止形、形容動詞の語幹＋「な」、名詞＋「の」に付いて、当然、確信、予定の意を表す *Katsuyō-go no shūshikei, keiyōdōshi no gokan + "na", meishi + "no" ni tsuite, tōzen • kakushin • yotei no i wo arawasu* Added to Base 3 of conjugables, to stem of adjectival nouns + *na,* and to nouns + *no,* expresses the idea of fitness, conviction, expectation:

- 君なら合格するはずだ。 *Kimi nara gōkaku suru hazu da.* You are sure to pass.
- 安いはずだ。量産車だから。 *Yasui hazu da. Ryōsansha da kara.* Of course it's cheap; it's a mass-produced car.
- 運動選手であるはずがない。 *Undō senshu de aru hazu ga nai.* He can't be an athlete.
- 知らないはずはない。 *Shiranai hazu wa nai.* He can't but know about it.
- 六時到着のはずだ。 *Rokuji tōchaku no hazu da.* They are due to arrive at six.
- なくしたはずの本は、ここにあった。 *Nakushita hazu no hon wa, koko ni atta.* The book I thought I had lost was here.
- そんなはずではなかった。 *Sonna hazu de wa nakatta.* That isn't what I expected.
- 簡単なはずだ。 *Kantan na hazu da.* It ought to be simple.

-hiki[1] 匹　接尾語　suffix

獣・魚・虫などを数える語 *Kemono • sakana • mushi nado wo kazoeru go* Counter for small animals, fishes, insects, etc.

- 犬二匹と金魚三匹を飼っている。 *Inu ni-hiki to kingyo san-biki wo katte iru.* He keeps two dogs and three goldfish.

NOTE. For larger animals, the counter is 頭 *-tō;* the cut-off point is given as "man-size", but there is great latitude. For birds and rabbits the counter is 羽 *-wa*, and for fishes there is also the special 尾 *-bi*. Formerly, *-hiki* served also to count lengths of cloth (= 2-*tan*), and as a monetary unit. 疋 is an *ate-ji* for *-hiki*.

-hiki[2] **(-biki, -ppiki)** 引き　接尾語 suffix

動詞「引く」の連用形で、色々な意味を示す *Dōshi "hiku" no ren'yōkei de, iroiro na imi wo shimesu* Base 2 of the verb *hiku*, expresses various meanings:

- 逢い引き *ai-biki* rendezvous; 相引き *ai-biki* mutual withdrawal; 後引き *ato-hiki* desire for more drink; 福引 *fuku-biki* lottery; 字引 *ji-biki* dictionary; 地引き網 *ji-biki ami* dragnet; 駆け引き *kake-hiki* bargaining; 風邪引き *kaze-hiki* catching cold; 首っ引き *kubippiki* constant reference; くじ引き *kuji-biki* drawing of lots; 間引き *mabiki* thinning out; 万引き *man-biki* shoplifting; 水引 *mizu-hiki* red and white string; 股引 *momo-hiki* drawers; 値引き *ne-biki* price reduction; 根引き *ne-biki* uprooting; 岡っ引き *okappiki* thief catcher (hist.); 置き引き *oki-biki* swiping another's baggage; 差し引き *sashi-hiki* balance, deduction; 友引 *tomo-biki* unlucky day; 割引 *wari-biki* discount.

NOTE. Other ideographs with the same reading are:

- 弾き、found in ピアノ弾き *piano-hiki* piano-player, piano-playing.
- 挽き、found in 木挽き *ko-biki* sawyer, sawing of wood.

hinshi 品詞

The parts of speech, with explanations, will be found in the Introduction (I). Note that there are ten of them in Japanese grammar (counting nouns and pronouns as one). The extras are: adjectival nouns, adnouns and particles. These last correspond, in part, with our prepositions. Note that auxiliary verbs are considered as a distinct part of speech.

hito 人　名詞 noun

The ideograph has many irregular readings: *futari, hitori, kurōto, nakōdo, otona, shirōto, -udo;* as a prefix: *jin-, nin-, hito-,*

1. The reading *hito:*
   - 帰らぬ人 *kaeranu hito,* 亡き人 *naki hito* the deceased; 内の人 *uchi no hito* family members, (my) husband.
2. The reading *-bito:*
   - 船人 *funa-bito* boat passenger, boatman; 人々 *hito-bito* people, each

one; 小人 *ko-bito (shō-jin)* dwarf; 恋人 *koi-bito* lover; 国人 *kuni-bito* native, the nation; 待ち人 *machi-bito* expected visitor; 宮人 *miya-bito* courtier, Shinto priest; 昔人 *mukashi-bito* ancients, deceased, old friends, old-fashioned person; 村人 *mura-bito* villagers; 何人 *nani-bito?* who?; 盗人 *nusu-bito* thief; 里人 *sato-bito* countryfolk; 旅人 *tabi-bito* traveller; 尋ね人 *tazune-bito* person being sought; 供人 *tomo-bito* attendant; 罪人 *tsumi-bito* sinner; 山人 *yama-bito* mountain folk, hermit; 詠み人 *yomi-bito* author (of poem).

3. The reading *-pito:*

- 何人 *nan-pito* (in pos. context) everybody; (in neg. context) nobody.

hito- 一 接頭語 prefix

1. 一つの、一回の *Hitotsu no, ikkai no* A single . . ., once:

- 一雨 *hito-ame* a shower of rain; 一晩 *hito-ban* one night, all night.

2. 少し、ちょっと *Sukoshi, chotto* Slight, brief, temporary:

- 一安心 *hito-anshin* a temporary relief; 一寝入り *hito-neiri* a nap.

3. はっきり定めず指す *Hakkiri sadamezu sasu* Refer to in a vague way:

- 一入 *hito-shio* still more; 一通り *hito-toori* in the main.

hitori 一人 名詞 noun

一人 is read *ichi-nin* in modern Japanese in:

- 一人称 *ichinin-shō* first person (gram.); 一人前 *ichinin-mae* one helping, growing up, full-fledged.

hō 方 形式名詞として As a formal noun:

比較して、一つを指すのに使う語 *Hikaku shite, hitotsu wo sasu no ni tsukau go* Word used to designate one of the choices of a comparison:

- 君の方が正しい。 *Kimi no hō ga tadashii.* You are in the right.
- どちらの方が好きですか。 *Dochira no hō ga suki desu ka?* Which do you prefer?
- 父は静かな方だ。 *Chichi wa shizuka na hō da.* My father is on the quiet side.
- 私はたばこを吸わない方だ。 *Watashi wa tabako wo suwanai hō da.* I'm not much of a smoker.
- 高橋先生はアメリカの方で有名だ。 *Takahashi sensei wa Amerika no hō de yūmei da.* Professor Takahashi is better known in America.
- 自分で料理をする方が楽しいのだ。 *Jibun de ryōri wo suru hō ga tanoshii no da.* She enjoys it more if she does the cooking herself.
- 暗くなるから早く帰った方がいい。 *Kuraku naru kara hayaku kaetta*

hō ga ii. I suggest you go home early, as it is getting dark.

- バスに乗るよりは歩く方が早いくらいだ。 *Basu ni noru yori wa aruku hō ga hayai kurai da.* Rather than take the bus, you will probably get there sooner on foot.
- 夕方よりも朝の方が電車は込んでいる。 *Yūgata yori mo asa no hō ga densha wa konde iru.* The trains are more crowded in the morning than in the evening.
- きれいなのよりも頑丈な方の椅子が欲しい。 *Kirei na no yori mo, ganjō na hō no isu ga hoshii.* What I am after is a strongly-built chair rather than a pretty one.

NOTE. 行方 is read *yukue,* whereabouts.

-hōdai 放題 接尾語 suffix

動詞の連用形や、助動詞「たい」またはある種の形容動詞の語幹に付いて、「全く制限しない」という意味を添える *Dōshi no renyōkei ya, jodōshi "-tai" Mata wa aru shu no keiyōdōshi no gokan ni tsuite, "mattaku seigen shinai" to iu imi wo soeru* Added to Base 2 of verbs, to the auxiliary *-tai* and to the stem of certain kinds of adjectival nouns, adds the idea of doing without restriction:

- 荒れ放題 *are-hōdai* being let go to ruin; 出放題 *de-hōdai* being left running; 食い放題・食べ放題 *kui-hōdai* • *tabe-hōdai* eating one's fill; し放題 *shi-hōdai* doing as one pleases; 好き放題 *suki-hōdai* doing whatever one likes; 取り放題 *tori-hōdai* taking as much as one wants; 休み放題 *yasumi-hōdai* resting as much as one wants; 言いたい放題のことを言う *iitai-hōdai no koto wo iu* have one's full say; 言いなり放題になる *iinari-hōdai ni naru* be at a person's beck and call; 我がまま放題をした報いだ。 *Wagamama-hōdai wo shita mukui da.* It is the result of (his) having had his own way in everything.

hodo 程 副助詞 adverbial particle

色々の語に付く *Iro-iro no go ni tsuku* Is added to various parts of speech.

1. およその分量を表す *Oyoso no bunryō wo arawasu* Denotes approximate amount:

- 十日ほど休んだ。 *Tooka hodo yasunda.* I took about ten days off.

2. 例示して、比較の基準を示す *Reiji shite, hikaku no kijun wo shimesu* Cites an example so as to set the standard of comparison:

- 去年ほど暑くない。 *Kyonen hodo atsuku nai.* It isn't as hot as last year.

3. 「…ば…ほど」の形で、「ますますそうなっていく」という意を表す *". . . -ba . . . hodo" no katachi de, "masu-masu sō natte iku" to iu i wo* *arawasu* In . . . *-ba* . . . *hodo* form, translates "the more . . . the more . . .":

- 安ければ安いほどいい。 *Yasukereba yasui hodo ii.* The cheaper the better.
- 見れば見るほど美しく思われる。 *Mireba miru hodo utsukushiku omowareru.* The more I look at it the prettier it seems.

hojo-dōshi 補助動詞 supplementary verb

To call these verbs "auxiliaries" is rather misleading. The list of auxiliaries is strictly limited, both in *bungo* and in *kōgo*. Japanese grammar defines a supplementary verb as a kind of auxiliary that, losing its own original meaning, helps (to define) the meaning of other verbs:

- 私には分かりかねます。 *Watashi ni wa wakari-kanemasu.* It is beyond me.
- 明日までに読み切れない。 *Asu made ni yomi-kirenai.* I can't finish (reading) it by tomorrow.
- 戦い抜く覚悟だ。 *Tatakai-nuku kakugo da.* He is determined to fight it out.

NOTE. Some verbs have to be considered content words or function words according to context:

- 真珠を箱に入れてしまった。 *Shinju wo hako ni irete shimatta.*
  As a content word: She locked the pearls away in the box.
  As a function word: She ended up putting the pearls in the box.

NOTE. In this work, *hojo-dōshi* are called "supplementary verbs", to distinguish them from the auxiliaries, which do not lose their original meaning.

hoka 外・他 形式名詞・副助詞 formal noun, adverbial particle

1. 形式名詞として *Keishiki meishi to shite* As a formal noun:

- 外で探しましょう。 *Hoka de sagashimashō.* Let's look someplace else.

2. 副助詞として、否定語を伴う *Fuku joshi toshite hiteigo wo tomonau* As an adverbial particle, followed by a negative:

- 彼のほかにこの仕事が出来る人は居ない。 *Kare no hoka ni kono shigoto ga dekiru hito wa inai.* He is the only one here that can do the job.
- そうするほかにしかたがなかった。 *Sō suru hoka ni shikata ga nakatta.* That was the only course open.

NOTE. Strictly speaking, 他 is the antonym of 自 *ji* (self) and 外 is the antonym of 内 *uchi* (inside). Thus we have 他の人 *hoka no hito* (another person) and 外の国 *hoka no kuni* (another country); many people, however, write the latter in hiragana, ほかの国。

-hon 本 接尾語（助数詞 *jo-sūshi)* suffix (counter)

1. 細長いものを数える語 *Hoso-nagai mono wo kazoeru go* Counter for long, slender objects:
   • 鉛筆三本 *enpitsu san-bon* three pencils; ビール六本 *biiru roppon* six bottles of beer.
2. 電話をしたり・葉書を出したりした回数 *Denwa wo shitari • hagaki wo dashitari shita kaisū* Counter for number of phone-calls made, or postcards sent:
   • 電話一本で片付けた。 *Denwa ippon de katazuketa.* We fixed it up with a single phone-call.
3. 映画の作品を数える語 *Eiga no sakuhin wo kazoeru go* Counter for film features:
   • 三本立てを見てきた。 *Sanbon-date wo mite kita.* I have been to see a triple feature.
4. 柔道・剣道などの勝負を数える語 *Jūdō • kendō nado no shōbu wo kazoeru go* Counter for bouts in the martial arts:
   • 一本勝負 *ippon shōbu* a one-game match; 一本勝ち *ippon-gachi* a win by a single feat.

NOTE. The ideograph 本 is read *-bon* or *-pon* in many compounds dealing with books; → *-bon, -pon.*

I

i- 以 接頭語 prefix

This prefix is found in a wide range of words of place, order, direction, etc. In such compounds the starting-point is included; e.g. 名古屋以西 *Nagoya isei* means "Nagoya and points west":

• 以遠 *i-en* beyond; 以外 *i-gai* excluding; 以後 *i-go* since, after; 以北 *i-hoku* north of; 以上 *i-jō* above, over, more than, "That's all", once (this is done. . .); 以下 *i-ka* under, less than, what follows; 以降 *i-kō* from there on, from then on (意向 *i-kō* intention); 以内 *i-nai* within; 以南 *i-nan* south of; 以往 *i-ō* since, after 以来 *i-rai* since; 以西 *i-sei* west of; 以東 *i-tō* east of; 以前 *i-zen* before.

ichi 一（イツ、イッ、ひと、ひとつ）

• 一月 *ichi-gatsu;* 一応 *ichi-ō;* 一喜一憂 *ikki-ichiyū;* 万一 *man-ichi;*

統一 *tō-itsu;* 均一 *kin-itsu;* 一足 *hito-ashi;* 一先ず *hito-mazu;* 一つ話 *hitotsu-banashi;* 一日 *tsuitachi, ichi-jitsu, ichi-nichi;* 一人 *hitori;* 一人称 *ichi-ninshō.*

This word has a wide range of connotations.

1. 別に変わったところがない *Betsu ni kawatta tokoro ga nai* No particular one:

- 一介の *ikkai no* a mere . . .; 一読者 *ichi-dokusha* one of our readers.

2. 一まとまりの全体 *Hito-matomari no zentai* All included:

- 一任する *ichi-nin suru* entrust entirely to . . .

3. 最上のもの *Saijō no mono* Of the highest order:

- 一位 *ichi-i* first rank; 一流 *ichi-ryū* first class.

4. ものごとの始め *Monogoto no hajime* Origin:

- 一次の *ichi-ji no* primary; 一にも二にも *ichi ni mo ni ni mo* before everything else.

5. 小さな一つ一つの *Chiisa na hitotsu hitotsu no* Detailed, itemized:

- 逐一 *chiku-ichi* in detail.

6. 僅か一つだけ *Wazuka hitotsu dake* Merely:

- 一見して *ikken shite* at a glance; 一刻 *ikkoku* (even) one moment.

7. 無視できない *Mushi dekinai* Not negligible:

- 一大事 *ichi-daiji* most important event; 一陣の風 *ichi-jin no kaze* gust of wind.

NOTE. Here are some doublets:

- 一分一厘 *ichi-bu ichi-rin* the least bit; 一言一句 *ichi-gon ikku* a single word; 一問一答 *ichi-mon ittō* question and answer; 一挙一動 *ikkyo ichidō* one's every move; 一夫一婦 *ippu ippu* monogamy; 一進一退 *isshin ittai* hanging in balance; 一朝一夕 *itchō isseki* short time; 一長一短 *ichō ittan* merits and demerits; 一得一失 *ittoku isshitsu* gains and losses.

NOTE. 一言 is read *ichi-gon,* but 一言居士 is read *ichigen koji* ready critic.

ide- 出で

Ide-, as found in *ide-tachi, ide-yu,* etc. comes from the *bungo* verb 出づ *izu,* the old form for 出る *deru,* 出す *dasu.* → *oide.*

iie いいえ 感動詞 interjection

1. 否定の答えの時、一番初めに使う語 *Hitei no kotae no toki, ichiban hajime ni tsukau go* Prefatory word in negative replies:

- いらっしゃいますか。いいえ、参りません。 *Irasshaimasu ka? Iie, mairimasen.* Are you going? No, I'm not.

• いらっしゃいませんか。いいえ、参ります。 *Irasshaimasen ka? Iie, mairimasu.* Won't you come? Yes, I will.

2. 礼を言われたり、あやまられた時の返事に使う語 *Rei wo iwaretari, ayamarareta toki no henji ni tsukau go* Prefatory word in reply to a compliment or apology:

• どうもお世話になりました。いいえ、どう致しまして。 *Dōmo o-sewa ni narimashita. Iie, dō itashimashite.* Thanks very much for your kindness. (Not at all,) Don't mention it.

NOTE. *Iie* is not meant to be used in isolation, as if it were the equivalent of English "no".

iku 行く 動詞 verb

1. • 学校へ行く *gakkō e iku* go to school; 海岸を行く *kaigan wo iku* go along the beach; 嫁に行く *yome ni iku* marry into; 稽古に行く *keiko ni iku* take lessons; 年が行く *toshi ga iku* the years pass; 行く水 *iku mizu* flowing water.

2. 「て行く」の形で、補助動詞で、継続・進行を示す。 *"-te iku" no katachi de, hojo-dōshi de, keizoku • shinkō wo shimesu.* In *-te iku* form, serves as a supplementary verb, and expresses the idea of continuation or progression:

• 空が暗くなっていった。 *Sora ga kuraku natte itta.* The sky gradually darkened.

• 数が日ごとに増えていく。 *Kazu ga hi-goto ni fuete iku.* The number increases daily.

NOTE. In early Japanese, *iku* was used to express the will of an agent, while *yuku* told of natural events; in modern Japanese, *iku* is considered more colloquial, *yuku* more literary. It is only natural that the *yuki-* form should have remained in many compounds:

• 行き当たり *yuki-atari* dead end; 行き方 *yuki-kata • iki-kata* one's way or course; 行き方 *yuki-gata* whereabouts; 行き交う *yuki-kau* come and go; 行き暮れる *yuki-kureru* be benighted; 行き付けの *yuki-tsuke no, iki-tsuke no* favorite (barber, restaurant, etc.).

NOTE. The form of prohibition: *-ikenai, ikemasen,* comes from the potential *ikeru* of this verb. Its positive forms have the following meanings.

1. 行くことが出来る *Iku koto ga dekiru* Can go:

• 月曜日に行けると思う。 *Getsuyōbi ni ikeru to omou.* I think I can go on Monday.

2. かなり上手である *Kanari jōzu de aru* Be fairly good at:

• スポーツなら何でもいける。 *Supōtsu nara nan de mo ikeru.* He is good at all sports.

3. 質・味などがなかなかいい *Shitsu · aji nado ga naka-naka ii* Quality, taste, etc. is really good:

- このブランデーはなかなかいける。 *Kono burandē wa naka-naka ikeru.* This brandy tastes really good!

4. 「いける口」の形で、「相当飲める」という意味を表す。*"Ikeru kuchi" no katachi de, "sōtō nomeru" to iu imi wo arawasu.* In *ikeru kuchi* form, describes a heavy drinker:

- いける口だ。 *Ikeru kuchi da.* He is a heavy drinker.

NOTE. The *ikeru* of *ike-bana* is 活ける・生ける。 An older use is the *ikeru* of:

- 生ける人と死せる人と *ikeru hito to shi-seru hito to* the living and the dead.

NOTE. A 唐 (*Tō*) reading of 行 *an,* is found in:

- 行灯 *an-don* paper-shaded lamp; 行脚 *an-gya* pilgrimage; 行宮 *an-gū* temporary palace; 行火 *an-ka* foot-warmer; 行在所 *an-zaisho* temporary palace.

-te iku · -te kuru

A. With verbs indicating the acquiring or applying of a skill, *-te iku* refers to future time, *-te kuru* to past time:

- これからもっと注意していく。 *Kore kara motto chūi shite iku.* I'll be more careful from now on.
- 今までそうやってきた。 *Ima made sō yatte kita.* That's what I've been doing all along.

B. In the sequence: "go, do and return", English lists the first two, Japanese, the last two:

- 新聞を買ってくる。 *Shinbun wo katte kuru.* I'll go and buy a paper.
- 友達がおいていった犬だ。 *Tomodachi ga oite itta inu da.* It's a dog a friend of mine (came and) left.

imasu 在す・座す 動詞 (古) verb in its own right, in *bungo*
「あり」「おり」「行く」「来」の尊敬語 *"Ari", "ori", "yuku", "ku" no sonkeigo* Honorific form for the *bungo* verbs *ari, ori, iku,* and *ku:*

- 右大将の宇治へいますること、なほ絶えずや。 *Udaishō no Uji e imasuru koto, nao taezu ya?* Does the Udaishō still keep going to Uji? (Base 4 before formal noun *koto*)

NOTE. The principal *bungo* honorific verbs one is likely to meet with are:

- 遊ばす *asobasu = suru;* 御覧ず *goran-zu = miru;* いまそかり= *aru, iru;* 聞こし召す *kikoshimesu = kiku;* 聞こす *kikosu = kiku, kuu;* ましします *mashi-masu = aru, oru, iku, kuru;* ます = *aru, oru, iku, kuru;* 召す *mesu = maneku, kuu, kiru, noru;* みそなわす = *miru;* 宣わす *notamawasu = iu;* 宣う *notamō (notamau) = iu;* 思し召す *oboshimesu = omou;* おぼす *obosu = omou;* 思ほす *omoosu = omou;* 仰す（おほす） *oosu = iu;* おはします *owashimasu = aru, oru, iku, kuru;* 知らす *shirasu = shiru, osameru;* 知ろし召す *shiroshimesu = shiru, osameru.*

ina 否　感動詞　interjection (= modern *iie*)

打ち消し・不同意を表す語 *Uchi-keshi • fu-dōi wo arawasu go* Word expressing denial or disagreement:

• 当地、否、日本の誇りである。 *Tōchi, ina, Nippon no hokori de aru.* It is the pride of this district, nay, of all Japan.

NOTE. It is sometimes nominalized:

• 否の態度を取った。 *Ina no taido wo totta.* He took a negative stance.

ina ya 否や　連語　phrase

1. 名詞として、不同意を表す *Meishi to shite, fudōi wo arawasu* As a noun, expresses the idea of disagreement:

• 払うことには否やはない。 *Harau koto ni wa, ina ya wa nai.* I have no objection to paying.

2. 「や否や」「と否や」の形で、「と同時に」「とすぐに」という意味を表す *"Ya ina ya" "to ina ya" no katachi de, "to dōji ni" "to sugu ni" to iu imi wo arawasu* In *ya ina ya* and *to ina ya* forms, translates "no sooner . . . than . . .":

• 床へ入るや否や、眠ってしまった。 *Toko e hairu ya ina ya, nemutte shimatta.* No sooner had I got into bed than I fell asleep.

• ベルが鳴るや否や、仕事を始める。 *Beru ga naru ya ina ya, shigoto wo hajimeru.* They start work immediately when the bell rings.

3. 「かどうか」の意味を表す *"Ka dō ka" no imi wo arawasu* Translates ". . . or not":

• 結婚するや否や分からない。 *Kekkon suru ya ina ya wakaranai.* I don't know whether he will marry or not.

ippai 一杯　形容動詞・名詞　adjectival noun

1. 名詞として *Meishi to shite* Used as a noun:

• 一杯いかがですか。 *Ippai ikaga desu ka?* How about a drink?

2. 充満の意味を表す *Jūman no imi wo arawasu* Denotes fullness, abundance:

- 力一杯 *chikara ippai* with all one's might; 三月一杯 *sangatsu ippai* all through March; 腹一杯 *hara ippai* one's fill; 若さいっぱいな人だ。*Wakasa ippai na hito da.* He is full of youthful vigor.

3.「たっぷり」という意味を表す *"Tappuri" to iu imi wo arawasu* Expresses the idea of being full to capacity:

- 言いたいことがいっぱいある。*Iitai koto ga ippai aru.* I have lots of things to tell you.
- いっぱい食わせてやる。*Ippai kuwasete yaru.* I'll put one over on him.

irassharu いらっしゃる 動詞 verb

1.「居る」「来る」「行く」の丁寧語 *"Iru", "kuru", "yuku" no teinei-go* Honorific form for the verbs *iru, kuru,* and *yuku:*

- 奥様はいらっしゃいますか。*Okusama wa irasshaimasu ka?* Is the lady of the house in? (Are you going to go?)
- お客様がいらっしゃいました。*Okyaku-sama ga irasshaimashita.* The guests have arrived.

2. 尊敬の意を表す補助動詞 *Sonkei no i wo arawasu hojo-dōshi* Supplementary verb expressing respect:

- お元気でいらっしゃいますか。*O-genki de irasshaimasu ka?* Are you well?
- お父さんは新聞を読んでいらっしゃる。*O-tōsan wa shinbun wo yonde irassharu.* Father is reading the newspaper.

NOTE. The four verbs *irassharu, kudasaru, nasaru* and *ossharu* follow these rules:

1. Belonging to the *go-dan* conjugation, they add *-nai* to the *-ra* of Base 1 to form the ordinary negative present:

- *irassharanai, kudasaranai, nasaranai, ossharanai.*

2. Base 2 has three endings: *ri, i,* and *tsu* (っ):

(i) *Ri* is used before a pause, with the *ni* of purpose, and before the auxiliaries *tai, tagaru,* and *sō da.*

- *irasshari, nasaritai, nasaritagaru, kudasarisō da.*

(ii) The *i* form serves as an abrupt style of imperative, and precedes *masu:*

- *Irasshai.* Come here, Welcome!
- *Irasshaimase.* Welcome!

(iii) The *tsu* form is found before *ta* and *te:*

- *irasshatta, nasatte, kudasatta, osshatte.*

NOTE. The forms *irasshita* and *irasshite* are now usual.

NOTE. An old imperative form is found in *kudasare, nasare, osshare* only.

-ire 入れ 接尾語 suffix

1. 入れる操作、またはその結果 *Ireru sōsa, mata wa sono kekka* The act, or the effect, of inserting:

- 出し入れ *dashi-ire* taking out and putting in; 書き入れ *kaki-ire* filling in; 刈り入れ *kari-ire* harvest, harvesting; 借入 *kari-ire* borrowing, a loan; 心入れ *kokoro-ire* attention, concern; 輿入れ *koshi-ire* (= *yome-iri*) bride's entering groom's house; 口入れ *kuchi-ire* mediation, interference; 組み入れ *kumi-ire* inclusion; 倉入れ *kura-ire* warehousing; 鍬入れ *kuwa-ire* ground-breaking; 乗り入れ *nori-ire* running on the same line as another railroad, extension (of rail, etc.); 思い入れ *omoi-ire* contemplation; 差し入れ *sashi-ire* gift, insertion: 仕入れ *shi-ire* stocking up; 質入れ *shichi-ire* pawning; 底入れ *soko-ire* touching bottom price; 漉入れ *suki-ire* watermarking; 手入れ *te-ire* repairing, raid; てこ入れ *teko-ire* promotion; 取り入れ *tori-ire* taking in, harvest(ing); 受け入れ *uke-ire* acceptance; 焼き入れ *yaki-ire* tempering (of steel).

2. 入れ物、容器 *Iremono, yōki* Receptacle, container:

- 茶入れ *cha-ire* tea caddy; 筆入れ *fude-ire* pen case; 花入れ *hana-ire* flower vase; 火入れ *hi-ire* fire pan, heating; 紙入れ *kami-ire* billfold, paper-holder; 金入れ *kane-ire* purse, billfold; 水入れ water-holder, jug; 肉入れ *niku-ire* seal-pad case; 押入れ *oshi-ire* closet; 札入れ *satsu-ire* billfold; 銭入れ *zeni-ire* purse.

3. その他の意味 *Sono hoka no imi* Miscellaneous meanings:

- 申し入れ *mōshi-ire* proposal; 投げ入れ *nage-ire* freestyle flower arrangement; 綿入れ *wata-ire* wadded clothes.

-ireru 入れる 接尾語 suffix

Compounds are very numerous; here are just a few samples:

- 聞き入れる *kiki-ireru* accede (to a request); 乗り入れる *nori-ireru* ride into, run on the same line as another railroad, extend railroad into; 呼び入れる *yobi-ireru* call in.

-iri 入り 接尾語 suffix

The modern *hairu* was *iru* in *bungo,* and this has carried over in many compounds.

体言に付く *Taigen ni tsuku* Is added to nouns.

1. 収容できる *Shūyō dekiru* Capable of holding:

- 二リットル入りの瓶 *ni rittoru-iri no bin* two-litre bottle; 百グラム入りの袋 *hyaku guramu-iri no fukuro* bag to hold 100 grams.

2. あるものが入っている *Aru mono ga haitte iru* Containing:

- 五万円入りの財布　*goman'en-iri no saifu* purse containing ¥50,000; 牛乳入りのコーヒー　*gyūnyū-iri no kōhī* café au lait.

3. その場所に入ること　*Sono basho ni hairu koto* Entry into:
   - 土俵入り　*dohyō-iri* sumō parade; お国入り *okuni-iri* entry into one's fief, going home.

NOTE. *Iri* is also used on its own as a noun:

- 土用の入り　*doyō no iri* first of dog days; 彼岸の入り *higan no iri* first day of equinoctial week; 日の入り *hi no iri* sunset; 月の入り *tsuki no iri* moonset; 梅雨の入り　*tsuyu no iri* onset of rainy season.

i-ro-ha

Besides the *gojūon-zu,* there is also the *i-ro-ha uta,* another arrangement of the *kana* syllabaries. It is a poem describing the Buddhist teaching that in this life we cannot really understand fully, something like Paul's: "Now we see indistinctly, as in a mirror." (I Cor. 13: 12) It was formerly in common use, to the extent that the headwords in dictionaries were listed in *i-ro-ha* order, but has now been superseded by the *gojūon.* The *kana* orthography is old style, and *nigori* (voicing) is ignored. Each letter is used once only. *N* is omitted.

1. The list in *hiragana:*
   いろはにほへと　ちりぬるを　わかよたれそ　つねならむ　うゐのおくやま　けふこえて　あさきゆめみし　ゑひもせす
2. The list in *kana-majiri:*
   色は匂へど散りぬるを、我が世誰ぞ常ならむ。有為の奥山今日越えて、浅き夢見じ。酔ひもせず。
3. The meaning is, roughly:
   The flowers that bloom so sweetly wither and fall. Our human life, too, is fleeting. Today, again, I will cross the mountain pass of this uncertain world, and will not entertain shallow dreams or give way to drunkenness.

iru 居る　動詞（上一段） verb (*kami-ichidan*)

A. 生物がある場所に存在することを表す　*Seibutsu ga aru basho ni sonzai suru koto wo arawasu* Denotes location, in case of animates (→ *aru*):

- この部屋に誰も居ない。 *Kono heya ni dare mo inai.* This room is unoccupied.
- ペン・フレンドはイタリアに居ます。 *Pen-furendo wa Itaria ni imasu.* My pen friend is in Italy.
- 庭に犬が二匹居る。 *Niwa ni inu ga ni-hiki iru.* There are two dogs in the garden.

B. 「ている」の形で、補助動詞 *"-Te iru" no katachi de, hojo-dōshi* In *-te iru* form, acts as a supplementary verb.

1. 動作の継続を表す *Dōsa no keizoku wo arawasu* Denotes the progressive:

- 友人の到着を待っている。 *Yūjin no tōchaku wo matte iru.* I am waiting for my friends to arrive.
- 仕事がなくてぶらぶらしている。 *Shigoto ga nakute, bura-bura shite iru.* He is out of work, and just hangs around.
- じっとしていられない。 *Jitto shite irarenai.* I cannot stay still.
- 彼は居ても立ってもいられなかった。 *Kare wa ite mo tatte mo irarenakatta.* He was quite restless.

2. 動作の結果の存続を表す *Dōsa no kekka no sonzoku wo arawasu* Denotes that the result of the action continues:

- 窓が開いている。 *Mado ga aite iru.* The windows are open.
- カナリアが死んでいる。 *Kanaria ga shinde iru.* The canary is dead.
- もう家に帰っているだろう。 *Mō ie ni kaette iru darō.* They are probably home by now.

3. 現在の状態を表す *Genzai no jōtai wo arawasu* Denotes present state:

- 道が曲がっている。 *Michi ga magatte iru.* The road is crooked.

NOTE. In this context, it is usual for this *-te iru* to be translated by "be + adjective":

- *futoru* put on weight *futotte iru* be stout.
- *hareru* clear up *harete iru* be fine.
- *hara ga heru* become hungry *hara ga hette iru* be hungry.
- *nodo ga kawaku* become thirsty *nodo ga kawaite iru* be thirsty.
- *kumoru* become cloudy *kumotte iru* be cloudy.
- *tsukareru* become tired *tsukarete iru* be tired.
- *yaseru* become thin *yasete iru* be thin

NOTE. There is some overlapping of *iru* and *aru* to denote existence and possession:

- 神がいる・あるとは信じられない。 *Kami ga iru • aru to wa shinjirarenai.* I can't believe in the existence of a God.
- 彼には娘が三人いた・あった。 *Kare ni wa musume ga sannin ita • atta.* He had three daughters.

NOTE. In the case of some verbs, the progressive and non-progressive forms will differ even in meaning:

- *motsu* take hold of *motte iru* possess, have.
- *oboeru* commit to memory *oboete iru* remember, recall.
- *shiru* come to know *shitte iru* know, be aware.

- *sumu* take up residence *sunde iru* dwell, live.
- *uru* sell *utte iru* be on (for) sale.

NOTE. The progressive form applies also to the causative, passive and imperative:

- 仕事を専門家にさせている。 *Shigoto wo senmonka ni sasete iru.* I am having an expert do the job. (causative)
- 見ていられるとやりにくい。 *Mite irareru to yari-nikui.* It is hard to do it while one is being watched. (passive)
- 黙っていなさい。 *Damatte i-nasai.* Be quiet, please. (imperative)

NOTE. While *-te iru* is used with both transitive and intransitive verbs, *-te aru* is usual only with transitives:

- 電灯が点いている。 *Dentō ga tsuite iru.* The lights are on.
- 電灯が点けてある。 *Dentō ga tsukete aru.* The lights are (have been switched) on.
- 本を読んでいる。 *Hon wo yonde iru.* They are reading books.

itadaku 頂く　動詞 verb

補助動詞として「ありがたく受ける」気持ちを表す *Hojo-dōshi to shite "arigataku ukeru" kimochi wo arawasu* Used as a supplementary verb, expresses the idea of being grateful for a favour received:

- 明日も来ていただきたい。 *Asu mo kite itadakitai.* I want you to (be so kind as to) come again tomorrow.
- この手紙を投函して頂けませんか。 *Kono tegami wo tōkan shite itadakemasen ka?* Would you be so kind as to drop this letter in the post for me?

NOTE. There is a sub-standard use of the potential of *itadaku* to express acceptability:

- この葡萄酒はいただける。 *Kono budōshu wa itadakeru.* This wine tastes good.
- その意見はいただけない。 *Sono iken wa itadakenai.* I don't fall for that idea.

itasu 致す　動詞 verb

1. 「する」「行う」の謙譲語 *"Suru", "okonau" no kenjō-go* Deferential form for *suru, okonau:*

- 何に致しましょうか。 *Nani ni itashimashō ka?* What will you have?

2. 「お」「ご」＋動詞の連用形または動作を表す名詞に付いて、丁寧を表す。*"O", "go" + dōshi no ren'yōkei, mata wa, dōsa wo arawasu meishi ni tsuite, teinei wo arawasu* Following *o* or *go* + Base 2 of verbs, or nouns denoting action, expresses respect:

- 御願いいたします。 *O-negai itashimasu.* I pray you.
- 日程が決まり次第ご連絡いたします。 *Nittei ga kimari-shidai, go-renraku itashimasu.* I will let you know as soon as the schedule has been fixed.

NOTE. This construction is restricted to first and second persons.

3. 影響を及ぼす（多く、よくない結果の場合に用いる） *Eikyō wo oyobosu (ooku, yoku nai kekka no baai ni mochiiru)* Exert influence (mostly in the case of undesirable results):

- 皆私の不徳の致すところです。 *Mina watashi no futoku no itasu tokoro desu.* It was entirely my fault.
- それに思いを致さなかったのは、私の失敗だ。 *Sore ni omoi wo itasanakatta no wa, watashi no shippai da.* It was wrong of me not to give thought to the matter.

itsu いつ（何時） 代名詞・副詞 pronoun / adverb

不定の時間を示す *Futei no jikan wo shimesu* Denotes indeterminate time:

- いつおいでになりますか。 *Itsu oide ni narimasu ka?* When will you go?
- いつから始まりますか。 *Itsu kara hajimarimasu ka?* When does it begin?
- いつごろ出来上がりますか。 *Itsu goro deki-agarimasu ka?* About when will it be ready?
- いつの間にか見えなくなった。 *Itsu no ma ni ka mienaku natta.* He disappeared unnoticed.

→ *itsu demo, itsuka, itsu mo*

-itsu 一 接尾語 suffix

This is an *on* reading, so the つ is not written in:

- 同一 *dō-itsu* identity, equality; 合一 *gō-itsu* unity; 画一 *kaku-itsu* uniformity; 均一 *kin-itsu* uniformity; 専一 *sen-itsu* devotion; 単一 *tan-itsu* simplicity; 統一 *tō-itsu* unification; 唯一 *yui-itsu* uniqueness.

itsu demo いつでも 副詞 adverb

- いつでも出発出来るように準備が整っている。 *Itsu de mo shuppatsu dekiru yō ni junbi ga totonotte iru.* We are ready to leave at a moment's notice.

itsu ka いつか 副詞 adverb

1. 知らないうちに *Shiranai uchi ni* Unexpectedly, unnoticed:

• いつか夜になっていた。 *Itsu ka yoru ni natte ita.* Night took us by surprise.

2. 過去の動詞を伴って、「以前」の意味を表す *Kako no dōshi wo tomonatte, "izen" no imi wo arawasu* With past-tense verbs, means "formerly":

• いつかお目にかかりましたね。 *Itsu ka o-me ni kakarimashita ne.* I believe we have met before.

3. 未来の動詞に伴って、「そのうちに」の意味を表す。 *Mirai no dōshi ni tomonatte, "sono uchi ni" no imi wo arawasu.* With future-tense verbs, means "sooner or later":

• 正しいことをやれば、きっといつか報いられる。 *Tadashii koto wo yareba, kitto itsu ka mukuirareru.* If you do the right thing, you are bound to be rewarded eventually.

itsu mo いつも　副詞・名詞 adverb/noun

• いつも六時に起きることにしている。 *Itsu mo roku-ji ni okiru koto ni shite iru.* I make it a rule to get up at six.

• いつものことをいつもの通りやった。 *Itsu mo no koto wo itsu mo no toori yatta.* He did the usual things in the usual way.

• いつもと違って、タクシーで帰ってきた。 *Itsu mo to chigatte, takushii de kaette kita.* He came home by taxi, something unusual for him.

iu 言う　動詞 verb

This is the traditional romanisation of 言う、pronounced long but not given the macron. It was いふ in *bungo*. The romanisation of 夕、友、有、etc. is yū, while that of the verb 結う is *yuu*, the stem *yu-* remaining and the final *-u* conjugating.

As for the ideograph, 言う is the one used in modern Japanese; 云う is now archaic; 曰く is found as *iwaku* in Kanbun, and 謂れ as *iware*.

NOTE. Although usually used as a transitive verb, it has also a special use.

自動詞として、「そういう音を立てる」意味を表す *Jidōshi to shite, "sō iu oto wo tateru" imi wo arawasu.* As an intransitive verb, means: "make this sound":

• 箪笥をがたぴし言わせて、衣類を取り出した。 *Tansu wo gatapishi iwasete, irui wo tori-dashita.* Opening the drawer with a creaking sound, she took out some clothes.

• ごぼごぼ言うだけで、水が出てこなかった。 *Gobo-gobo iu dake de, mizu ga dete konakatta.* There was a gurgle, but no water came out.

NOTE. For idioms involving *iu* (*to ieba, to ii . . . to ii, to wa ie,* etc.,) see ***to***[2].

J

ja (jā) じや、(じゃあ)　連語　phrase (colloquial)
「だ」の連用形に、係助詞「は」 *"Da" no ren'yōkei ni, kakari-joshi "wa"* Base 2 of the auxiliary verb *-da* + bound particle *wa*.

1. 接続助詞「それでは」 *Setsuzoku-joshi "sore de wa"* Conjunctive particle:
   - じゃ、遠足は延期か。 *Ja, ensoku wa enki ka?* So the outing is postponed, then?
2. 感動詞「それならば」 *Kandōshi "sore naraba"* Interjection:
   - じゃあ、ここで失礼致します。 *Jā, koko de shitsurei itashimasu.* Well, I'll be off now.
3. 連語「では」の変化 *Rengo "de wa" no henka* Colloquial form for *de wa:*
   - いいえ、親戚じゃない。 *Iie, shinseki ja nai.* No, he is no relation.
   - あの人はお宅にいましたかと聞いているのじゃありません。 *Ano hito wa o-taku ni imashita ka to kiite iru no ja arimasen.* It isn't a question of: "Was he at your place?"
4. 接続助詞「ちゃ、じゃ」 *Setsuzoku-joshi "-cha, -ja"* Conjunctive particle:
   - 転んじゃいけない。 *Koronja ikenai.* Mind you don't fall!
5. (古) 助動詞 *Jodōshi* Auxiliary verb (*da* in Kanto, *ja* in Kansai):
   - 行きましたじゃ。 *Ikimashita ja.* He went, I tell you.

-jaku 弱　接尾語　suffix
ある数量よりちょっと少ないことを示す *Aru sūryō yori chotto sukunai koto wo shimesu* Denotes that the amount falls just short of that stated:
• 人数は百名弱だ。 *Ninzū wa hyakumei-jaku da.* There are close on a hundred people. →強、*-kyō* slightly more than.

jihatsu 自発　spontaneity
Jihatsu denotes that the action comes about independently of the subject's will. It is restricted to verbs of thinking and feeling, and is expressed by adding *-rareru* or *-reru* to Base 1.

jodōshi 助動詞　auxiliary verb
活用のある付属語で *Katsuyō no aru fuzoku-go de* Conjugated dependent words:

1. 用言に付いて、色々の意味を加え、叙述を助ける *Yōgen ni tsuite, iro-iro no imi wo kuwae, jojutsu wo tasukeru* With conjugables, they add various meanings and help with predication.

2. 体言その他の語について、叙述の意味を加える *Taigen sono hoka no go ni tsuite, jojutsu no imi wo kuwaeru* With nominals and other parts of speech, they add the element of predication.

jō 上 体言・接頭語・接尾語 nominal, prefix, suffix

1. 名詞として *Meishi to shite* As a noun:

• 成績は中の上だ。 *Seiseki wa chū no jō da.* His record is above average

2. 接頭語として *Settō-go to shite* As a prefix.

1. upper, as opposed to lower:

• 上部 *jō-bu* upper part; 上段 *jō-dan* upper berth; 上半身 *jō-hanshin* torso; 上流 *jō-ryū* upper reaches, upper classes.

2. first of a series:

• 上中下の三巻 *jō-chū-ge no san-kan* all three volumes; 上下二巻の本 *jō-ge ni-kan no hon* work in two volumes.

3. first class, excellent:

• 上品な *jō-hin na* refined; 上等の *jō-tō no* of superior quality.

4. with a *Kan-go* suffix + *suru,* makes verbal compounds:

• 上映する *jō-ei suru* screen, show; 上演する *jō-en suru* stage; 上京する *jō-kyō suru* proceed to capital; 上陸する *jō-riku suru* come or go ashore.

3. 接尾語として *Setsubi-go to shite* As a suffix:

1. on surface of, in view of:

• 海上自衛隊 *Kaijō-jieitai* Maritime Self-defence Forces; 山上の垂訓 *San-jō no suikun* Sermon on the Mount; 席上 *seki-jō* at or during a meeting; 史上最大の *shi-jō saidai no* greatest ever; 紙上 *shi-jō* on paper, in print; 至上の *shijō no* supreme; 身上書 *shinjō-sho* personal information form; 長上 *chō-jō* one's superior; 発展途上国 *hatten tojō-koku* developing nations.

2. with a *Kan-go* prefix + *suru,* makes verbal compounds:

• 炎上する *en-jō suru* go up in flames; 逆上する *gyaku-jō suru* fly into a rage; 返上する *hen-jō suru* send back; 計上する *kei-jō suru* add up, appropriate; 献上する *ken-jō suru* present; 向上する *kō-jō suru* improve; 参上する *san-jō suru* visit; 呈上する *tei-jō suru* present.

jōgo 畳語

同じ単語を重ねて作った複合語 *Onaji tango wo kasanete tsukutta*

fukugō-go Repetitive word, used in making plurals, for emphasis, and, most of all, in onomatopoeic expressions:

- *yama-yama* mountains; *ware-ware* we; *hitotsu-hitotsu* one by one; *bata-bata* flapping; *goro-goro* rumbling; *hyū-hyū* whizzing.

joshi 助詞 particle

活用しない付属語で、色々な語について、その語と他の語との関係を示したり、ある意味を添えたりする。 *Katsuyō shinai fuzoku-go de, iro-iro na go ni tsuite, sono go to hoka no go to no kankei wo shimeshitari, aru imi wo soetari suru.*

Particles are invariable, independent words, added to various other parts of speech, showing their relationship to them or adding a certain meaning. They are divided into four main classes, two of these classes being subdivided (by some authorities), giving six altogether. The disconcerting point for the student is that several particles belong to more than one category.

1. 格助詞 *Kaku-joshi* Case particles (those that correspond most closely to English prepositions):

- *ga, no, wo, ni, e, to, yori, kara, de, ya.*

2. 接続助詞 *Setsuzoku-joshi* Conjunctive particles:

- *ba, de, ga, kara, keredomo, nagara, nari, node, noni, shi, tari, te, temo, to, tsutsu.*

3. 副助詞 *Fuku-joshi* Adverbial particles:

- *bakari, dake, datte, demo, kurai, hodo, ka, kiri, koso, made, mo, nado, nari, sae, shi, shika, toka, ha, yara.*

4. 終助詞 *Shū-joshi* Final particles:

- *ka, koto, na, ne, no sa, tomo, wa, yo, ze, zo.*

NOTE. Some people classify *koso, mo* and *ha* as 係助詞 *kei-joshi* or *kakari-joshi* (bound particle), and *ne* and *sa* as 間投助詞 *kantō-joshi* (interjectional particle).

josūshi 助数詞

数を表す語に付いて、物の種類を示す接尾語 *Kazu wo arawasu go ni tsuite, mono no shurui wo shimesu setsubi-go* Suffix added to numerals, denoting the nature of the items counted:

- 鉛筆三本 *enpitsu san-bon* three pencils; ビラ百枚 *bira hyaku-mai* one hundred flyers; 牛二頭 *ushi ni-tō* two cows.

  English still retains some few counters, but the Japanese array presents the student with a formidable task. The more important ones are listed. → Appendix C.

NOTE. There is another 序数詞 *jo-sūshi,* that turns cardinal numbers into ordinals:

- 第五 *dai-go* fifth; 八番 *hachi-ban* eighth; 三号 *san-gō* third (car); 七人目 *shichinin-me* seventh (person).

jū- 十 ジュウ（ジッ、とお、と）

- 十月 *jū-gatsu* October; 十人十色 *jū-nin to-iro* so many men, so many minds; 十日 *too-ka* the tenth; 二十歳 *hatachi, ni-jissai* twenty years old; 二十日 *hatsuka* the twenth.

-jū 中 接尾語 suffix

1. 時間を表す語に付いて、その期間全体の意味を添える *Jikan wo arawasu go ni tsuite, sono kikan zentai no imi wo soeru* With time words, means "throughout that period":

- 冬中 *fuyu-jū* all winter long; 一晩中 *hitoban-jū* all night long; 一日中 *ichinichi-jū* all day long; 一年中 *ichinen-jū* all the year round; 今月中 *kongetsu-jū* all this month.

NOTE. The addition of *ni* narrows the extent.

- 今週中 *konshū-jū* all this week; 今週中に *konshū-jū ni* within the week.

2. 場所を表す語に付いて、その空間全体の意味を添える *Basho wo arawasu go ni tsuite, sono kūkan zentai no imi wo soeru* With space words, indicates "throughout that space":

- 京都中 *Kyōto-jū* all over Kyoto; そこら中 *sokora-jū* all over the place; 国中至る所 *kuni-jū itaru tokoro* throughout the country; 体中にぶつぶつがいっぱいできた。 *Karada-jū ni butsu-butsu ga ippai dekita.* A rash broke out all over his body.

→ ***-chū***

jūbako-yomi

Compounds in which the *on* reading comes first:

- 気持ち *ki-mochi* feeling; 台所 *dai-dokoro* kitchen.

NOTE. The opposite of *jūbako-yomi* is 湯桶読み *yutō-yomi.*

→ Appendix A

K

ka[1] か 終助詞 final particle

1. 疑問を表す *Gimon wo arawasu* Signals a question:

- 今何時ですか。 *Ima nan-ji desu ka?* What time is it now?
- そんなことがあるものか。 *Sonna koto ga aru mono ka?* That's impossible!
- 本当かどうか分からない。 *Hontō ka dō ka wakaranai.* I don't know whether it is true or not.

2. 念を押す意を表す *Nen wo osu i wo arawasu* Expresses the idea of pressing a point:

- 集合は十五時、いいか。 *Shūgō wa jūgoji, ii ka?* We assemble at 3 p.m., OK?

3. 提案・依頼を表す *Teian・irai wo arawasu* Expresses a proposition or recommendation:

- 見に行こうか。 *Mi ni ikō ka?* Let's go and have a look.
- お茶はいかがですか。 *O-cha wa ikaga desu ka?* How about a cup of tea?

ka[2] か 副助詞 adverbial particle

1. 不確実を表す *Fu-kakujitsu wo arawasu* Expresses uncertainty:

- いつかやってみたい。 *Itsu ka yatte mitai.* I should like to try it sometime.
- 五十歳かそこらだろう。 *Gojissai ka sokora darō.* He must be about fifty.
- 目黒かどこかで働いている。 *Meguro ka doko ka de hataraite iru.* He works in Meguro or somewhere round there.
- 家を出るか出ないうちに雨が降り出した。 *Ie wo deru ka denai uchi ni ame ga furidashita.* No sooner had I left (the house) than it began to rain.

2. 列挙したもののうちのどれかが成り立つ意を表す *Rekkyo shita mono no uchi no dore ka ga nari-tatsu i wo arawasu* denotes a choice:

- 君が来るか僕が行くかだ。 *Kimi ga kuru ka boku ga iku ka da.* It is a question of your coming here, or my going there.
- 正しいか否かが問題だ。 *Tadashii ka ina ka ga mondai da.* The question is whether it is right or not.
- 今月の下旬か来月の上旬に完成する。 *Kongetsu no gejun ka raigetsu no jōjun ni kansei suru.* It will be ready late this month or early next month.

ka- か 接頭語 prefix

形容詞の上に付いて、調子を整え、意味を強める *Keiyōshi no ue ni tsuite, chōshi wo totonoe, imi wo tsuyomeru* Prefixed to adjectives, adjusts the tone, and strengthens the meaning:

• か細い腕 *ka-bosoi ude* slender arms; か黒い髪 *ka-guroi kami* dark hair; か弱い声 *ka-yowai koe* weak voice.

-ka か 接尾語 suffix

Of the many *-ka* suffixes, three are very common:

1. 下 (also read *ge, shita, shimo, moto, sa-garu, kuda-ru, o-riru*)

• 地下 *chi-ka* underground; 治下 *chi-ka* under rule of; 眼下 *gan-ka* under eyes of; 陛下 *Heika* His Majesty; 氷点下 *hyōten-ka* below freezing-point; 階下 *kai-ka* downstairs; 閣下 *kak-ka* Excellency: 目下 *mok-ka* at present (目下 *me-shita* one's subordinates); 落下傘 *rak-kasan* parachute; 廊下 *rō-ka* corridor; 低下 *tei-ka* decline, depreciation; 天下 *ten-ka* the whole country.

2. 化 (also read *ke, bakeru*)

• 悪化 *ak-ka* worsening; 美化 *bi-ka* beautification; 文化 *bun-ka* civilization; 分化 *bun-ka* differentiation; 電化 *den-ka* electrification; 同化 *dō-ka* assimilation; 映画化 *eiga-ka* cinematization; 液化 *eki-ka* liquefaction; 合理化 *gōri-ka* rationalization; 自由化 *jiyū-ka* liberalization; 気化 *ki-ka* evaporation; 帰化 *ki-ka* naturalization; 近代化 *kindai-ka* modernization; 強化 *kyō-ka* strengthening; 民主化 *minshu-ka* democratization; 軟化 *nan-ka* softening; 緑化 *ryok-ka* afforestation; 進化 *shin-ka* evolution.

3. 家 (also read *ke, ie, -ya*)

• 画家 *ga-ka* painter; 一家 *ik-ka* house, family, "school" *(ik-ke* family, relatives); 自家 *ji-ka* one's own house; 実家 *jik-ka* one's parents' home or family; 旧家 *kyū-ka* old family or house; 名家 *mei-ka* prestigious family, great master; 民家 *min-ka* private house; 農家 *nō-ka* farmhouse, farmer; 作家 *sak-ka* writer.

ka-, -ka 個・箇 接頭語・接尾語 prefix, suffix

1. 物を数える語 *Mono wo kazoeru go* Counter (limited range):

• 五箇月 *go-ka-getsu* five months; 一箇年 *ik-ka-nen* one year; 二箇国 *ni-ka-koku* two countries.

2. 物事を一つ一つ指し示す語 *Mono-goto wo hitotsu-hitotsu sashi-shimesu go* Word used to refer to things individually:

• 箇条 *kajō* item, article; 箇所 *ka-sho* part, section; 三箇日 *san-ga-nichi* first 3 days of New Year.

NOTE. The two ideographs are more or less interchangeable, 箇 being read *ka*, and 個 being read *ko*. Both are often substituted by ヶ or even か。

ka dō ka かどうか　連語　phrase

• 来るかどうか彼に聞いてくれ。 *Kuru ka dō ka kare ni kiite kure.* Ask him whether he is coming or not.

ka na[1] かな　終助詞（古） final particle (*bungo*)

感動を表す *Kandō wo arawasu* Expresses strong emotion:

• 絵にいとよく似たるかな。 *E ni ito yoku ni-taru ka na!* (What a beautiful scene it is!) It is as if it were a painting! (This is the *ka na* of poetry.)

ka na[2] かな　連語　phrase

疑問の終助詞「か」に、詠嘆の終助詞「な」 *Gimon no shū-joshi "ka" ni, eitan no shū-joshi "na"* Final interrogative particle *ka* + final exclamative particle *na:*

1. 自問を表す *Jimon wo arawasu* Denotes a question addressed to oneself:

• 待った方がいいかな。 *Matta hō ga ii ka na?* Should I wait, I wonder?

2. 打ち消しを伴って、願望を表す *Uchikeshi wo tomonatte, ganbō wo arawasu* With a negative, expresses a wish:

• 早く来ないかな。 *Hayaku konai ka na!* I wish he would hurry up!

ka shira かしら　終助詞　final particle

Ka shira comes from か知らぬ、and is found as a suffix in 何かしら、誰かしら、etc.

体言・用言の連体形・形容動詞の語幹に付く。 *Taigen • yōgen no rentaikei • keiyō-dōshi no gokan ni tsuku* Is added to nominals, to Base 4 of verbals and to stem of adjectival nouns.

1. 疑ったり怪しんだりするときに使う語 *Utagattari, ayashindari suru toki ni tsukau go* Word used to convey the idea of doubt or suspicion:

• 今日は何日かしら。 *Kyō wa nan-nichi ka shira?* What day (of the month) is it today, I wonder?

• 雨が降るかしら。 *Ame ga furu ka shira?* I wonder if it will rain?

• どちらが適当かしら。 *Dochira ga tekitō ka shira?* I wonder which is the more suitable?

2. 婉曲な依頼を表す *Enkyoku na irai wo arawasu* Expresses a request indirectly:

• 窓を閉めていただけないかしら。 *Mado wo shimete itadakenai ka-shira?* Would you be so kind as to close the window?

3. 「…ないかしら」の形で、願望を表す *". . . -nai ka shira" no katachi de, ganbō wo arawasu* In . . . *-nai ka shira* form, expresses a wish:
   - 早く春が来ないかしら。 *Hayaku haru ga konai ka shira!* How I wish it were spring!

NOTE. Besides the final particles properly so called, there are some ten words classed as 終助詞に準ずるもの *shū-joshi ni junzuru mono* words treated as final particles: *i, e, ka shira, tara, te, tte, teba, teyo,* and *mono ka.*

-kaeru 返る　補助動詞 supplementary verb
程度の甚だしいことを表す *Teido no hanahadashii koto wo arawasu* Denotes intense degree:
   - 踏ん反りかえる *funzori-kaeru* throw one's head back in a haughty attitude; むせかえる *muse-kaeru* be choked; 煮え返る *nie-kaeru* seethe; 力み返る *rikimi-kaeru* strain; 冴え返る *sae-kaeru* be very clear; 静まり返る *shizumari-kaeru* become very quiet; 沸き返る *waki-kaeru* boil up; 呆れ返る *akire-kaeru* get disgusted.

-kaesu 返す・反す　接尾語 suffix verb
動詞の連用形に付く *Dōshi no ren'yokei ni tsuku* Is added to Base 2 of verbs.

1. 「反復する」という意味を添える *"Hanpuku suru" to iu imi wo soeru* Adds the idea of repetition:
   - 繰り返す *kuri-kaesu* repeat, re-wind; 見返す *mi-kaesu* look back, return another's look; 読み返す *yomi-kaesu* re-read.
2. 他からの働き掛けにたいして、こちらからも同じことをする *Ta kara no hatarakikake ni taishite, kochira kara mo onaji koto wo suru* Do the same in reverse:
   - 射返す *i-kaesu* shoot back; にらみ返す *nirami-kaesu* glare back at.

kagiri 限り　形式名詞 formal noun

1. 接続助詞の様に *Setsuzoku-joshi no yō ni* Used like a conjunctive particle:
   - 私の知っている限りでは、*watashi no shitte iru kagiri de wa,* to the best of my knowledge; 見渡すかぎり *mi-watasu kagiri* as far as the eye can see.
   - 仕事があるかぎり帰らない。 *Shigoto ga aru kagiri kaeranai.* He won't go home as long as there is work to be done.
2. 接尾語として *Setsubi-go to shite* As a suffix:

- 命限り *inochi-kagiri* as long as one lives; 身代限り *shindai-kagiri* bankruptcy.

NOTE. Distinguish *kagiri-nai* from *kagiranai:*

- 限りない称賛に値する。 *Kagiri-nai shōsan ni atai suru.* No praise is too good for him.
- 金持は必ずしも幸福とは限らない。 *Kanemochi wa kanarazu shi mo kōfuku to wa kagiranai.* The rich are not necessarily happy.

kahen Short for か行変格活用 *ka-gyō henkaku katsuyō;* in modern Japanese applies only to the one verb *kuru.* → *sahen*

-kai

Of the many *-kai* suffixes, the following are the most common:

- 回 number of times: 二回繰り返す *ni-kai kuri-kaesu* repeat (twice).
- 階 stories: 五階建てのビル *go-kai-date no biru* 5-story building.
- 会 meeting, group: 忘年会 *bōnen-kai* end-of-year party.
- 界 boundary, circle: 世界 *se-kai* world, circle(s).
- 介 being in between: 仲介 *chū-kai* mediation.
- 快 pleasant feeling: 不快な *fu-kai na* unpleasant.
- 改 change, renew: 朝令暮改 *chōrei bo-kai* inconsistency of policy.
- 解 divide, understand: 誤解 *go-kai* misunderstanding.
- 開 open, begin: 打開 *da-kai* solution; 満開 *man-kai* full bloom.
- 海 sea, waters: 沿海 *en-kai* coastal waters; 航海 *kō-kai* navigation.

-kakaru 掛かる 接尾語 suffix verb

動詞の連用形に付く *Dōshi no ren'yōkei ni tsuku* Is added to Base 2 of verbs.

1. 相手に向かって動作をする *Aite ni mukatte dōsa wo suru* Direct the action against another person:

- 切り掛かる *kiri-kakaru* attack with sword; 殴り掛かる *naguri-kakaru* hit out at; 襲い掛かる *osoi-kakaru* fall upon; 飛び掛かる *tobi-kakaru* fly at.

2. 動作を始める *Dōsa wo hajimeru* Begin the action:

- 出掛かる *de-kakaru* be on the point of going out, be about to rise (of sun, moon); 暮れ掛かる *kure-kakaru* night is about to fall; 沈み掛かる *shizumi-kakaru* be about to set (of sun); 行き掛かる *yuki-kakaru* be on the point of going.

3. 状態が始まる *Jōtai ga hajimaru* State begins:

- 壊れ掛かる *koware-kakaru* begin crumbling; 死に掛かる *shini-kakaru* face death.

4. たまたまそこを通る *tama-tama soko wo tooru* happen to pass by:
- 通り掛かる *toori-kakaru* happen to be passing (only with synonyms of *tooru*).

-kake 掛け 接尾語 suffix

A. 動詞の連用形に付いて、「...する途中」という意味を添える *Dōshi no ren'yōkei ni tsuite, ". . . suru tochū" to iu imi wo soeru* With Base 2 of verbs, adds the meaning: "be in the process of doing":
- 食べ掛けの御飯 *tabe-kake no gohan* meal one has just begun; 飲み掛けのお茶 *nomi-kake no o-cha* tea left half drunk; 吸い掛けのたばこ *sui-kake no tabako* half-smoked cigarette; 読み掛けの本 *yomi-kake no hon* book one has begun to read.

B. 名詞に付く *Meishi ni tsuku* Is added to nouns.

1. ものを置く道具 *Mono wo oku dōgu* Appliance to rest things on:
- 衣紋掛け *emon-kake* dress-hanger; 肘掛け *hiji-kake* elbow rest; 稲掛け *ine-kake, ina-kake* rice-plant rack; 腰掛け *koshi-kake* chair, temporary post; 手拭い掛け *tenugui-kake* towel rack; 洋服掛け *yō-fuku-kake* coat hanger.

2. 装飾となる布・板など *Sōshoku to naru nuno • ita, nado* Decorative covering:
- 壁掛け *kabe-kake* tapestry; 窓掛け *mado-kake* window-curtain; 祭壇掛け *saidan-kake* altar-cloth; 寝台掛け *shindai-kake* bedspread; テーブル掛け *tēburu-kake* tablecloth.

3. 料理で使う粉類 *Ryōri de tsukau kona-rui* Powdered additives in cookery
- 餡掛け *an-kake* dressed with a thick, starchy sauce; 振り掛け *furi-kake* dried condiment for sprinkling on rice

4. 動詞用法の「掛け」の熟語 *Dōshi-yōhō no "-kake" no juku-go* Compounds using *-kake* in its verbal sense:
- 願掛け *gan-kake* making a vow to a deity; 帆掛け舟 *ho-kake-bune* sailing-ship; 見掛け *mi-kake* outward appearance; 見せ掛け *mise-kake* pretence; 差し掛け *sashi-kake* holding over; 呼び掛け *yobi-kake* appeal.

-kakeru 掛ける 接尾語 suffix verb

動詞の連用形に付く *Dōshi no ren'yōkei ni tsuku* Is added to Base 2 of verbs.

1. 動作を始める *Dōsa wo hajimeru* Begin the action:

- 英語で話し掛けた。 *Eigo de hanashi-kaketa.* I addressed him in English.
- 急に問い掛けられた。 *Kyū ni toi-kakerareta.* A sudden question was flung at me.
- 食べ掛けたところへ友達が来た。 *Tabe-kaketa tokoro e tomodachi ga kita.* A friend came just after I had begun my meal.
- 読み掛けた本をどこかに置き忘れた。 *Yomi-kaketa hon wo doko ka ni oki-wasureta.* I have mislaid the book I had begun to read.

2. 「もう少しで...する」 *"Mō sukoshi de . . . suru"* Be about to . . . :

- 垣根が倒れ掛けている。 *Kakine ga taore-kakete iru.* The fence is on the verge of collapse.
- 殴られ掛けたので、急いで逃げた。 *Nagurare-kaketa no de, isoide nigeta.* I was about to be thrashed, so I took to my heels.

-kakkō 格好 接尾語 suffix

1. 年齢を表す数字に付いて、「ぐらい」の意を示す *Nenrei wo arawasu sūji ni tsuite, "gurai" no i wo shimesu* With numbers indicating age, denotes approximate amount:

- 四十格好の人 *shijū-kakkō no hito* a person of about forty.

NOTE. The suffix is usually added to numbers indicating middle age or above.

2. 名詞に付いて、外観を示す *Meishi ni tsuite, gaikan wo shimesu* Added to nouns, denotes outward appearance:

- 背格好 *se-kakkō, sei-kakkō* stature, build.

kaku joshi 格助詞 case particle

体言や体言の資格を持つ語と、文中の他の語との関係を示す助詞 *Taigen ya taigen no shikaku wo motsu go to, bunchū no ta no go to no kankei wo shimesu joshi* Particles that indicate the relationship of nominals or nominal equivalents to other words in the sentence:

- 雪が降り始めた。 *Yuki ga furi-hajimeta.* It has started to snow. (grammatical subject).
- 形の美しい山だ。 *Katachi no utsukushii yama da.* It is a beautifully shaped mountain. (possessive).
- 年を取るに連れて *toshi wo toru ni tsurete* as we get old (direct object).
- 生徒に英語を教える *seito ni Eigo wo oshieru* teach English to students (indirect object).
- 学校から帰る *gakkō kara kaeru* return from school (ablative).

- 東京へ向かっている *Tōkyō e mukatte iru* going to Tokyo (destination).
- 本と雑誌 *hon to zasshi* books and magazines (conjunction).
- 兄より背が高い *ani yori se ga takai* be taller than one's brother (comparison).
- 庭で遊んでいる *niwa de asonde iru* be playing in the garden (location).
- 青いのや赤いのや *aoi no ya akai no ya* blues and reds (conjunction).

→ *joshi*.

kami-ichidan 上一段（活用）

The conjugation for most verbs ending in *-iru*. *Shimo-ichidan* is the conjugation for most verbs ending in *-eru*. Those verbs that end in *-iru*, *-eru* but belong to the *go-dan* conjugation are listed in the Introduction (III).

- 居る *iru, imasu* be (present) . . . is a *kami-ichidan* verb.
- 要る *iru, irimasu* be necessary . . . is a *go-dan* verb.

-kan

Of the many *-kan* suffixes, the following are worth noting:

- 巻（まき）巻物、書物、映画などを数える語 *Maki-mono, shomotsu, eiga nado wo kazoeru go* Counter for scrolls, books, films, etc.

→ *-maki*

- 管（くだ）笛などを数える語 *Fue nado wo kazoeru go* Counter for wind instruments such as flutes.
- 貫（つらぬ-く）重さ・貨幣の昔の単位、また、地行高の換算に用いた語 *Omosa • kahei no mukashi no tan'i, mata, chigyō-daka no kansan ni mochiita go:* Former unit of weight and currency, and also a word used in reckoning yield of fief.
- 間（あいだ）名詞に付いて、「…と…のあいだ」 *Meishi ni tsuite, ". . . to . . . no aida"* Added to nouns, denotes time or space between: 過去十年間 *kako jūnen-kan* for the last ten years; 東京横浜間の鉄道 *Tōkyō-Yokohama-kan no tetsudō* the Tokyo-Yokohama railway.

-kaneru 兼ねる 補助動詞 supplementary verb (*shimo-ichidan*)

動詞の連用形に付いて、「出来ない」「しにくい」という意味を添える *Dōshi no ren'yōkei ni tsuite, "dekinai", "shi-nikui" to iu imi wo soeru* With Base 2 of verbs, adds the idea of the action's being impossible or at least very difficult:

• ご依頼に応じかねます。 *Go-irai ni ōji-kanemasu.* I can't comply with your request.
• それだけはしかねる。 *Sore dake wa shi-kaneru.* I'll do anything but that.
• あの人はどんなことでもしかねない。 *Ano hito wa donna koto de mo shi-kanenai.* That fellow will stop at nothing.

kara[1] から 格助詞 case particle

体言または体言の資格を作る「の」に付く *Taigen mata wa taigen no shikaku wo tsukuru "no" ni tsuku* Is added to nominals and nominalizing "no."

1. 動作・作用の起点を示す *Dōsa • sayō no kiten wo shimesu* Indicates point of origin of action:

• 外国から帰ってきた。 *Gaikoku kara kaette kita.* He has returned from abroad.
• 太陽は東から昇る。 *Taiyō wa higashi kara noboru.* The sun rises in the east.
• 授業は九時から始まる。 *Jugyō wa kuji kara hajimaru.* Class begins at nine.

2. 経由の場所を示す *Keiyu no basho wo shimesu* Indicates route of action:

• 木の間から光が差し込む。 *Ko-no-ma kara hikari ga sashi-komu.* Light shines in through the trees.
• 泥棒は裏から入ったらしい。 *Dorobō wa ura kara haitta-rashii.* The thief seems to have got in from the rear.

3. 原因・理由・根拠・動機などを示す *Gen'in • riyū • konkyo • dōki nado wo shimesu* Indicates cause, reason, basis, motive, etc.:

• お前の不注意から出たことだ。 *O-mae no fu-chūi kara deta koto da.* It is the result of your carelessness.
• 極度の興奮から泣き出した。 *Kyokudo no kōfun kara naki-dashita.* She was so excited that she burst into tears.
• ちょっとしたいたずらから大怪我をした。 *Chotto shita itazura kara oo-kega wo shita.* A slight prank led to his being seriously injured.

4. 原料・材料などを示す *Genryō • zairyō nado wo shimesu* Indicates (raw) material:

• 水は水素と酸素からなる。 *Mizu wa suiso to sanso kara naru.* Water consists of hydrogen and oxygen.
• チーズは牛乳から作る。 *Chiizu wa gyūnyū kara tsukuru.* Cheese is made from milk.

5. 勘定の基準を示す *Kanjō no kijun wo shimesu* Indicates basis for calculation:

- こういう本は五千円からする。 *Kō iu hon wa gosen'en kara suru.* A book like this will cost upwards of ¥5000.

6. 受け身の相手を示す *Ukemi no aite wo shimesu* Denotes the agent in passive construction:

- 先生から叱られた。 *Sensei kara shikarareta.* I was scolded by the teacher.
- 級友からいじめられることもある。 *Kyūyū kara ijimerareru koto mo aru.* He is sometimes teased by his classmates.

NOTE. *kara* may be used only when the agent is a person; *ni* is more usual:

- 雨に降られるよ。 *Ame ni furareru yo.* You will be caught in the rain.

kara～yori

Yori is more literary than *kara* and is often used in announcements:

- 本日十五時より職員会議がある。 *Honjitsu jūgo-ji yori shokuin-kaigi ga aru.* There will be a staff meeting at 3:00 p.m. today.

kara～wo

With verbs of motion . . . *kara* implies transfer from one place to another, while *wo* suggests motion within the same sphere; there are exceptions, as these examples will show:

- 坂を降りる *saka wo oriru* descend a slope; 窓から逃れる *mado kara nogareru* escape by the window; 大学を卒業する *daigaku wo sotsugyō suru* graduate from university; 大学から社会へと飛び出す *daigaku kara shakai e to tobi-dasu* dash from university into society.

NOTE. For *-te kara* and *-ta ato* → *ato*.

kara² から 接続助詞 conjunctive particle

用言の終止形に付く *Yōgen no shūshikei ni tsuku* Is added to Base 3 of conjugables.

1. 原因・理由を表す *Gen'in・riyū wo arawasu* Expresses cause or reason:

- 雨が降ってきたから止めた。 *Ame ga futte kita kara yameta.* We stopped because it began to rain.
- 悲しいから泣いているのです。 *Kanashii kara naite iru no desu.* I am crying because I am sad.

2. （そこで中止して）決意・断定を表す *(Soko de chūshi shite) ketsui・*

dantei wo arawasu (Ending with *kara*) adds an air of finality:

• ただではおかないから。 *Tada de wa okanai kara!* You won't get away with this!

• そんなことをすると先生に言い付けるから。 *Sonna koto wo suru to sensei ni ii-tsukeru kara!* If you do such a thing I'll tell the teacher!

kara～no de

Kara introduces a subjective, *no de* an objective reason:

• 風が強いから窓を閉めよう。 *Kaze ga tsuyoi kara mado wo shimeyō.* The wind is strong, so let's close the windows. (subjective reason)

• 風が強いので埃が立つ。 *Kaza ga tsuyoi no de hokori ga tatsu.* The strong wind is raising the dust. (objective reason)

kara ni wa からには 接続助詞 conjunctive particle

用言の連体形に付いて、「...する・した以上は」という意味を表す *Yōgen no rentaikei ni tsuite, ". . . suru • shita ijō wa" to iu imi wo arawasu* With Base 4 of verbals, expresses the idea of "for the simple reason that . . .":

• 決めたからにはどうしてもやり遂げなければならない。 *Kimeta kara ni wa dōshite mo yari-togenakereba naranai.* Now that I have decided, I must go through with it.

NOTE. The corresponding *bungo* phrase meant: . . . *suru to sugu* immediately on doing. . .

kara shite からして 連語 phrase

助詞「から」の強調的な表現 *Joshi "kara" no kyōchō-teki na hyōgen* Emphatic form for both case particle and the conjunctive particle *"kara":*

• この点からして賛成できない。 *Kono ten kara shite sansei dekinai.* On this point I can't agree.

• 出発は十時だからして、急がなくてもいい。 *Shuppatsu wa jūji da kara shite, isoganakute mo ii.* Since departure is at ten, there's no need to rush.

-kare かれ 形容詞の命令形（古） Base 6 (imperative) of adjectives in *bungo*.

Adjectives, too, had an imperative form in classical Japanese, and this has carried over in stock phrases like:

• 多かれ少なかれ *oo-kare sukuna-kare* more or less; 遅かれ早かれ *osokare haya-kare* sooner or later; 善かれ悪しかれ *yokare ashikare* right or wrong.

-karō かろう　助動詞　auxiliary verb

形容詞の未然形「かろ」に、推量の助動詞「う」、推量を表す *Keiyōshi no mizenkei "-karo" ni, suiryō no jodōshi "-u," suiryō wo arawasu* Base 1, *-karo* of adjectives + conjectural auxiliary *-u*, expresses conjecture:

- この調子では、明日も天気がよかろう。 *Kono chōshi de wa, asu mo tenki ga yokarō.* At this rate, it looks as if tomorrow will be fine, too.

NOTE. This construction is now replaced mostly by Base 3 + *darō;* e.g., 高かろう → 高いだろう。 It is still retained in certain phrases:

- 寒かろうが暑かろうが、行くことに決めた。 *Samukarō ga atsukarō ga, yuku koto ni kimeta.* I am determined to go, regardless of the weather.
- 高かろうと安かろうと、とにかく買いたい。 *Takakarō to yasukarō to, to ni kaku kaitai.* I want to buy it, no matter what it costs.

-kata 方　接尾語　suffix

体言・動詞の連用形に付く *Taigen • dōshi no ren'yōkei ni tsuku* Is added to nominals and to Base 2 of verbs.

1. 手段・方法を示す *Shudan • hōhō wo shimesu* Denotes means or method:

- 使い方はまだ分からない。 *Tsukai-kata wa mada wakaranai.* I don't know yet how to use it.
- 着物の着方がうまい。 *Kimono no ki-kata ga umai.* She dresses tastefully.

2.「係員」の意味を示す *"Kakari-in" no imi wo shimesu* Denotes "person in charge":

- 賄い方を捜している。 *Makanai-kata wo sagashite iru.* We are looking for a cook.

3. 他人の家に住んでいるとき、主人の名の下に添える語 *Tanin no ie ni sunde iru toki, shujin no na no shita ni soeru go:* Equivalent to "c/o":

- 山田二郎方 *Yamada Jirō-kata* c/o Jiro Yamada.

4. 人数を数えるときの尊敬の言い方 *Ninzū wo kazoeru toki no sonkei no ii-kata* Polite counter for persons:

- お二方がお見えになりました。 *O-futa-kata ga o-mie ni narimashita.* The two (visitors) have arrived.

5. 二つのうちの一方 *Futatsu no uchi no ippō* One of a pair:

- 母方の祖父が亡くなった。 *Haha-kata no sofu ga nakunatta.* My maternal grandfather has died.

6. 複雑な用法 *Fukuzatsu na yōhō* Various applications:

- 目方 *me-kata* weight; 味方 *mi-kata* ally (見方 viewpoint); 親方

oya-kata master; 里方 *sato-kata* relatives of bride or adopted child; 馬方 *uma-kata* packhorse driver.

→ *-gata*[1]

katei-kei 仮定形 Base 5, or "conditional form"

In *bungo* it was called 已然形 *izen-kei.*

- 今すぐ行けば間に合う。 *Ima sugu ikeba ma ni au.* If I go immediately I'll be in time.
- 当たらずと言えども遠からず。 *Atarazu to ie-domo tookarazu.* It isn't far from the truth.

katsuyō 活用 conjugation

Taking the word as a noun, it refers to the three conjugations of verbs (*go-dan, kami-ichidan* and *shimo-ichidan*), and to those of adjectives and adjectival nouns. In its verbal sense, it refers to the six "forms" (*mizen-kei, ren'yō-kei, shūshikei, rentai-kei, katei-kei, meirei-kei*) that follow the stemof the three kinds of conjugables. The verbs *kuru* and *suru* follow their own conjugations.

-katta かった 助動詞 auxiliary verb

形容詞・動詞の連用形に、過去の助動詞「た」 *Keiyōshi* • *dōshi no ren'yō-kei + kako no jodōshi "-ta"* Base 2 of adjectives/verbs + past auxiliary-*ta:* 形容詞・動詞の過去形を作る *Keiyōshi* • *dōshi no kako-kei wo tsukuru* Forms past tense of adjectives/verbs:

- 行ってきてよかったね. *Itte kite yokatta ne.* It was a good thing that you went, isn't it?
- いいえ、呼ばなかった。 *Iie, yobanakatta.* No, I didn't call you. (Adj. *nai*)
- 読みたかったのですか。 *Yomitakatta no desu ka?* Did you want to read it?
- 放火らしかった。 *Hōka-rashikatta.* It looked like (a case of) incendiarism.

ke- 気 接頭語 prefix

多く、形容詞の上に付いて、「何となく」という意味を表す *Ooku, keiyōshi no ue ni tsuite, "nan to naku" to iu imi wo arawasu* Prefixed mostly to adjectives, gives the meaning "somehow", "vaguely":

- 気振り *ke-buri* air, look; 気高い *ke-dakai* noble; 気だるい *ke-darui* languid; 気押される *ke-osareru* be overawed; 気色 *ke-shiki* sign, look; 気疎い *ke-utoi* disagreeable.

-ke[1] 気　接尾語　suffix

形容詞の語幹に付いて、名詞を作り、「…という感じ」の意味を添える *Keiyōshi no gokan ni tsuite, meishi wo tsukuri, ". . . to iu kanji" no imi wo soeru* Added to stem of adjectives, nominalizes them and adds the meaning: "the feeling of . . .":

- 吐き気 *haki-ke* nausea; 人気のない *hito-ke no nai* deserted; 脚気 *kakke* beriberi; 眠気 *nemu-ke* drowsiness; 寒気 *samu-ke* chill, *kan-ki* the cold; 湿気 *shikke* humidity; 塩気 *shio-ke* saltiness (潮気 *shio-ke* sea air).

→ *-ge*[1]

-ke[2] 家　接尾語　suffix

姓名や官職に付いて、家族や一族の意を表す *Seimei ya kanshoku ni tsuite, kazoku ya ichi-zoku no i wo arawasu* Added to names and titles, adds the meaning of "the whole family", "the whole clan":

- 徳川家 *Tokugawa-ke* the House of Tokugawa; 鈴木家 *Suzuki-ke* the Suzuki's; 分家 *bun-ke* branch family; 本家 *hon-ke* head family; 一家 *ik-ke* whole family, relatives (一家 *ik-ka* a house, a family, a "school", an authority); 出家 *shuk-ke* entering Buddhist priesthood.

keishiki meishi 形式名詞　formal noun

名詞としての実質を失って、形式的に用いられるもの *Meishi to shite no jisshitsu wo ushinatte, keishiki-teki ni mochiirareru mono* Nouns that, losing their semantic meaning, serve only in a formal capacity.

These nouns are listed in all dictionaries, but their use as function words is not mentioned, still less explained. The most common ones are: *aida*; *ato*; *hazu*; *hodo*; *koro*; *koto*; *mae*; *mama*; *naka*; *sai*; *tabi*; *tame*; *toki*; *tokoro*; *uchi*; *ue*; *wake*; *yō*; *yue*.

It is now recommended that these nouns be written in *kana*, to distinguish the formal use from their semantic role. Note also that the verbal preceding them is Base 4, not Base 3; this shows up only in the case of adjectival nouns:

- 簡単なはずだ。 *Kantan na hazu da*. It ought to be simple.

keiyōdōshi 形容動詞　adjectival nouns

This category is not recognized by all grammarians.

A. Definition.

活用する自立語で、それだけで述語になることができ、ものごとの性質・状態を表す *Katsuyō suru jiritsu-go de, sore dake de jutsu-go ni naru koto ga deki, monogoto no seishitsu • jōtai wo arawasu.* Conjugated independent words that can, by their nature, become predicates, and describe the nature or state of things.

B. Origin

本来副詞であったものに、文語動詞「あり」が付いてできた。 *Honrai fukushi de atta mono ni, bungo dōshi "ari" ga tsuite dekita.* The *bungo* verb *ari* was added to what were originally adverbs:

- 静かに＋あり…静かなり…静かな *shizuka ni + ari . . . shizuka nari . . . shizuka na;* 堂々と＋あり…堂々たり…堂々と *dō-dō to + ari . . . dō-dō tari . . . dō-dō to.*

The latter, so-called "subjective" adjectival nouns, now appear only in the forms *-to* and *-taru (danko to shite kyozetsu suru, reizen taru taido).*

C. Conjugation

1. *darō* 2. *datt* (だっ)、*de, ni* 3. *da* 4. *na* 5. *nara* 6. —.

D. Use of each of the six Bases

1. Base 1 未然形 *mizenkei:*

助動詞「う」に続いて、推量を表す *Jodōshi "-u" ni tsuzuite, suiryō wo arawasu* Followed by the auxiliary *-u,* expresses conjecture:

- 今日、波は静かだろう。 *Kyō, nami wa shizuka darō.* The sea will probably be calm today.

2. Base 2 連用形 *ren'yōkei:*

a.「だっ」

助動詞「た」、接続助詞「たり」「て」「ても」に続く *Jodōshi "-ta", setsuzoku-joshi "-tari", "-te", "-te mo" ni tsuzuku* Is followed by the auxiliary verb *-ta,* and by the conjunctive particles *-tari, -te, -te mo:*

- 言ってみたけれども、だめだった。 *Itte mita keredomo, dame datta.* I tried to tell him, but it was no good.
- ちょっと粗末だって構わない。 *Chotto somatsu datte kamawanai.* It doesn't matter if it is a bit rough.

b.「で」

1. 動詞「ある」、形容詞「ない」に続く *Dōshi "aru", keiyōshi "nai" ni tsuzuku* Is followed by the verb *aru* and the adjective *nai:*

- 純粋であるとは信じがたい。 *Junsui de aru to wa shinji-gatai.* It is difficult to believe that it is genuine.
- 便利でない場合もある。 *Benri de nai baai mo aru.* It isn't always convenient.

NOTE. A *wa* may intervene between the *de* and the *nai.*

2. 中止法の意を表す *Chūshi-hō no i wo arawasu* Signals a pause:

- 風は温かで、空も青い。 *Kaze wa atataka de, sora mo aoi.* The wind is warm, and the sky is blue.

3. 並列を表す *Heiretsu wo arawasu* Denotes listing:

- 勤勉で正直な生徒です。 *Kinben de shōjiki na seito desu.* He is a hardworking, honest student.

c. 「に」
連用修飾語を作る *Ren'yō-shūshokugo wo tsukuru* Makes modifiers (adverbs):

- 贅沢に暮らしている。 *Zeitaku ni kurashite iru.* He lives in luxury.

3. Base 3 終止形 *shūshikei:*
文章を言い切る *Bunshō wo ii-kiru* Ends the sentence:

- 見るのも嫌だ。 *Miru no mo iya da.* I can't stand the sight of it.

NOTE. This *da* may be followed by the final particles: *ga, kara, keredomo, na (nā), ne (nē), shi, tomo, yo, zo.*

- 私の場合も同様だけれども。 *Watashi no baai mo dōyō da keredomo.* I am in the same boat, though.

4. Base 4 連体形 *rentaikei:*
連体修飾語を作る *Rentai-shūshokugo wo tsukuru* Makes adjectival modifiers:

- 僅かな人しか知らないことだ。 *Wazuka na hito shika shiranai koto da.* It is something very few people know.

a. 助動詞「ようだ」に続く *Jodōshi "yō da" ni tsuzuku* Is followed by the auxiliary verb *yō da:*

- 学問に熱心なようだ。 *Gakumon ni nesshin na yō da.* He seems to be in earnest about his studies.

b. 助詞「の」「のに」「ので」に続く *Joshi "no", "no ni", "no de" ni tsuzuku* Is followed by the particles *no, no ni, no de:*

- 静かなのが好きだ。 *Shizuka na no ga suki da.* I like the peacefulness of it.
- 海が穏やかなのにだれも泳いでいない。 *Umi ga odayaka na no ni dare mo oyoide inai.* Nobody is swimming despite the fact that the sea is calm.
- 秘密なので今何も言えない。 *Himitsu na no de ima nani mo ienai.* I can't say anything just now, because it's a secret.

5. Base 5 仮定形 *kateikei:*

a. そのままか、助詞「ば」に連なって、仮定条件を表す *Sono mama ka, joshi "-ba" ni tsuranatte, katei-jōken wo arawasu* With or without the particle *-ba*, expresses a condition:

- 本当ならいいのだが。 *Hontō nara ii no da ga.* I hope it is true.
- 退屈ならば止めよう。 *Taikutsu naraba yameyō.* If it's boring, let's stop.

b. 並列を表す *Heiretsu wo arawasu* Denotes listing:

• 声も同じなら、顔も同じだ。 *Koe mo onaji nara, kao mo onaji da.* Both the voice and the facial appearance are the same.

6. Base 6, imperative, is not used in modern Japanese, although it did exist in *bungo:*

• 波静かなれ。 *Nami, shizuka nare.* Waves, be still.

E. The stem of adjectival nouns is used as follows.

1. 述語として *Jutsu-go to shite* As predicate:

• 見事、見事。 *Migoto! Migoto! Splendid! Splendid!*

2. 助動詞「そうだ」(様態)に続く *Jodōshi "sō da" (yōtai) ni tsuzuku* Is followed by the auxiliary verb *sō da* (appearance):

• 退屈そうにテレビを見ている。 *Taikutsu-sō ni terebi wo mite iru.* He is watching television, looking bored.

3. 助動詞「らしい」に続く *Jodōshi "rashii" ni tsuzuku* Is followed by the auxiliary verb *rashii:*

• 近頃元気らしい。 *Chika-goro genki-rashii.* He seems to be keeping well of late.

4. 接尾語「さ」を付けて、抽象名詞を作る *Setsubigo "sa" wo tsukete, chūshō meishi wo tsukuru* Is followed by the suffix *-sa* to make abstract nouns:

• 正確さを欠く。 *Seikaku-sa wo kaku.* It lacks precision.

• 鶏が朝の静けさを破って鳴いた。 *Niwatori ga asa no shizukesa wo yabutte naita.* The fowl crowed and broke the morning silence. (also *shizuka-sa*)

NOTE. Although the *keiyōdōshi* is basically a noun, it may not be used alone as subject or object of a sentence; this is the reason for the addition of *-sa* here.

NOTE. The most vexing problem about *keiyōdōshi* is whether to use *na* or *no* to make qualifiers of them. When *na* is used, they are being treated as adjectival nouns, when *no* is used, they are being treated as ordinary nouns. Sometimes the choice entails a difference in meaning:

• 五千円相当の品物 *gosen'en-sōtō no shinamono* goods to the value of ¥5000.

• 相当な暮らしをしている。 *Sōtō na kurashi wo shite iru.* They make a decent living.

NOTE. Some words have a true adjectival form and an adjectival noun form also:

• *atatakai, atataka na* warm; *chiisai, chiisa na* little; *ki-iroi, ki-iro na* yellow; *komakai, komaka na* small, fine; *makkuroi, makkuro na* jet black; *man-marui, man-maru na* perfectly round; *ookii, ooki na* big; *okashii, okashi na* funny; *yawarakai, yawaraka na* soft.

NOTE. Some loanwords, even those already adjectival, are found followed by *na:*

• *furesshu na* fresh; *handi na* handy; *romanchikku na* romantic.

keiyōshi 形容詞 adjectives

A. Definition

自立語で、それだけで述語になることができる用言 *Jiritsu-go de, sore dake de jutsu-go ni naru koto ga dekiru yōgen* Verbals that are independent and can of themselves form predicates.

B. Form

活用をし、口語では言い切ったとき、「い」で終わる。 *Katsuyō wo shi, kōgo de wa, ii-kitta toki, "i" de owaru* Conjugate, and, in modern Japanese, have their final form in *-i.*

C. Meaning

物事の性質・状態を表す *Monogoto no seishitsu • jōtai wo arawasu* Describe the nature or state of things.

D. Conjugation

(kōgo) 1. *karo* 2. *katt* (かっ), *ku* 3. *i* 4. *i* 5. *kere* 6. —; *(bungo)* 1. *ku, kara* 2. *ku, kari,* 3. *shi* 4. *ki, karu,* 5. *kere* 6. *kare.*

E. Euphonic change

Adjectives undergo a euphonic change before *gozaimasu* and *zonjimasu:*

• ちょっと短うございます。 *Chotto mijikō gozaimasu.* It is slightly short.

• 嬉しゅう存じます。 *Ureshū* (also *ureshiku*) *zonjimasu.* I am most happy.

F. Use of each of the six bases

1. Base 1 未然形 *mizenkei:*

推量の助動詞「う」に連なる *Suiryō no jodōshi "-u" ni tsuranaru* Is followed by the conjectural auxiliary *-u:*

• これでよかろう。 *Kore de yokarō.* This will do.

2. Base 2 連用形 *ren'yōkei:*

a. かっ

助動詞「た」、接続助詞「たり」に連なる *Jodōshi "-ta", setsuzoku-joshi "-tari" ni tsuranaru* Is followed by the past tense auxiliary *-ta* and the conjunctive particle *-tari:*

• 危なかった。 *Abunakatta!* It was a close call!

• 暑かったり寒かったりする。 *Atsukattari samukattari suru.* It is hot and cold by turns.

b. く

1. 副詞法に用いる *Fukushi-hō ni mochiiru* Is used adverbially:

- 気持ちよく引受けた。 *Kimochi-yoku hiki-uketa.* He took it on willingly.

補助形容詞「ない」、動詞「ある」に連なる *Hojo-keiyōshi "nai", dōshi "aru" ni tsuranaru* Is followed by the supplementary adjective *nai,* and by the verb *aru:*

- 値段は高くない。 *Nedan wa takaku nai.* It isn't expensive.
- 面白くはあるが、読みでがない。 *Omoshiroku wa aru ga, yomide ga nai.* It is interesting reading, but there isn't much in it.

2. 中止法に用いる *Chūshi-hō ni mochiiru* Signals a pause:
   - 品もよく、値段も安い。 *Shina mo yoku, nedan mo yasui.* They are of good quality, and cheap into the bargain.
3. 接続助詞「て」「ても」、係助詞「さえ」などに連なる *Setsuzoku-joshi "te", "te mo", kei-joshi "sae" nado ni tsuranaru* Is followed by the conjunctive particles *te* and *te mo*, and by the bound particle *sae:*
   - ちょっと長くても構わない。 *Chotto nagakute mo kamawanai.* It doesn't matter if it's a bit too long.

3. Base 3 終止形 *shūshikei:*

a. 言い切りに用いる *Ii-kiri ni mochi-iru* Is used to end a sentence:

- 私には小さい。 *Watashi ni wa chiisai.* It is (too) small for me.

b. 助動詞「だろ」「でしょ」「なら」「らしい」「そうだ²」に連なる *Jodōshi´ "daro", "desho", "nara", "rashii", "sō da²" ni tsuranaru* Is followed by the auxiliaries *daro, desho, nara, rashii, sō da²*.:

- 試験は難しいだろ。 *Shiken wa muzukashii daro.* The exam must be difficult.
- あちらはもう暖かいでしょ。 *Achira wa mō atatakai desho.* It must be warm over there already.
- 病気が重いそうだ。 *Byōki ga omoi sō da.* It seems his illness is serious.

c. 色々な助詞に連なる *Iro-iro na joshi ni tsuranaru* Is followed by various particles:

- 面倒臭いからしたくない。 *Mendō-kusai kara shitaku nai.* It's too much trouble so I don't want to do it.
- 読みやすいのに読めない。 *Yomi-yasui no ni yomenai.* He can't read it even though it's easy.
- 痛いけれども我慢できます。 *Itai keredomo gaman dekimasu.* It hurts, but I can bear it.

4. Base 4 連体形 *rentaikei:*

a. 体言に連なる *Taigen ni tsuranaru* Is followed by nominals (very often, formal nouns):

- あまり寒いときは外出しない。 *Amari samui toki wa gaishutsu shinai.* He doesn't go out when it's too cold.
- 若いころはよく風邪をひいたものだ。 *Wakai koro wa yoku kaze wo hiita mono da.* When I was young I used to catch cold very often.

b. 助動詞「ようだ」に連なる *Jodōshi "yō da" ni tsuranaru.* Is followed by the auxiliary *yō da:*

- 正しいようだ。 *Tadashii yō da.* It seems to be correct.

NOTE. In modern Japanese Bases 3 and 4 a re identical, but in classical Japanese they were different.

5. Base 5 仮定形 *kateikei:*

接続助詞「ば」に連なって、仮定条件または並列を示す *Setsuzoku-joshi "-ba" ni tsuranatte, katei jōken mata wa heiretsu wo shimesu* Followed by the conjunctive particle *-ba,* indicates condition as well as listing:

- 天気がよければ行きます。 *Tenki ga yokereba yukimasu.* We will go if the weather is fine.
- 頭もよければ、容貌も美しい。 *Atama mo yokereba, yōbō mo utsukushii.* He is not only clever, but handsome, too.

6. Base 6 命令形 *meireikei:*

In modern Japanese adjectives do not have an imperative. Classical Japanese had an imperative form that expressed hope and invitation as well as command:

- 今宵の月清かれ。 *Koyoi no tsuki kiyokare.* May the moon be clear this night.

NOTE. The stem of adjectives serves many purposes.

1. 感動を込めた叙述になる *Kandō wo kometa jojutsu ni naru* Serves as an exclamatory predicate:

- ああ、痛。 *Aa, ita!* Ouch!

2. 格助詞「の」を伴って、連体修飾語となる *Kaku-joshi "no" wo tomonatte, rentaishūshoku-go to naru* Is followed by the case particle *no* to form qualifiers:

- 懐かしのメロディー *natsukashi no merodii* tunes that bring back memories

3. 様態を表す助動詞「そうだ1」に連なる *Yōtai wo arawasu jodōshi "sō da1" ni tsuranaru* Is followed by the auxiliary *sō da*1, expressing semblance:

- 強そうだ。 *Tsuyo-sō da.* He looks strong.
- 重たそうな足取りで登校する。 *Omota-sō na ashi-dori de tōkō suru.*

Unwillingly, they slowly creep to school.

4. 合成語を作る *Gōsei-go wo tsukuru* Makes compound words:

- 赤字 *aka-ji* deficit; 細長い *hoso-nagai* slender; 遠回り *too-mawari* detour; 気短 *ki-mijika* hot-tempered; 高さ *taka-sa* height; 軽々と *karu-garu to* lightly.

ken- 兼 接頭語 prefix

掛け持ちをすること *Kake-mochi wo suru koto* Holding two positions concurrently:

- 居間と食堂の兼用だ。 *I-ma to shoku-dō no ken-yō da.* It serves as both living-room and dining-room.
- 総理大臣兼外務大臣を勤める。 *Sōridaijin ken-gaimudaijin wo tsutomeru.* He holds the portfolios of both Prime Minister and Minister for Foreign Affairs.

-ken[1] 件 接尾語 suffix

事柄・出来事を数える語 *Koto-gara • deki-goto wo kazoeru go* Counter for matters and incidents:

- 交通事故三件 *kōtsū jiko san-ken* three traffic accidents

-ken[2] 軒 接尾語 suffix

戸数を数える語 *Ko-sū wo kazoeru go* Counter for houses, shops, etc.:

- 角から三軒目です。 *Kado kara san-genme desu.* It's the third house from the corner.

-ken[3] 間 接尾語 suffix

日本の建築で、柱と柱とのあいだ *Nippon no kenchiku de, hashira to hashira to no aida* In (traditional) Japanese buildings, space between pillars:

- 三十三間堂 *Sanjūsan-gendō* the building of that name, in Kyōto

長さの単位 *Nagasa no tan'i* Unit of length, equals about 1.8m.

-ken[4] 券 接尾語 suffix

1. 約束の証拠とする割り符 *Yakusoku no shōko to suru warifu* A tally:
   - 株券 *kabu-ken* stock certificate; 証券 *shō-ken* bond.
2. 切符類 *Kippu-rui* Ticket:
   - 乗車券 *jōsha-ken* boarding-ticket; 回数券 *kaisū-ken* coupon ticket; 入場券 *nyūjō-ken* admission ticket; 旅券 *ryo-ken* passport.

-ken[5] 権 接尾語 suffix

他人を支配することの出来る力・資格 *Tanin wo shihai suru koto no dekiru chikara • shikaku* Right(s):

- 分権 *bun-ken* decentralization; 人権 *jin-ken* human rights; 民権 *min-ken* civil rights; 所有権 *shoyū-ken* ownership; 職権 *shok-ken* official authority; 特権 *tok-ken* privilege; 全権 *zen-ken* full powers.

-ken[6] 見 接尾語 suffix

1. 見ること・見えること *Miru koto • mieru koto* Seeing or appearing:

- 発見 *hak-ken* discovery; 露見 *ro-ken* disclosure; 散見 *san-ken* scattered appearances; 拝見 *hai-ken* having the honor of seeing.

2. 考え *Kangae* Opinion:

- 偏見 *hen-ken* prejudice; 意見 *iken* opinion; 定見 *tei-ken* fixed opinion.

3. 人に会うこと *Hito ni au koto* Meeting:

- 謁見 *ek-ken* audience; 会見 *kai-ken* interview.

-kereba けれぱ

文語の助動詞「けり」の已然形に、接続助詞「ば」 *Bungo no jodōshi "keri" no izenkei ni, setsuzoku-joshi "-ba"* Base 5 of the *bungo* auxiliary *keri* plus the conjunctive particle *-ba.*

It is now used to form the conditional of adjectives, and so we find it in:

- もう帰らなければならない。 *Mō kaeranakereba naranai.* I must go home now.
- 見たければどうぞ。 *Mitakereba dōzo.* Take a look if you want to.
- 男らしければ男らしいほどいい。 *Otoko-rashikereba otoko-rashii hodo ii.* The more manly he looks, the better.

NOTE. This is the *kere-* of *keredo, keredomo,* the *-do* being a *bungo* conjunctive particle. A shortened form, *kedo,* is conversational.

-ki[1] 基 接尾語 suffix

据え付けてあるものを数える語 *Sue-tsukete aru mono wo kazoeru go* Counter for pieces of equipment set up on bases:

- 高炉一基 *kōro ikki* one blast furnace; 三基の石碑 *san-ki no seki-hi* three stone monuments; 二基の灯籠 *ni-ki no tōrō* two stone lanterns.

-ki[2] 機 接尾語 suffix

航空機を数える語 *Kōkūki wo kazoeru go* Counter for aeroplanes:

- 敵機三機を撃墜した。 *Tekki san-ki wo geki-tsui shita.* They shot down three enemy planes.

-ki[3] 騎 接尾語 suffix

馬に乗った人を数える語 *Uma ni notta hito wo kazoeru go* Counter for cavalrymen:

- 一万騎の兵を率いて争った。 *Ichiman-ki no hei wo hikiite arasotta.* He went into battle at the head of ten thousand cavalry.

-ki[4] き

Base 3 of a classical auxiliary verb, slightly defective:

- ほとりには松もありき。 *Hotori ni wa matsu mo ariki.* There were also pines round about.

NOTE. For the *-ki* of adjectives, see under *keiyōshi,* 4, conjugation.

-kireru 切れる 接尾語 suffix verb

補助動詞「切る」の可能形・動詞の連用形に付く *Hojo-dōshi "-kiru" no kanōkei. Dōshi no renyōkei ni tsuku* Potential form of the complementary verb *-kiru.* Is added to Base 2 of verbs.

1. 肯定的に、「終わりまで出来る」という意味を添える *Kōtei-teki ni, "owari made dekiru" to iu imi wo soeru* In a positive context, adds the idea of being able to see something through:

- 明日までに読み切れると思う。 *Asu made ni yomi-kireru to omou.* I think I can finish reading it by tomorrow.

2. 打ち消しを伴って、「出来る限度を越える」という意味を添える *Uchi-keshi wo tomonatte, "dekiru gendo wo koeru" to iu imi wo soeru* In a negative context, adds the idea that something is beyond one's power:

- 褒めきれない *home-kirenai* be beyond praise; 数えきれない *kazoe-kirenai* be innumerable; 曲がりきれないカーブ *magari-kirenai kābu* curve too sharp to negotiate; 一日で見切れない *ichi-nichi de mi-kirenai* too much to see in one day;
  し切れない *shi-kirenai* be beyond one; 食べきれない *tabe-kirenai* be too much for one to eat; 使いきれない *tsukai-kirenai* be more than one can use.

-kiri きり（ぎり、っきり） 副助詞 adverbial particle

体言・副詞・助詞や、活用語の連体形に付く *Taigen • fukushi • joshi ya, katsuyōgo no rentaikei ni tsuku* Is added to nominals, adverbs and particles, and to Base 4 of conjugables.

1. それだけと限って、分量や程度を表す *Sore dake to kagitte, bunryō ya teido wo arawasu* Denotes that amount or degree is restricted:

- 今一人きりで住んでいる。 *Ima hitori-kiri de sunde iru.* He now lives alone.
- 朝から水きり飲んでいない。 *Asa kara mizu-kiri nonde inai.* He has drunk nothing but water since morning.
- ここで外国人は私きりです。 *Koko de gaikoku-jin wa watashi-kiri desu.* I am the only foreigner here.

2. 打ち消しを伴って、それで最後であることを示す *Uchi-keshi wo tomonatte, sore de saigo de aru koto wo shimesu* With a negative, denotes that this was or is the last time:

- 去年分かれたきり、一度も会わない。 *Kyonen wakareta-kiri, ichido mo awanai.* I haven't met him again since we parted last year.
- 出掛けたきり帰ってこない。 *Dekaketa-kiri kaette konai.* He left and hasn't returned.

3. ずっとそのまま続いていることを示す *Zutto sono mama tsuzuite iru koto wo shimesu* Denotes the continuance of a state or action:

- 母は寝たきりだ。 *Haha wa neta-kiri da.* My mother is bedridden.
- 付きっきりで看病している。 *Tsukik-kiri de kanbyō shite iru.* She nurses him full time.

-kiru 切る 補助動詞 supplementary verb

動詞の連用形に付いて、「し終える」「するのを止める」という意味を添える *Dōshi no ren'yōkei ni tsuite, "shi-oeru", "suru no wo yameru" to iu imi wo soeru* Added to Base 2 of verbs, gives the meaning of termination and completion:

- 出切る *de-kiru* be used up, be out of *(de-kitte iru)*; 張り切る *hari-kiru* be in high spirits; 言い切る *ii-kiru* tell all, state positively; 借り切る *kari-kiru* charter; 貸し切る *kashi-kiru* charter; 困り切る *komari-kiru* be greatly embarrassed; 見切る *mi-kiru* give up, sell cheap; 苦り切る *nigari-kiru* look disgusted; 擦り切る *suri-kiru* cut by rubbing, use up; 詰め切る *tsume-kiru* stuff full; 分かり切る *wakari-kiru* understand fully; 読み切る *yomi-kiru* read right through; 弱り切る *yowari-kiru* be completely at a loss, be exhausted; 体力を使い切った。 *Tairyoku wo tsukai-kitta.* I am dead beat.

kiseru 着せる 動詞 verb

Like *miseru* and *niseru,* this is a verb in its own right, and not a causative; its causative form is *ki-saseru:*

- 子供に着物を着せた。 *Kodomo ni kimono wo kiseta.* She dressed the child.
- 子供に着物を着させなさい。 *Kodomo ni kimono wo ki-sase nasai.* Get the child to dress himself.
- 部下に罪を着せた *Buka ni tsumi wo kiseta.* He laid the blame on his subordinate.

-kko[1] っ子 接尾語 suffix
名詞や動詞の連用形に付いて、「そういう子供」の意味を添える *Meishi ya dōshi no ren'yōkei ni tsuite, "sō iu kodomo" no imi wo soeru* With nouns and Base 2 of verbs, adds the meaning of "such a child":
- 駄々っ子 *dadak-ko* spoilt child; 江戸っ子 *Edok-ko* Edoite; 一人っ子・独りっ子 *hitorik-ko (hitori-go)* only child; いじめっ子 *ijimek-ko* bully; 鍵っ子 *kagik-ko* latchkey child; 売れっ子 *urek-ko* popular person.

-kko[2] っこ 接尾語 suffix
動詞の連用形に付いて、「することはない」という意味を添える *Dōshi no ren'yōkei ni tsuite, "suru koto wa nai" to iu imi wo soeru* With Base 2 of verbs, expresses a strong denial of the possibility:
- 出来っこない *dekik-ko nai* out of the question; 帰りっこない *kaerik-ko nai* will certainly not return; なりっこない *narik-ko nai* will certainly not become; しっこない *shik-ko nai* will certainly not do or make; 分かりっこない *wakarik-ko nai* will never understand.

-kko[3] っこ 接尾語 suffix
動詞の連用形に付いて、「競争してする」「お互いにする」という意味を添える *Dōshi no ren'yōkei ni tsuite, "Kyōsō shite suru", "o-tagai ni suru" to iu imi wo soeru* With Base 2 of verbs, adds the meaning of competing in doing, doing to each other:
- 頭をぶつけっこする *atama wo butsukek-ko suru* butt each other; 駆けっこ *kakek-ko* race; 背中の流しっこ *senaka no nagashik-ko* washing each other's back; 睨めっこ *niramek-ko* outstaring each other; 取り返っこ *torikaek-ko* swapping, exchange.

NOTE. In many cases the action is to be considered a game.

-kkoi っこい 接尾語 suffix
名詞に付いて、形容詞を作り、「たくさん含んでいる」という意味を添える *Meishi ni tsuite, keiyōshi wo tsukuri, "takusan fukunde iru" to iu*

imi wo soeru Added to nouns, forms adjectives, and adds the idea that the quality abounds:

- 脂っこい *aburak-koi* greasy, oily; 冷やっこい *hiyak-koi* chilly; まだるっこい *madaruk-koi* sluggish; 丸っこい *maruk-koi* roundish; 懐っこい *natsuk-koi (natsukoi)* affable; 粘っこい *nebak-koi* sticky; 滑っこい *subek-koi* slippery, smooth; 脂っこい *yanik-koi* gummy.

NOTE. This *-kkoi* derives from 濃い *koi* (thick, strong).

ko-1 小 接頭語 prefix

1. 小さい *Chiisai* In its literal meaning of "small", "toy", "young of":

- 小人 *ko-bito* dwarf (→ *shōjin, shōnin*); 小振り *ko-buri* small in size; 小降り *ko-buri* light rain; 小柄 *ko-gara* small stature (also read *kozuka* dagger); 小刀 *ko-gatana* pocket knife; 小弓 *ko-yumi* toy bow.

2. 僅か *Wazuka* Slightly, somewhat:

- 小当たりに当たってみる *ko-atari ni atatte miru* put out a feeler; 小馬鹿にする *ko-baka ni suru* poke fun at; 小走りに走る *ko-bashiri ni hashiru* go at a trot; 小太り *ko-butori* plumpness; 小金 *ko-gane* small sum; 小ぎれいな *ko-girei na* trim, neat; 恥ずかしい *ko-hazukashii* be slightly ashamed; 小言 *ko-goto* rebuke; 小暗い *ko-gurai* dim; 小生気な *ko-iki na* chic; 小急ぎに歩く *ko-isogi ni aruku* hurry along; 小気味のよい *ko-kimi no yoi* smart, pleasant; 小人数 *ko-ninzū, ko-ninzu* small group; 小銭 *ko-zeni* (loose) change.

NOTE. Under this heading come some set phrases involving a part of the body + a verb:

- 小足に歩く *ko-ashi ni aruku* walk with mincing steps; 小腹が立つ *ko-bara ga tatsu* be slightly offended; 小腰を屈める *ko-goshi wo kagameru* bow slightly; 小膝を打つ *ko-hiza wo utsu* pat one's knee; 小首を傾げる *ko-kubi wo kashigeru* bend one's head slightly to one side; 小股に歩く *ko-mata ni aruku* mince one's steps; 小耳に挟む *ko-mimi ni hasamu* happen to hear.

3. 大体・殆ど *Daitai • hotondo* (with time and place words) Roughly, almost:

- 小半日 *ko-hannichi* almost half a day; 小半時 *ko-hantoki* almost half an hour; 小昼 *ko-hiru* almost noon; 小一日 *ko-ichinichi* almost a day.

4. 軽べつの意を表す *Keibetsu no i wo arawasu* Adds a tone of contempt:

• 小賢しい *ko-gashikoi* shrewd; 小難しい *ko-muzukashii* tortuous, peevish; 小生意気な *ko-namaiki na* impertinent; 小憎らしい *ko-nikurashii* provoking; 小面憎い *ko-zuranikui* loathsome; 小物 *ko-mono* small fry; 小細工 *ko-zaiku* cheap tricks; 小憎 *ko-zō* errandboy.

5. 語調を整える *Go-chō wo totonoeru* Adjusts the tone:

• 小揚げ *ko-age* unloading (of ship); 小鼻 *ko-bana* wings of nose; 小鬢 *ko-bin* sidelocks; 小幅物 *ko-habamono* single-width cloth; 小春日和 *koharu-biyori* Indian summer; 小舅 *ko-jūto* brother-in-law; 小姑 *ko-jūtome* sister-in-law; 小回りが利く *ko-mawari ga kiku* be able to make a sharp turn, be quick-witted; 小間使 *ko-mazukai* maid; 小躍り *ko-odori* dancing for joy; 小脇 *ko-waki* armpit; 小割り *ko-wari* batten; 小楊枝 *ko-yōji* toothpick; 小遣い *ko-zukai* pocket money; 小使い *ko-zukai* office servant.

NOTE. Following is a list of various readings for 小:

1. *Shō* is the only *on* reading:

• 小説 *shō-setsu* novel; 縮小 *shuku-shō* reduction.

2. *Chiisai* (adj.) and *chiisa na* (adjvl. noun) are the most frequent *kun* readings.

3. Both *ko-* and *o-* (*kun* readings) are found in:

• 小舟・小船 *ko-bune* • *o-bune* boat; 小川 *ko-gawa* • *o-gawa* brook; 小暗い *ko-gurai* • *o-gurai* dusky.

4. *O-* alone is found in:

• 小母さん *o-basan* "aunt"; 小父さん *o-jisan* "uncle".

5. *Sa-* is found in:

• 小夜 *sa-yo* night; 小百合 *sa-yuri* lily.

6. *Sasa-* is found in:

• 小栗 *sasa-guri* small chestnut; 小鳴き *sasa-naki* low twittering; 小濁り *sasa-nigori* slightly muddy; 小波（細波、漣）*sasa-nami* • *saza-nami* ripples.

NOTE. Listed here are some irregular readings:

• 小豆 *azuki* "adzuki" bean (but: 小豆島 *Shōdo-shima*); 小火 *boya* small fire; 小路 *kō-ji* lane; 小酷い *koppidoi* harsh.

ko-² 木 接頭語 prefix

The ideograph 木 is read *ko- (ko-no-)* in many compounds:

• 木羽（小羽）*ko-ba* shingles; 木端 *ko-ba, koppa* wood scraps; 木挽き *ko-biki* sawyer, sawing; 木深い *ko-bukai* densely wooded; 木立 *ko-dachi* grove; 木霊 *ko-dama* dryad; echo; 木隠れ *ko-gakure* hiding among trees; 木枯し *ko-garashi* wintry wind; 木口 *ko-guchi* the cut end; 木暮れ *ko-gure* darkness of a forest; 木肌 *ko-hada* tree bark; 木蔭 *ko-kage* bower; 木舞 *ko-mai* laths; 木叢 *ko-mura* clump of trees; 木末 *kozue, ko-nure* twigs at treetops.

-ko[1] 個 接尾語 suffix

Is used as a counter for small articles that have no counter of their own:

- 梨三個 *nashi san-ko* three pears; 石鹼二個 *sekken ni-ko* two pieces of soap.

NOTE. This *-ko* serves as a prefix in many compounds: 個々 *koko* individuals; 個人 *kojin* individual 個性 *kosei* individuality; 個別 *kobetsu* individualism 個室 *koshitsu* single room.

It also is read *ka* in 個条 *ka-jō* article, item.

-ko[2] 戸 接尾語 suffix

家を数える語 *Ie wo kazoeru go* Counter for dwellings:

- 住宅五十戸 *jūtaku gojik-ko* fifty dwellings.

-ko[3] 粉 接尾語 suffix

「こな」の略 *"Kona" no ryaku* Short for *kona:*

- 小麦粉 *komugi-ko* flour; パン粉 *pan-ko* flour; メリケン粉 *meriken-ko* flour.

-ko[4] 子 接尾語 suffix

This suffix has many unexpected meanings:

- 船子 *funa-ko* boatman; 振り子 *furi-ko* pendulum; 張り子 *hari-ko* papier-mâché; 舞子 *mai-ko* fledgling *geisha;* 鳴子 *naru-ko* bird-clapper; 踊り子 *odori-ko* female dancer; 氏子 *uji-ko* parishioner; 呼び子 *yobi-ko* whistle.

NOTE. Listed here are some irregular readings:

- 帽子 *bō-shi* headgear; 分子 *bun-shi* molecule; 原子 *gen-shi* atom; 利子 *ri-shi* interest; 扇子 *sen-su* folding fan; 様子 *yō-su* state, appearance.

-ko[5] こ 接尾語 suffix

1. 擬声語・擬態語に付いて、「...の状態」の意味を表す *Giseigo・gitai-go ni tsuite, ". . . no jōtai" no imi wo arawasu* With onomatopoeics, expresses the idea of "in the state of . . .":

- ぺちゃんこになる *pechan-ko ni naru* be flattened out, be beaten hollow; どんぶりこ *donburi-ko* with a splash (also *donbura-ko*).

2. 名詞に付いて、俗な言い方を造る *Meishi ni tsuite, zoku na ii-kata wo tsukuru* Attached to nouns, makes familiar expressions:

- 餡こ *an-ko* bean-jam; ちゃんちゃんこ *chanchan-ko* padded sleeveless coat; 変わり番こに *kawariban-ko ni* by turns; うんこ *un-ko* nursery word for *daiben*.

kō こう 副詞 adverb

他称、近称。状態を表す *Tashō, kinshō. Jōtai wo arawasu* 3rd. person, proximal. Denotes manner (referring to matters close at hand):

- こうやればいいのだ。 *Kō yareba ii no da.* This is the way to do it.
- 実はこうだ。 *Jitsu wa kō da.* This is how the matter stands.
- こういう形の箱が欲しい。 *Kō iu katachi no hako ga hoshii.* I'd like a box of this shape.
- こうなってはもうお仕舞いだ。 *Kō natte wa mō o-shimai da.* Now that it has come to this, it's all over.

→ *ā, dō, sō.*

kō- 接頭語 prefix

Prefixes worth noting are:

- 広 *hiroi:* 広範囲 *kō-han'i* wide range; 好 *suki:* 好成績 *kō-seiseki* good results; 後 *ato* 後半 *kō-han* latter half; 抗 *kō suru:* 抗生物質 *kō-seibusshitsu* antibiotics; 高 *takai:* 高齢者 *kō-reisha* the elderly; 交 *majiwaru:* 交差点 *kō-saten* intersection; 光 *hikari:* 光学 *kō-gaku* optics; 向 *mukau:* 向上 *kō-jō* improvement; 考 *kangaeru:* 考案 *kō-an* plan; 効 *kiku:* 効果 *kō-ka* effect; 幸 *saiwai:* 幸福 *kō-fuku* happiness; 厚 *atsui:* 厚意 *kō-i* favor; 降 *furu:* 降車 *kō-sha* alighting.

-kō 接尾語 suffix

Suffixes worth noting are:

- 口 *kuchi:* 火口 *ka-kō* crater; 工 *takumi:* 加工 *kakō* processing; 功 *isao:* 成功 *sei-kō* success; 交 *majiwaru:* 外交官 *gai-kō-kan* diplomat; 光 *hikari:* 観光 *kan-kō* sightseeing; 向 *mukau:* 傾向 *kei-kō* tendency; 好 *suki:* 絶好の *zekkō no* optimum; 考 *kangaeru:* 参考 *san-kō* reference; 行 *okonau:* 実行 *jikkō* execution; 効 *kiku:* 無効 *mu-kō* invalidity; 校 *kō:* 登校 *tō-kō* going to school; 高 *takai:* 崇高 *sū-kō* grandeur; 港 *minato:* 漁港 *gyo-kō* fishing-port.

kochira こちら 代名詞 pronoun

他称、近称。方角を示す *Tashō, kinshō. Hōgaku wo shimesu* 3rd. person, proximal. Denotes direction.

1. 話し手に近い方角 *Hanashi-te ni chikai hōgaku* Direction nearer to speaker:

- こちらへお入りください。 *Kochira e o-hairi kudasai.* Come this way, please.

2. 話し手に近いもの *Hanashi-te ni chikai mono* Objects nearer to speaker:

- こちらの方が丈夫そうだ。 *Kochira no hō ga jōbu-sō da.* This one looks the stronger.

3.「ここ」より丁寧な言い方 *"Koko" yori teinei na ii-kata* Polite alternative for *koko:*

- こちらはまだ寒うございます。 *Kochira wa mada samū gozaimasu.* It is still cold here.

4.「自分」を指す語 *"Jibun" wo sasu go* Word indicating oneself:

- もしもし、こちらは清水です。 *Moshi, moshi, kochira wa Shimizu desu.* Hello, this is Shimizu speaking.

5.「こちらさま」の形で、話し相手を指す *"Kochira-sama" no katachi de, hanashi-aite wo sasu* In *kochira-sama* form, refers to the other party:

- こちら様に、先刻お目にかかりましたね。 *Kochira-sama ni, senkoku o-me ni kakarimashita ne.* I believe we have already met.

NOTE. *Kochi, kotchi* are alternative forms.

→ *achira, dochira, sochira*

kogo 古語

現在では使われなくなったことば *Genzai de wa tsukaware-naku natta kotoba* Archaic word or language. Distinguish from 口語、next entry.

kōgo 口語

話しことばも現代日本語の書きことばも *Hanashi-kotoba mo gendai Nihongo no kaki-kotoba mo* Includes not only the spoken language, but also the written modern language.

→ *bungo*

koko ここ 代名詞 pronoun

他称、近称。場所を示す *Tashō, kinshō. Basho wo shimesu* 3rd. person, proximal; refers to place.

1. 話し手に近いところを示す *Hanashi-te ni chikai tokoro wo shimesu* Denotes place close to speaker:

- ここから五分しか掛からない。 *Koko kara go-fun shika kakaranai.* It takes only five minutes from here.

2. 話し手に近いものを示す *Hanashi-te ni chikai mono wo shimesu* Denotes things close to speaker:

- お答えはここが違っている。 *O-kotae wa koko ga chigatte iru.* Your answer is wrong on this point.

3. 現在を中心に、近い過去または未来を含む *Genzai wo chūshin ni, chikai kako mata wa mirai wo fukumu* With present time as basis, includes immediate past as well as future:

- ここ二、三日は暖かいですね。 *Koko ni, san-nichi wa atatakai desu ne.* It has been warm these past few days, hasn't it?
- ここ当分は忙しい。 *Koko tōbun wa isogashii.* I shall be busy for some time.

4. 「このような状態」の意を示す *"Kono yō na jōtai" no i wo shimesu* Expresses the idea of "this state of affairs":

- 事ここに至っては手の施しようがない。 *Koto koko ni itatte wa te no hodokoshi-yō ga nai.* Now that things have come to this pass, nothing can be done.

kokora ここら 代名詞 pronoun

代名詞「ここ」に、接尾語「ら」 *Daimeishi "koko" ni, setsubi-go "ra"* Pronoun *koko* and suffix *-ra:*

- ここらに公衆電話はないでしょうか。 *Kokora ni kōshū denwa wa nai deshō ka?* I wonder if there is a public telephone anywhere round here?

NOTE. *Koko-ira* is a variant. There was also *bungo* *kokora* meaning "generally".

→ **-ra**

-koku 石 接尾語 suffix

1. 米などの量をはかる語 *Kome nado no ryō wo hakaru go* Measure for rice and other grains. Hence its use to measure worth of fiefs, in feudal times.

2. 船の容積をはかる語 *Fune no yōseki wo hakaru go* Measure of capacity of ships.

3. 材木の嵩をはかる語 *Zaimoku no kasa wo hakaru go* Measure for volume of timber.

koku-ji 国字

Ideographs coined in Japan are termed *koku-ji.* The following are listed among *jōyō kanji,* the 1945 *kanji* recommended for daily use in

1981. (*Tōyō kanji* are the 1850 recommended for daily use from 1946.):

- 畑 *hatake* field; 働く *hataraku* work (given the *on* reading of *dō,* as in 労働 *rō-dō,* the noun); 塀 *hei* fence; 込む *komu* be crowded; 匁 *monme* former unit of weight; 〆 *shime* total; 峠 *tōge* mountain pass; 枠 *waku* frame.

NOTE. The series of *koku-ji* covering the units of the metric system has now been abandoned in favour of *katakana.*

-komu 込む　補助動詞　supplementary verb

1. 中に入る・入れる *Naka ni hairu • ireru* Enter, insert:

- 会議が昼休みに食い込んだ。 *Kaigi ga hiru-yasumi ni kui-konda.* The meeting encroached on our lunch-time.
- プラグをソケットに差し込んでみなさい。 *Puragu wo soketto ni sashi-konde mi nasai.* Try putting the plug in the socket.

2. 一途にする *Ichizu ni suru* Do something to the exclusion of all else:

- 黙り込む *damari-komu* fall silent; 話し込む *hanashi-komu* have a long talk with; 冷え込む *hie-komu* be or feel very cold; 着込む *ki-komu* be wrapped in; 決め込む *kime-komu* take for granted; 丸め込む *marume-komu* wheedle; 眠り込む *nemuri-komu* fall fast asleep; 老いこむ *oi-komu* dote; 追い込む *oi-komu* drive in; 思い込む (i) be firmly convinced; (ii) resolve firmly.

-konasu 熟す　補助動詞　supplementary verb

「その動作を要領よく、巧みにする」意味を添える *"Sono dōsa wo yōryō yoku, takumi ni suru" imi wo soeru* Adds the meaning of doing skilfully:

- 弾きこなす *hiki-konasu* play well; 着こなす *ki-konasu* dress tastefully; 噛みこなす *kami-konasu* chew well; appreciate; しこなす *shi-konasu* manage well; 読みこなす *yomi-konasu* read and digest.

konna da こんなだ　形容動詞・連体詞　adjectival noun, adnoun

他称、近称。状態を表す *Tashō, kinshō; jōtai wo arawasu* 3rd. person, proximal; refers to state:

- こんなことは初めてだ。 *Konna koto wa hajimete da.* This is the first time a thing like this has happened.
- 雨がこんなのに出掛けるのですか。 *Ame ga konna na no ni dekakeru no desu ka?* Are you going out in this rain?
- こんなに大きな被害をもたらした台風はかつてなかった。 *Konna ni*

ooki na higai wo motarashita taifū wa katsute nakatta. Never before has there been such a disastrous typhoon.

NOTE. For the debated question of classification, see *anna da.*
→ *anna da, donna da, sonna da*

kono この 連体詞 adnoun

他称、近称。関係を表す *Tashō, kinshō; kankei wo arawasu* 3rd. person, proximal; denotes relationship.

1. 話し手に近い位置、事柄、時間を示す *Hanashi-te ni chikai ichi, kotogara, jikan wo shimesu* Denotes location, objects, time close to speaker:

- この傘を貸してください。 *Kono kasa wo kashite kudasai.* Please lend me this umbrella.
- この一週間は雨が多かった。 *Kono isshūkan wa ame ga ookatta.* It has been rather wet this last week.

2. 直前に述べた言葉またはこれから言う言葉を指す *Chokuzen ni nobeta kotoba mata wa kore kara iu kotoba wo sasu* Refers to something just mentioned or about to be mentioned:

- この問題は解決しにくい。 *Kono mondai wa kaiketsu shi-nikui.* This problem (just mentioned, or about to be mentioned) is a difficult one to solve.

kore[1] これ 代名詞 pronoun

指示代名詞、他称、近称。事物を示す *Shiji-daimeishi, tashō, kinshō. Jibutsu wo shimesu* Demonstrative pronoun, 3rd. person, proximal; denotes objects:

1. 話し手の近くにある物を指す *Hanashi-te no chikaku ni aru mono wo sasu* Refers to objects close to the speaker:

- これはだれの靴ですか。 *Kore wa dare no kutsu desu ka?* Whose shoes are these?

2. 前に述べたことを示す *Mae ni nobeta koto wo shimesu* Denotes things previously mentioned:

- まだ帰ってこないところを見ると、これは、何か事故に遭ったのかも知れない。 *Mada kaette konai tokoro wo miru to, kore wa, nani ka jiko ni atta no ka mo shirenai.* Seeing that he isn't back yet, it may mean that he has met with an accident.

3. 「現在」を示す *"Genzai" wo shimesu* Refers to the present moment:

- これまでのことは、水に流してください。 *Kore made no koto wa, mizu ni nagashite kudasai.* Let bygones be bygones, please.

4. 例外として、妻子、身近の目下の者を指す *Reigai to shite, saishi,*

mijika no meshita no mono wo sasu As an exception, refers to one's wife or children, or immediate subjects:

- これは倅です。 *Kore wa segare desu.* This is my son. (deferential)

kore[2] これ 感動詞 interjection

呼びかけたり、注意したりするときに使う語 *Yobi-kaketari, chūi shitari suru toki ni tsukau go* Word used in hailing or calling attention:

- これ、どこへ行くの。 *Kore, doko e iku no?* Hi, where are you off to?

koro 頃 形式名詞 formal noun

1. ある決まった時間の前後を指す *Aru kimatta jikan no zengo wo sasu* Indicates approximate time:

- もう、寝るころだ。 *Mō, neru koro da.* It's about bed-time.

2. だいたいその時期であることを示す *Daitai sono jiki de aru koto wo shimesu* Indicates approximate period:

- 子供の頃からやってきている。 *Kodomo no koro kara yatte kite iru.* I've been doing it since childhood.

3. 時節を示す *Jisetsu wo shimesu* Denotes period or season:

- 花の散るころでした。 *Hana no chiru koro deshita.* It was the season when the (cherry-)blossoms were falling.

4. あることにちょうどよい時期を示す *Aru koto ni chōdo yoi jiki wo shimesu* Denotes a favourable opportunity:

- 頃を見計らって家に帰って行った。 *Koro wo mi-hakaratte, ie ni kaette itta.* He left for home when he saw his chance.

→ *-goro*

-koshi[1] 腰 接尾語 suffix

刀・えびら・袴など、腰に帯びるものを数える語 *Katana・ebira・hakama nado, koshi ni obiru mono wo kazoeru go* Counter for objects secured to the waist, like swords, quivers, *hakama,* etc.:

- 太刀一腰 *tachi hito-koshi* one (long) sword.

-koshi[2] 越し 接尾語 suffix

名詞や動詞の連用形に付いて、「それを隔てて」という意味を添える *Meishi ya dōshi no ren'yōkei ni tsuite, "sore wo hedatete" to iu imi wo soeru* With nouns and Base 2 of verbs, adds the meaning of "on the other side of":

- 引っ越し *hik-koshi* house-moving; 勝ち越し *kachi-koshi* winning overall; 借り越し *kari-koshi* debt balance; 貸し越し *kashi-koshi* credit balance; 繰り越し *kuri-koshi* amount carried forward; 負け越し *make-koshi* losing overall; 見越し *mi-koshi* speculation; 持ち越し *mochi-koshi* carry-over; 申し越し *mōshi-koshi* sending word; 乗り越し *nori-koshi* riding past one's destination; お越し *o-koshi* polite for *iku, kuru,* etc.; 取り越し苦労 *tori-koshi gurō* being over-anxious; 年越し *toshi-koshi* seeing the old year out.

NOTE. *Koshi* was the old name for *Hokuriku-dō*, and this has carried over in the place-names such as 越前 *Echizen,* 越中 *Etchū,* and 越後 *Echigo.*

koso こそ　副助詞　adverbial particle

体言・用言の連用形・色々の語に付いて、意味を強める *Taigen • yōgen no ren'yōkei • iro-iro no go ni tsuite, imi wo tsuyomeru* With nominals, Base 2 of conjugables, and various parts of speech, strengthens the meaning:

- これこそ長い間捜していたものだ。 *Kore koso nagai aida sagashite ita mono da.* This is just what I have been looking for all along.
- こちらこそお詫びしなければなりません。 *Kochira koso o-wabi shi-nakereba narimasen.* It is I that ought to beg pardon.
- 今年こそ海外旅行に行く。 *Kotoshi koso kaigai-ryokō ni iku.* It is this year or never for a foreign tour.

NOTE. In *bungo, koso* was a 係助詞 *(kei-joshi, kakari-joshi),* followed invariably by a Base 5 verb, formerly called *izenkei.* Traces of this usage are found in modern Japanese:

- 先生は喜びこそすれ、怒るはずはない。 *Sensei wa yorokobi koso sure, okoru hazu wa nai.* The teacher will be glad; there is no reason why he should be angry.
- 誉めこそすれ、けなすことはない。 *Home koso sure, kenasu koto wa nai.* They will praise, not disparage him.

NOTE. Other particles still classed by some as "bound particles" are: *datte, demo, mo, sae, shika,* and *wa.*

koto[1] 事　体言　nominal

A. (written in *kanji*)

1. 自然・人事の無形の現象を表す *Shizen • jinji no mukei no genshō wo arawasu:* Denotes abstract matters, whether natural or human:

- 金銭の事は私に頼んでもだめ。 *Kinsen no koto wa, watashi ni tanonde mo dame.* It's no use asking me for money.

2. 事件・一大事の意味を表す *Jiken • ichi-daiji no imi wo arawasu* Denotes a serious matter:

- 百万円がなくなった。これは事だ。 *Hyakuman-en ga nakunatta.*

Kore wa koto da. A million yen has disappeared. This is a serious matter.

3. 「仕事」の意味を表す *"Shigoto" no imi wo arawasu* Denotes a task to be done:

- 私の知った事ではない。 *Watashi no shitta koto de wa nai.* It is none of my business.

4. 「事実」の意味を表す *"Jijitsu" no imi wo arawasu* Denotes the facts of a case:

- 事の真相を確かめてください。 *Koto no shinsō wo tashikamete kudasai.* Please find out what is really the matter.

5. ある事に関連を持っている事柄 *Aru koto ni kanren wo motte iru kotogara* The topic under consideration:

- 試験の事はもう話すのを止めよう。 *Shiken no koto wa mō hanasu no wo yameyō.* Let's stop talking about exams.

B. (written in *kana*)

活用語の連体形に付いて、名詞化して、色々な構文に現われる *Katsuyō-go no rentaikei ni tsuite, meishi-ka shite, iro-iro na kōbun ni arawareru* Added to Base 4 of conjugables, nominalizes them and appears in various constructions.

1. 「**...**することは**...**だ」の形で、主語を作る *". . . suru koto wa. . . da" no katachi de, shugo wo tsukuru* In *. . . suru koto wa . . . da* form, makes the subject of a sentence:

- 一人で水泳することは危険だ。 *Hitori de suiei suru koto wa kiken da.* It is dangerous to go swimming alone.

2. 「**...**することがある」の形で、「時々起こる」という意味を表す *". . . suru koto ga aru" no katachi de, "toki-doki okoru" to iu imi wo arawasu* In *. . . suru koto ga aru* form, denotes occasional occurrence:

- ピクニックに行くことがありますか。 *Pikunikku ni iku koto ga arimasu ka?* Do you ever go on a picnic?

3. 「**...**たことがある」の形で、過去の経験を表す *". . . -ta koto ga aru" no katachi de, kako no keiken wo arawasu* In *. . . ta koto ga aru* form, denotes past experience:

- 一回も負けたことがない。 *Ikkai mo maketa koto ga nai.* We have never lost a match.

NOTE. 「**...**たことがあった」の形で、元の経験を表す *". . . -ta koto ga atta" no katachi de, moto no keiken wo arawasu* In *. . . ta koto ga atta* form, denotes previous experience:

- それまでに日本に来たことがなかった。 *Sore made ni Nippon ni kita koto ga nakatta.* He hadn't been to Japan previously.

4. 「**...**することが多い・少ない」の形で、ことの起こる頻度を表す

". . . suru koto ga ooi • sukunai" no katachi de, koto no okoru hindo wo arawasu In *. . . suru koto ga ooi/sukunai* form, denotes frequency of occurrence:

- 雪が降った翌日は晴れることが多い。 *Yuki ga futta yokujitsu wa, hareru koto ga ooi.* It is often fine the day after a snowfall.

5. 「**…**することが出来る」の形で、能力・権利を示す *". . . suru koto ga dekiru" no katachi de, nōryoku • kenri wo shimesu* In *. . . suru koto ga dekiru* form, denotes ability or capacity:

- ここでは降りることが出来ません。 *Koko de wa oriru koto ga dekimasen.* You can't get off here. (→ *dekiru.*)

6. 「**…**することになっている」の形で、約束・取り決めを示す *". . . suru koto ni natte iru" no katachi de, yakusoku • tori-kime wo shimesu* In *. . . suru koto ni natte iru* form, denotes a promise or arrangement:

- 近くの喫茶店で会うことになっていた。 *Chikaku no kissaten de au koto ni natte ita.* We had arranged to meet at a nearby tearoom.

7. 「**…**することにする」の形で、決定を示す *". . . suru koto ni suru" no katachi de, kettei wo shimesu* In *. . .suru koto ni suru* form, denotes determination:

- 郊外を歩いてみることにした。 *Kōgai wo aruite miru koto ni shita.* We decided to try taking a walk in the suburbs.

8. 「**…**することにしている」の形で、習慣を示す *"...suru koto ni shite iru" no katachi de, shūkan wo shimesu* In *. . . suru koto ni shite iru* form, denotes habitual action:

- 朝夕歯を磨くことにしている。 *Asayū ha wo migaku koto ni shite iru.* I (make it a rule to) brush my teeth morning and evening.

9. 「**…**とのことだ」の形で、伝聞を示す *". . . to no koto da" no katachi de, denbun wo shimesu* In *. . . to no koto da* form, denotes hearsay:

- 数十人が負傷したとのことだ。 *Sūjūnin ga fushō shita to no koto da.* It is said that scores of people were injured.

10. 「**…**することだ」の形で、軽い義務を示す *". . . suru koto da" no katachi de, karui gimu wo shimesu* In *. . . suru koto da* form, denotes a mild obligation:

- 何でも食べることだ。 *Nan de mo taberu koto da.* One should eat (a bit of) everything.

11. 「**…**すること。」の形で、忠告を示す *". . . suru koto." no katachi de, chūkoku wo shimesu* In *. . . suru koto.* form, denotes a strong recommendation:

- 必ず窓を閉めること。 *Kanarazu mado wo shimeru koto.* Make sure you close the windows.

12. 「**…**することがあるか」「**…**することはない」の形で、必要を意味す

る "... *suru koto ga aru ka?*", "... *suru koto wa nai" no katachi de, hitsuyō wo imi suru* In ... *suru koto ga aru ka?* or ... *suru koto wa nai* form, denotes necessity:

- 何を泣くことがあるか。 *Nani wo naku koto ga aru ka?* What is there to cry about?
- 急ぐことはない。 *Isogu koto wa nai.* There's no need to hurry.

C. Special usage:

1. 人の名を挙げて、その人を強く指す気持ちを表す *Hito no na wo agete, sono hito wo tsuyoku sasu kimochi wo arawasu* After a person's name, denotes strong emphasis:
   - 田中のことだから、三時きっかりにやってくるよ。 *Tanaka no koto da kara, san-ji kikkari ni yatte kuru yo!* If I know Tanaka, he will be here at three on the dot!
2. 「形容詞＋こと」の形で、副詞になる *"Keiyōshi + koto" no katachi de, fukushi ni naru* In the adjective + *koto* form, makes adverbs of the adjectives:
   - えらく早いこと片付けてしまったものだ。 *Eraku hayai koto katazukete shimatta mono da.* How fast they tidied up!
3. ペン・ネーム、芸名、通称などを掲げて、あとに本名を出す時の繋ぎの語にする *Pen-nēmu, geimei, tsūshō nado wo kakagete, ato ni honmyō wo dasu toki no tsunagi no go ni suru* Serves to link a nom de plume, stage or screen name, etc., with the real name:
   - 南州こと西郷隆盛 *Nanshū koto Saigō Takamori* Saigo Takamori, alias Nanshu.

koto ~ mono

The former is more abstract, the latter more concrete; here is the Japanese description:

「こと」はものの働き、性質、ものとものとの関係や、動詞・形容詞で表すものを受け持つ *"Koto" wa mono no hataraki, seishitsu, mono to mono to no kankei ya, dōshi • keiyōshi de arawasu mono wo uke-motsu* "*Koto*" represents the action, nature, mutual relationship of objects, and what is normally expressed by verbs and adjectives.

「もの」は、形のある物体や、形がなくても、名詞で表すものを受け持つ *"Mono" wa, katachi no aru buttai ya, katachi ga nakute mo, meishi de arawasu mono wo uke-motsu. Mono* represents concrete objects, or at least, what are usually expressed by nouns.

koto suffix in compounds and phrases:

A. Written 事、pronounced *-koto:*

- あらぬ事 *aranu-koto* something extraordinary; 一つ事 *hitotsu-koto* one and the same thing; いい事 *ii-koto* happy event; いっその事 *isso no koto* would rather; もしもの事 *moshi mo no koto* emergency; 付かぬ事 *tsukanu koto* abrupt question.

B. Written こと、pronounced *koto:*

- 尚のこと *nao no koto* still more; しょうことなしに *shō koto nashi ni* reluctantly; すんでのことに *sunde no koto ni* almost; てなこと *te na koto (= tō iu yō na koto)* "something like . . .".

C. Written 事、pronounced *-goto,* refers to various genres of theatre, especially in *kabuki:*

- 荒事 *ara-goto* part played by ruffian; 振り事 *furi-goto* pantomime; 実事 *jitsu-goto* serious part; 濡れ事 *nure-goto* lover's part; 所作事 *shosa-goto;* 和事 *wa-goto* love-scene.

D. Other common compounds:

- 当てごと *ate-goto* expectations; 出来事 *deki-goto* event; 古ごと *furu-goto* tradition; 芸事 *gei-goto* accomplishments; 賭事 *kake-goto* gambling; 考え事 *kangae-goto* worry; 稽古ごと *keiko-goto* accomplishments; 奇麗ごと *kirei-goto* whitewashing; こしらえごと *koshirae-goto* fabrication; 人事 *hito-goto* other people's affairs; 粋ごと *iki-goto* love affair; 色ごと *iro-goto* love affair; 祝い事 *iwai-goto* happy event; 事々 *koto-goto* affairs; 曲ごと *kuse-goto* injustice; ままごと *mama-goto* playing house; 真似事 *mane-goto* mockery; 見事 *mi-goto* excellence; 雅ごと *miyabi-goto* elegant pursuits; もめ事 *mome-goto* trouble; 物事 *mono-goto* things; 無駄事・徒事 *muda-goto* twaddle; 何事 *nani-goto* what(-ever); 願い事 *negai-goto* wish, petition; 大事 *oo-goto* grave matter; 仕事 *shi-goto* work; 忍びごと *shinobi-goto* secret; 痴れごと *shire-goto* folly; 勝負事 *shōbu-goto* gamble; 好きごと *suki-goto* curiosity, lewdness; 杯ごと *sakazuki-goto* pledge with *sake;* 作り事 *tsukuri-goto* fabrication; 笑い事 *warai-goto* laughing matter; 私事 *watakushi-goto* private affair; 余所事 *yoso-goto* other people's affairs.

NOTE. *Hakarigoto* (謀) plot, *matsurigoto* (政) government, and *mikoto* (尊・命) prince, are written with single ideographs.

koto² こと 終助詞 final particle

活用語の終止形に付いて、感動を柔らかに表したり、人を軽く誘ったり、柔らかく同意を求めたりする気持ちを表す *Katsuyō-go no shūshikei ni tsuite, kandō wo yawaraka ni arawashitari, hito wo karuku sasottari, yawarakaku dōi wo motometari suru kimochi wo arawasu* Added to Base

3 of conjugables, expresses mild emotion, gentle enticement, or the sense of mildly seeking approval:

- まあ、かわいい人形だこと。 *Mā, kawaii ningyō da koto!* My, what a pretty doll!

NOTE. This *koto* is used mostly in women's speech.

-koto 言

1. Pronounced *-koto:*
   - 二言目 *futa-koto-me* same old story; 一言 *hito-koto* • *ichi-gen* • *ichi-gon* a word; 片言 *kata-koto* prattle; 御言 *mi-koto* imperial edict; 大御言 *oo-mi-koto* Imperial edict.
2. Pronounced *-goto:*
   - 徒言 *ada-goto* insincere utterance; 誓い言 *chikai-goto* oath; 人言 *hito-goto* rumour; 一人言 *hitori-goto* soliloquy; 託言 *ka-goto* complaint; 繰り言 *kuri-goto* tedious talk; 雅言 *miyabi-goto* refined speech; 睦言 *mutsu-goto* lovers' talk; 泣き言 *naki-goto* complaint; 寝言 *ne-goto* somniloquy; 根無し言 *nenashi-goto* unfounded report; 空言*sora-goto* falsehood; 称え言 *tatae-goto* eulogy; 戯言 *tawa-goto* silly talk; 戯れ言 *zare-goto* joke; 詫び言 *wabi-goto* apology; 世迷言 *yomai-goto* grumbling.

ku 来 動詞（古） verb (classical)

In *bungo,* Base 3 of this verb was *ku, kuru* being Base 4. The conjugations are as follows: *kōgo* (spoken) → 1. *ko* 2. *ki* 3. *kuru* 4. *kuru* 5. *kure* 6. *koi; bungo* (written) 1. *ko* 2. *ki* 3. *ku* 4. *kuru* 5. *kure* 6. *koyo.*

NOTE. *Kitaru,* written 来る, 来たる (next, coming) is an example of 現代文語 *gendai bungo* (modern language). It is a *rentaishi,* adnoun, the antonym of 去る *saru* (last). 明くる・翌る *akuru* refers to a time following an event in the past.

-ku[1] く 形容詞の連用形 Base 2 of adjectives

1. 動詞に連なり、副詞のように修飾する *Dōshi ni tsuranari, fukushi no yō ni shūshoku suru* Preceding a verb, modifies it in the manner of an adverb:
   - 船はひどく左右に揺れていた。 *Fune wa hidoku sayū ni yurete ita.* The ship was rolling heavily.
2. 「て」に連なる *-Te ni tsuranaru* Is followed by *-te:*
   - 嬉しくて夢中になった。 *Ureshikute muchū ni natta.* He was beside himself for joy.

3. 中止法に用いる *Chūshi-hō ni mochiiru* Is used to signal a pause:

• 声もよく、節もよい。 *Koe mo yoku, fushi mo yoi.* Her voice is good, and the tune is in keeping.

4.「ない」「ありません」に連なり、打ち消しを作る *"Nai", "arimasen" ni tsuranari, uchi-keshi wo tsukuru* Is followed by *nai, arimasen,* to form negatives:

• 駅までは遠くありません。 *Eki made wa tooku arimasen.* It isn't far to the station.

• そんなに高くはない。 *Sonna ni takaku wa nai.* It isn't so expensive.

5. ある形容詞を名詞化する *Aru keiyōshi wo meishi-ka suru* Nominalizes a few special adjectives:

• 近くまで寄る *chikaku made yoru* come close; 遠くから見る *tooku kara miru* watch from a distance; 早くから起きている *hayaku kara okite iru* be out of bed early; 遅くまで働く *osoku made hataraku* work late; 家の奥深くまでのぞく *ie no oku-fukaku made nozoku* peer into the depths of the house.

→ *keiyōshi*

-ku[2] く

A very old suffix that nominalized conjugables, still surviving in a few expressions:

• 曰く *iwaku* as . . . says; 願わくは *negawaku wa* I pray; 宣はく *notamawaku* polite form for *iwaku;* 思惑 (当て字 *ateji*) *omowaku* thought, speculation, popularity.

kudasaru 下さる 動詞 verb

1.「与える」「呉れる」の尊敬語 *"Ataeru", "kureru" no sonkei-go* Respect word for *ataeru* and *kureru:*

• 先生がこの時計をくださった。 *Sensei ga kono tokei wo kudasatta.* My teacher gave me this watch.

2. 補助動詞として、「お」「ご」の付いた漢語・動詞の連用形などに付いて、「呉れる」の尊敬語となる *Hojo-dōshi to shite, "o-", "go-" no tsuita kan-go • dōshi no ren'yōkei nado ni tsuite, "kureru" no sonkei-go to naru* As a complementary verb, with Chinese words, or Base 2 of verbs, etc., serves as a respect verb for *kureru:*

• この写真を御覧ください。 *Kono shashin wo go-ran kudasai.* Please look at this photo.

• 少々お待ち下さい。 *Shōshō o-machi kudasai.* Please wait a moment.

NOTE. For the conjugation of *kudasaru,* see under *irassharu.*

-kundari くんだり　接尾語　suffix

「下り」の音便で、「遠く離れた土地」を指す *"Kudari" no on-bin de, "tooku hanareta tochi" wo sasu* Euphonic variation of *kudari*, denotes a remote location:

- 長崎くんだりまで行ってきた。 *Nagasaki-kundari made itte kita.* I have been to faraway Nagasaki.

kurai くらい (位)　副助詞　adverbial particle

1. 程度を示す *Teido wo shimesu* Denotes degree:

- 一時間くらい掛かるだろう。 *Ichi-jikan kurai kakaru darō.* It will probably take about an hour.
- 寝たきりになるくらいなら、死んだ方がましだ。 *Neta-kiri ni naru kurai nara, shinda hō ga mashi da.* I should prefer to be dead rather than be bedridden.

2. 比較の基準を示す *Hikaku no kijun wo shimesu* Sets the standard of comparison:

- そのくらいのことは僕だって出来る。 *Sono kurai no koto wa boku datte dekiru.* Even I could do that.
- 葉書一枚くらい出しておきなさい。 *Hagaki ichi-mai kurai dashite oki-nasai.* Send them a postcard, at least.

→ *gurai*

kureru 呉れる　動詞　verb

1. 人に物を与える *Hito ni mono wo ataeru* Corresponds with English "give":

- お茶を一杯呉れませんか。 *O-cha wo ippai kuremasen ka?* Won't you give me a cup of tea?
- 金に目もくれない。 *Kane ni me mo kurenai.* He has no interest in money.

2. 補助動詞として、動詞の連用形+「て」に付いて、人が自分あるいは関係者のために、その動作をする意を表す *Hojo-dōshi to shite, dōshi no ren'yōkei + "-te" ni tsuite, hito ga jibun aruiwa kankeisha no tame ni, sono dōsa wo suru i wo arawasu* As a complementary verb, is added to Base 2 of verbs + *-te*, and expresses the idea that another person does the action in favour of me or us:

- 親切に駅まで送ってくれた。 *Shinsetsu ni eki made okutte kureta.* He was kind enough to see me to the station.

NOTE. A less frequent usage is the act of giving viewed from the giver's standpoint; it then has a tone of contempt:

- お金をくれてやる。 *O-kane wo kurete yaru.* I'll give (the blighter) some money.

NOTE. The imperative *kure,* without *-yo*, implies that the request is made to one's peer or an inferior:

- 僕にもやらせてくれ。 *Boku ni mo yarasete kure.* Let me have a try, too.

kuru 来る　カ行変格活用動詞　special conjugation *(ka-gyō henkaku katsuyō)* verb

For conjugation, see under *ku*. This verb is irregular in that its Base 1 is *ko-,* whereas *go-dan* verbs have Base 1 ending in *a-, kami-ichidan* verbs have *i-,* and *shimo-ichidan* verbs have *e-*. The only other really irregular verb is *suru.*

A. 一般動詞として *Ippan-dōshi to shite* As a main verb:

- 早く来ないかな。 *Hayaku konai ka na!* I wish he would hurry up (and come)!

B. 補助動詞として、連用形+「て」を受ける *Hojo-dōshi to shite, ren'-yōkei + "-te" wo ukeru* Is a complementary verb, after Base 2 + *-te.*

1. 動作をしながら、移動する意味を表す *Dōsa wo shi-nagara, idō suru imi wo arawasu* Implies locomotion while action is in progress:

- たばこを買ってくる。 *Tabako wo katte kuru.* I'll go and buy some cigarettes.

2. ことのある方向に進む意味を表す *Koto no aru hōkō ni susumu imi wo arawasu* Denotes movement towards where the action is:

- まもなく雨が降ってくるだろう。 *Ma mo naku ame ga futte kuru darō.* It will probably turn to rain before long.

3. 体言+「とくると」「ときたら」「ときては」の形で、「それに関すること」を意味する *Taigen + "to kuru to", "to kitara", "to kite wa" no katachi de, "sore ni kansuru koto" wo imi suru* In . . . *to kuru to,* . . . *to kitara,* and . . . *to kite wa* translates as "when it is a matter of . . .":

- 水泳と来ると、全然だめだ。 *Suiei to kuru to, zenzen dame da.* When it comes to swimming, I'm hopeless at it.
- 将棋ときたら、得意だ。 *Shōgi to kitara, tokui da.* As for shogi, it's his forte.

kusa- 草　接頭語　prefix

本格的でないものを表す *Honkaku-teki de nai mono wo arawasu* "Not the real thing":

• 草競馬 *kusa-keiba* local horse-race; 草野球 *kusa-yakyū* sandlot baseball; 草相撲 *kusa-zumō* amateur sumo wrestling.

-kute くて　接尾語　suffix
形容詞の連用形＋接続助詞「て」 *Keiyōshi no ren'yōkei + setsuzoku-joshi "-te"* Base 2 of adjectives + the conjunctive particle *-te*.
1. 並列を表す *Heiretsu wo arawasu* Denotes listing:
• 軽くて、丈夫で運びやすい。 *Karukute, jōbu de hakobi-yasui.* It is light, strong, and easy to carry.
2. 理由を示す *Riyū wo shimesu* Indicates reason why:
• 高くて買えない。 *Takakute kaenai.* It is too expensive (for me) to buy.
3. 「―くても」の形で、譲歩を表す *"-kute mo" no katachi de, jōho wo arawasu* In *-kute mo* form, denotes concession:
• 安くても買わない。 *Yasukute mo kawanai.* Even if (*or* though) it is cheap I won't buy it.
NOTE. The adjective-type conjugation auxiliaries *-nai* and *-tai* become *-nakute* and *-takute:*
• 行かなくて済んだ。 *Ikanakute sunda.* I didn't have to go after all.
• 見たくてたまらない。 *Mitakute tamaranai.* I'm dying to see it.
NOTE. A construction similar to *-kute mo* is *-ku to mo,* translated in English as "at the + a superlative":
• 早くとも *hayaku to mo* at the earliest; 多くとも *ooku to mo* at (the) most; 遅くとも *osoku to mo* at the latest; 少なくとも *sukunaku to mo* at (the) least.
NOTE. For *-nakute* and *-naide,* see under *-nai.*

kuten, kutōten 句点、句読点　punctuation marks
→ Appendix D.

-kyaku 脚　接尾語　suffix
脚の付いた道具を数える語 *Ashi no tsuita dōgu wo kazoeru go* Counter for items of furniture that stand on legs:
• 机三脚 *tsukue san-kyaku* three desks.
NOTE. There is also: 二人三脚 *ni-nin san-kyaku* 3-legged race, cooperation.

-kyō 強　接尾語　suffix
ある数量よりちょっと多いことを示す *Aru sūryō yori chotto ooi koto wo shimesu* Indicates a quantity slightly greater than that quoted:

• 体重は五十キロ強だ。 *Taijū wa gojikkirō-kyō da.* He weighs just over 50 kgs.

NOTE. The antonym of *-kyō* is *-jaku.*

kyū- 九 キュウ（ここのつ、ここの、ク）

• 九月 *ku-gatsu* September; 九寸五分 *ku-sun go-bu* dagger; 九死に一生 *kyū-shi ni isshō* narrow escape from death.

NOTE. 九重 *kokonoe* ninefold, the Imperial Palace; 九日 *kokonoka* the ninth.

M

ma 間 名詞 noun

With readings *kan, ken, aida, ma,* this ideograph figures in very many expressions.

1. Interval of time or place:

• 間合い *ma-ai* time interval; 間引き *ma-biki* thinning out; 間違い *ma-chigai* mistake; まだるい *ma-darui* tedious; 間遠い *ma-dooi* remote, distant; 間際 *ma-giwa* verge; 間口 *ma-guchi* frontage; 間近い *ma-jikai* close; 間延び *ma-nobi* long interval, stupid look; 間切り *ma-giri* tacking (nautical).

2. Words relating to rooms:

• 間代 *ma-dai* room rent (真鯛 sea bream); 間借り *ma-gari* renting of rooms; 間貸し *ma-gashi* letting of rooms; 間数 *ma-kazu* number of rooms; 茶の間 *cha no ma* sitting-room; 板の間 *ita no ma* wooden-floor(ed room); 客間 *kyaku-ma* parlour; 床の間 *toko no ma* alcove; 洋間 *yō-ma* Western-style room.

3. The various sizes of *tatami*; lengths between pillars:

• 江戸間 *Edo-ma* c. 1.75m.; 京間 *Kyō-ma* c. 1.91m.; 田舎間 *inaka-ma* c. 1.82m.

Note: Length is always double the width. There are other sizes, too.

4. Miscellaneous:

• 間柱 *ma-bashira* intervening pillar; 小間物 *koma-mono* haberdashery; 間抜け *ma-nuke* stupidity; 間ぬるい *ma-nurui* sluggish; 仲間 *naka-ma* comrades; 手間 *te-ma* time, trouble; 間尺に合わない *ma-shaku ni awanai* doesn't pay.

ma-[1] 目 接頭語 prefix

The ideograph 目 is read *ma-* in many compounds:

• 目映い *ma-bayui* dazzling; 目庇 *ma-bisashi* visor; 目縁 *ma-buchi* eyelid; 目深に *ma-buka ni* pulled down over eyes; 目陰 *ma-kage* shading one's eyes; 目見える *ma-mieru* have interview.

NOTE. 瞬き *matataki, mabataki* blinking; まなじり *manajiri* corner of one's eye; 眼 *manako* eyes, eyeball; まなざし *manazashi* a look.

ma-² 真　接頭語　prefix

1. 真実を示す *Shinjitsu wo shimesu* Denotes truth:
   • 真顔 *ma-gao* serious look; 真心 *ma-gokoro* sincerity.
2. 正確さを示す *Seikakusa wo shimesu* Denotes precision:
   • 真上 *ma-ue* directly overhead; 真裏 *ma-ura* directly behind.
3. 純粋を示す *Junsui wo shimesu* Denotes genuineness:
   • 真名 *ma-na* ideographs, as opposed to *ka-na*; 真水 *ma-mizu* fresh water; 真綿 *ma-wata* floss silk.
4. 動植物の名に付いて、標準的なものを示す *Dōshokubutsu no na ni tsuite, hyōjunteki na mono wo shimesu* With animal and plant names, denotes the true type:
   • 真鯛 *ma-dai* red sea-bream; 真竹 *ma-dake* long-jointed bamboo.

NOTE. ま becomes まっ in many compounds:

• 真っ向 *mak-kō* right in front; 真っ裸 *map-padaka* stark nakedness; 真っ平 *map-pira* (not) by any means; 真っ昼間 *map-piruma* broad daylight; 真っ二つ *map-putatsu* clean in halves; 真っ最中 *mas-saichū* at height of; 真っ正面 *mas-shōmen* right opposite; 真っすぐに *mas-sugu ni* dead straight; 真只中 *mat-tadanaka* very centre.

赤い becomes 真っ赤な *mak-ka na* crimson; 青い becomes 真っ青な *mas-sao na* deadly pale; 黒い becomes 真っ黒い *and* 真っ黒な *mak-kuroi, mak-kuro na* jet black; 暗い becomes 真っ暗い and 真っ暗な *mak-kurai, mak-kura na* pitch dark; 白い becomes 真っ白い and 真っ白な *mas-shiroi, mas-shiro na* snow white.

NOTE. There are also:

• 真ん丸の *man-maru no* and 真ん丸い *man-marui* perfectly round; 真ん中 *man-naka* dead centre; 真ん前 *man-mae* right in front.

NOTE. The use of 真 as an independent word is probably limited to 真に受ける *ma ni ukeru* take seriously.

NOTE. 馬 is read *ma* in 絵馬 *ema* votive tablet, 伝馬船 *tenmasen* barge, and 馬子 *ma-go* packhorse driver.

mada 未だ　副詞　adverb

Formerly *imada,* was also used as an adjectival noun:

1. 否定の言葉を伴って、その事態が今なお実現していないことを表す

Hitei no kotoba wo tomonatte, sono jitai ga ima nao jitsugen shite inai koto wo arawasu With negative expressions, indicates that the condition has not yet arisen:

- 火事はまだ消えない。 *Kaji wa mada kienai.* The fire has not been put out yet.
- まだ授業が始まらない。 *Mada jugyō ga hajimaranai.* Class hasn't begun yet.

2. 肯定の言葉を伴って、その状態がなお続いていることを表す *Kōtei no kotoba wo tomonatte, sono jōtai ga nao tsuzuite iru koto wo arawasu* With positive expressions, indicates that the condition endures:

- 子供はまだ寝ている。 *Kodomo wa mada nete iru.* The children are still in bed.

3.「充分でないが、どちらかと言えば」という意味を表す *"Jūbun de nai ga, dochira ka to ieba" to iu imi wo arawasu* Denotes the lesser of two evils:

- これでもまだましな方だ。 *Kore de mo mada mashi na hō da.* This is still the better of the two.

4. さらに、もっと *Sara ni, motto* Still more:

- 話したいことはまだ山ほどある。 *Hanashitai koto wa mada yama hodo aru.* There is no end to the things I have to tell you.

5. どうやら *Dō yara* Somehow (or other):

- この程度ならまだ我慢出来る。 *Kono teido nara, mada gaman dekiru.* I can put up with this much.

NOTE. *Mada* is sometimes used as a negative reply:

- 帰ってきたのですか。まだです。 *Kaette kita no desu ka? Mada desu.* Has he returned? Not yet.

made まで 副助詞 adverbial particle

1. 場所・時間・数量などの範囲・限度を示す *Basho • jikan • sūryō nado no han'i • gendo wo shimesu* Indicates the range in place, time, quantity to which an action extends:

- 駅まで送ってきた。 *Eki made okutte kita.* I saw him off to the station.
- 夜遅くまで勉強する。 *Yoru osoku made benkyō suru.* They study late into the night.
- 十人のうち、八人まで感染した。 *Jūnin no uchi, hachinin made kansen shita.* As many as eight out of ten were infected.

2. 極端な場合を挙げて強調し、一般的な場合を暗示する *Kyokutan na baai wo agete kyōchō shi, ippanteki na baai wo anji suru* Provides and emphasizes an extreme case, suggesting what is ordinary:

- 親友にまで愛想を尽かされた。 *Shin-yū ni made aisō wo tsukasareta.* He has been deserted even by his best friends.

3. 程度を表す *Teido wo arawasu* Denotes degree:

- 私を気違いとまで言った。 *Watashi wo ki-chigai to made itta.* He went so far as to say I was mad.

NOTE. While *made* indicates a period of time, *made ni* indicates a cut-off point:

- 五時まで待ちましょう。 *Go-ji made machimashō.* Let's wait until five.
- 五時までに帰宅する。 *Go-ji made ni kitaku suru.* I'll be home by five.

NOTE. *Made* mostly replaces the particles *ga, wa, wo,* and follows other particles:

- 皿までなめた。 *Sara made nameta.* He even licked the plate.
- 兄さんまでそんなことをしてはいけない。 *Niisan made sonna koto wo shite wa ikenai.* Not even your elder brother is allowed to do things like that.
- 夢にまで見る。 *Yume ni made miru.* I see it even in my dreams.
- 十二時までが営業時間です。 *Jūni-ji made ga eigyō-jikan desu.* They are open until twelve o'clock.
- 十二時までを営業時間にしている。 *Jūni-ji made wo eigyō jikan ni shite iru.* Twelve o'clock is our closing-time.

NOTE. *Made* is one of the particles that may come between a verb and its auxiliary:

- 聞いてまでみたが、だめだった。 *Kiite made mita ga, dame datta.* I went so far as to inquire, but it was of no avail.

→ *bakari*

mae 前 形式名詞として As a formal noun

動詞の終止形に付いて、その時よりも早い時期を指す *Dōshi no shūshi-kei ni tsuite, sono toki yori mo hayai jiki wo sasu* With Base 3 of verbs, indicates an earlier time than that mentioned as the standard:

- 帰る前に窓を閉めなさい。 *Kaeru mae ni mado wo shime nasai.* Close the windows before you go home.

NOTE. The negative *-nai mae ni (= -nai uchi ni)* is translated with a positive expression:

- 雨が降らない前に帰ろう。 *Ame ga furanai mae ni kaerō.* Let's go home before it rains.

NOTE. In the case of a past event, this negative construction may not be used if the event actually took place:

• 雨が降り出す前に帰ってきた。 *Ame ga furi-dasu mae ni kaette kita.* We came home before it began to rain.

→ *saki*

-mae 前 接尾語 suffix

1. その人数に相当する分量 *Sono ninzū ni sōtō suru bunryō* Amount suited to that number of persons:

• 寿司を五人前注文した。 *Sushi wo gonin-mae chūmon shita.* He ordered *sushi* for five.

2. それ相当の優れたもの *Sore sōtō no sugureta mono* Something worthy of . . . :

• 男前 *otoko-mae* man's (good) looks; 腕前 *ude-mae* ability.

mai- 毎 接尾語 prefix

そのたびごとに *Sono tabi-goto ni* Every time . . . :

• こんなことは毎日はない。 *Konna koto wa mai-nichi wa nai.* This sort of thing doesn't happen every day.

NOTE. Although *mai-* is an *on* reading, we get:

• 毎朝 *mai-asa* every morning; 毎夜 *mai-yo* every night; 毎夕 *mai-yū* every evening; 毎月 *mai-getsu* • *mai-tsuki* every month; 毎年 *mai-nen* • *mai-toshi* every year. → *-goto ni*

-mai[1] まい 助動詞 auxiliary verb

Deriving from *bungo "maji",* this *-mai* now retains only Bases 3 and 4 (which are identical); this is why it is classed with *-u* and *yō* as *fu-henkei,* non-conjugated.

五段動詞、「たがる」「ます」の終止形に、その他の動詞・助動詞の未然形に付いて、 *Godan dōshi, "tagaru", "masu" no shūshikei ni, sono ta no dōshi • jodōshi no mizenkei ni tsuite* Added to Base 3 of *godan* verbs, *-tagaru* and *-masu* and to Base 1 of all the other verbs and auxiliaries.

1. 打ち消しの推量を表す *Uchikeshi no suiryō wo arawasu* Expresses negative conjecture:

• 雨はもう降るまい。 *Ame wa mō furumai.* It probably won't rain again.

• 食べたがるまい。 *Tabetagarumai.* He probably won't want to eat it.

• そんなことはありますまい。 *Sonna koto wa arimasumai.* That can't be.

2. 打ち消しの意志を表す *Uchikeshi no ishi wo arawasu* Expresses negative volition:

• こんな誤りは二度としまい。 *Konna ayamari wa ni-do to shimai.* You won't catch me making the same mistake again.

-mai² 枚 接尾語 suffix
薄くて平たいものを数える語 *Usukute hiratai mono wo kazoeru go* Counter for thin, flat objects:
• 百円切手五枚ください *Hyaku-en kitte go-mai kudasai.* Five ¥100 stamps, please.
• この皿は六枚で一揃いです。 *Kono sara wa roku-mai de hito-soroi desu.* These plates are six to the set.

mairu 参る 動詞 verb
1. 補助動詞として、「来る」「行く」を丁重に言う *Hojo-dōshi to shite, "kuru", "yuku" wo teichō ni iu* As a supplementary verb, a courteous substitute for *kuru, yuku:*
• 雨が降ってまいりました。 *Ame ga futte mairimashita.* It has begun to rain.
2. 「来る」「行く」の謙譲語 *"Kuru", "yuku" no kenjō-go* A deferential substitute for *kuru, yuku:*
• どちらへいらっしゃいますか。 *Dochira e irasshaimasu ka?* Where are you going?
公園へ参ります。 *Kōen e mairimasu.* I'm going to the park.

-maki 巻 接尾語 suffix
書物・巻物を数える語 *Shomotsu • maki-mono wo kazoeru go* Counter for (sections of) books and scrolls:
• 下の巻にある。 *Ge no maki ni aru.* It is in the second (third) volume.
• 掛け軸三巻 *kake-jiku mi-maki (san-kan)* three scrolls.
→ *-kan*

-maku 幕 接尾語 suffix
劇などの一段落を数える語 *Geki nado no ichi-danraku wo kazoeru go* Counter for sections of drama:
• 三幕物 *san-maku mono* play in three acts.
→ *-ba²*

-makuru 捲る 補助動詞 supplementary verb
動詞の連用形に付いて、動作を休みなく、激しくする *Dōshi no ren'yō-*

kei ni tsuite, dōsa wo yasumi naku, hageshiku suru Added to Base 2 of verbs, denotes that the action is done indiscreetly or incessantly:

- 吹きまくる *fuki-makuru* rage, brag; 言いまくる *ii-makuru* talk glibly; 書きまくる *kaki-makuru* write incessantly; 切りまくる *kiri-makuru* mow down; 追いまくる *oi-makuru* put to flight; 押しまくる *oshi-makuru* push violently.

mama まま 形式名詞 formal noun

1. その通り *Sono toori* In that state:
   - 靴を履いたまま部屋に入った。 *Kutsu wo haita mama heya ni haitta.* He entered the room with his shoes on.
   - どうぞ、掛けたままでいらっしゃいませ。 *Dōzo, kaketa mama de irasshaimase.* Please remain seated.
   - 出掛けたまま帰らない。 *Dekaketa mama kaeranai.* He left and hasn't come back.
2. 思う通り *Omou-toori* As one pleases:
   - 思うままに生きたいと思っている。 *Omou mama ni ikitai to omotte iru.* He wants to live his life to please himself.

mama- 継 接頭語 prefix

血の繋がりのない親・子 *Chi no tsunagari no nai oya • ko* Parent-child relationship other than that of blood:

- 継父 *mama-chichi* step-father; 継母 *mama-haha* step-mother; 継子 *mama-ko* step-child; 継兄弟 *mama-kyōdai* step-brothers, step-sisters; 継親 *mama-oya* step-parent(s).

HOMONYMS. ままごと *mama-goto* playing "house"; 飯炊き *mama-taki* cooking rice; 儘ならぬ *mama-naranu* unable to have one's own way; ままよ *mama yo* I don't care; 間々 *ma-ma* occasionally; ママ from English "mama".

-maru まる 接尾語 suffix

1. Some adjectives drop their final *-i* and add *-maru* to form intransitive verbs, *-meru* to form transitive verbs:
   - *fukai* → *fukamaru* (become deeper), *fukameru* (make deeper)
   - *hiroi* → *hiromaru* (be diffused), *hiromeru* (diffuse)
   - *katai* → *katamaru* (solidify), *katameru* (harden)
   - *marui* → *marumaru* (become round), *marumeru* (round off)
   - *takai* → *takamaru* (be raised), *takameru* (heighten)
   - *tsuyoi* → *tsuyomaru* (become stronger), *tsuyomeru* (strengthen)

2. Some adjectives add *-mu* and *-meru:*
   - *itai* → *itamu* (be painful), *itameru* (hurt)
   - *kurushii* → *kurushimu* (feel pain), *kurushimeru* (cause pain)
   - *nurui* → *nurumu* (become tepid), *nurumeru* (take chill off)
   - *yurui* → *yurumu* (relax), *yurumeru* (slacken)
3. A few adjectival nouns drop their final *-ka* and add *-maru, -meru.*
   - *atataka* → *atatamaru* (become warm), *atatameru* (make warm)
   - *shizuka* → *shizumaru* (subside), *shizumeru* (calm, ease)

-masu ます　助動詞（特殊型） auxiliary verb (special conjugation)
The conjugation is as follows: 1. *mase, mashō* 2. *mashi* 3. *masu* 4. *masu* 5. *masure* 6. *mase, mashi.*
動詞の連用形に付いて、丁寧を表す　*Dōshi no ren'yōkei ni tsuite, teinei wo arawasu* Added to Base 2 of verbs, expresses politeness:
- ここは雪がよく降ります。 *Koko wa yuki ga yoku furimasu.* It snows a lot here.
- 申し上げますことをお聞きください。 *Mōshi-agemasu koto wo o-kiki kudasai.* Please listen to what I have to say.
- いらっしゃいませ。 *Irasshaimase!* Welcome!

NOTE. This imperative form is now used only with the four verbs *irassharu, kudasaru, nasaru* and *ossharu.* The conditional, *-masure,* is now replaced with *-mashitara. Mashimasu* comes from a now obsolete verb *masu,* still earlier *imasu.*

-me- 女　接頭語・接尾語　prefix, suffix
人を指す語に付いて、「女の」 *Hito wo sasu go ni tsuite, "onna no"* With words indicating human beings, denotes the female:
- 女神　*me-gami* goddess; 女雛 *me-bina* lady doll; 乙女 *oto-me* girl, virgin; 醜女 *shiko-me* ugly woman.

NOTE. In the case of inanimates, 女、*me-* refers to the weaker of a pair:
- 女滝 *me-daki* lesser waterfall; 男滝 *o-daki* greater waterfall; 女波 *me-nami* smaller wave; 男波 *o-nami* larger wave.

NOTE. Of the two ideographs 雌 and 牝、the former originally referred to the female of birds only, the latter to that of other beasts. The distinction has blurred:
- 雌雄　*shi-yū, mesu-osu* 牝牡 *mesu-osu* female and male; 牝鹿 *me-jika* doe, hind; 雌馬 *me-uma* mare; 雌鳴 *men-dori* hen.

-me[1] 目　接尾語　suffix
1. 順序を示す語　*Junjo wo shimesu go* Word used to express order:

• 角から三軒目です。 *Kado kara sangen-me desu.* It is the third house from the corner.

2. 主に動詞の連用形に付いて、一番大事な点を示す *Omo ni dōshi no ren'yōkei ni tsuite, ichi-ban daiji na ten wo shimesu* Added mainly to Base 2 of verbs, denotes the most important point:

• 切れ目 *kire-me* gap; 切り目 *kiri-me* cut; 結び目 *musubi-me* knot; 折れ目 *ore-me* crease; 折り目 *ori-me* crease; 境目 *sakai-me* border; 死に目 *shini-me* point of death; 割れ目 *ware-me* crack.

3. 量・程度に関する形容詞の語幹に付いて、どちらかと言えば、その性質を持つ意を表す *Ryō • teido ni kansuru keiyōshi no gokan ni tsuite, dochira ka to ieba, sono seishitsu wo motsu i wo arawasu* Added to stem of adjectives of quantity or degree, denotes that the quality is present to some extent:

• 近め *chika-me* close; 太め *futo-me* on the stout side; 早めに *haya-me ni* somewhat early; 細めに切る *hoso-me ni kiru* cut into thin slices; 低めに *hiku-me ni* slightly low.

NOTE. Many of these compounds have also the ideograph 目、with a different meaning:

• 近目 *chika-me* = *kingan* myopia; 細目 *hoso-me* narrow eyes, etc.

→ *ma*[1]

-me[2] 奴 (*yatsu*) 接尾語 suffix

体言に付く *Taigen ni tsuku* Is attached to nouns.

1. 相手に用いて、罵る意を表す *Aite ni mochiite, nonoshiru i wo arawasu* Applied to others, expresses a sense of vituperation:

• 馬鹿ものめ *bakamono-me* silly fool; 偽善者評論家め *gizensha hyōronka-me* stupid hypocrite of a critic.

2. 自分に付けて、謙譲を表す *Jibun ni tsukete, kenjō wo arawasu* Applied to oneself, expresses deference:

• 私め *watakushi-me* your humble servant.

-mei-[1] 名 接頭語・接尾語 prefix, suffix

1. 呼び名 *Yobi-na* Literal meaning of "name":

• 別名 *betsu-mei* pseudonym; 病名 *byō-mei* name of a disease; 地名 *chi-mei* geographical name; 題名 *dai-mei* title (cf. 大名 *dai-myō*); 学名 *gaku-mei* scientific name; 芸名 *gei-mei* stage name; 偽名 *gi-mei* false name; 人名 *jin-mei* person's name; 除名 *jo-mei* expulsion; 仮名 *ka-mei* assumed name; 家名 *ka-mei* family name; family reputation; 改名 *kai-mei* change of one's name; 旧名 *kyū-mei* former name; 無名 *mu-mei* anonymity; obscure name; 姓名 *sei-mei* full name; 氏名 *shi-mei* full name; 指名 *shi-mei* (of 指名手配 *shimei tehai*) designation; 署名 *sho-mei* signature; 書名 *sho-mei* name of a book; 和名 *wa-mei* Japanese name (as opposed to *gaku-mei*).

2. 評判 *Hyōban* Reputation:

• 悪名 *aku-mei* bad reputation; 著名な *cho-mei na* famous; 有名な *yū-mei na* famous.

3. 人数を数える語 *Ninzū wo kazoeru go* Counter for persons (= *-nin*).

NOTE. The reading *myō* is found in a few compounds:

• 名号 *myō-gō* title of Buddha; 名字 *myō-ji* surname; 名代 *myō-dai* proxy; 名田 *myō-den* unit of land measurement in feudal times.

NOTE. The following have two readings:

• 名目 *mei-moku, myō-moku* title, pretext; 名聞 *myō-mon, mei-bun* fame; 名利 *myō-ri, mei-ri* name and wealth.

-mei-[2] 命 *(inochi)* 接頭語・接尾語 prefix, suffix

1. いのち *Inochi* Life:

• 亡命 *bō-mei* taking refuge; 長命 *chō-mei* long life; 延命 *en-mei* prolonging life; 一命 *ichi-mei* one's life; 人命 *jin-mei* human life; 助命 *jo-mei* clemency; 革命 *kaku-mei* revolution; 懸命 *ken-mei* utmost endeavour; 救命 *kyū-mei* life-saving; 生命 *sei-mei* life; 使命 *shi-mei* mission; 短命 *tan-mei* short life; 天命 *ten-mei* destiny; 運命 *un-mei* destiny; 余命 *yo-mei* one's remaining days; 絶命 *zetsu-mei* dying.

2. 言い付け *Ii-tsuke* Command:

• 幕命 *baku-mei* order of Shogun; 命令 *mei-rei* command.

NOTE. 寿命 *ju-myō* lifespan; 宣命 *sen-myō* Imperial edict written in old style.

-mekasu めかす 接尾語 suffix verb (causative of *-meku*)

名詞などの下に付いて、「それらしく見えるようにする」 *Meishi nado no shita ni tsuite, "sore-rashiku mieru yō ni suru"* Added to nouns and other parts of speech, gives the meaning "cause to look like":

• 秘密めかす *himitsu-mekasu* make (one's remark, etc.) look like a secret; ほのめかす *hono-mekasu* drop a hint; ときめかす *toki-mekasu* cause to palpitate; 時めかす *toki-mekasu* make (a person) look prosperous.

-meku めく 接尾語 suffix verb

名詞などに付いて、「それらしく見える」 *Meishi nado ni tsuite, "sore-*

rashiku mieru" Added to nouns and other parts of speech, gives the meaning "look like":

- 秋めく *aki-meku* have a touch of fall (is added also to the names of the other three seasons); どよめく *doyo-meku* reverberate; はためく *hata-meku* flutter; 色めく *iro-meku* be tinged with; 唐めく *Kara-meku* be in Chinese style; ときめく *toki-meku* palpitate; 時めく *toki-meku* be at the height of one's prosperity; 揺らめく *yura-meku* sway; よろめく *yoro-meku* stagger; 逆説めくかも知れませんが、*gyakusetsu-meku ka mo shiremasen ga,* paradoxical as it may seem, . . .

NOTE. There is also an adjectival form *mekashii:*

- 今めかしい *ima-mekashii* up-to-date; 古めかしい *furu-mekashii* old-looking.

meshi- 召し 「召す」の連用形 Base 2 of verb *mesu* (used as prefix)

Originally, 召す meant "summon by calling", while 招く meant "summon by waving the hand". From the former derived the polite prefix to verbs substituting for *miru, taberu, nomu, kiru* (put on), *hiku (kaze wo)* and others:

- 召し上がる *meshi-agaru* eat, drink; 召し上げる *meshi-ageru* confiscate, summon; 召し出す *meshi-dasu* summon (the religious term for vocation is *meshi-dashi,* more technically 召命、*shōmei*); 召し変える *meshi-kaeru* change (clothes); 召し使う *meshi-tsukau* take into one's service.

NOTE. As a suffix, *-mesu* is found only in compounds now considered archaic:

- 聞こし召す *kikoshi-mesu = kiku, taberu, nomu, osameru, okonau* (hear, eat, drink, conduct, perform).
- 思し召す *oboshi-mesu = omou* (think).
- 知ろし召す *shiroshi-mesu = shiru, osameru.* (know, conduct).

mi-[1] 御 接頭語 prefix

名詞の上に付いて、尊敬・丁寧の意を表す *Meishi no ue ni tsuite, sonkei • teinei no i wo arawasu* Prefixed to nouns, expresses respect and politeness. The majority of words with this prefix pertain to religious or Imperial matters:

- 御灯 *mi-akashi* light offered; 御堂 *mi-dō* main monastery temple; 御稜威 *mi-itsu* Imperial virtue; 帝・御門 *Mi-kado* His Imperial Majesty; 御影 *mi-kage* spirit of the dead (御影石 *mikage-ishi* granite);

神酒・御酒 *mi-ki* wine offering; 御子 *mi-ko* Imperial child; 御心 *mi-kokoro* divine will (Cath. religious term "Sacred Heart"); 神輿・御輿 *mi-koshi* portable shrine; 御言 *mi-koto* Imperial command; 御くじ *mi-kuji* sacred lot; 御国 *Mi-kuni* Japan; 御前 *mi-mae* sacred presence; 御旨 *mi-mune* divine will; 御簾 *mi-su* bamboo blind; 御霊 *mi-tama* spirit of the departed; 御手洗 *mi-tarai* "lavabo"; 御世・御代 *mi-yo* Imperial reign.

→ *go-*[1], *gyo-*, *o-*[1], *on-*

mi-[2] 美・深 接頭語 prefix

名詞の上に付いて、美称の意を表す *Meishi no ue ni tsuite, bishō no i wo arawasu* Prefixed to nouns (often place-names), embellishes them:

- 美空 *mi-sora* the (beautiful) sky; 美吉野 *mi-Yoshino Yoshino*

mi-[3] 未 接頭語 prefix

名詞などの上に付いて、「まだそうしない」「まだそうならない」意味を表す *Meishi nado no ue ni tsuite, "mada sō shinai", "mada sō naranai" imi wo arawasu* Prefixed to nouns and other parts of speech, tells that the action or state has not yet come about:

- 未払いの *mi-harai no* unpaid; 未熟な *mi-juku na* unripe, immature; 未解決の *mi-kaiketsu no* pending; 未婚の *mi-kon no* unmarried; 未明 *mi-mei* predawn; 未来 *mi-rai* future; 未成年 *mi-seinen* minority; 未亡人 *mi-bōjin* widow.

NOTE. The antonym 既 *ki-* (*sude ni*) may be prefixed to some of the above:

- 既決 *ki-ketsu* settled; 既婚 *ki-kon* already married.

-mi[1] 味 (あじ) 接尾語 suffix

形容詞・形容動詞の語幹に付いて、体言化する *Keiyōshi・keiyōdōshi no gokan ni tsuite, taigen-ka suru* Added to stem of adjectives and adjectival nouns, nominalizes them.

1. 程度・状態を表す *Teido・jōtai wo arawasu* Expresses degree or state:

- 青み *ao-mi* blueness; 温かみ *atataka-mi* warmth; ありがたみ *ari-gata-mi* blessing; 嫌味 *iya-mi* bad taste, sarcasm; 臭み *kusa-mi* stench; 寂しみ *sabishi-mi* loneliness; 渋み *shibu-mi* astringency, elegant simplicity; 辛み *tsura-mi* bitter feeling.

2. 「そのような状態である場所・部分」 *"Sono yō na jōtai de aru basho・bubun* Place or part having that quality:

- 浅み *asa-mi* shallows; 深み *fuka-mi* depth (s); 茂み・繁み *shige-mi* thicket; 明るみに出る *akaru-mi ni deru* come to light.

- そこが彼の強み（弱み）だ。 *Soko ga kare no tsuyo-mi • yowa-mi da.* That is where his strength (weakness) lies.
- 有段者の重みがある。 *Yūdansha no omo-mi ga aru.* He has the prestige of a grade-holder.

→ *-ge*[1], *-sa*

-mi[2] 見 接尾語 suffix

見たり・予報したりする操作、また、それをする人、見る道具などの意味を表す *Mitari • yohō shitari suru sōsa, mata, sore wo suru hito, miru dōgu nado no imi wo arawasu* Expresses the idea of viewing, forecasting, the person who does this, and the instruments used in viewing:

- 花見 *hana-mi* cherry-blossom viewing; 菊見 *kiku-mi* chrysanthemum-viewing; 物見 *mono-mi* sightseeing; 月見 *tsuki-mi* moon-viewing; 梅見 *ume-mi* plum-blossom viewing; 雪見 *yuki-mi* snow-viewing; 味見 *aji-mi* foretaste; ちょっと見 *chotto-mi* glance; 八卦見 *hakke-mi* fortune-teller; 早見表 *hayami-hyō* chart; 火の見櫓 *hi no mi yagura* fire watchtower; 日和見 *hiyori-mi* a wait-and-see attitude; 垣間見 *kaima-mi* glimpse; 形見 *kata-mi* keepsake; 風見 *kaza-mi* weather vane; 人相見 *ninsō-mi* physiognomist; のぞき見 *nozoki-mi* peeking; 盗み見 *nusumi-mi* furtive glance; 下見 *shita-mi* preliminary inspection; 外見 *soto-mi* outward appearance; 姿見 *sugata-mi* large mirror; 隙見 *suki-mi* peeping through; 立ち見席 *tachi-mi-seki* gallery; 遠見 *too-mi* distant view; 脇見 *waki-mi* looking aside; よそ見 *yoso-mi* looking aside, connivance; 夢見 *yume-mi* dreaming.

→ *-ken*[7]

mieru 見える 動詞 verb

With *kikoeru, omoeru,* this is a verb in its own right, and the form *mireru* is sub-standard. (See notes to *-eru • -uru*) Besides its primary use, it also serves as a respect verb for *kuru*:

- お客様が見えました。 *O-kyakusama ga miemashita.* The guests have arrived.

mi-idasu 見出す 動詞 verb

From *bungo* 出す *idasu;* see also *oide.*

miru[1] 見る 補助動詞 supplementary verb

1. 動詞の連用形＋「てみる」の形で、「試しに…する」という意味を表す *Dōshi no ren'yōkei + "-te miru" no katachi de, "tameshi ni . . . suru" to iu imi wo arawasu* In Base 2 of verbs + *-te miru* form, expresses the idea of doing something on an experimental basis:

- この靴を履いてみなさい。 *Kono kutsu wo haite mi-nasai.* Try these shoes on.
- いつか会ってみたい。 *Itsu ka atte mitai.* I should like to meet him sometime.

2. 「てみると」「てみれば」「てみたら」の形で、順態の確定条件を表す *"-te miru to", "-te mireba", "-te mitara" no katachi de, juntai no kakutei jōken wo arawasu* In *-te miru to, -te mireba,* and *-te mitara* forms, states an actual fact "did something, and this was the result":

- 登校してみると、窓がたくさん懐れていた。 *Tōkō shite miru to, mado ga takusan kowarete ita.* When I went to school I found many windows broken.
- 枚数を数えてみたら、一枚足りなかった。 *Maisū wo kazoete mitara, ichi-mai tarina-katta.* I counted them (the tickets), and found we were one short.

NOTE. The verb preceding *miru* is usually volitional, but exceptions are met with:

- 親があってみれば、あんまり自由には出来ない。 *Oya ga atte mireba, anmari jiyū ni wa dekinai.* Having my parents still, I am not as free as I should like to be.
- 朝になってみると、濃霧がすっかり晴れていた。 *Asa ni natte miru to, nōmu ga sukkari harete ita.* When morning came the thick fog had completely dispersed.

NOTE. The verb may also be a passive or causative:

- 行かせてみたらどうですか。 *Ikasete mitara dō desu ka?* How about letting him go?
- そう言われてみると、 *Sō iwarete miru to, . . .* Now that you mention it, . . .

miru² 診る 動詞 verb

This is the ideograph for *miru* in:

- 医者に診てもらおう。 *Isha ni mite moraō.* I'll see a doctor. 病気の様子を診る *byōki no yōsu wo miru* examine the patient; 脈を診る *myaku wo miru* take the pulse.

miseru 見せる

With *kiseru* and *niseru,* this is a verb in its own right.

The causative of *miru,* according to rule, would be *mi + saseru.*

- 入場券を見せてください。 *Nyūjōken wo misete kudasai.* Please show me your ticket.

NOTE. Do not confuse Base 1 of *miseru* with the *mise* of "shop":

- 見せびらかす *mise-birakasu* show off; 店開き *mise-biraki* shop opening.

mitai na みたいな 形容動詞 adjectival noun
「見たような」から変化した表現；体言または用言の連体形に付く *"Mita yō na" kara henka shita hyōgen; taigen mata wa yōgen no rentaikei ni tsuku* The modified form of "*mita yō na*"; added to nominals and to Base 4 of verbals.

1. 比況を表す *Hikyō wo arawasu* Expresses a comparison:
   - 夢みたいな話だ。 *Yume mitai na hanashi da.* It seems like a dream.
   - 明るくて昼みたいだ。 *Akarukute hiru mitai da.* It is bright enough to be taken for daytime.
2. 不確実な断定を表す *Fu-kakujitsu na dantei wo arawasu* Expresses a vague assertion:
   - まるで遠足にでも行くみたいに楽しそうだ。 *Maru de ensoku ni de mo yuku mitai ni tanoshisō da.* They look as pleased as if they were going on a picnic (or something).
   - どうも熱があるみたいだ。 *Dōmo, netsu ga aru mitai da.* I suspect he has a fever.
3. 例示を表す *Reiji wo arawasu* Furnishes an example:
   - 豚みたいによく食べる。 *Buta mitai ni yoku taberu.* He eats enough for a pig.

NOTE. *Yō na* and *-rashii,* are synonyms, but *mitai na* can express a sense of contempt lacking in the other two, as in the last example.

mo も 係助詞 (*kei-joshi, kakari-joshi*) bound particle

1. 同じような事実のうちの一つを挙げて言う *Onaji yō na jijitsu no uchi no hitotsu wo agete iu* Singles out a particular item from a series of similar ones:
   - あの人もそう言った。 *Ano hito mo sō itta.* He said so, too.
2. 並列の意を表す *Heiretsu no i wo arawasu* Denotes listing:
   - 数学も語学も上手だ。 *Sūgaku mo gogaku mo jōzu da.* He is good at both maths and languages.
   - 痛くも痒くもない。 *Itaku mo kayuku mo nai.* It doesn't affect me at all.
3. 強調を表す *Kyōchō wo arawasu* Expresses emphasis:
   - やってみもしないで、批判ばかりする。 *Yatte mi mo shinaide, hihan bakari suru.* He won't touch it himself, but never stops criticising.
   - 雪は二メートルも積もった。 *Yuki wa ni-mētoru mo tsumotta.* As much as two meters of snow piled up.

4. 不定を表す語に付いて、全面的な肯定または否定を表す *Futei wo arawasu go ni tsuite, zenmen-teki na kōtei mata wa hitei wo arawasu* With indefinites, expresses overall assertion or denial:

- 平野は幾マイルも続いている。 *Heiya wa iku-mairu mo tsuzuite iru.* The plain goes on for mile after mile.
- 教室にはだれも居ない。 *Kyōshitsu ni wa dare mo inai.* There is nobody in the classroom.

5. 同じ動詞を挟んで、程度の激しいことを表す *Onaji dōshi wo hasande, teido no hageshii koto wo arawasu* Placed between a verb and the repetition of the same verb, denotes that the action is intense:

- 食べも食べたり、御飯を十杯も平らげた。 *Tabe mo tabetari, gohan wo jippai mo tairageta.* He ate and ate until he had put away ten bowls of rice.

NOTE. This *mo* is now preferably considered an adverbial particle.

mo and case particles

Mo replaces *ga, wa, wo,* and almost invariably follows other particles:

- 明日もいい天気でしょう。 *Asu mo ii tenki deshō.* It will probably be fine tomorrow, too. (replacing *wa*)
- 明後日もいい天気なら、試合をしよう。 *Asatte mo ii tenki nara, shiai wo shiyō.* If the day after tomorrow is fine, too, let's have a match. (replacing *ga*)
- 新聞も読まないし、テレビも見ない。 *Shinbun mo yomanai shi, terebi mo minai.* He neither reads the newspaper nor watches television. (replacing *wo*)
- 私の他にもお客が居た。 *Watashi no hoka ni mo o-kyaku ga ita.* There were other clients there besides me.
- 休暇中どこへも行かなかった。 *Kyūka-chū doko e mo ikanakatta.* I didn't go anywhere during the holidays.

NOTE. An exception where *mo* does not follow the particle is:

- だれもが知っていることだ。 *Dare mo ga shitte iru koto da.* Everybody knows that.

-modoki 擬 接尾語 suffix

体言に付いて、「あるものに似せて作ったもの」という意味を添える *Taigen ni tsuite, "aru mono ni nisete tsukutta mono" to iu imi wo soeru* Added to nominals, means "after the fashion of . . . ":

- 雁もどき *gan-modoki* a kind of fritter; 芝居もどきに *shibai-modoki ni* as in a play; お伽話もどきに *otogibanashi-modoki ni* as in a fairy-tale.

NOTE. The ideograph is the *gi* of 擬声語 *gi-seigo* onomatopoeia, and 模擬試験 *mogi-shiken* mock exam.

-mon 文　接尾語 suffix
足袋・靴・靴下などの底の長さを計る単位 *Tabi • kutsu • kutsushita nado no soko no nagasa wo hakaru tan'i* Former unit of measurement for (length of soles of) *tabi,* shoes, socks, etc. The word comes from the custom of laying *ichi-mon* coins in line as a measure. One *mon* equals 2.4 cm.

mono[1] 物　体言 nominal
A. (written in *kanji*)
感覚で感知できる有形の物体・物質 *Kankaku de kanchi dekiru yūkei no buttai • busshitsu* Concrete object capable of being perceived by the senses:
- この土地は私の物だ。 *Kono tochi wa watashi no mono da.* This piece of land is mine.

B. (written in *kana*)
1. 存在すると考えられる無形の事柄 *Sonzai suru to kangaerareru mukei no kotogara* Abstract things that are thought to exist:
- 親切というものは人の心を明るくする。 *Shinsetsu to iu mono wa hito no kokoro wo akaruku suru.* Kindness is such that it cheers the heart.

2. 次に来る語によって、ある特殊な「もの」と分かる場合 *Tsugi ni kuru go ni yotte, aru tokushu na "mono" to wakaru baai* When the meaning is specified by the word(s) following:
- 一日中ものを食べないで、何かを考えている。 *Ichinichi-jū mono wo tabenaide, nani ka wo kangaete iru.* He spends the day thinking, without eating a thing.
- いざとなれば、腕力がものを言う。 *Iza to nareba, wanryoku ga mono wo iu.* In an emergency, it is force that counts.
- この布は、ものがいい。 *Kono nuno wa, mono ga ii.* This cloth is of good quality.

3. 特に取り立てていうほどのこと *Toku ni tori-tatete iu hodo no koto* Something worthy of special mention:
- 嵐をものともせずにやってきた。 *Arashi wo mono to mo sezu ni yatte kita.* He came despite the storm.

4. 立派な状態 *Rippa na jōtai* An excellent outcome:
- これはものになるだろう。 *Kore wa mono ni naru darō.* This will be a great success.
- この研究を何とかしてものにしたい。 *Kono kenkyū wo nan to ka shite mono ni shitai.* I am determined to make a success of my research at all costs.

5. 理屈・道理を表す *Rikutsu・dōri wo arawasu* Signifies reasonableness:

- 実にものの分かった人だ。 *Jitsu ni mono no wakatta hito da.* He is indeed a sensible type of person.
- 赤ん坊はもうものが分かりはじめた。 *Akanbō wa mō mono ga wakari-hajimeta.* The baby has already begun to take notice.

mono² 者 体言 nominal

人物を指し、単独では使わない *Jinbutsu wo sashi, tandoku de wa tsukawanai* Refers to persons, and is not used in isolation:

- 残りたい者は残れ。 *Nokoritai mono wa nokore.* Those who want to remain are free to do so.
- 負傷した者もあるらしい。 *Fushō shita mono mo aru-rashii.* It seems there are some casualties, too.

mono³

「ものだ」「ものです」の形で *"Mono da" "mono desu" no katachi de* In *mono da* and *mono desu* forms.

1. 一般的な傾向を表す *Ippan-teki na keikō wo arawasu* Denotes a general trend:

- 犬はよく吠えるものだ。 *Inu wa yoku hoeru mono da.* Dogs (tend to) bark a lot.
- 冬には火事が起こりやすいものだ。 *Fuyu ni wa kaji ga okori-yasui mono da.* In winter, fires are likely to occur.

2. 意見の押しつけを表す *Iken no oshi-tsuke wo arawasu* Expresses the forcing of an opinion:

- 年寄りの言うことは聞くものだ。 *Toshiyori no iu koto wa kiku mono da.* One should listen to one's elders.
- 陰口を言うものではない。 *Kage-guchi wo iu mono de wa nai.* One should not indulge in backbiting.

3. 過去には度々起こったことを懐かしく回想する意味を表す *Kako ni wa tabi-tabi okotta koto wo natsukashiku kaisō suru imi wo arawasu* Denotes fond recollections:

- 若いころそこへよく行ったものだ。 *Wakai koro soko e yoku itta mono da!* How often I went there in my youth!
- 川でよく遊んだものだ。 *Kawa de yoku asonda mono da!* How we used to play in the river!

4. 難しいことに成功したのに驚く意を表す *Muzukashii koto ni seikō shita no ni odoroku i wo arawasu* Expresses surprise at success in doing something difficult:

- 一日五百円でよく暮らせるものだ。 *Ichi-nichi gohyaku-en de yoku kuraseru mono da!* How well he manages to live on ¥500 a day!
- こんな子供がよく一人で来たものだ。 *Konna kodomo ga yoku hitori de kita mono da!* To think that such a child should (manage to) come on his own!

5. 「だから」「ですから」を伴って、理由の意を強調する *"Da kara", "desu kara" wo tomonatte, riyū no i wo kyōchō suru* Followed by *da kara* and *desu kara,* emphasises the idea of cause or reason:

- 小さかったものだから、よく覚えていない。 *Chiisakatta mono da kara, yoku oboete inai.* I was so young that I don't remember rightly.
- 急に寒くなったものだから、風邪をひいてしまった。 *Kyū ni samuku natta mono da kara, kaze wo hiite shimatta.* It got cold so suddenly that I caught a cold.

6. 可能動詞＋「なら」、「おう・よう」＋「なら」を伴って、仮定条件を表す *Kanō-dōshi + "nara", "-ō・-yō + nara" wo tomonatte, katei-jōken wo arawasu* With a potential verb + *nara,* or *-ō, -yō + nara,* expresses an open condition:

- 出来るものなら、今すぐしてあげたいけれども。 *Dekiru mono nara, ima sugu shite agetai keredomo.* If at all possible, I should like to do it for you right now.
- 私に黙って勝手なことをしようものなら、決して許しません。 *Watashi ni damatte katte na koto wo shiyō mono nara, kesshite yurushimasen.* If you get up to your tricks behind my back, I certainly will not forgive you.

NOTE. The consequence is almost invariably something undesirable.

7. しみじみと感慨を表す *Shimijimi to kangai wo arawasu* Reveals deep emotion:

- 人間とは弱いものだ。 *Ningen to wa yowai mono da.* What a weakling man is!

8. 「たいものだ」の形で、切なる希望を表す *"-tai mono da" no katachi de, setsu naru kibō wo arawasu* In *-tai mono da* form, expresses a fervent wish:

- その話を聞きたいものだ。 *Sono hanashi wo kikitai mono da.* How I long to hear about it!

mono⁴ もの 終助詞 final particle

不満・不平などの気持を含めて、強く主張する *Fu-man・fu-hei nado no kimochi wo fukumete, tsuyoku shuchō suru* Makes a strong assertion, with overtones of complaint or dissatisfaction:

- 切符はみんな行列して買っているんですもの。 *Kippu wa minna*

gyōretsu shite katte irun desu mono! They are all lined up buying tickets (I tell you)!

- あなたなら、分かってくださると思っていましたもの。 *Anata nara, wakatte kudasaru to omotte imashita mono!* I thought that at least *you* would understand!

NOTE. This use of *mono* is mostly women's speech.

mono[5] (in compounds)

A. 接頭語として *Settō-go to shite* As a prefix.

1. 形容詞・形容動詞の上に付いて、「何となく」という意味を表す *Keiyōshi • keiyōdōshi no ue ni tsuite, "nan to naku" to iu imi wo arawasu* Prefixed to adjectives and adjectival nouns, acts as a (usually) mild intensifier:

- 物悲しい *mono-ganashii* sorrowful; 物寂しい *mono-sabishii* lonesome; 物足りない *mono-tarinai* not quite satisfactory; 物珍しい *mono-mezurashii* curious, strange; 物静か *mono-shizuka* quiet; 物凄い *mono-sugoi* ghastly; 物柔らか *mono-yawaraka* gentle.

2. 動詞の連用形に付いて、その動詞との複雑な関係を表す *Dōshi no ren'yōkei ni tsuite, sono dōshi to no fukuzatsu na kankei wo arawasu* With Base 2 of verbs, expresses various relationships with the verbs:

- 物干し *mono-hoshi* airing-frame, airing-place, airing; 物見 *mono-mi* sightseeing, watchtower, scout; 物知り *mono-shiri* well-informed person; 物取り *mono-tori* robbery, robber.

B. 接尾語として *Setsubi-go to shite* As a suffix.

1. 形容詞に付く例 *Keiyōshi ni tsuku rei* Examples with adjectives:

- 青物 *ao-mono* vegetables; 荒物 *ara-mono* kitchen utensils; 古物 *furu-mono* second-hand articles; 大物 *oo-mono* V.I.P. (not 大者).

2. 名詞に付く例 *Meishi ni tsuku rei* Examples with nouns:

- 刃物 *ha-mono* edged tools; 端物 *ha-mono* remnants; 屑物 *kuzu-mono* odds and ends; 際物 *kiwa-mono* seasonable goods; 品物 *shina-mono* goods; 反物 *tan-mono* (pieces of) textiles.

3. 動詞に付く例 *Dōshi ni tsuku rei* Examples with verbs:

NOTE. As a general rule, the writing in of *okuri-gana* shows the consciousness of the verbal force of the compound, while its omission recognizes the compound as a nominal.

1. Verbs of only one syllable cannot have *okuri-gana:*
   - 獲物 *e-mono* game, booty; 得物 *e-mono* weapon, one's forte; 鋳物 *i-mono* (metal) casting; 着物 *ki-mono* clothes; 見物 *mi-mono* sight worth seeing (*ken-butsu* sightseeing).
2. The following do not have *okuri-gana:*

- 絵巻物 *emaki-mono* picture scroll; 毛織物 *keori-mono* woolen fabrics; 巻物 *maki-mono* scroll; 置物 *oki-mono* ornament; 織物 *ori-mono* textiles; 敷物 *shiki-mono* carpet; 建物 *tate-mono* building.

3. With the following, *okuri-gana* is optional:

- 編み物 *ami-mono* knitting; 買い物 *kai-mono* shopping; 飲み物 *nomi-mono* beverage; 縫い物 *nui-mono* sewing; 塗り物 *nuri-mono* lacquer-ware; 贈り物 gift; 染め物 *some-mono* dyed goods; 売り物 *uri-mono* item for sale; 読み物 *yomi-mono* reading-matter.

NOTE. Reversing *mono* compounds changes the meaning:

- 干し物 *hoshi-mono* articles to be aired; 物干し airing-frame.
- 見物 *mi-mono* sight worth seeing; 物見 sightseeing.
- 持ち物 *mochi-mono* possessions; 物持ち rich person, care of property.
- 貰い物 *morai-mono* something received; 物貰い beggar, stye.
- 置物 oki-mono ornament; 物置 storeroom.
- 売り物 *uri-mono* item for sale; 物売り vendor.
- 笑い物 *warai-mono* laughing-stock; 物笑い act or object of derision.
- 忘れ物 *wasure-mono* thing left behind; 物忘れ forgetfulness.

mono[6], butsu, motsu

Mono is the *kun* reading, *butsu,* the *kan,* and the old *go* reading *mochi* has given way to an "accepted" reading, *motsu.* This last is rarely found as a prefix:

- 物相飯 *mossō-meshi* prison rations; 物怪・勿怪 *mokke* something unexpected. 勿体・物体 *mottai* solemnity.
- 物価 *bukka* commodity prices; 物貨 *bukka* commodities.
- 供物 *ku-motsu* offerings; 書物 *sho-motsu* book; 荷物 *ni-motsu* baggage; 貨物 *ka-motsu* freight; 禁物 *kin-motsu* prohibition, prohibited item; 穀物 *koku-motsu* grain; 食物 *shoku-motsu* food (食べ物 *tabe-mono* food; 植物 *shoku-butsu* plant; 飲食物 *inshoku-butsu* food and drink).

NOTE. Extra readings:

- 御物 *gomotsu, gyo-motsu, gyo-butsu* Imperial household possessions.
- 宝物 *hō-motsu, takara-mono* treasure.
- 作物 *saku-motsu* crops; 作物 *saku-butsu* work (of art, etc.).

mono ka もの か 終助詞 final particle

強く打ち消す気持ちを表す *Tsuyoku uchi-kesu kimochi wo arawasu* Expresses a strong sense of denial:

- そんなことがあるものか。 *Sonna koto ga aru mono ka?* That's impossible!
- 彼が学者なものか。 *Kare ga gakusha na mono ka?* Him, a scholar!

mono no¹ 物の 連体詞 adnoun

時間や距離の量がごく僅かであることを示す *Jikan ya kyori no ryō ga goku wazuka de aru koto wo shimesu* Denotes that the amount of time or distance is negligible:

- 物の一分も経たないうちに、もう大きないびきが聞こえた。 *Mono no ippun mo tatanai uchi ni, mō ooki na ibiki ga kikoeta.* Not even a minute had passed before a loud snoring was heard.
- 物の十人も居ない。 *Mono no jū-nin mo inai.* There are scarcely ten persons there.

mono no² ものの 接続助詞 conjunctive particle

活用語の連体形に付いて、前に述べたことと、後に述べることが、食い違う意を表す *Katsuyō-go no rentaikei ni tsuite, mae ni nobeta koto to, ato ni noberu koto ga, kui-chigau i wo arawasu* Added to Base 4 of conjugables, denotes the incompatibility of what was said earlier with what is said later:

- 作ってはみたものの、良い出来ではなかった。 *Tsukutte wa mita mono no, yoi deki de wa nakatta.* I did try making one, but it didn't turn out well.
- 上機嫌ではあったものの、やはり、どこか気抜けしたようだった。 *Jōkigen de wa atta mono no, yahari, doko ka ki-nuke shita yō datta.* Really he was in quite good spirits, but somehow he felt depressed.

NOTE. The form is slightly literary, and milder than *no ni.*

-morau 貰う 補助動詞として as a supplementary verb

連用形＋「て」に付いて、人に頼んで好意ある動作を受ける *Ren'yōkei + "-te" ni tsuite, hito ni tanonde kōi aru dōsa wo ukeru* In Base 2 + *-te* form, means "have something desirable done for one":

- だれかに手伝ってもらおう。 *Dare ka ni tetsudatte moraō.* I'll get somebody to lend a hand.
- それについて話さないでもらいたい。 *Sore ni tsuite hanasanaide moraitai.* I don't want you to talk about the matter.
- 出て行ってもらってください。 *Dete itte moratte kudasai.* Please get them to leave.

mōsu 申す　動詞 verb

1. 「言う」「つげる」などの謙譲語 *"Iu", "tsugeru" nado no kenjōgo* Deferential form for verbs of saying:

- 田中と申します。 *Tanaka to mōshimasu.* My name is Tanaka.
- 申すまでもございません。 *Mōsu made mo gozaimasen.* There is no need to say it.

2. 「お」「ご」＋連用形や、「漢語＋申す」の形で、「する」の謙譲語になる *"O-", "go-" + ren'yōkei ya, "Kan-go + mōsu" no katachi de, "suru" no kenjōgo ni naru* In *o-/go-* + Base 2 and Chinese-based word + *mōsu* forms, serves as a deferential form for *suru:*

- 後ほどお知らせ申し上げます。 *Nochi hodo o-shirase mōshi-agemasu.* We shall notify you later on.
- ご協力をお願い申し上げます。 *Go-kyōryoku wo o-negai mōshi-agemasu.* I beg your kind co-operation.
- では、ご案内申しましょう。 *De wa, go-annai mōshimashō.* Well, then, let me show you around.

motte 以て　連語 phrase

A. 「持つ」の連用形＋接続助詞「て」の音便で、上を受けて調子を強める *"Motsu" no ren'yōkei + setsuzoku-joshi "-te" no onbin de, ue wo ukete chōshi wo tsuyomeru* Euphonic adaptation of Base 2 of the verb *motsu* and the conjunctive particle *-te* (used to be *mochite*), strengthens the tone in view of what has preceded:

- どうした理由か、今もって私にも分からない。 *Dōshita riyū ka, ima motte watashi ni mo wakaranai.* For what reason, to this day I can't (for the life of me) understand.

NOTE. The *motte* of the following phrases is an intensifier:

- 今以て *ima motte* even yet; 前以て *mae motte* beforehand; 全く以て *mattaku motte* in reality; 先ず以て *mazu motte* first and foremost.

B. 「をもって」の形で *"Wo motte" no katachi de* In *wo motte* form:

1. 理由・原因を示す *Riyū • gen'in wo shimesu* Denotes cause or reason:

- 天才をもって世間に聞こえが高い。 *Tensai wo motte seken ni kikoe ga takai.* He is known worldwide for his genius.
- 豪勇をもって鳴る *gōyū wo motte naru* be known for valor
- 雨降りをもって中止する。 *Ame-furi wo motte chūshi suru.* We will call it off because of the rain.

2. 手段・道具・方法を示す *Shudan • dōgu • hōhō wo shimesu* Denotes means, tools used, method, etc.:

- 書面をもってご返事します。 *Shomen wo motte go-henji shimasu.* I shall reply in writing.
- 毒をもって毒を制する。 *Doku wo motte doku wo sei-suru.* Set a thief to catch a thief.

→ *de*[3]

NOTE. でもって *de motte* is a stylish alternative for で *de*.

-muke, -muki 向け、向き 接尾語として as suffixes

A. 向け *muke*

送り先や対象を表す語 *Okuri-saki ya taishō wo arawasu go* Word designating a destination or a target of action:

- 中国向けの輸出 *Chūgoku-muke no yushutsu* exports to China 老人向けの放送 *rōjin-muke no hosō* broadcast aimed at the elderly.

NOTE. Some compounds using *-muke:*

- 顔向けが出来ない *kao-muke ga dekinai* can't face people; 仕向地 *shi-mukechi* destination; 手向け *ta-muke* (religious) offering.

B. 向き *muki*

1. ある方向に向いていること *Aru hōkō ni muite iru koto* Facing . . .

- 前向きに腰掛けていた。 *Mae-muki ni koshi-kakete ita.* They sat facing forward.

2. ある事柄・種類に適合すること *Aru koto-gara • shurui ni teki-gō suru koto* Suited to a particular category:

- 子供向きの本 *kodomo-muki no hon* books suited to children.

NOTE. Some compounds using *-muki:*

1. 向いている方向、進んでいく方向 *Muite iru hōkō, susunde iku hōkō* Direction in which one is facing or proceeding:

- 仰向き *ao-muki* (also *ao-muke*) supine; うつ向き *utsu-muki, utsu-muke* prone; 左向き *hidari-muki* facing left; 東向き *higashi-muki* facing east; 後ろ向き *ushiro-muki* looking backwards; 横向き *yoko-muki* facing sideways.

2. 適している・合っている *Teki shite iru • atte iru* Suited to . . . :

- 誂え向き *atsurae-muki* ideal; 万人向き *bannin-muki* meeting all tastes; 冬向き *fuyu-muki* for winter use; 当世向き *tōsei-muki* suited to people of present day; 若向き *waka-muki* suited to the young.

3. 色々 *Iro-iro* Miscellaneous:

- 奥向き *oku-muki* domestic affairs; 表向き *omote-muki* open, formal, ostensible; 風向き *kaza-muki* wind direction, situation, humor; 勝手向き *katte-muki* financial circumstances; 暮らし向き *kurashi-muki* financial circumstances; 勤め向き *tsutome-muki,* 用向き *yō-muki* one's business; 見向きもしない *mi-muki mo shinai* not even look towards; 直向きに生きる *hita-muki ni ikiru* live intently; 一向きに励む *hito-muki ni hagemu* strive might and main; 役向き *yaku-muki* nature of one's office.

N

-n ん 「ぬ」「む」「の」の略 contraction for *-nu, -mu, no*

1. 「ぬ」の変化で、打ち消しの助動詞 *"-nu" no henka de, uchi-keshi no jodōshi* Corruption of *-nu,* serves as a negative auxiliary:

- いいえ、分かりません。 *Iie, wakarimasen.* No, I don't know.

2. 「む」の変化で、推量の助動詞 *"-mu" no henka de, suiryō no jōdōshi* Corruption of *-mu,* serves as a conjectural auxiliary (archaic):

- そうならんと願う。 *Sō naran to negau.* May it come to pass!

3. 「の」の変化で、格助詞 *"No" no henka de, kaku-joshi* Corruption of *no,* serves as a case particle:

- ぼくんとこにはない。 *Bokun toko ni wa nai. (Boku no tokoro ni wa nai.)* I don't have one (at home).
- 試験は今日なんだ。 *Shiken wa kyō nan da.* The exam is today (I tell you).

na[1] な 終助詞 final particle

1. 動詞の終止形に付いて、禁止を表す *Dōshi no shūshikei ni tsuite, kinshi wo arawasu* With Base 3 of verbs, expresses prohibition:

- ドアをばたんと閉めるな。 *Doa wo batan-to shimeru na!* Don't slam the door!

2. 動詞の連用形に付いて、気軽な感じの命令を表す *Dōshi no ren'yōkei ni tsuite, kigaru na kanji no meirei wo arawasu* With Base 2 of verbs, expresses an offhand sort of command:

- そんなこと止めな。 *Sonna koto yame na!* Stop it! (men's speech)

3. 「ちょうだい」「いらっしゃい」「ください」「なさい」に付いて、命令の調子を和らげる *"Chōdai", "irasshai", "kudasai", "nasai" ni tsuite, meirei no chōshi wo yawarageru* Added to *chōdai, irasshai, kudasai,* and *nasai,* softens the tone of command:

- ちょっとこちらへいらっしゃいな。 *Chotto kochira e irasshai na.* Would you come here a moment, please?

4. 感動を表す *Kandō wo arawasu* Expresses emotion:

- うまく出来るな。 *Umaku dekiru na!* Isn't he good (at it)!

5. 念を押す気持ちを表す *Nen wo osu kimochi wo arawasu* Expresses feeling of making sure:

- 間違っていると思うな。 *Machigatte iru to omou na?* I think it is wrong, don't you?

na² な 間投助詞 (*kantō-joshi*) interjectional particle
言葉の切れ目に付けて、調子を整える *Kotoba no kire-me ni tsukete, chōshi wo totonoeru* Placed at junctures in the sentence, adjusts the tone:

- 貸してくれたあの本な、なかなか面白い。 *Kashite kureta ano hon na, naka-naka omoshiroi.* That book you lent me, now, it's really good.

NOTE. For *ka na* → *kana*[1,2].

na³ な
形容動詞の連体形 *keiyōdōshi no rentaikei* Base 4 of adjectival nouns:

- 海が穏やかなので泳ぎに行く。 *Umi ga odayaka na no de oyogi ni iku.* The sea is calm, so I am going for a swim.

NOTE. For the theory of adjectival nouns, their conjugation and usage, see under *keiyōdōshi.*

na⁴ な 「には」の略 contraction of *ni wa*
The etymology is doubtful, and the word is now found in only a few phrases:

- 朝な朝な *asa-na asa-na (asa-na sa-na)* morning after morning; 朝な夕な *asa-na yū-na* morning and evening, all the time; 夜な夜な *yo-na yo-na* night after night; 病院を夜な夜な抜け出して飲み歩いているとか . . . *byōin wo yo-na yo-na nukedashite nomi aruite iru to ka . . .* (Rumor has it that) he has been slipping out of the hospital night after night and painting the town red. . .

na⁵ な
Traces of a Nara era case particle meaning "of" are still found in some words:

- まなかい (目交い) before one's eyes; まなこ (目の子) pupil of eye; みなくち (水口) point where water enters a ricefield; みなもと (源) source; みなそこ (水底) bottom (of water); たなごころ (掌) palm of hand.

nā¹ なあ 終助詞 final particle
1. 感動・願望の気持ちを表す *Kandō • ganbō no kimochi wo arawasu* Expresses a sense of emotion or wish:

- 今週は変な天気だなあ。 *Konshū wa hen na tenki da nā!* What strange weather we are having this week!
- 車があったらなあ。 *Kuruma ga attara nā!* How I wish I had a car!

2. 念を押す気持ちを表す *Nen wo osu kimochi wo arawasu* Expresses a sense of making sure:

- 行き過ぎのようだなあ。 *Yuki-sugi no yō da nā!* That's going too far, don't you think?

nā[2] なあ 間投助詞 interjectional particle

言葉の切れ目に付けて、調子を整える *Kotoba no kire-me ni tsukete, chōshi wo totonoeru* Placed at junctures in the sentence, adjusts the tone:

- このお寺はなあ、昔からここにあったものだ。 *Kono o-tera wa nā, mukashi kara koko ni atta mono da.* This temple, now, has been on this site since ancient times.

nado 等 (*nazo, nanzo, nando*) 副助詞 adverbial particle

1. 例示して、他に同類のものがある意を表す *Reiji shite, hoka ni dōrui no mono ga aru i wo arawasu* Gives an example to suggest that other similar cases exist:

- 動物園で象、虎、猿などを見た。 *Dōbutsu-en de zō, tora, saru nado wo mita.* At the zoo we saw elephants, tigers, monkeys, and so on.

2. ぼかして軟らかく述べる *Bokashite yawarakaku noberu* Softens the diction by being less precise:

- 病気見舞には、お花などがいいでしょう。 *Byōki mimai ni wa, o-hana nado ga ii deshō.* When visiting the sick, something like flowers make a nice present.

3. 自分にとって謙譲を、他人にとって軽べつを表す *Jibun ni totte kenjō wo, tanin ni totte keibetsu wo arawasu* Expresses deference in one's own case, contempt in the case of others:

- そんな高価なものは、私などに勿体ない。 *Sonna kōka na mono wa, watashi nado ni mottai nai.* Such an expensive item is too good for the likes of me.
- あいつなどが出来るもんか。 *Aitsu nado ga dekiru mon ka?* He just isn't up to it.

NOTE. *Nado* is one of the particles that may come between a verb and its auxiliary:

- 別に疲れてなどいない。 *Betsu ni tsukarete nado inai.* I'm not particularly tired.

→ *-tō*[1]

-nagara (乍)　接続助詞　conjunctive particle
動詞の連用形、形容詞の終止形、形容動詞の語幹に付く *Dōshi no ren'-yōkei, keiyōshi no shūshikei, keiyōdōshi no gokan ni tsuku* Is added to Base 2 of verbs, to Base 3 of adjectives, and to stem of adjectival nouns.

1. 動作の平行を表す *Dōsa no heikō wo arawasu* Denotes simultaneous actions:

- お茶を飲みながらおしゃべりをした。 *O-cha wo nomi-nagara o-shaberi wo shita.* We had a chat over a cup of tea.
- 歌を歌いながら仕事をする。 *Uta wo utai-nagara shigoto wo suru.* They sing at their work.

2. 食い違う動作・状態を表す *Kui-chigau dōsa • jōtai wo arawasu* Denotes incompatible actions or states:

- 悪いと知っていながら、止められない。 *Warui to shitte i-nagara, yamerarenai.* Even though I know it is wrong, I can't give it up.
- 近くに住みながら互いに口もきかなかった。 *Chikaku ni sumi-nagara tagai ni kuchi mo kikanakatta.* Even though they were neighbours, they never spoke to each other.
- 貧しいながら幸福だ。 *Mazushii-nagara kōfuku da.* They are poor but happy.
- 残念ながら失敗した。 *Zannen-nagara shippai shita.* Unfortunately, he failed.

3. 「そのまま」の意味を表す *"Sono mama" no imi wo arawasu* Expresses the idea of "unchanged", "inherently":

- 生まれながらの盲人 *umare-nagara no mōjin* one blind from birth.

4. 「共に」「そっくり全部」の意味を表す *"Tomo ni", "sokkuri zenbu" no imi wo arawasu* Expresses the idea of "together", "in its entirety":

- 兄弟三人ながら天才だ。 *Kyōdai sannin-nagara tensai da.* All three brothers are geniuses.
- りんごを皮ながら食べる。 *Ringo wo kawa-nagara taberu.* He eats apples peel and all.

→ *-goto.*

NOTE. *Nagara* will sometimes be found attached to nominals:

- 陰ながら *kage-nagara* secretly; 昔ながらの建物 *mukashi-nagara no tatemono* building that has remained unchanged; 失礼ながら *shitsu-rei-nagara* pardon me but . . . ; 余所ながら *yoso-nagara* from a distance, casually: 我ながら *warenagara* even if it is I that did it.

nai 無い　(補助)形容詞　(complementary) adjective
The conjugation is as follows: 1. *nakaro* 2. *nakatt* (なかっ)、*naku* 3. *nai* 4. *nai* 5. *nakereba* 6. —.

1. 存在を否定する意を表す *Sonzai wo hitei suru i wo arawasu* Negates existence:

- お金がないから困る。 *O-kane ga nai kara komaru.* I am hard up for cash.
- 根拠のないことを言いふらすな。 *Konkyo no nai koto wo ii-furasu na.* Don't spread false rumors.

2. 形容詞・形容動詞の連用形に付いて、打ち消しの意を表す *Keiyōshi・keiyōdōshi no ren'yōkei ni tsuite, uchi-keshi no i wo arawasu* Added to Base 2 of adjectives and adjectival nouns, expresses negation:

- 重くない方を頂きます。 *Omoku nai hō wo itadakimasu.* I'll take the lighter one.
- 本当でないかも知れません。 *Hontō de nai ka mo shiremasen.* Perhaps it isn't true.

NOTE. The negative form of the verb 有る・在る is, strange to say, the adjective *nai*. The only difference in form is that the auxiliary verb *-nai* has an extra Base 2 form, *-naide*. The reasons for the distinction become apparent when we compare:

- 書か—ない Base 1 of *kaku* + auxiliary verb *-nai*.
- よく—ない Base 2 of *yoi* + complementary adjective *nai*.
- 書か—ない nothing may be inserted between Base 1 and the auxiliary.
- よくはない particles like *wa, mo,* etc. may be inserted.
- 書かない＝書かぬ Here, the *-nai* may be changed to *-nu*.
- よくない Here, such a change is impossible.

NOTE. The adjectives *nai* and *yoi* take the suffix *-sa* before adding *-sō da*[1]*:*

- 「馬鹿だな」と情けなさそうに言った。 *"Baka da na" to nasake-nasa-sō ni itta.* "You stupid!" he said heartlessly:
- 見込はなさそうだ。 *Mi-komi wa nasa-sō da.* There seems to be little likelihood.

NOTE. The literary negative *aranu* has carried over in stock phrases:

- あらぬ方を見る *aranu kata wo miru* look off into the distance.
- あらぬことを想像する *aranu koto wo sōzō suru* think of something outlandish.
- あらぬ噂を立てられる *aranu uwasa wo taterareru* be the object of false rumor.

NOTE. The construction "Base 2 of transitive verb + *-te* + *aru*" becomes "*-te nai*" in the negative:

- 窓はまだ閉めてない。 *Mado wa mada shimete nai.* The windows haven't been closed yet.

-nai ない　助動詞　auxiliary verb

The conjugation is as follows: 1. *nakaro* 2. *nakatt* (なかっ)、*naku, naide* 4. *nai* 3. *nai* 5. *nakere* 6. —. This *-nai*, together with *-tai* and *-rashii,* conjugates like an adjective, and in modern Japanese, has no imperative form.

動詞の未然形に付いて、打ち消しを表す *Dōshi no mizenkei ni tsuite, uchi-keshi wo arawasu* Added to Base 1 of verbs, expresses negation:

- 買わないことに決めた。 *Kawanai koto ni kimeta.* I've decided not to buy it.
- 読まないとだめですよ。 *Yomanai to dame desu yo.* You must read it.
- 今日は来ないだろう。 *Kyō wa konai darō.* He won't come today.

NOTE. 愛する *ai suru* (to love) may have either 愛しない or 愛さない in modern Japanese. 信ずる *shin-zuru* (to believe) has only 信じない。 (→ *su*)

NOTE. A few words like *kudaranai, tamaranai, tsumaranai,* although in derivation negative verbs, are now treated only as adjectives:

- くだらないことを言っている。 *Kudaranai koto wo itte iru.* He is talking nonsense.
- 読書がつまらなくなってきた。 *Dokusho ga tsumaranaku natte kita.* I have got tired of reading.

NOTE. Some idioms using the auxiliary *-nai:*

- 英国へ行かない代わりにフランスへ行った。 *Eikoku e ikanai kawari ni Furansu e itta.* Instead of going to England he went to France.
- 雨が降らない前に帰りたい。 *Ame ga furanai mae ni kaeritai.* I should like to go home before it starts to rain.

-nai- 内　接頭語・接尾語　prefix, suffix

- 内外の *nai-gai no* internal and external; 校内暴力 *kō-nai bōryoku* violence in schools.

NOTE. Irregular readings:

- 内裏 *dai-ri* Imperial Palace; 入内 *ju-dai* bride entering Imperial Court; 海内 *kai-dai,* interior, whole country; 境内 *kei-dai* shrine precincts; 参内 *san-dai* proceeding to Imperial Palace; 宇内 *u-dai* whole world.

NOTE. The *kun* reading *uchi* is also common:

- 内弁慶 *uchi-Benkei* lion at home but a mouse abroad; 内祝い *uchi-iwai* family celebration; 幕内 *maku-uchi* top division of sumo; 身内 *mi-uchi* relatives, one's men.

-naide ～ -nakute

The standard form is *-nakute,* Base 2 + particle *-te,* but in modern times the form *-naide* has come into use.

- 帽子を被らないで出掛けた。 *Bōshi wo kaburanaide dekaketa.* He went out bareheaded. (also *kaburazu ni*)
- 学校に行かないで家にいた。 *Gakkō ni ikanaide ie ni ita.* Instead of going to school he stayed at home. (also *ikazu ni*)
- 御飯を食べないで寝てしまった。 *Gohan wo tabenaide nete shimatta.* He went to bed without having his meal. (also *tabezu ni*)

NOTE. Only *-naide* may be used in the case of commands and prohibitions:

- まだ発表しないでください。 *Mada happyō shinaide kudasai.* Please don't announce it yet.
- そんな本を読まないでほしい。 *Sonna hon wo yomanaide hoshii.* I don't want you to read books of that sort.

NOTE. In other cases, the choice is open:

- 掃除をしなくてもいい。掃除をしないでもいい。 *Sōji wo shinakute • shinaide mo ii.* You don't have to do the cleaning.
- 借りれば買わなくても済む。借りれば買わないでも済む。 *Karireba kawanakute • kawanaide mo sumu.* Borrow one and you won't need to buy it.
- 御飯が食べられなくて困る。御飯が食べられないで困る。 *Gohan ga taberarenakute • taberarenaide komaru.* I'm worried because I can't eat.

NOTE. Use of the five Bases:

1. 雨はもう降らなかろう。 *Ame wa mō fura-nakarō.* It probably won't rain any more.

NOTE. This form is now replaced by *-nai darō.*

2. どうして行かなかったのですか。 *Dōshite ika-nakatta no desu ka?* Why didn't you go?
3. 行かなくてもよかったからです。 *Ika-nakute mo yokatta kara desu.* Because I didn't have to.
4. もう、たばこを吸わない。 *Mō, tabako wo suwa-nai.* I don't smoke any longer.
5. お酒を飲まない人もあります。 *O-sake wo noma-nai hito mo arimasu.* There are some non-drinkers, too.
6. 急がなければ間に合わない。 *Isoga-nakereba ma ni awanai.* If you don't hurry you'll be late.

naka 中　形式名詞として as a formal noun

物事の進行している最中 *Monogoto no shinkō shite iru saichū* "In the midst of":

- お忙しい中を済みません。 *O-isogashii naka wo sumimasen.* Pardon my interrupting your work.
- 都市ガスのタンクが爆発する中をくぐり抜けて、ようやく長崎駅前にたどりついた。 *Toshi-gasu no tanku ga bakuhatsu suru naka wo kuguri-nukete, yōyaku Nagasaki-eki mae ni tadori-tsuita.* Picking my way among the exploding city gas tanks, at long last I reached the entrance to Nagasaki Station.

naku 無く (補助) 形容詞「ない」の連用形 Base 2 of (supplementary) adjective *nai*

This is found in many useful phrases:

- どことなく *doko to naku* somehow; 端なくも *hashi naku mo* unexpectedly; ほどなく *hodo naku* shortly; 遺憾なく *ikan naku* satisfactorily; 幾許もなく *ikubaku mo naku* shortly; いつとなく *itsu to naku* before one knows, at any time; 過不及なく *ka-fukyū naku* moderately; 心置きなく *kokoro-oki naku* without reserve; 隈なく *kuma naku* all over; 間もなく *ma mo naku* shortly; 万遍なく *man-ben naku* thoroughly, without exception; 漏れなく *more-naku* without omission; なにくれとなく *nani-kure to naku* in various ways; 難なく *nan-naku* easily; 何となく *nan to naku* somehow; 臆面もなく *okumen mo naku* audaciously; 性懲りもなく *shōkori mo naku* without contrition; しょうことなく *shō-koto naku* reluctantly; それとなく *sore to naku* indirectly; 手もなく *te mo naku* easily; やむなく *yamu naku* against one's will; 容赦なく *yōsha naku* without mercy; 余念なく *yonen naku* intently; 我にもなく *ware ni mo naku* unconsciously.

-nami[1] 並(み) 接尾語 suffix

名詞に付く *Meishi ni tsuku* Is added to nouns.

1. 普通の程度を示す *Futsū no teido wo shimesu* Denotes the average or ordinary:

- 人並み以上の努力をしている。 *Hito-nami ijō no doryoku wo shite iru.* He is making extraordinary efforts.
- 世間並に暮らしている。 *Seken-nami ni kurashite iru.* They make a decent living.

2.「…ごとに」という意味を添える "*. . . -Goto ni" to iu imi wo soeru* Adds the meaning "each and every . . . ":

- 近所の家は軒並み空き巣にやられた。 *Kinjo no ie wa noki-nami akisu ni yarareta.* Every single house in the neighbourhood was broken into.

NOTE. Compounds with 並(み) :

• 足並み *ashi-nami* pace, step; 歯並み *ha-nami* alignment of teeth; 羽並み *ha-nami* plumage; 日並み *hi-nami* sequence of days; 等し並み *hitoshi-nami* equality; 穂並み *ho-nami* waving ears (of rice); 十人並み *jūnin-nami* mediocrity; 町並み *machi-nami* row of houses; 人間並み *ningen-nami* common run of men; 手並み *te-nami* skill; 年並み *toshi-nami* ordinary year; 月並み *tsuki-nami* monthly, conventional; 常並み *tsune-nami* commonplace; 屋並み・家並み *ya-nami* • *ie-nami* row of houses; 山並み *yama-nami* mountain range.

-nami[2] 波・浪 接尾語 suffix

• 徒波 *ada-nami* noisy waves; 荒波 *ara-nami* high waves; 土用波 *doyō-nami* high midsummer waves; 人波 *hito-nami* surge of people; 穂波 *ho-nami* waving ears (of rice); 磯波 *iso-nami* surf; 小波 *ko-nami*, *saza-nami* ripples; 女波 *me-nami* smaller wave; 男波 *o-nami* larger wave; 大波 *oo-nami* billow; 細波 *saza-nami* • *sasara-nami* • *sazare-nami* wavelets; 三角波 *sankaku-nami* cross-waves; 白波 *shira-nami* foam; 高波 *taka-nami* high sea; 年波 *toshi-nami* old age; 縦波 *tate-nami* longitudinal wave; 津波 *tsu-nami* tidal wave; 横波 *yoko-nami* side wave; transverse wave; 夕波 *yūnami* evening waves.

nani, nan 何 代名詞 pronoun

Nani optionally (in speech, usually) contracts to *nan-* before words beginning with d, t, n; occasionally also before words beginning with s, z, r:

• 何ですか。 *Nan desu ka?* What is it?

• 何と言いますか。 *Nan to iimasu ka?* What is it called?

• 何の話ですか。 *Nan no hanashi desu ka?* What are you talking about?

NOTE. *Nani* is used also when the meaning is "Which?":

• 何大学。 *Nani-daigaku?* Which university?; 何新聞。 *Nani-shinbun?* Which newspaper?; 何町。 *Nani-machi?* Which town?; 何色。 *Nani-iro?* What color?;

• 何人 (i) *Nani-jin?* What nationality? (ii) *nani-bito* anyone, someone (iii) *Nan-nin?* How many persons?

NOTE. *Nani* is sometimes used adverbially, as in:

• 何不自由なく暮らしている。 *Nani fu-jiyū naku kurashite iru.* He leads a comfortable life.

nani (nāni) な(あ)に 感動的に as an interjection

1. 問い返す時のことば *Toi-kaesu toki no kotoba* Serves to reverse a question:

- なあに、それでいいの。 *Nāni, sore de ii no?* You mean to say it's all right?

2. 意に介しない気持ちを表す *I ni kai shinai kimochi wo arawasu* Denotes unconcern:

- なあに、かまうもんか。 *Nāni, kamau mon ka?* What the hell do I care?

nan da なんだ 連語 phrase

助動詞「だ」の連体形＋助詞「の」＋助動詞「だ」 *Jodōshi "da" no rentaikei + joshi "no" + jodōshi "da"* Base 4 of the auxiliary verb *da* + the particle *no* + the auxiliary verb *da*.

Colloquial form of *na no da (na no desu)*, derives from the fact that Base 4 of the auxiliary *da* is used only before *no, node* and *noni* (see under *-da*[1] 4). The expression denotes strong assertion:

- これこそが問題なんだ。 *Kore koso ga mondai nan da.* This is just where the trouble is. (In women's speech, *na no yo, na no ne* are common.)

nan ka 何か 副助詞 adverbial particle

1. 同じような物事を幾つか並べて示す *Onaji yō na monogoto wo ikutsu ka narabete shimesu* Is used at the end of a list of similar items:

- テレビとかラジオ何かでよくやっている。 *Terebi to ka rajio nan ka de yoku yatte iru.* It is a regular feature of TV, radio, etc.

2. 表現を和らげる *Hyōgen wo yawarageru* Softens the diction:

- 何か嬉しそうな顔だ。 *Nan ka ureshisō na kao da.* He looks somewhat pleased.

3. 謙遜や軽べつを表す *Kenson ya keibetsu wo arawasu* Expresses deference (in one's own case) or contempt (in the case of others):

- 僕なんかには分からない。 *Boku nan ka ni wa wakaranai.* It is beyond the likes of me.
- 君の泣き言なんか聞きたくない。 *Kimi no naki-goto nan ka kikitaku nai!* I don't want to hear any of your whimpering!

4. 打ち消しの気持ちを強める *Uchikeshi no kimochi wo tsuyomeru* Strengthens the sense of negation:

- そんなことなんか言っていない。 *Sonna koto nan ka itte inai!* I never said such a thing!

NOTE. This *nan ka* is one of the particles that may come between a verb and its auxiliary:

- 威張ってなんかいないよ。 *Ibatte nan ka inai yo!* Don't think I am giving myself airs!

nante なんて　副助詞　adverbial particle

1. 意外な気持ちを表す *Igai na kimochi wo arawasu* Expresses surprise:

• 千円もするなんておかしい。 *Sen'en mo suru nante okashii.* It's ridiculous (to think) that it should cost as much as ¥1000.

2. 軽視する気持ちを表す *Keishi suru kimochi wo arawasu* Denotes an air of nonchalance:

• 宿題なんて嫌だ。 *Shukudai nante iya da!* I hate such things as homework!

NOTE. This *nante* is one of the particles that may come between a verb and its auxiliary:

• 真に受けてなんていないよ。 *Ma ni ukete nante inai yo!* Do you think I would fall for such a story?

-naosu 直す　接尾語　suffix verb

動詞の連用形に付いて、改めてもう一度する *Dōshi no ren'yōkei ni tsuite, aratamete mō ichi-do suru* Added to Base 2 of verbs, expresses the idea off repetition, usually with some improvement:

• 出直す *de-naosu* make a fresh start; 言い直す *ii-naosu* rephrase; 書き直す *kaki-naosu* rewrite; 考え直す *kangae-naosu* reconsider; 聞き直す *kiki-naosu* ask again; 見直す *mi-naosu* think better of, reconsider; 思い直す *omoi-naosu* reconsider; し直す *shi-naosu* start afresh, brush up; やり直す *yari-naosu* start afresh, brush up; 染め直す *some-naosu* redye; 建て直す *tate-naosu* rebuild; 焼き直す *yaki-naosu* rebake, reprint, rehash.

nara なら　助動詞　auxiliary verb

断定の助動詞「だ」の仮定形 *Dantei no jodōshi "da" no kateikei* Base 5 (conditional) of the auxiliary of assertion *da*.

体言またはある種の助詞、動詞・形容詞・助動詞の終止形に付いて、条件の意を表す *Taigen mata wa aru shu no joshi, dōshi • keiyōshi • jodōshi no shūshikei ni tsuite, jōken no i wo arawasu* With nominals and some kinds of particles, and with Base 3 of verbs, adjectives and auxiliaries, expresses the idea of condition:

• 行くなら早く行きなさい。 *Iku nara hayaku iki nasai.* If you are going, go early.

• 眠いならもう寝てもいい。 *Nemui nara mō nete mo ii.* If you are sleepy, you may go to bed now.

• 私ならそうはしないのだが。 *Watashi nara sō wa shinai no da ga.* I wouldn't do such a thing. (I wouldn't do it that way.)

• お出になりますなら、早めにお出なさい *Oide ni narimasu nara,*

hayame ni oide nasai. If you intend to come, please come a little early.

- 彼が合格したなら、パーティーを開こう。 *Kare ga gōgaku shita nara, pātii wo hirakō.* If he has passed, let's have a party.
- 言えぬなら言えぬと言えよ。 *Ienu nara ienu to ie yo.* If it's something you can't say, just let us know.

NOTE. The auxiliaries to which *nara* may be added are:

1. Verb-type conjugation *reru, rareru, seru,* and *saseru.*
2. Adjective-type conjugation *nai, tai,* and *rashii.*
3. Special conjugation such as *ta, nu,* and *masu* (but not *desu*).

NOTE. The particles to which *nara* may be added are: *bakari, dake, kurai, hodo, kara, made, nado, no,* and *yara.*

NOTE. While the conjunctive particle *-ba* is necessary with the conditional of other verbs and adjectives, it is optional with *nara:*

- お暇なら(ば)いらしてください。 *O-hima nara(ba) irashite kudasai.* Please come if you have the time.

NOTE. The subject of the verb with *nara* is usually not the first person:

- そんなことを言うなら、僕にも言い分がある。 *Sonna koto wo iu nara, boku ni mo ii-bun ga aru.* If you talk like that, I, too, will have my say.
- 私が行けば、鈴木さんもいらっしゃいますか。 *Watashi ga ikeba, Suzuki-san mo irasshaimasu ka?* If I go, will you come, too, Mr. Suzuki? (not: *Watashi ga iku nara,...*)

NOTE. Placed after a noun, *nara* singles this out:

- 花なら桜。 *Hana nara, sakura.* The cherry blossom reigns supreme among flowers.
- 父なら、今出掛けたばかりです。 *Chichi nara, ima dekaketa bakari desu.* If it's my father you are looking for, he has just gone out.

nara de wa ならでは　連語　phrase

指定の助動詞「なり」の未然形に、打ち消しの接続助詞「で」＋係助詞「は」 *Shitei no jodōshi "nari" no mizenkei ni, uchikeshi no setsuzoku-joshi "de" + kei-joshi "wa"* Base 1 of the assertive auxiliary *nari* + the negative conjunctive particle *-de* + the bound particle *wa:*

- 専門家ならでは出来ない仕事だ。 *Senmonka nara de wa dekinai shigoto da.* It is a job that only an expert could do (a job for an expert).
- 先生ならではの気遣いだ。 *Sensei nara de wa no kizukai da.* Nobody but a teacher could show such concern.

NOTE. *Nara de wa* corresponds with the modern *de* + *nakute* + *wa.*

-nareru 慣れる・馴れる 接尾語 suffix verb

動詞の連用形・名詞に付いて *dōshi no ren'yōkei • meishi ni tsuite* Added to Base 2 of verbs and to nouns.

1. 熟達する *Jukutatsu suru* Become skillful;

• 漢字も書き慣れてきた。 *Kanji mo kaki-narete kita.* I have got used to writing characters, too.

2. 程よくなる *Hodo-yoku naru* Become moderate:

• 履き慣れた靴を履いていく。 *Haki-nareta kutsu wo haite iku.* I'll go in the shoes I'm used to wearing.

NOTE. For the ideographs: 慣れる、become accustomed to, through repetition; 馴れる、become domesticated.

• 通い慣れた道 *kayoi-nareta michi* familiar road; 聞き慣れた声 *kiki-nareta koe* familiar voice; 住み慣れた土地 *sumi-nareta tochi* place where one has lived long; 使い慣れた道具 *tsukai-nareta dōgu* tools one is used to; 場慣れた *ba-nareta* "at home"; 世慣れた人 *yo-nareta hito* man of the world; 人馴れのしない鳥 *hito-nare no shinai tori* wild birds; 人馴れした態度 *hito-nare shita taido* sociable manner; 口慣れる *kuchi-nareru* (i) be in habit of saying; (ii) get used to taste of; 目慣れる *me-nareru* get used to seeing; 耳慣れる *mimi-nareru* get used to hearing; 手慣れる *te-nareru* (i) get used to using; (ii) become good at.

nari[1] なり 接続助詞 conjunctive particle

終止形に付く *Shūshikei ni tsuku* Is added to Base 3.

1. 一つの動作が成立すると同時に、次の動作が行なわれるという意味を表す *Hitotsu no dōsa ga seiritsu suru to dōji ni, tsugi no dōsa ga okonawareru to iu imi wo arawasu* Denotes that one action follows immediately on completion of the previous one:

• 家に鞄を置くなり、遊びに飛び出す。 *Ie ni kaban wo oku nari, asobi ni tobi-dasu.* No sooner has he dropped his bag in home than he is out playing.

2.「たなり」の形で、「そのままの状態で」という意味を表す *"-Ta nari" no katachi de, "sono mama no jōtai de" to iu imi wo arawasu* In *-ta nari* form, expresses the idea of "in that state":

• 本を机の上に置いたなり、うたた寝をしている。 *Hon wo tsukue no ue ni oita nari, utata-ne wo shite iru.* He is taking a nap, with his books on the desk.

3. 並列した中から一つを選ぶ意味を表す *Heiretsu shita naka kara hitotsu wo erabu imi wo arawasu* Indicates a choice from among a list:

• 煮て食うなり、焼いて食うなり、したいようにしろ。 *Nite kuu nari,*

yaite kuu nari, shitai yō ni shiro. Do as you please with it.

4. 「なりと」「なりとも」の形で、最小の限度を示す *"Nari to", "nari to mo" no katachi de, saishō no gendo wo shimesu* In *nari to, nari to mo* forms, denotes the minimum:

- 私になりと相談してもらえたらいいな。 *Watashi ni nari to sōdan shite moraetara ii na.* I wish they would consult the likes of me.

NOTE. *Doko nari to mo = doko de arō to mo = doko de mo* (anywhere). Also, *itsu nari to mo = itsu de arō to mo = itsu de mo* (any time).

nari² なり 接尾語 suffix

体言に付いて、その形・状態・様子であることを示す *Taigen ni tsuite, sono katachi • jōtai • yōsu de aru koto wo shimesu* Attached to nominals, denotes the shape, condition, or appearance:

- 妹なりの考え方だ。 *Imōto-nari no kangae-kata da.* It is just like my sister to think like that.
- 日本の場合、それにはそれなりの理由が幾つかある。 *Nippon no baai, sore ni wa sore-nari no riyū ga ikutsu ka aru.* In Japan's case, there are several particular reasons for that.

nari³ なり 体言 nominal

1. 体付きを示す *Karada-tsuki wo shimesu* Denotes bodily build:

- 大きななりをしている。 *Ooki na nari wo shite iru.* He is of large build.

2. 服装・格好を示す *Fukusō • kakkō wo shimesu* Denotes dress or appearance:

- そんななりで出掛けると、笑われるよ。 *Sonna nari de dekakeru to, warawareru yo.* If you go out dressed like that, people will laugh at you.

nari⁴ 生り・成り 体言 nominal

実のなること、結果が出ること *Mi no naru koto, kekka ga deru koto* Ripening of fruits, appearing of results:

- 今年は梨の生りが悪い。 *Kotoshi wa nashi no nari ga warui.* Pears have done poorly this year.

nari⁵ 也 断定の助動詞（古） auxiliary of assertion (classical) The conjugation is as follows: 1. *nara* 2. *nari, ni* 3. *nari* 4. *naru* 5. *nare* 6. —.

- 世には心得ぬこと多きなり。 *Yo ni wa kokoro-enu koto ooki nari.* There are a lot of things in this world that are hard to understand.

- 賢が子賢ならず。 *Ken ga ko ken narazu.* The son of a wise man is not necessarily wise.
- 顔回なる者ありき。 *Gankai naru mono ariki.* There was a man called Gankai.

NOTE. This is the *nari* used in *soroban* exercises as a punctuator.

NOTE. Almost indistinguishable from the above is the *nari* used with adjectival nouns. It differs in form in that it has an imperative, *nare*:

- あはれなり *aware nari* be pitiful; かたくななり *katakuna nari* be stubborn; きよらなり *kiyora nari* be beautiful; せちなり *sechi nari* be urgent; しづかに *shizuka ni* quietly; あきらかに *akiraka ni* clearly.

naru なる 補助動詞 supplementary verb

「お・ご…になる」の形で、敬意を表す *"O-・go-. . . ni naru" no katachi de, keii wo arawasu* In *o-・go-* form, expresses respect:

- お分かりになりましたか。 *O-wakari ni narimashita ka?* Do you understand?
- 三月にご卒業になるでしょう。 *Sangatsu ni go-sotsugyō ni naru deshō.* He will probably graduate in March.

NOTE. The construction ". . . *ni naru*" has very many applications:

1. 動詞の終止形＋ことになる *Dōshi no shūshikei + koto ni naru* Base 3 of verbs + *koto ni naru*. . . translates the English future perfect:

- 今年で日本語を三年間習うことになる。 *Kotoshi de Nihongo wo san-nen-kan narau koto ni naru.* This year I shall have studied Japanese for three years.
- また見れば三回見たことになる。 *Mata mireba san-kai mita koto ni naru.* Once more and I shall have seen it three times.

2. 動詞の連体形＋ことになっている *Dōshi no rentaikei + koto ni natte iru* In Base 4 of verbs + *koto ni natte iru* form, denotes the usual procedure:

- 日曜日に教会に行くことになっている。 *Nichiyōbi ni kyōkai ni iku koto ni natte iru.* We are in the habit of going to church on Sundays.

3. 動詞の連体形＋ことになった *Dōshi no rentaikei + koto ni natta* In Base 4 of verbs + *koto ni natta* form, denotes an arranged procedure:

- 四月に入学することになった。 *Shigatsu ni nyūgaku suru koto ni natta.* He is to enter school in April.
- 駅前で会うことになった。 *Eki-mae de au koto ni natta.* We are to meet in front of the station.

4. 動詞の連体形＋ことにならない *Dōshi no rentaikei + koto ni naranai*

In Base 4 of verbs + *koto ni naranai* form, denotes that the action or state cannot be taken for granted:

- こうしても文章をよくすることにはならない。 *Kōshite mo bunshō wo yoku suru koto ni wa naranai.* It cannot be said that this will improve the style.

5. 動詞の連形体+ようになる *Dōshi no rentaikei + yō ni naru* In Base 4 of verbs + *yō ni naru* form, denotes the start of a habit or condition:

- お酒を飲むようになったのは、最近のことだ。 *O-sake wo nomu yō ni natta no wa, saikin no koto da.* It is only recently that he has taken to drink.

6. 可能動詞+ようになる *Kanō-dōshi + yō ni naru* In a potential verb + *yō ni naru* form, denotes the acquisition of a skill:

- 赤ちゃんがもう歩けるようになった。 *Akachan ga mō arukeru yō ni natta.* The baby has begun to (= become able to) walk.

NOTE. The difference between *ni naru* and *to naru* is so slight that one has to rely on examples; the many stock phrases tend to cloud the issue.

1. Examples of *ni naru:*

- 当てにならない *ate ni naranai* be unreliable; 馬鹿にならない人 *baka ni naranai hito* a man not to be trifled with; 話にならない *hanashi ni naranai* be not worth talking about; 相撲にならない *sumō ni naranai* be no match for; 力になる *chikara ni naru* be of assistance; ちょんになる *chon ni naru* come to an end; 絵になる *e ni naru* make a good picture; 骨になる *hone ni naru* die; いい子になる *ii ko ni naru* take all the credit; 意地になって *iji ni natte* obstinately; 一緒になって *issho ni natte* united; 金になる *kane ni naru* be lucrative; 気になる *ki ni naru* weigh on one's mind; 苦になる *ku ni naru* give trouble; 首になる *kubi ni naru* be fired; 癖になる *kuse ni naru* become a habit; 薬になる *kusuri ni naru* do somebody good; 実になる *mi ni naru* be nutritious; 身二つになる *mi-futatsu ni naru* become a mother; 物になる *mono ni naru* come to something; 無になる *mu ni naru* come to nought; むきになる *muki ni naru* turn serious; 懇ろになる *nengoro ni naru* become intimate with; おちょこになる *o-choko ni naru* be blown inside out (of umbrella, taking shape of *sake* cup); 公になる *ooyake ni naru* come to light; 晒し者になる *sarashi-mono ni naru* be pilloried; お世話になる *o-sewa ni naru* be indebted to; ためになる *tame ni naru* be beneficial, be instructive; 天狗になる *tengu ni naru* become conceited; 虎になる *tora ni naru* get dead drunk; 厄介になる *yakkai ni naru* become dependent on; 人の厄介にならない *hito no yakkai ni naranai* be self-reliant.

2. Examples of *to naru:*

- 仇となる *ada to naru* turn out harmful; 暴風雨となる *bōfū-u to naru* turn into a storm; 白玉楼中の人となる *hakugyokurō-chū no hito to naru* be numbered with the dead (of a literary man); 人となる *hito to naru* attain manhood; 氷となる *koori to naru* turn into ice; 藻屑となる *mo-kuzu to naru* drown (in sea); 勝利となる *shōri to naru* turn into victory; 習性となる *shūsei to naru* become a habit; 土となる *tsuchi to naru* die.

NOTE. Because the *to naru* version is more classical, it will be found in proverbs:

- 後は野となれ、山となれ。 *Ato wa no to nare, yama to nare.* After us, the deluge!
- 塵も積もれば山となる。 *Chiri mo tsumoreba yama to naru.* Many a little makes a mickle.
- 鶏口となるも、牛後となるなかれ。 *Keikō to naru mo, gyūgo to naru nakare.* Better be the head of a dog than the tail of a lion.

NOTE. The *to naru* form is also used to lend dignity:

- こうして夕べとなり、朝となった。 *Kō shite yūbe to nari, asa to natta.* Evening came and morning followed (—the fourth day). (Gen. I, 19)

NOTE. Also found are the phrases *to naru to* and *to nattara:*

- 食い物となると、そうはいかない。 *Kuimono to naru to, sō wa ikanai.* This doesn't hold true in the matter of eating.
- 酒となったら、目がないのですが。 *Sake to nattara, me ga nai no desu ga.* When it comes to *sake,* I just can't resist.

na-sa 無さ　名詞　noun

形容詞「ない」の語幹に、接尾語「さ」、「ないこと」「ない度合い」の意味を表す *Keiyōshi "nai" no gokan ni, setsubigo "-sa", "nai koto", "nai do-ai" no imi wo arawasu* Stem of the adjective *nai* + suffix *-sa,* expresses the idea of lack, or degree of lack:

- 意気地のなさに呆れる。 *Ikuji no na-sa ni akireru.* I am amazed at his lack of gumption.

NOTE: Several compounds involve not this *nai* but the auxiliary *-nai:*

- はかなさ *hakana-sa* transience; いたらなさ *itarana-sa* shortcomings; くだらなさ *kudarana-sa* worthlessness; 分からなさ *wakarana-sa* failure to understand.

nasaru 為さる　動詞　verb

The conjugation is as follows: 1. *nasara, nasaro* 2. *nasari, nasatt* (なさっ)、*nasai* 3. *nasaru* 4. *nasaru* 5. *nasare* 6. *nasare, nasai.*

A.「する」「なす」の敬語 *"Suru", "nasu" no kei-go* Polite equivalent of *suru, nasu:*

- 静かになさい。 *Shizuka ni nasai.* Be quiet.
- お父さんは何をなさいましたか。 *O-tōsan wa nani wo nasaimashita ka?* What did your father do?

B. 補助動詞として、「お・ご＋なさる」の形で、動詞の連用形・漢語に付いて、尊敬の意を表す *Hojo-dōshi to shite, "o-" • "go-" + "nasaru" no katachi de, dōshi no ren'yōkei • Kango ni tsuite, sonkei no i wo arawasu* As a supplementary verb, in *o-/go- + nasaru* form, added to Base 2 of verbs and Chinese words, expresses respect:

- お帰りなさいませ、 *O-kaeri nasaimase!* Welcome home!
- ご心配なさらないでください。 *Go-shinpai nasaranaide kudasai.* Please don't worry.

NOTE. After single Chinese words, the *suru* is retained.

- 隣人を愛する *rinjin wo ai-suru* 隣人を愛しなさい。 *Rinjin wo ai-shinasai.* Love your neighbour.
- 本を訳する *hon wo yaku-suru* 本を訳しなさった。 *Hon wo yaku-shi nasatta.* He translated the book.

NOTE. *Nasari* is used before the auxiliaries *-sō da*[1], *-tagaru* and *-tai,* with the *ni* of purpose, and before a pause.

NOTE. *Nasai* alone, as the imperative, is considered abrupt; the full form is *nasai-mase.*

nasa-sō da なさそうだ 連語 phrase

形容詞「無い」の語幹に、接尾語「さ」に、様態の助動詞「そうだ」 *Keiyōshi "nai" no gokan ni, setsubigo "-sa" ni, yōtai no jodōshi "sō da"* Stem of the adjective *nai* + the suffix *-sa* + the auxiliary *-sō da*[1] (evidential):

- 回復の見込みはあまりなさそうだ。 *Kaifuku no mikomi wa amari nasasō da.* There seems to be little chance of his recovering.

→*sō da*[1]

nasu 成す・為す 動詞 verb

「する」「行なう」の古い言い方 *"Suru", "okonau" no furui ii-kata* Old version of *suru, okonau:*

- 我々のなすがままだ。 *Ware-ware no nasu ga mama da.* They are at our mercy.
- なすことは我にありて、成ることは天命なり。 *Nasu koto wa ware ni arite, naru koto wa tenmei nari.* Man proposes, God disposes.

ni[1] に 格助詞 case particle

1. 動作•作用が行なわれる位置を静的に示す *Dōsa • sayō ga okonawareru ichi wo seiteki ni shimesu* Denotes static location:

- 大抵の薬屋にある。 *Taitei no kusuri-ya ni aru.* Most drugstores have it.
- 午前中家に居ります。 *Gozenchū ie ni orimasu.* I am at home in the morning.

2. 帰着点を示す *Kichaku-ten wo shimesu* Denotes point of arrival:

- 教室に入っていった。 *Kyōshitsu ni haitte itta.* They went into the classroom.
- 船はもう港に着いていた。 *Fune wa mō minato ni tsuite ita.* The ship was already in port.

NOTE. In this connection, while *ni* implies entry into a place, *e* suggests only the direction.

3. 時刻を示す *Jikoku wo shimesu* Denotes point of time:

- 三時十分に到着する。 *San-ji jippun ni tōchaku suru.* We arrive at 3:10.
- 朝何時に起きますか。 *Asa nanji ni okimasu ka?* At what time do you get up?

NOTE. With verbs implying a beginning, Japanese prefers *kara* in these cases:

- 授業は八時から始まる。 *Jugyō wa hachi-ji kara hajimaru.* School begins at 8.

NOTE. With words that indicate wide bands of time, *ni* is usually omitted:

- 将来大人物になるに違いない。 *Shōrai daijinbutsu ni naru ni chigai nai.* He will be a great man later on, without a doubt.
- 昔、ここらにお寺があった。 *Mukashi, kokora ni o-tera ga atta.* There used to be a temple hereabouts, long ago.

4. 動作•作用の及ぶ対象を示す *Dōsa • sayō no oyobu taishō wo shimesu* Denotes target of action:

- 途中でだれかに会うかも知れない。 *Tochū de dare ka ni au ka mo shirenai.* You may meet somebody on the way.
- これが君に話した本だ。 *Kore ga kimi ni hanashita hon da.* This is the book I told you about.

5. 動作•作用が行なわれるありさまを示す *Dōsa • sayō ga okonawareru arisama wo shimesu* Denotes circumstances of action:

- 箱を横に並べなさい。 *Hako wo yoko ni narabe nasai.* Lay the boxes side by side.

- 晴れ間もなしに降り続ける。 *Harema mo nashi ni furi-tsuzukeru.* It keeps on raining without a break.
- 喜怒哀楽の表情に乏しい。 *Kido-airaku no hyōjō ni toboshii.* They are loth to express their feelings.

6. 動作の変化の結果を示す *Dōsa no henka no kekka wo shimesu* Denotes effect of change:

- 金持ちになりたいなあ。 *Kanemochi ni naritai, nā!* How I should like to be rich!
- 兄の子を養子にする。 *Ani no ko wo yōshi ni suru.* He is adopting his brother's child.
- 二組に分けた方がいい。 *Futa-kumi ni waketa hō ga ii.* It would be better to divide them into two groups.

7. 動詞の連用形に付いて、動作の目的を示す *Dōshi no ren'yōkei ni tsuite, dōsa no mokuteki wo shimesu* With Base 2 of verbs, denotes purpose of action:

- 泳ぎに行こうよ。 *Oyogi ni ikō yo.* Let's go for a swim.
- 僕のパソコンを見にきた。 *Boku no pasokon wo mi ni kita.* He came to see my personal computer.

NOTE. This construction requires that the main verb be one of coming or going.

8. 受け身の場合に、動作主を示す *Ukemi no baai ni, dōsa-nushi wo shimesu* In the case of the passive construction, denotes the agent:

- 先生に叱られるよ。 *Sensei ni shikarareru yo!* You'll catch it from the teacher!
- 雨に降られると困る。 *Ame ni furareru to komaru.* I shouldn't like to be caught in the rain.
- 犬に手を噛まれた。 *Inu ni te wo kamareta.* I had my hand bitten by a dog.

NOTE. When the agent is a person, *kara* may replace *ni:*

- お医者さんから言われたことだ。 *O-isha-san kara iwareta koto da.* That's what the doctor told me (to do).

9. 使役の場合に、作用の相手を示す *Shieki no baai ni, sayō no aite wo shimesu* In the causative construction, denotes the person made or allowed to act:

- 私に持たせてください。 *Watashi ni motasete kudasai.* Let me take it, please.
- 画家に描かせた絵だ。 *Gaka ni egakaseta e da.* It's a picture I got an artist to paint.

10. 原因・理由を示す *Gen'in•riyū wo shimesu* Denotes cause or reason:

- その知らせに驚いた。 *Sono shirase ni odoroita.* I was surprised at the news.
- 住宅不足に悩んでいる。 *Jūtaku-busoku ni nayande iru.* They suffer from a shortage of housing.
- これからどうしたらよいのか途方に暮れている。 *Kore kara dō shitara yoi no ka tohō ni kurete iru.* We are at a loss as to what to do next.
- サラリーマンは重税に苦しんでいる。 *Sarariiman wa jūzei ni kurushinde iru.* Office-workers are weighed down with taxes.

11. 並列・添加を示す *Heiretsu • tenka wo shimesu* Denotes listing or addition:

- 春に、夏に、秋に、冬を四季と言う。 *Haru ni, natsu ni, aki ni, fuyu wo shi-ki to iu.* Spring, summer, fall and winter are called the four seasons.
- 鉛筆に、ノートに、消しゴムを買った。 *Enpitsu ni, nōto ni, keshigomu wo katta.* I bought a pencil, a notebook and an eraser.

12. 割合・割当の基準を示す *Wariai • wariate no kijun wo shimesu* Denotes standard of distribution, active and passive:

- 週に三回ゴルフをやる。 *Shū ni san-kai gorufu wo yaru.* I play golf three times a week.
- 十人に一人が病欠している。 *Jūnin ni hitori ga byōketsu shite iru.* One in ten is absent through illness.

13. 「は」を伴って、尊敬の意を表す *"Wa" wo tomonatte, sonkei no i wo arawasu* Followed by *wa,* attaches a sense of respect to subject of sentence:

- 先生にはお変わりありませんか。 *Sensei ni wa, o-kawari arimasen ka?* I hope you are well. (said or written to a teacher or other person worthy of the title)

14. 動詞の連用形＋に＋終止形の形で、動詞の意味を強める *Dōshi no ren'yōkei + ni + shūshikei no katachi de, dōshi no imi wo tsuyomeru* In Base 2 of verbs + *ni* + Base 3 of verbs form, strengthens meaning of verbs:

- 雨が降りに降った。 *Ame ga furi ni futta.* It rained cats and dogs.
- 赤ん坊はただ泣きに泣くばかりだ。 *Akanbō wa tada naki ni naku bakari da.* The baby cries its eyes out all the time.

ni² に

形容動詞活用の連用形 *Keiyōdōshi-katsuyō no ren'yōkei* Base 2 of conjugation of adjectival nouns:

- 見事に目的を果たした。 *Migoto ni mokuteki wo hatashita.* He achieved his goal splendidly.
- 空は俄かに曇った、 *Sora wa niwaka ni kumotta.* The sky suddenly darkened.
- その本を大事にしてください。 *Sono hon wo daiji ni shite kudasai.* Please take good care of that book.

→ ***keiyōdōshi***

ni- 二 (ジ、ふた、ふたつ)

- 二月 *ni-gatsu* February; 二年 *ni-nen* two years; 二人三脚 *ni-nin san-kyaku* three-legged race; 無二 *mu-ni* peerless; 二心 *futa-gokoro* double-dealing; 二つ目 *futatsu-me* second . . . But: 二日 *futsuka* the second; 二十日 *hatsuka* the twentieth; 二人 *futari* two people.

-nikui にくい 接尾語 suffix

動詞の連用形に付いて、形容詞を作り、「することが難しい」という意味を添える *Dōshi no ren'yōkei ni tsuite, keiyōshi wo tsukuri, "suru koto ga muzukashii" to iu imi wo soeru* Added to Base 2 of verbs, makes adjectives of them and adds the idea that the action is difficult:

- 読みにくい漢字までも読める。 *Yomi-nikui kanji made mo yomeru.* He can read even ideographs that are hard to read.
- 勉強しにくい環境だ。 *Benkyō-shi-nikui kankyō da.* The environment doesn't lend itself to study.
- この車のエンジンはかかりにくい。 *Kono kuruma no enjin wa kakari-nikui.* The engine of this car is slow to start.

→ ***-gatai, -zurai***

-nin- 人 接頭語・接尾語 prefix, suffix

人を数える語 *Hito wo kazoeru go* Counter for persons (mostly as suffix):

- 十人十色。 *Jū-nin to-iro.* So many people, so many minds; 悪人 *aku-nin* villain; 同人 *dō-nin* • *dō-jin* same person; 芸人 *gei-nin* artist; 本人 *hon-nin* person himself, said person; 女人 *nyo-nin* woman, women; 商人 *shō-nin* merchant; 証人 *shō-nin* witness; 上人 *shō-nin* saint (Buddh.); 他人 *ta-nin* others, unrelated person; 役人 *yaku-nin* public servant; 善人 *zen-nin* good person.

NOTE. *Nin-*, not *jin-* is found as prefix in:

- 人偏 *nin-ben* the radical indicating "person"; 人間 *nin-gen* human being; 人魚 *nin-gyo* mermaid; 人形 *nin-gyō* doll; 人参 *nin-jin* carrot, ginseng; 人気 *nin-ki* popularity; 人相 *nin-sō* physiognomy; 人足 *nin-*

soku labourer; 人非人 *nin-pi-nin* brute, fiend; 人夫 *nin-pu* labourer; 人称 *nin-shō* person (gram.); 人体 (i) *jin-tai* human body; (ii) *nin-tei* personal appearance; 人数 *nin-zū* number of persons.

NOTE also:

- 人足 *hito-ashi* traffic; 人数 *hito-kazu* = *nin-zū*; 人気 *hito-ke* indication of human presence; *hito-ge* humaneness.

→ *hito*

ninshō daimeishi 人称代名詞 personal pronoun

These will be found in the Introduction (II), where they are called *jin-daimeishi*. They form part of the paradigm covering all *ko-so-a-do* words. Note that *Kokugo*, when untainted by translation, is sparing in the use of personal pronouns. The reason is that the first person pronoun is usually rendered unnecessary by the use of the deferential form of verb, the second, by the use of respect forms, and the third by the use of nouns. Note also that for each of the few pronouns listed in the Introduction, there are many others, dating back to various eras.

- ただ今戻って参りました。 *Tadaima modotte mairimashita.* I have just got back.
- どちらへいらっしゃいますか。 *Dochira e irasshaimasu ka?* Where are you going?
- 先生の本です。 *Sensei no hon desu.* It's your book, sir.

かれ、and still more かのじょ、owe their currency to the influence of English.

no[1] の 格助詞 case particle

体言または体言に準ずるものに付いて、連体修飾語を作る *Taigen mata wa taigen ni jun-zuru mono ni tsuite, rentai shūshoku-go wo tsukuru* Added to nouns and to nominalized words, makes qualifiers of them.

1. 所有を示す *Shoyū wo shimesu* Denotes possession:
   - だれのものですか。 *Dare no mono desu ka?* Whose is it?
2. 所属を示す *Shozoku wo shimesu* Denotes affiliation:
   - 学校の先生です。 *Gakkō no sensei desu.* She is a schoolteacher.
3. 所在を示す *Shozai wo shimesu* Denotes location:
   - あそこの建物にある。 *Asoko no tatemono ni aru.* It's in that building.
4. 所産を示す *Shosan wo shimesu* Denotes origin of a product:
   - 青森県の林檎です。 *Aomori-ken no ringo desu.* They are apples from Aomori Prefecture.
5. 述語が連体形で終わる文章の主語を表す *Jutsu-go ga rentaikei de*

owaru bunshō no shugo wo arawasu Denotes subject of a qualifying clause:

- 雨の降る日は、外出しない。 *Ame no furu hi wa, gaishutsu shinai.* They don't go out on rainy days.

NOTE. In some cases, the word preceding this *no* will translate into English as the object:

- 入場券の入用な方はありませんか。 *Nyūjōken no nyūyō na kata wa arimasen ka?* Isn't there anybody needing an admission ticket?
- 運転の出来る人を捜している。 *Unten no dekiru hito wo sagashite iru.* We are looking for somebody who can drive.

6. 同格を示す *Dōkaku wo shimesu* Denotes apposition:

- 友人の鈴木さんから貰った。 *Yūjin no Suzuki-san kara moratta.* I got it from my friend Mr. Suzuki.
- 薬屋の川岸が勧めたものだ。 *Kusuri-ya no Kawa-gishi ga susumeta mono da.* It was recommended to me by Kawagishi the druggist.

7. 並列を示す *Heiretsu wo shimesu* Denotes listing:

- なんのかのとうるさい人だ。 *Nan no ka no to urusai hito da.* What with one thing or another, he is a nuisance.
- 貸したの借りないのと、言い合っている。 *Kashita no karinai no to, ii-atte iru.* The one says he lent it, the other says he didn't borrow it, and the argument goes on.

→ *da no*

8. 準体言を作る *Jun-taigen wo tsukuru* Nominalizes verbs:

- 起きるのにはまだ早い。 *Okiru no ni wa mada hayai.* It is still too early to get up.
- 注意しなければならないのは右折だ。 *Chūi shinakereba naranai no wa usetsu da.* What one has to be careful about is right turns.

9. 「だ」「です」を伴って、断定・説明をする。 *"Da", "desu" wo tomonatte, dantei • setsumei wo suru* With *"Da", "desu",* adds a sense of assertion or explanation:

- 寝坊した。頭が痛いのだ。 *Nebō shita; atama ga itai no da.* I got up late; I have a headache, you see.
- 窓はだれが壊したのか。 *Mado wa dare ga kowashita no ka?* Who was it that broke the window?

no² の 終助詞 final particle

活用語の連体形に付く *Katsuyō-go no rentaikei ni tsuku* Is added to Base 4 of conjugables.

1. 軽い断定の意を表す *Karui dantei no i wo arawasu* Adds a mild sense of assertion:

- 本当に何も食べたくないの。 *Hontō ni nani mo tabetaku nai no.* I really don't feel like eating anything.
- 新校舎に移ることになりましたのよ。 *Shin-kōsha ni utsuru koto ni narimashita no yo.* We are to move into the new school building.

2. 柔らかい疑問を作る *Yawarakai gimon wo tsukuru* Forms a mild question:
- どこへ行くの。 *Doko e iku no?* Where are you off to?
- どちらが美味しいの。 *Dochira ga oishii no?* Which is the tastier?

nochi 後 形式名詞として as a formal noun

1. あることが済んでから *Aru koto ga sunde kara* After something has taken place:
- 雨、のち晴れ。 *Ame, nochi hare.* Rain, later fine.
- 長い時間歩いたのち、やっと山小屋に着いた。 *Nagai jikan aruita nochi, yatto yama-goya ni tsuita.* After walking for a long time, we finally reached the hut.

2. これから先 *Kore kara saki* From here on, in future:
- 後のことを心配している。 *Nochi no koto wo shinpai shite iru.* He is worried for his future.

3. 死んでからの世 *Shinde kara no yo* The hereafter:
- 後の世 *nochi no yo* (i) future generations; (ii) the life to come.

→ *ato, go*[2], *-go.*

no de ので 接続助詞 conjunctive particle

活用語の連体形に付いて、原因・理由を表す *Katsuyō-go no rentaikei ni tsuite, gen'in • riyū wo arawasu* Added to Base 4 of conjugables, expresses cause or reason:

- 風が強いので、埃が立つ。 *Kaze ga tsuyoi no de, hokori ga tatsu.* The wind is strong, so a lot of dust is in the air.
- 傾斜がなだらかなので、わりに疲れない。 *Keisha ga nadaraka na no de, wari ni tsukarenai.* The slope is gentle, so one doesn't get so tired.
- 雨が降るので、外出を見合わせた。 *Ame ga furu no de, gaishutsu wo mi-awaseta.* It is raining, so I have put off going out.

→ *kara*[1][3], *kara*[2][1]

nomi のみ 副助詞 adverbial particle

体言・活用語の連体形に付いて、限定の意を表す *Taigen • katsuyōgo no rentaikei ni tsuite, gentei no i wo arawasu* Added to nominals and to Base 4 of conjugables, denotes restriction:

- 静かで、波の音のみ聞こえる。 *Shizuka de, nami no oto nomi kikoeru.* It is quiet, with only the sound of waves to be heard.
- 英語のみならず、フランス語も話す。 *Eigo nomi narazu, Furansugo mo hanasu.* He speaks not only English, but French as well.
- 人間にのみ考える力がある。 *Ningen ni nomi kangaeru chikara ga aru.* Man alone has the power to think.

Homonyms: 飲み Base 2 of verb *nomu:* 蚤 flea; 鑿 a chisel.
NOTE. *Nomi* is the literary form for *bakari, dake.*

no ni[1] のに 接続助詞 conjunctive particle
活用語の連体形に付く *Katsuyō-go no rentaikei ni tsuku* Is added to Base 4 of verbals.
1. 順応しない結果な表す *Junnō shinai kekka wo arawasu* Denotes adversative conjunction:

- 風がないのに、花が散る。 *Kaze ga nai no ni, hana ga chiru.* The blossoms are falling even though there is no wind.
- 打ち合わせをしていたのではないのに、声を揃えて言った。 *Uchiawase wo shite ita no de wa nai no ni, koe wo soroete itta.* We spoke in unison, even though we had made no previous arrangement.
- 兄が金持ちなのに、私は貧乏だ。 *Ani ga kanemochi na no ni, watashi wa binbō da.* Despite the fact that my brother is rich, I am poor.

2. 終助詞のように、意外な気持ちや、不満の意を表す *Shū-joshi no yō ni, igai na kimochi ya, fuman no i wo arawasu* Used like a final particle, expresses a feeling of surprise or disappointment:

- 黙っていればよかったのに。 *Damatte ireba yokatta no ni!* You could have kept your mouth shut!
- あんなに約束しておいたのに。 *Anna ni yakusoku shite oita no ni!* To think that he had promised so firmly!

no ni[2] のに
準体助詞「の」+格助詞「に」 *Juntai-joshi "no" + kaku-joshi "ni"* Nominalizing *no* + case particle *ni:*

- 来るのに三時間もかかる。 *Kuru no ni san-jikan mo kakaru.* It takes all of three hours to get here.
- もっと奇麗なのに取り替えよう。 *Motto kirei na no ni tori-kaeyō.* Let me change it for a prettier one.

-nu ぬ 助動詞 auxiliary verb
The conjugation is as follows: 1. — 2. *zu* 3. *nu (n)* 4. *nu (n)* 5. *ne* 6. —.
動詞型活用語や「ます」の未然形に付いて、打ち消しの意を表す *Dōshi-*

gata katsuyō-go ya "masu" no mizenkei ni tsuite, uchi-keshi no i wo arawasu Added to Base 1 of verb-type conjugables and of the auxiliary *-masu,* adds the idea of negation:

- 歩けぬ者は申し出なさい。 *Arukenu mono wa mōshi-de nasai.* Would those who can't walk please make yourselves known.
- どうしても行かねばならぬ。 *Dōshite mo ikaneba naranu.* I must go at all costs.
- 知らず知らずに眠ってしまった。 *Shirazu-shirazu ni nemutte shimatta.* In spite of myself I fell asleep.

NOTE. This *-nu* mostly contracts to *-n; suru* becomes *senu,* and *kuru* becomes *konu.* There was also a classical auxiliary *-nu* expressing completion (modern *-ta*), emphasis (modern *tashika ni . . . , kitto . . .*) and listing (modern *-tari . . . -tari*).

-nuki 抜き 接尾語 suffix

1. 名詞に付いて、「抜くこと」「ないこと」の意味を表す *Meishi ni tsuite, "nuku koto", "nai koto" no imi wo arawasu* With nouns, expresses omission or lack:

- あく抜き *aku-nuki* removal of bitter taste; 牛ぼう抜き *gobō-nuki* pulling straight out; 骨抜き *hone-nuki* boning, emasculating; 居抜きで買う *i-nuki de kau* buy as a going concern; 居合抜き *iai-nuki* quick drawing of sword; 息抜き *iki-nuki* respite; 毛抜き *ke-nuki* tweezers; 口抜き・栓抜き *kuchi-nuki* • *sen-nuki* bottle opener; 釘抜き *kugi-nuki* nail puller; 空気抜き *kūki-nuki* ventilator; 目抜き通り *me-nuki doori* main street; 煮抜き *ni-nuki* rice glue, boiled egg; 疎抜き *oro-nuki* thinning out; 背抜き *se-nuki* unlined coat; 渋抜き *shibu-nuki* removal of astringency; 染み抜き *shimi-nuki* removal of stains; 手抜き *te-nuki* cutting corners; 刺抜き *toge-nuki* tweezers.

2. 人数を表す漢語に付いて、その人数だけ負かす意を示す *Ninzū wo arawasu Kango ni tsuite, sono ninzū dake makasu i wo shimesu* With Chinese words denoting a number of persons, expresses the idea of a series of wins over that number:

- 五人抜きをした。 *Gonin-nuki wo shita.* He beat five opponents in a row.

3. 動詞の連用形に付いて、いろいろな意味を表す *Dōshi no ren'yōkei ni tsuite, iroirona imi wo arawasu* With base 2 of verbs, expresses various meanings:

- 選り抜き *eri-nuki, yori-nuki* choosing, the choice; 吹き抜き *fuki-nuki* stairwell, ventilating; 踏み抜き *fumi-nuki* having a nail pierce one's foot; piercing with foot; 生え抜き *hae-nuki* born and bred; 張り

抜き *hari nuki* papier mache; 引き抜き・引っこ抜き *hiki-nuki* • *hikko-nuki* picking (and buying) of players; 掘り抜き *hori-nuki* artesian well; 勝ち抜き *kachi-nuki* series of wins; 書き抜き *kaki-nuki* extract; 切り抜き *kiri-nuki* cutting (from paper, etc.); 染め抜き *some-nuki* leaving a pattern undyed, dyeing fast; 打ち抜き *uchi-nuki* punching (holes).

-nuku 抜く　補助動詞　supplementary verb

動詞の連用形に付いて、「最後まで…する」意味を添える *Dōshi no ren'yōkei ni tsuite, "saigo made . . . suru" imi wo soeru* With Base 2 of verbs, adds the idea of seeing something through:

- 出し抜く *dashi-nuku* forestall; 生き抜く *iki-nuku* live through, outlive; 困り抜く *komari-nuku* be greatly embarrassed; 見抜く *mi-nuku* see through (a person, scheme); 追い抜く *oi-nuku* outrun; 知り抜く *shiri-nuku* know thoroughly; すっぱ抜く *suppa-nuku* disclose; 戦い抜く *tatakai-nuku* fight to bitter end.

NOTE. Besides these, there are also the many compounds in which *-nuku* has its primary meaning of "extract". See *-nuki,* above.

O

o-[1] 御　接頭語　prefix

体言・用言の上に付く *Taigen • yōgen no ue ni tsuku* Prefixed to both nominals and verbals.

1. 尊敬の意を表す *Sonkei no i wo arawasu* Expresses a sense of respect:

- お手紙ありがとうございました。 *O-tegami arigatō gozaimashita.* Thank you so much for your letter.

2. へりくだった意を表す *Herikudatta i wo arawasu* Expresses a sense of deference:

- お願いいたします。 *O-negai itashimasu.* I pray you.

3. 丁寧の意を表す *Teinei no i wo arawasu* Expresses a sense of politeness:

- お早うございます。 *O-hayō gozaimasu.* Good morning.

4. 女性の名の上に付いて、親しみの意を表す *Josei no na no ue ni tsuite, shitashimi no i wo arawasu* Prefixed to girls' names, expresses a sense of familiarity:

- お花さんは来ましたか。 *O-Hana-san wa kimashita ka?* Has Hanasan arrived?

NOTE. This *o-* is prefixed mostly to *Yamato-kotoba* (Japanese words). while *go-* is prefixed to *Kango* (Chinese words). However, Chinese words in daily use are an exception:

• お肉 *o-niku* meat; お電話 *o-denwa* phone; お世辞 *o-seji* flattery.

NOTE. There are many cases in which the honorific is now essential to the meaning:

1. 料理・食事関係のことば *Ryōri • shokuji kankei no kotoba* Words concerning cooking and meals:

• おでん *o-den* hotchpotch; お鉢 *o-hachi* rice-tub; おはぎ *o-hagi* dumplings; お昼 *o-hiru* lunch; お浸し *o-hitashi* boiled greens; おひつ *o-hitsu* rice-tub; お代わり *o-kawari* second helping; おかず *o-kazu* side-dish; お強 *o-kowa* steamed rice with adzuki beans; お握り *o-nigiri* rice-balls; お八つ *o-yatsu* (afternoon) snack.

2. 日常生活に関することば *Nichi-jō seikatsu ni kansuru kotoba* Words concerning daily (family) life:

• お包み *o-kurumi* wadded baby-wrapper; おまる *o-maru* chamber pot; おめでた *o-medeta* happy event; おめざ *o-meza* sweets given to a child on awakening; おむつ *o-mutsu* diapers; おなか *o-naka* tummy; おせっかい *o-sekkai* meddling, busybody; おしゃべり *o-shaberi* gossip, a gossip; おしゃぶり *o-shaburi* teething-ring; おしゃれ *o-share* foppery, a fop; おしめ *o-shime* diapers; おざなり *o-zanari* perfunctoriness.

3. 教宗関係のことば *Shūkyō-kankei no kotoba* Religious terms:

• 御札 *o-fuda* amulet; 御祓い *o-harai* purification (rite); 御飾り *o-kazari* decorations; 御参り *o-mairi* temple visit; 御供え *o-sonae* offering.

4. 様々 *Sama-zama* Miscellaneous:

• お化け *o-bake* bogy, ghost; おでき *o-deki* abscess; おはじき *o-hajiki* marbles; おまけに *o-make ni* in addition; おしろい *o-shiroi* face powder.

→ *go-¹, gyo-, mi-¹.*

o-² 小 接頭語 prefix

1. 小さい *Chiisai* Literal meaning of "small":

• 小川 *o-gawa* brook; 小舟 *o-bune, ko-bune* boat.

2. 少しの *Sukoshi no* Small quantity of:

• 小暗い *o-gurai* dusky; 小止み *o-yami, ko-yami* slight let-up (in rain).

3. 語調を和らげる *Go-chō wo yawarageru* Softens diction:

• 小母 *o-ba* Mrs. 小父 *o-ji* Mr.; 小田 *o-da* paddy field; (in place names) 小田原 *Odawara;* 小笠原 *Ogasawara.*

-ō, -yō

NOTE. The use of romaji makes it possible to list here the conjectural auxiliary *-u*. When it is added to Base 1 of *go-dan* verbs, adjectives, and adjectival nouns, and to most auxiliaries, we get the ending *-ō;* when it is added to Base 1 of *kami-ichidan* and *shimo-ichidan* (*-iru, -eru*) verbs, and the four auxiliaries *-reru, -rareru, seru, -saseru,* we get *-yō:*

- 買おう *kaō* (*kau,* buy); 行こう *ikō* (*iku,* go); 話そう *hanasō* (*hanasu,* speak); 勝とう *katō* (*katsu,* win); なかろう *nakarō* (*nai,* not).
- 見よう *miyō* (*miru,* see); 上げよう *ageyō* (*ageru,* give); 書かせよう *kakaseyō* (*kakaseru,* make write); 来させよう *kosaseyō* (*kosaseru* make come).

1. 推量を表す *Suiryō wo arawasu* Expresses conjecture:

- これでよかろう。 *Kore de yokarō.* This will do.
- もう東京へ着いたでしょう。 *Mō Tōkyō e tsuita deshō.* He will have arrived in Tokyo by this.

2. 意志を表す *Ishi wo arawasu* Expresses volition:

- 休み中、読書しようと思っている。 *Yasumi-chū, dokusho shiyō to omotte iru.* I intend to do some reading during the holidays.
- 出席しようと予定している。 *Shusseki shiyō to yotei shite iru.* He intends to be present.

3. 勧誘を表す *Kan'yū wo arawasu* Expresses enticement:

- 皆で校歌を歌おう。 *Mina de kōka wo utaō.* Let's all sing our school song.
- もう、その話を止めよう。 *Mō, sono hanashi wo yameyō.* Let's drop the subject.

-ō ga . . . -ō ga おう/ようが…おう/ようが

- 勝とうが負けようが、頑張るつもりだ。 *Katō ga makeyō ga, ganbaru tsumori da.* Win or lose, I intend to do my best.

-ō ga . . . -mai ga おう/ようが…まいが

- 結婚しようがしまいが、僕には関係ない。 *Kekkon shiyō ga shimai ga, boku ni wa kankei nai.* Whether he marries her or not, it doesn't concern me.

-ō ka . . . -mai ka おう/ようか…まいか

- 帰ろうか帰るまいか、考えが決まらなかった。 *Kaerō ka kaerumai ka, kangae ga kimaranakatta.* She hadn't made up her mind whether to go home or not.

-ō to おう/ようと

After question word:

- どんな反対があろうと、歯牙に掛けるような彼ではなかった。 *Donna hantai ga arō to, shiga ni kakeru yō na kare de wa nakatta.* It wasn't like him to worry, no matter what opposition he met with.

-ō ni mo おう/ようにも

- 慰めようにも、慰める術を知らない。 *Nagusameyō ni mo, nagusameru sube wo shiranai.* However much I want to comfort her, I don't know how.

-ō to suru おう/ようとする

1. 努力をする意を表す *Doryoku wo suru i wo arawasu* Denotes effort:

- 戸を開けようとしたが、開かなかった。 *To wo akeyō to shita ga, akanakatta.* He tried to open the door, but it wouldn't open.

2. 動作・状態が起こりかけていることを表す *Dōsa • jōtai ga okorikakete iru koto wo arawasu* Denotes that something is just about to happen:

- 第二学期も終わろうとしている。 *Dai ni gakki mo owarō to shite iru.* The second term, too, is drawing to a close.
- 出掛けようとしているところへ、電話が掛かった。 *Dekakeyō to shite iru tokoro e, denwa ga kakatta.* Just as I was about to leave, the phone rang.

-ō to mo shinai おう/ようともしない

- 起きようともしなかった。 *Okiyō to mo shinakatta.* He made no move to get up.

-ō to mo omowanai おう/ようとも思わない

- 早く帰ろうとも思わなかった。 *Hayaku kaerō to mo omowanakatta.* I had no intention of coming home early.

-ō ga (-ō to) kamawanai おう/ようが（おう/ようと）構わない

- 死のうが構わない。 *Shinō ga kamawanai.* I don't care if he dies.
- 危険があろうと構わない。 *Kiken ga arō to kamawanai.* It doesn't matter whether there is danger or not.

-oeru 終える 補助動詞のように used like a supplementary verb

Both the transitive *-oeru* and the intransitive *-owaru* will be found in this context:

- 書き終えた封筒を枕元に置いた。 *Kaki-oeta fūtō wo makura-moto ni oita.* He put the envelope he had finished writing (addressing) beside his pillow.
- 本を昨夜読み終わった。 *Hon wo yūbe yomi-owatta.* I finished reading the book last night.

oide 御出で 動詞（古） verb (classical)

The conjugation is as follows: 1. *ide* 2. *ide* 3. *izu*（いづ）4. *izuru*（いづる）5. *izure*（いづれ）6. *ideyo.*

古語の「出づ」の名残で、「ある」「居る」「行く」「くる」の尊敬の言い方 *Kogo no "izu" no nagori de, "aru", "iru", "iku", "kuru" no sonkei no ii-kata* Carry-over from classical *izu,* is a polite alternative for *aru* (have), *iru* (is), *iku* (go), and *kuru* (come):

- またのお出でをお待ちしております。 *Mata no oide wo o-machi shite orimasu.* We are looking forward to your coming again.
- 会へお出でになるでしょうか。 *Kai e oide ni naru deshō ka?* I wonder if he will come to the meeting?
- 静かにしてお出で（なさい）。 *Shizuka ni shite oide (nasai).* Please be quiet.

-oki 置き　　接尾語　suffix

数量を表す語に付いて、それだけずつの間を隔てること *Sūryō wo arawasu go ni tsuite, sore dake zutsu no aida wo hedateru koto* With quantity words, adds the idea of leaving that amount of interval:

- 一行置きに書いてください。 *Ichigyō-oki ni kaite kudasai.* Please write on alternate lines.
- 三時間置きに薬を飲む。 *Sanjikan-oki ni kusuri wo nomu.* I take my medicine at three-hour intervals.
- 二メートル置きに杭を打った。 *Ni-mētoru-oki ni kui wo utta.* They drove in a peg every two meters.

-oku 置く　　補助動詞　supplementary verb

連用形やそれに「て」の付いた形などを受ける *Ren'yōkei ya sore ni "-te" no tsuita katachi nado wo ukeru* Follows Base 2, or Base 2 + *-te.*

1. 何かをして、そのままにする *Nani ka wo shite, sono mama ni suru* Do something and leave it so:

- お金を金庫にしまっておこう。 *O-kane wo kinko ni shimatte okō.* I'll lock the money away in the safe.
- 遊ばしておくことは出来ない。 *Asobashite oku koto wa dekinai.* I can't afford to leave him idle.
- 本を読まないでおいた。 *Hon wo yomanaide oita.* I left the book unread.

2. 前以て用意する *Maemotte yōi suru* Prepare beforehand:

- 少し多めに買っておかないとだめ。 *Sukoshi ōme mi katte okanai to dame.* You had better buy in some extra.
- 今のうちに寝ておきなさい。 *Ima no uchi ni nete oki-nasai.* Get in some sleep now (while you have time).

-okureru 遅れる・後れる　　補助動詞　supplementary verb

1. 時間的に間に合わない *Jikan-teki ni ma ni awanai* Fail to do something because one is late:

• 電車に乗り遅れるよ。 *Densha ni nori-okureru yo!* You'll miss your train!

2. 他より遅れて...する *Hoka yori okurete. . . suru* Do something later than somebody else:

• 夫に十年ほど死に後れた。 *Otto ni jūnen hodo shini-okureta.* She outlived her husband by as much as ten years.

omoeru 思える　動詞　verb

1. 思うことが出来る *Omou koto ga dekiru* Be conceivable:

• 雪が降るとはとても思えない。 *Yuki ga furu to wa totemo omoenai.* A snowfall is inconceivable.

2. 思われる *Omowareru* Expresses spontaneity

• 一生の仕事のように思えてきた。 *Isshō no shigoto no yō ni omoete kita.* It has come to seem to me like my life's work.

ookare sukunakare 多かれ少なかれ　more or less → *-kare*

-oroka 疎か　副詞　adverb

「...は疎か」の形で、「言うまでもなく」という意味を示す *". . . wa oroka" no katachi de, "iu made mo naku" to iu imi wo shimesu* In . . . *wa oroka* form, means "needless to say":

• 自動車は疎か、自転車さえ買えない。 *Jidōsha wa oroka, jitensha sae kaenai.* I can't afford a bicycle, let alone a car.

NOTE. 疎 is the *so-* of *sokai* (evacuation, dispersal).

ooseru おおせる（果せる）　補助動詞　supplementary verb

動詞の連用形に付いて、「すっかりやり遂げる」という意味を添える *Dōshi no ren'yōkei ni tsuite, "sukkari yari-togeru" to iu imi wo soeru* With Base 2 of verbs, adds the idea of bringing to completion, managing to do:

• 書きおおせる *kaki-ooseru* finish writing; 隠しおおせる *kakushi-ooseru* manage to hide; 逃げおおせる *nige-ooseru* effect one's escape; しおおせる *shi-ooseru* bring to completion

oru 居る　動詞　verb

「いる」の改まった言い方 *"Iru" no aratamatta ii-kata* A more formal alternative for *iru:*

- 五年間東京におりました。 *Gonenkan Tōkyō ni orimashita.* We spent five years in Tokyo.

NOTE. With the *-te* form, *oru* has a dignity lacking in *iru:*

- ずっと田舎に住んでおります。 *Zutto inaka ni sunde orimasu.* I have been living in the country all along.

NOTE. With the *-masu* forms, *oru* implies a first-person subject:

- だれかおるか。 *Dare ka oru ka?* Is there anybody at home?
  午前中は家におります。 *Gozenchū wa ie ni orimasu.* I am at home in the morning.

NOTE. With 2nd and 3rd person subjects, *oru* can imply a sense of contempt.

oshi- 押し　接頭語　prefix

1.「無理に…する」という意味を表す *"Muri ni . . . suru" to iu imi wo arawasu* Adds the idea of doing. . . forcibly or unreasonably:
   - 押し入る *oshi-iru* break in; 押し流す *oshi-nagasu* sweep away; 押し通す *oshi-toosu* push through; 押し売り *oshi-uri* high-pressure sales(man).
2. 意味を強める *Imi wo tsuyomeru* Strengthens meaning:
   - 津波が押し寄せてきた。 *Tsunami ga oshi-yosete kita.* The tidal wave came surging on.

osokare hayakare 遅かれ早かれ　sooner or later → *-kare*

ossharu おっしゃる　動詞　verb

「言う」の尊敬の言い方 *"Iu" no sonkei no ii-kata* Respect verb for *iu:*

- おっしゃるとおりです。 *Ossharu toori desu.* It's just as you say.

NOTE. For conjugating *ossharu,* see *gozaru.*

-otosu 落とす　補助動詞　supplementary verb

動詞の連用形に付いて、「その動作に失敗する」という意味を添える *Dōshi no ren'yōkei ni tsuite, "sono dōsa ni shippai suru" to iu imi wo soeru* With Base 2 of verbs, adds the meaning of failure in the action:

- 言い落とす *ii-otosu* fail to mention; 書き落とす *kaki-otosu* forget to write; 聞き落とす *kiki-otosu* fail to hear; 見落とす *mi-otosu* fail to notice; 取り落とす *tori-otosu* let fall, lose, omit by mistake; 釣り落とす *tsuri-otosu* fail to land (a fish).

→ *-sokonau*

-owaru → *-oeru*

P

-pokkiri ぽっきり　接尾語　suffix
数量を表す体言に付いて、「ちようどそれだけ」「僅かそれだけ」という意味を添える *Sūryō wo arawasu taigen ni tsuite, "chōdo sore dake", "wazuka sore dake" to iu imi wo soeru* With quantity nominals, adds the meaning of precisely or merely that amount:

- 千円ぽっきりしか入っていなかった。 *Sen'en-pokkiri shika haitte inakatta.* It contained a paltry ¥1000.

-pon 本
After the *hatsu-on* ん and the *soku-on* っ、 the ideograph is read *-pon* in compounds dealing mostly with books:

- 別本 *beppon* different book; 珍本 *chin-pon* rare book; 円本 *en-pon* one-yen edition; 粉本 *fun-pon* sketch; 合本 *gappon* bound volumes; 原本 *gen-pon* original work; 版本 *han-pon* woodblock-printed book; 返本 *hen-pon* returned copies; 印本 *in-pon* printed book; 院本 *in-pon jōruri* libretto; 刊本 *kan-pon* published work; 完本 *kan-pon* complete work; 官本 *kan-pon* government publication; 献本 *ken-pon* complimentary copy; 欠本 *keppon* missing volume; 藍本 *ran-pon* original work; 臨本 *rin-pon* calligraphy copy-book; 新本 *shin-pon* newly-published book; 春本 *shun-pon* obscene book; 点本 *ten-pon* punctuated *Kanbun* text; 残本 *zan-pon* remainders; 全本 *zen-pon* full set; 善本 *zen-pon* authenticated book, well-preserved book.

NOTE. *-pon.* A few compounds not connected with books are:

- 抜本的な *bappon-teki na* drastic; 元本 *gan-pon* principal (econ.); 根本的に *konpon-teki ni* basically.

-ppanashi っ放し　接尾語　suffix
動詞の連用形に付いて、「その動作をして、そのままにしておく」という意味を添える *Dōshi no ren'yōkei ni tsuite, "sono dōsa wo shite, sono mama ni shite oku" to iu imi wo soeru* With Base 2 of verbs, adds the meaning of doing an action and leaving it like that:

- 窓を開けっ放しにしておいた。 *Mado wo ake-ppanashi ni shite oita.* They left the windows wide open.
- 彼の開けっ放しな態度が好きだ。 *Kare no ake-ppanashi na taido ga suki da.* I like his forthright manner.
- 勝ちっぱなし *kachi-ppanashi* having a series of wins; 掛けっぱなし *kake-ppanashi* left switched on or running; 借りっぱなし *kari-ppa-*

nashi borrowed and not repaid; 負けっぱなし *make-ppanashi* having a series of defeats; 置きっぱなし *oki-ppanashi* left and forgotten; 敷きっぱなし *shiki-ppanashi* left spread out; つけっぱなし *tsuke-ppanashi* left switched on or running; 受取りっぱなし *uketori-ppanashi* left unanswered (of a letter, etc.); やりっぱなし *yari-ppanashi* left half done; 垂れっぱなし *tare-ppanashi* dribbling.

→ *-banashi*[2]

-ppara っ腹　接尾語　suffix

朝っぱら *asa-ppara* so early in the morning; 中っ腹 *chū-ppara* a huff; 土手っ腹 *dote-ppara* belly; 太っ腹 *futo-ppara* broadmindedness; 向っ腹 *muka-ppara* getting angry; 空きっ腹 *suki-ppara* empty stomach; 自棄っ腹 *yake-ppara* desperation; 横っ腹 *yoko-ppara* flank.

→ *-bara, -hara*

-pparai っ払い　接尾語　suffix

• 掻っ払い *ka-pparai* swiping, snatcher; 酔っ払い *yo-pparai* getting drunk, drunkard.

→ *-harai*

-ppari っ張り　接尾語　suffix

• 出っ張り *de-ppari* projection; 鼻っ張り *hana-ppari* feigned good form; 強情っ張り *gōjo-ppari* obstinacy, obstinate person; 引っ張り *hi-ppari* pulling; 意地っ張り *iji-ppari* obstinate, obstinate person; 見栄っ張り *mie-ppari* vanity, vain person; 突っ張り *tsu-ppari* prop, bluffing youngster, thrust; 上っ張り *uwa-ppari* overall; 宵っ張り *yoi-ppari* keeping late hours, night owl.

→ *-bari, -hari*

-ppochi っぽち　接尾語　suffix

指示代名詞や数量を表す語に付いて、「僅かそれだけ」という意味を添える *Shiji-daimeishi ya sūryō wo arawasu go ni tsuite, "wazuka sore dake" to iu imi wo soeru* With demonstrative pronouns and quantity words, adds the meaning of paucity:

• これっぽち *kore-ppochi* only this much; 百円ぽち *hyakuen-pochi* a paltry ¥100; 痩せっぽち *yase-ppochi* scrawny person.

-ppoi っぽい　接尾語　suffix

体言・動詞の連用形・形容詞や形容動詞の語幹に付いて、「その傾向が強い」という意味を添える *Taigen • dōshi no ren'yōkei • keiyōshi ya keiyōdōshi no gokan ni tsuite, "sono keikō ga tsuyoi" to iu imi wo soeru* Added to nominals, to Base 2 of verbs and to stem of adjectives and adjectival nouns, denotes a strong tendency (slightly pejorative):

- あだっぽい *ada-ppoi* coquettish; 飽きっぽい *aki-ppoi* fickle; 荒っぽい *ara-ppoi* rough; 哀れっぽい *aware-ppoi* pathetic; 埃っぽい *hokori-ppoi* dusty; 色っぽい *iro-ppoi* sexy; きざっぽい *kiza-ppoi* affected, snobbish; 水っぽい *mizu-ppoi* wishy-washy; 怒りっぽい *okori-ppoi* touchy; 湿っぽい *shime-ppoi* damp; 白っぽい *shiro-ppoi* whitish, amateurish; 忘れっぽい *wasure-ppoi* forgetful; 俗っぽい *zoku-ppoi* vulgar.
- 大人っぽくなってきた。 *Otona-ppoku natte kita.* He has begun to give himself airs.
- 何という子供っぽさであろう。 *Nan to iu kodomo-pposa de arō!* What childishness!

-ppuri っ振り　接尾語　suffix

- 女っぷり *onna-ppuri* woman's looks, womanliness; 男っぷり *otoko-ppuri* man's looks, manliness; 知らん振り *shiran-puri* feigned ignorance.

→ *-buri*[1]

R

-ra 等　接尾語　suffix

1. 体言・指示代名詞に付いて、複数を示す *Taigen • shiji-daimeishi ni tsuite, fukusū wo shimesu* With nominals and demonstrative pronouns, indicates the plural:

- 子供らを呼び寄せてください。 *Kodomo-ra wo yobi-yosete kudasai.* Assemble the children, please.
- これらはもうしまっておいてもいい。 *Korera wa mō shimatte oite mo ii.* These ones can be locked away now.

2. 一人の主立った人を挙げて、以下を略す時に使う語 *Hitori no omodatta hito wo agete, ika wo ryaku-su toki ni tsukau go* Word used when naming the leading member of a party and omitting the others:

- 安田さんらはもう帰りました。 *Yasudasan-ra wa mō kaerimashita.* Mr. Yasuda and the others have already gone home. (Also: The Yasuda's . . .)

3. 場所を示す指示代名詞に付いて、「その付近」という意味を添える

Basho wo shimesu shiji-daimeishi ni tsuite, "sono fukin" to iu imi wo soeru With demonstrative pronouns indicating place, adds the meaning of "thereabouts":

- もと、ここらに橋があった。 *Moto, kokora ni hashi ga atta.* There was a bridge somewhere round here long ago.

→ *-domo*[1], *-tachi*

-rai 来 接尾語 suffix

時間を示す語に付いて、「...から今まで」という意味を添える *Jikan wo shimesu go ni tsuite, ". . . kara ima made" to iu imi wo soeru* With time words, adds the meaning of "since . . . ":

- 二十年来の友人です。 *Nijūnen-rai no yūjin desu.* He is a friend of twenty years' standing.
- 今年の夏は五年来の暑さだ。 *Kotoshi no natsu wa gonen-rai no atsusa da.* This is the hottest summer we have had in five years.

→ *-buri*[1]

-raka らか 接尾語 suffix

形容詞の語幹に付いて、形容動詞を作り、「...である様子」の意を表す *Keiyōshi no gokan ni tsuite, keiyōdōshi wo tsukuri, ". . . de aru yōsu" no i wo arawasu* Added to stem of adjectives, makes adjectival nouns of them and adds the idea of semblance:

- 明らかな *akiraka na* clear; 荒らかな・粗らかな *araraka na* rough; 朗らかな *hogaraka na* cheerful; 軽らかな *karoraka na* light; きららかな *kiraraka na* glittering; 清らかな *kiyoraka na* clear, pure; なだらかな *nadaraka na* gentle; 滑らかな *nameraka na* smooth; 大らかな *ooraka na* magnanimous; 高らかな *takaraka na* loud; 麗らかな *uraraka na* bright; 安らかな *yasuraka na* peaceful; 柔らかな *yawaraka na* tender.

NOTE. The suffix *-raka* is slightly more direct and objective than *-yaka* (q.v.).

-rareru, -reru られる、れる 助動詞 auxiliary verbs

These two forms are of the same auxiliary, *-rareru* following Base 1 of *kamiichi-dan, shimoichi-dan* verbs and *kuru,* while *-reru* follows that of *go-dan* verbs and *suru*. The conjugation for *-rareru* is: 1. *rare* 2. *rare* 3. *rareru* 4. *rareru* 5. *rarere* 6. *rarero, rareyo;* for *-reru*: 1. *re* 2. *re* 3. *reru* 4. *reru* 5. *rere* 6. *rero, reyo.*

1. 受け身を表す *Ukemi wo arawasu* Denotes the passive voice:

- だれにも見られない。 *Dare ni mo mirarenai.* You won't be seen.

NOTE. *Mienai,* here, would mean: "You won't be visible to anybody."

- だれだって誉められれば嬉しい。 *Dare datte homerarereba ureshii.* There is nobody who doesn't like to be praised.

NOTE. Only in this case of passive voice do *-rareru, -reru* have an imperative form.

2. 可能の意味を表す *Kanō no imi wo arawasu* Denotes possibility or ability:

- そんなに早く起きられない。 *Sonna ni hayaku okirarenai.* I can't get up so early.
- 来られるかどうか分からない。 *Korareru ka dō ka wakaranai.* I don't know whether he can come or not.

3. 自発を表す *Jihatsu wo arawasu* Denotes spontaneity:

- 後になって、恥じられることがある。 *Ato ni natte, hajirareru koto ga aru.* It can happen that one feels ashamed later on.
- 最近故郷のことが思い出される。 *Saikin, kokyō no koto ga omoidasareru.* Thoughts of home have been coming to mind recently.

4. 尊敬を表す *Sonkei wo arawasu* Denotes respect:

- あの先生は英語を教えられる。 *Ano sensei wa Eigo wo oshierareru.* That teacher teaches English.

-rashii[1] らしい 助動詞 auxiliary verb

The conjugation is: 1. — 2. *rashikatt*(らしかっ), *rashiku* 3. *rashii* 4. *rashii* 5. *rashikere* 6. —.

動詞・形容詞の終止形、形容動詞の語幹、名詞などに付いて、推量して、断定する意味を表す *Dōshi • keiyōshi no shūshikei, keiyōdōshi no gokan, meishi nado ni tsuite, suiryō shite, dantei suru imi wo arawasu* Added to Base 3 of verbs and adjectives, to stem of adjectival nouns, to nouns and other parts of speech, expresses an assertion founded on inference:

- 午後は雨が降るらしい。 *Gogo wa ame ga furu-rashii.* It looks as if it will rain this afternoon.
- 海上は風が強いらしい。 *Kaijō wa kaze ga tsuyoi-rashii.* There seems to be a strong wind out to sea.
- 近頃元気らしい。 *Chika-goro genki-rashii.* He seems to be in good health of late.
- かれらは知らないらしい。 *Karera wa shiranai-rashii.* They seem to be unaware.
- 授業は八時かららしい。 *Jugyō wa hachi-ji kara-rashii.* Class begins at eight, it seems.
- どうも、風邪らしかった。 *Dōmo, kaze-rashikatta.* It seems it was a cold, after all.

NOTE. Because of its meaning, it is only in very rare cases that the *-rashii* construction can have a first person subject.
→ *mitai na, -yō da*

-rashii² らしい　接尾語　suffix
名詞に付いて、形容詞を作る *Meishi ni tsuite, keiyōshi wo tsukuru* Added to nouns, adjectivalizes them:

- どう見ても、学者らしい。 *Dō mite mo, gakusha-rashii.* He is a scholar through and through.
- そんなことをするなんて、君らしくない。 *Sonna koto wo suru nante, kimi-rashiku nai.* It isn't like you to do such a thing.
- あの声は妹らしゅうございます。 *Ano koe wa imōto-rashū gozaimasu.* That seems to be my sister's voice.

NOTE. For the distinction between the two parts of speech, compare:

- あちらから来るのは女でなくて、男らしい。 *Achira kara kuru no wa, onna de nakute, otoko-rashii.* The person coming towards us seems to be a man, not a woman. (auxiliary).
- 彼の態度は男らしい。 *Kare no taido wa otoko-rashii.* His attitude is manly. (suffix)

NOTE. Some compounds with the suffix *-rashii:*

- 阿呆らしい *aho-rashii* absurd; 愛らしい *airashii* sweet, cute; 馬鹿らしい *baka-rashii* ridiculous; 分別らしい *funbetsu-rashii* prudent-looking; 嫌らしい *iya-rashii* disagreeable, indecent; 子供らしい *kodomo-rashii* childlike; 勿体らしい *mottai-rashii* pompous; もっともらしい *mottomo-rashii* plausible; 女らしい *onna-rashii* womanly; 男らしい *otoko-rashii* manly; 子細らしく *shisai-rashiku* with a knowing look; 胡散らしい *usan-rashii* suspicious-looking; わざとらしい *wazato-rashii* forced.

NOTE. The following adjectives add *-rashii* to their stem:

- 可愛らしい *kawai-rashii* sweet, cute; 汚らしい *kitana-rashii* shabby; 恐らしい *kowa-rashii* fierce-looking; 憎らしい *niku-rashii* hateful.

-rei 例　接尾語　suffix
いつもと同じように *Itsu mo to onaji yō ni* The usual; as usual:

- 月例の *getsu-rei no* monthly; 定例の *tei-rei no* regular, ordinary; 通例 *tsū-rei* ordinarily.

rentaikei 連体形
Base 4 of the conjugation of all conjugables, found before nominals.

In modern Japanese, the only case where this base is evident is in adjectival nouns:

- 出掛けることにした。 *Dekakeru koto ni shita.* They decided to set out. (Here, the verb is the same as if it were Base 3.)
- 安全な所に隠した。 *Anzen na tokoro ni kakushita.* He hid it in a safe place. (Here, Base 3 would be *anzen da.*)

rentaishi 連体詞 adnoun

自立語で、活用がなくて、体言を修飾する *Jiritsu-go de, katsuyō ga nakute, taigen wo shūshoku suru* Independent, invariable words that qualify nominals. See Introduction (I).

Whereas adnouns qualify nominals, adverbs modify verbals.

- いかなる場合にも *ikanaru baai ni mo* in every case; ほんの冗談に *honno jōdan ni* just for fun; 来る日曜日に *kuru Nichiyōbi ni* next Sunday; そんなつもりではなかった。 *Sonna tsumori de wa nakatta.* I didn't mean it. とんだことになってしまった。 *Tonda koto ni natte shimatta.* It has got quite out of hand.

NOTE. The adnouns of classical Japanese were few: *aru, saru, kakaru, toaru, arayuru, iwayuru, ataru, kitaru.*

NOTE. Modern Japanese has more adnouns, classified according to their endings.

1. Adnouns with *no* endings: *ano, dono, kono, sono, honno, rei no, kudanno,* etc.
2. Adnouns with *na* endings: *anna, donna, konna, sonna, chiisana, ookina, ironna,* etc.
3. Adnouns with *ta/da* endings: *bakageta, taishita, tatta, tonda,* etc.
4. Adnouns with *ru* endings: *akuru, arayuru, aru, dōdōtaru, ikanaru, iwayuru, kitaru, saru,* etc.
5. Adnouns with *ga* endings: *waga* (see *ga*[4]).

ren'yōkei 連用形 Base 2 of the conjugation of all conjugables.

For a complete treatment of the matter, see under both *keiyōshi* and *keiyōdōshi.*

-reru See under *-rareru.*

-rin 輪 接尾語 suffix

1. 花を数える語 *Hana wo kazoeru go* Counter for flowers:

- 梅一輪 *ume ichi-rin* one plum blossom.

2. 車の車輪を数える語 *Kuruma no sha-rin wo kazoeru go* Counter for wheels:

• 三輪車 *sanrinsha* three-wheeler, tricycle.

-ro ろ 助詞 particle

Formerly a 間投助詞、*kantō-joshi,* interjectional particle, is now considered part of the imperative of some verbs (*kami-ichidan, shimo-ichidan, suru*). With these, either *yo* or *ro* is now necessary. While *yo* is more literary, *ro* sounds more conversational and is used preferably by men.

• もう七時だ。早く起きろ。 *Mō shichi-ji da. Hayaku oki-ro!* It's already seven o'clock. Get up at once!

NOTE. Modern *suru* has both *shi-ro* and *se-yo; kuru* has *koi* (rarely *koi-yo*).

roku- 六 (ロク、むつ、むっつ)

• 六月 *roku-gatsu* June; 六法 *roppō* six directions; 六つ目 *mutsu-me,* the sixth (one) (but: 六日 *muika* the sixth).

ryō- 両 接頭語 prefix

1. 相対して一組となるものの双方 *Ai-tai shite hito-kumi to naru mono no sōhō* Both elements of a pair:

• 両足・両脚 *ryō-ashi* both legs; 両岸 *ryō-gan, ryō-gishi* both banks; 両眼 *ryō-gan* both eyes; 両目 *ryō-me* both eyes; 両面 *ryō-men* both sides or faces; 両手 *ryō-te* both hands; 両端 *ryō-hashi, ryō-tan* both ends.

2. 二つ、二つながら *Futatsu, futatsu nagara* Two; co-:

• 一両日 *ichi-ryō-jitsu* one or two days; 両立する *ryō-ritsu suru* co-exist, be mutually consistent.

-ryō 両 接尾語 suffix

1. 昔の量目の単位 *mukashi no ryō-me no tan'i* Former unit of weight.

2. 薬の量目の単位 *Kusuri no ryō-me no tan'i* Unit of weight for medicines.

3. 昔の貨幣の単位 *Mukashi no kahei no tan'i* Former currency unit.

4. 車の台数を数える語 *Kuruma no dai-sū wo kazoeru go* Counter for vehicles:

• 八両連結 *hachi-ryō renketsu* eight-carriage train.

-ryū 流 接尾語 suffix

1. 師匠系統 *Shishō keitō* "School":

- 小笠原流の礼法 *Ogasawara-ryū no reihō* Ogasawara code of etiquette.

2. 特有の仕方 *Tokuyū no shikata* One's own style:

- 我流の歌い方 *ga-ryū no utai-kata* one's own style of singing.

3. 等級 *Tōkyū* Rank:

- 一流の人物 *ichi-ryū no jinbutsu* person of highest rank.

S

sa さ 終助詞 final particle

1. 軽く言い放つ意を表す *Karuku ii-hanatsu i wo arawasu* Gives an air of finality to the utterance:

- そんなことありっこないさ。 *Sonna koto arikkonai sa!* But that's impossible!

2. 疑問詞を伴って、抗議・詰問の意を表す *Gimonshi wo tomonatte, kōgi • kitsumon no i wo arawasu* With question words, expresses a sense of protest or cross-examination:

- 威張りくさって、何さ。 *Ibari-kusatte, nani sa?* So who on earth do you think you are?

sa- さ 接頭語 prefix

名詞・動詞・形容詞の上に付いて、語調を整える *Meishi • dōshi • keiyōshi no ue ni tsuite, go-chō wo totonoeru* Prefixed to nouns, verbs and adjectives, adjusts the tone:

- 小夜 *sa-yo* night; 小夜更けて *sa-yo fukete* in the small hours; さ迷う *sa-mayou* wander; さ霧 *sa-giri* fog.

NOTE. Another *sa-* adds the meaning of "early", "young":

- 早苗 *sa-nae* rice-sprouts; 早乙女 *sa-otome* (rice-planting) girl.

NOTE. The two ideographs 五月 (*go-gatsu, sa-tsuki*) are sometimes read *sa-*:

- 五月蝿 *sa-bae* swarms of flies in early summer; 五月雨 *sa-midare* early summer rain.

-sa さ 接尾語 suffix

形容詞・形容動詞の語幹・ある種の名詞に付いて、性質・状態・程度を表す *Keiyōshi • keiyōdōshi no gokan • aru shu no meishi ni tsuite, seishitsu • jōtai • teido wo arawasu* Added to stem of adjectives and adjectival nouns, and to certain kinds of nouns, expresses nature, state, degree:

- 高さ三十メートル以上ある。 *Taka-sa sanjū-mētoru ijō aru.* It is more than 30 meters in height.
- 嬉しさの余り、夢中になった。 *Ureshi-sa no amari, muchū ni natta.* He was beside himself for joy.
- その便利さに驚いた。 *Sono benri-sa ni odoroita.* I was surprised at its usefulness.

NOTE. There was formerly also a suffix attached to Base 3 of verbs, indicating the time or occasion when an action took place:

- 行くさ *yuku-sa* time when somebody goes . . . ; 帰るさ *kaeru-sa* time when somebody returns.

NOTE. For the *sa* of *na-sa-sō da* and *yo-sa-sō da,* see *nai* and *sō da.*

sae さえ 係助詞 bound particle

体言・用言の連用形、色々の語に付く *Taigen • yōgen no ren'yōkei, iro-iro no go ni tsuku* Is added to nominals and to Base 2 of conjugables, and to various parts of speech.,

1. 類推を表す *Ruisui wo arawasu* Denotes analogy:

- こんなことは子供にさえ分かる。 *Konna koto wa kodomo ni sae wakaru.* Even a child knows this.
- 封さえ切らずに手紙を捨てた。 *Fū sae kirazu ni tegami wo suteta.* He threw the letter away without even unsealing it.

2. 限定を表す *Gentei wo arawasu* Denotes limitation:

- 時間さえあれば、成し遂げられる。 *Jikan sae areba, nashi-togerareru.* If only we have enough time, we can finish it.
- 顔を出しさえすればいいよ。 *Kao wo dashi sae sureba ii yo.* All you have to do is put in an appearance.

3. 添加を表す *Tenka wo arawasu* Denotes addition:

- 北風が吹くのに雪さえ混じってきた。 *Kita-kaze ga fuku no ni yuki sae majitte kita.* A north wind was blowing, and then it snowed into the bargain.
- 事業に失敗した上に、病気にさえ掛かった。 *Jigyō ni shippai shita ue ni, byōki ni sae kakatta.* Not only did he fail in business, but he fell ill as well.

NOTE. *Sae* is one of the particles that may come between a verb and its auxiliary:

- もう少し早く来てさえいれば、会えたのだが。 *Mō sukoshi hayaku kite sae ireba, aeta no da ga.* If only I had come a little earlier, we might have met.

sa-hen サ変
Contraction of サ行変格活用 (*sa-gyō henkaku katsuyō*), in modern Japanese, involves only the verb *suru*. (*See ka-hen.*) Both classical *su* and modern *suru* are treated *in loco*.

sai 際 形式名詞 formal noun
「あることが起こったとき」という意味を表す *"Aru koto ga okotta toki" to iu imi wo arawasu* Expresses the idea of the timing of an action:
- 上京の際、お立ち寄りください。 *Jōkyō no sai, o-tachi-yori kudasai.* When you come to Tokyo, please drop in.
- お会いした際、詳細を申し上げます。 *O-ai shita sai, shōsai wo mōshi-agemasu.* I will give you the details when we meet.

→ *-giwa*

saki 先 形式名詞 formal noun
「それより前」という意味を表す *"Sore yori mae" to iu imi wo arawasu* Indicates priority:
- 就職しない先からボーナスのつかい道を考えていた。 *Shūshoku shinai saki kara, bōnasu no tsukaimichi wo kangaete ita.* He was thinking of how to use his bonus even before he got the job.

-saki 先 接尾語 suffix
1. 先端・末端 *Sentan • mattan* Tip, point, edge:
   - 縁先 *en-saki* edge of veranda; 筆先 *fude-saki* tip of brush; 鼻先 *hana-saki* tip of nose; 春先 *haru-saki* early spring; 舳(先) *he-saki* prow; 穂先 *ho-saki* (tip of) ear (of rice); 門先 *kado-saki* front of a house; 小手先 *kote-saki* fingers; 口先 *kuchi-saki* lip(s); 目先に *me-saki ni* under one's nose; 店先 *mise-saki* shopfront; 胸先 *muna-saki* pit of stomach; 庭先で *niwa-saki de* in the garden; 軒先で *noki-saki de* under the eaves; ペン先 *pen-saki* nib; 舌先 *shita-saki* tip of tongue; 手先 *te-saki* fingers; 筒先 *tsutsu-saki* muzzle, nozzle; 指先 *yubi-saki* fingertips; する矢先に *suru ya-saki ni* on point of . . . -ing.
2. 場所を示す *Basho wo shimesu* Denotes place where, whither or whence:
   - 宛先 *ate-saki* address, destination; 出先 *desaki* destination, place where one is staying; 水先案内 *mizu-saki annai* pilotage, (boat) pilot; 送り先 *okuri-saki* destination, consignee; 旅先 *tabi-saki* destination, journey; 立ち回り先 *tachimawari-saki* places where one puts in an appearance; 届け先 *todoke-saki* destination (of package); 嫁ぎ先 *totsugi-saki* house one marries into; 使い先 *tsukai-saki* place one

is sent on errand; 勤め先 *tsutome-saki* place of employment; 行き先 *iki-saki* • *yuki-saki* • 行く先 *iku-saki* • *yuku-saki* destination, future.

3. 色々の意味を示す *Iro-iro no imi wo shimesu* Various meanings:
 • 後先 *ato-saki* (reversing) order, consequences; 真っ先の *mas-saki no* foremost; 老い先 *oi-saki* one's remaining years; 生い先 *oi-saki* the life before one; 幸先 *sai-saki* good omen; 潮先 *shio-saki* time when tide begins to rise; 得意先 *tokui-saki* customer; 取引先 *tori-hiki-saki* business connection.

sakki さっき 副詞 adverb

「先」の促音化で、副詞的に使う *"Saki" no sokuon-ka de, fukushi-teki ni tsukau* Intensified form of *saki,* is used adverbially:
 • さっき帰ってきたばかりだ。 *Sakki kaette kita bakari da.* He has just arrived home.

-same 雨

Ame is read *-same* in some compounds:
 • 春雨 *haru-same* spring rain; 霧雨 *kiri-same* misty rain; 小雨 *ko-same* light rain; 村雨 *mura-same* sudden shower.

NOTE. Irregular readings:
 • 五月雨 *samidare* early summer rain; 時雨 *shigure* drizzle in late autumm and early winter; 梅雨 *tsuyu* • *baiu* rainy season.

san- 三 (サン、み、みつ、みっつ)
 • 三月 *san-gatsu* March; 三杯 *san-bai* three cups; 再三 *sai-san* again and again (but: 三日月 *mika-zuki* new moon; 三毛猫 *mike-neko* tortoise-shell cat; 三つ子 *mitsu-go* three-year-old child; 三味線 *shamisen* shamisen; 三人 *san-nin, mitari* three people).

-sao 竿 接尾語 suffix

旗・箪笥・長持ち・羊羹などを数える語 *Hata* • *tansu* • *nagamochi* • *yōkan nado wo kazoeru go* Counter for flags, chests of drawers, oblong chests, sticks of sweet bean-jelly, etc.:
 • 箪笥を二竿作ってあげた。 *Tansu wo futa-sao tsukutte ageta.* I made them two chests of drawers.

sareru される

「する」の受け身の形；受け身・可能・自発・尊敬を表す *"Suru" no*

ukemi no katachi ukemi • kanō • jihatsu • sonkei wo arawasu Passive form of the verb *suru;* expresses passive voice, potential, spontaneity and respect (see *-rareru, -reru*):

- 非難される場合もある。 *Hinan sareru baai mo aru.* He is sometimes criticized. (passive)
- 明日までに提出される。 *Asu made ni teishutsu sareru.* It may be handed in by tomorrow. (potential, but usually interpreted as passive)
- 将来のことが心配される。 *Shōrai no koto ga shinpai sareru.* The future gives cause for worry. (spontaneity)
- 市長も参列されるそうです。 *Shichō mo sanretsu sareru sō desu.* The mayor, too, will be present, it seems. (respect)

saseru させる

「する」の使役の形 *"Suru" no shieki no katachi* Causative form of the verb *suru.*

1. 「するように要求する」意を表す *"Suru yō ni yōkyū suru" i wo arawasu* Expresses the idea of causation:

- あまりにも勉強をさせ過ぎているのではないでしょうか。 *Amari ni mo benkyō wo sase-sugite iru no de wa nai deshō ka?* Don't you think you are making him study too much?

2. 許容の意を表す *Kyoyō no i wo arawasu* Expresses the idea of permission:

- 好きなようにさせるがいい。 *Suki na yō ni saseru ga ii.* Let him do as he pleases.

-saseru, -seru させる、せる 助動詞 auxiliary verb

The conjugation for *-saseru* is: 1. *sase* 2. *sase* 3. *saseru* 4. *saseru* 5. *sasere* 6. *sasero, saseyo*; for *-seru:* 1. *se* 2. *se* 3. *seru* 4. *seru* 5. *sere* 6. *sero, seyo*.

These two forms are of the same auxiliary, *-saseru* following Base 1 of *kami-ichidan, shimo-ichidan* verbs and *kuru, -seru* following Base 1 of *go-dan* verbs and *suru.*

1. 使役の意を表す *Shieki no i wo arawasu* Denotes causation:

- 田中君に集めさせよう。 *Tanaka-kun ni atsume-saseyō.* Let's get Tanaka to collect them.
- こちらへ来させようか。 *Kochira e ko-saseyō ka?* Shall I have them come here?
- もっと早くから準備させればよかった。 *Motto hayaku kara junbi*

sa-sereba yokatta. You ought to have got them to prepare sooner.
- 毎日歌を歌わせる。 *Mainichi uta wo utawaseru.* He has them sing songs every day.

2. 許容・放任を表す *Kyoyō • hōnin wo arawasu* Denotes permission or non-intervention:
- 漫画を読ませない。 *Manga wo yomasenai.* I don't let them read comics.
- 危ない所に行かせないでください。 *Abunai tokoro ni ikasenaide kudasai.* Don't let them go into dangerous places.
- 子供に飴をあまりたくさん食べさせてはいけない。 *Kodomo ni ame wo amari takusan tabe-sasete wa ikenai.* It isn't right to let children eat too much candy.
- 唇を震えさせながら惨事を語った。 *Kuchibiru wo furue-sase-nagara sanji wo katatta.* With quivering lips he told of the tragedy.

3.「られる」や「給う」を伴って、深い尊敬を表す *"-Rareru" ya "tamō" wo tomonatte, fukai sonkei wo arawasu* With *-rareru* or *tamō,* expresses profound respect:
- お手ずから植えさせられた記念樹です。 *O-tezukara ue-saserareta kinen-ju desu.* It is a memorial tree which he planted with his own hands.

-sasu 止す 補助動詞 supplementary verb

動詞の連用形に付いて、「途中で止める」という意味を添える *Dōshi no ren'yōkei ni tsuite, "tochū de yameru" to iu imi wo soeru* With Base 2 of verbs, adds the meaning of interrupting the action:
- 本を読みさしにして床に付いた。 *Hon wo yomi-sashi ni shite toko ni tsuita.* He went to bed without finishing (reading) the book.
- 言いさす *ii-sasu* check oneself; 書きさす *kaki-sasu* leave off writing; 飲みさす *nomi-sasu* leave off drinking or smoking; 燃えさし *moe-sashi* embers.

-satsu 冊 接尾語 suffix
- 書物などを数える語 *Shomotsu nado wo kazoeru go* Counter for such things as books:
- 休み中本を三冊読んだ。 *Yasumi-chū hon wo san-satsu yonda.* I read three books during the holidays.

HOMONYMS: 札 paper money; 刷 *(in-)* printing; 殺 *(-jin)* murder; 拶 *(ai-)* greeting; 察 *(kan-)* observation; 撮 *(-ei)* taking of photo; 擦 *(ma-)* friction.

-seki[1] 隻　接尾語　suffix

1. 対になるものの片方を数える語　*Tsui ni naru mono no katahō wo kazoeru go:* Counter for one of a pair:

- 屏風一隻　*byōbu isseki* one leaf of a folding screen.

NOTE. In this meaning, it is also used as a prefix.

- 隻眼　*seki-gan* one eye; 隻語　*seki-go* single word; 隻騎　*sekki* lone rider; 隻手　*seki-shu* one hand.

2. 船舶を数える語　*Senpaku wo kazoeru go* Counter for shipping:

- 外国船が数隻入港している。　*Gaikoku-sen ga sū-seki nyū-kō shite iru.* There are several foreign ships in port.

→ *-sō*[1,3]

-seki[2] 石　接尾語　suffix

時計の軸受けなどを数える語　*Tokei no jiku-uke nado wo kazoeru go* Counter for "jewels" of watches and the like:

- 二十三石の金時計　*nijūsan-seki no kin-dokei* 23-jewel gold watch.

→ *-koku*

setsubigo, settōgo　接尾語・接頭語　suffix, prefix

Setsubigo: 単語の後に付いて、意味を添えたり、品詞を変えたりする語　*Tango no ato ni tsuite, imi wo soetari, hinshi wo kaetari suru go* Word affixed to another word so as to add a meaning or change the part of speech.

Settōgo: 単語の前に付いて、語調を整えたり、意味を添えたりする語　*Tango no mae ni tsuite, go-chō wo totonoetari, imi wo soetari suru go* Word prefixed to another word so as to adjust the tone or add a meaning.

The student who has begun the study of Japanese through *romaji* will naturally tend to restrict his vocabulary to polysyllabic *Yamato-kotoba;* it is only when he has acquired a knowledge of a fair range of *kanji* that he will realise their usefulness in forming compound words.

Of special interest are the supplementary verbs; in many cases their import is not at all evident to the foreigner.

setsuzokushi　接続詞　conjunction

自立語で、活用のない、文、文節、語などを接続する品詞　*Jiritsu-go de, katsuyō no nai, bun, bunsetsu, go nado wo setsuzoku suru hinshi* Independent, unconjugated parts of speech that join sentences, clauses and words:

1. 対等の接続詞 *Taitō no setsuzokushi* Correlative conjunctions,
(i) 並列を表す *Heiretsu wo arawasu* Denote listing:
• *mata, narabi ni, oyobi, to.*
(ii) 選択を表す *Sentaku wo arawasu* Denote a choice:
• *arui wa, mata wa, moshiku wa, soretomo.*
(iii) 添加を表す *Tenka wo arawasu* Denote addition:
• *omake ni, sara ni, shikamo, sono ue.*
2. 条件的接続詞 *Jōken-teki setsuzokushi* Conditional conjunctions,
(i) 順接を表す *Junsetsu wo arawasu* Denote co-ordination:
• *dakara, shitagatte, soreyue, suru to.*
(ii) 逆接を表す *Gyakusetsu wo arawasu* Denote adversative conjunction:
• *da ga, demo, keredomo, tokoro ga.*

NOTE. Many words that are translated as conjunctions in English are actually formal nouns in Japanese: *aida, ato, kagiri, mae, tokoro,* etc. (→ *keishiki meishi*)

se yo せよ　動詞「する」の命令形 imperative form of the verb *suru.* 「…にせよ」の形で、「例え…とも」という意味を表す *"... ni se yo" no katachi de, "tatoe ... to mo" to iu imi wo arawasu* In *... ni se yo* form, expresses concession:

• いずれにせよ、よくないのだ。 *Izure ni se yo, yoku nai no da.* It is wrong, no matter what.
• 人権の問題にせよ、社会経済の問題にせよ、彼の影響は大きい。 *Jinken no mondai ni se yo, shakai keizai no mondai ni se yo, kare no eikyō wa ookii.* His influence is great, both in the matter of human rights and in that of social economy.

NOTE. The alternative form of *se yo* is *shi ro.*
→ *de are, shi ro,*

setsuzoku-joshi 接続助詞 See *joshi,* 2.

sezu せず
「する」の未然形に、打ち消しの助動詞「ず」 *"Suru" no mizenkei ni, uchi-keshi no jodōshi "-zu"* Base 1 of *suru* + negative auxiliary *-zu* (Bases 1, 2, 3):

• 降りもせず、晴れもしない。 *Furi mo sezu, hare mo shinai.* It is neither rainy nor sunny.
• この本は読者を魅了せずにはおかない。 *Kono hon wa dokusha wo*

miryō sezu ni wa okanai. This book is bound to fascinate the reader.
NOTE. Base 4 of this *-zu* is *-zaru,* giving *-sezaru.* (→ *-zaru)*

shi- 四 (シ、よ、よん、よつ、よっつ)
• 四月 *shi-gatsu* April; 四方八方に *shi-hō happō ni* in every direction; 再三再四 *sai-san sai-shi* repeatedly (but: 四隅 *yo-sumi* four corners; 四つ足 *yotsu-ashi* quadraped; 四日 *yokka* the fourth; 四等分 *yon-tōbun* quarter an apple.

shi し 接続助詞 conjunctive particle
活用語の終止形に付く *Katsuyōgo no shūshikei ni tsuku* Is added to Base 3 of conjugables.
1. 並列を表す *Heiretsu wo arawasu* Denotes listing:
• 絵も書くし、音楽もやる。 *E mo kaku shi, ongaku mo yaru.* He applies himself to both painting and music.
• 景色もいいし、食べ物もうまい。 *Keshiki mo ii shi, tabemono mo umai.* The scenery is beautiful, and the food is tasty as well.
2. 原因・理由を表す *Gen'in • riyū wo arawasu* Denotes cause or reason:
• 休日だし、天気もいいし、お客様がいらっしゃるだろう。 *Kyūjitsu da shi, tenki mo ii shi, o-kyaku sama ga irassharu darō.* It's a holiday, and the weather is fine, so we expect customers.
3. 相反する条件を列挙する *Ai-han suru jōken wo rekkyo suru* Joins matters mutually incompatible:
• 遊びに行きたいし、金はないし。 *Asobi ni ikitai shi, kane wa nai shi.* I should like to have a fling, but I have no money.

-shiburu 渋る 接尾語 suffix verb
「容易に事をしようとしない」という意味を添える *"Yōi ni koto wo shiyō to shinai" to iu imi wo soeru* Adds the idea of reluctance to do an action:
• 金を出し渋る人だ。 *Kane wo dashi-shiburu hito da.* He is tight with his money.
• 言い渋る *ii-shiburu* falter (in speech); 下げ渋る *sage-shiburu* hold steady (of market); 売り渋る *uri-shiburu* hoard goods.
→ *-oshimu*

shichi- 七 (シチ、なな、ななつ、なの、なぬ)
• 七月 *shichi-gatsu* July; 七宝 *shichihō* seven treasures (but: 七色 *nana-iro* prismatic colors; 七つ道具 *nanatsu-dōgu* one's

paraphernalia; 七日 *nanoka, nanuka* the seventh; 七夕 *Tanabata* Star Festival.

shidai 次第　形式名詞として as a formal noun

1. 名詞に付いて、「...によって決まる」という意味を添える *Meishi ni tsuite, ". . . ni yotte kimaru" to iu imi wo soeru* With nouns, adds the idea of dependence or conformity:

- 総ては君の決心次第だ。 *Subete wa kimi no kesshin shidai da.* Everything depends on your decision.
- 地獄の沙汰も金次第だ。 *Jigoku no sata mo kane shidai da.* Money opens all doors.

2. 動詞の連用形に付いて、「...するやいなや」という意味を添える *Dōshi no renyōkei ni tsuite, ". . . suru ya ina ya" to iu imi wo soeru* With Base 2 of verbs, denotes immediate sequence:

- ご到着になり次第、お電話をください。 *Go-tōchaku ni nari shidai, o-denwa wo kudasai.* Please give us a ring as soon as you arrive.
- チャンスがあり次第行きたい。 *Chansu ga ari shidai ikitai.* I want to go at the first opportunity.
- 手当たり次第に *te-atari shidai ni* at random

shika しか　副助詞 adverbial particle

打ち消しの言葉を伴って、「それと限る」という意味を表す *Uchi-keshi no kotoba wo tomonatte, "sore to kagiru" to iu imi wo arawasu* With a negative expression, denotes restriction:

- 四時間しか寝ていない。 *Yo-jikan shika nete inai.* I have been asleep for only four hours.
- 馬鹿としか思えない。 *Baka to shika omoenai.* One can only take him for a fool.
- 教科書しかだめだ。 *Kyōkasho shika dame da.* Nothing but the textbook will do. (with virtual negative *dame*)

NOTE. *Shika* usually replaces *ga, wa, wo,* may not accompany *mo,* and follows other particles.

→ *bakari, dake, -kiri, nomi*

-shiki[1] しき　接尾語 suffix

指示代名詞に付いて、「僅か...ほど」という意味を添ええる *Shiji daimeishi ni tsuite, "wazuka . . . hodo" to iu imi wo soeru* With demonstrative pronouns, expresses the idea that the amount is trifling:

- これしきの金では何も買えない。 *Kore-shiki no kane de wa nani mo kaenai.* What can I buy with such a small sum?

-shiki[2] 式　接尾語　suffix

1. 一定のやり方 *Ittei no yari-kata* Fixed procedure:

• 儀式 *gi-shiki* ceremony; 格式 *kaku-shiki* formality; 形式 *kei-shiki* form, formality; 挙式 *kyo-shiki* performing of ceremony.

2. 一定の作法が伴う行事 *Ittei no sahō ga tomonau gyōji* Various ceremonies:

• 除幕式 *jomaku-shiki* unveiling ceremony; 結婚式 *kekkon-shiki* wedding ceremony; 告別式 *kokubetsu-shiki* funeral ceremony; 入学式 *nyūgaku-shiki* school entrance ceremony; 落成式 *rakusei-shiki* inauguration ceremony; 成人式 *seijin-shiki* coming-of-age ceremony; 始業式 *shigyō-shiki* opening ceremony; 修業式 *shūgyō-shiki* closing ceremony; 葬式 *sō-shiki* burial ceremony; 卒業式 *sotsugyō-shiki* graduation ceremony; 戴冠式 *taikan-shiki* coronation ceremony.

3. 形式の種類 *Keishiki no shurui* Kinds of formality:

• 非公式 *hikō-shiki* unofficial; 本式 *hon-shiki* orthodox; 公式 *kō-shiki* official; 硬式 *kō-shiki* regulation (tennis, baseball); 旧式 *kyū-shiki* old-style; 軟式 *nan-shiki* (tennis, etc.) played with a soft ball; 略式 *ryaku-shiki* informal; 新式 *shin-shiki* new-style; 和式 *Wa-shiki* Japanese-style; 洋式 *Yō-shiki* Western-style.

4. 数字や符号で示したもの *Sūji ya fugō de shimeshita mono* Mathematical formulae:

• 方程式 *hōtei-shiki* equation; 数式 *sū-shiki* numerical expression; 等式 *tō-shiki* equation.

HOMONYMS. 色、as in 景色 *keshiki* scenery, 彩色 *saishiki* coloring; 識、as in 意識 *ishiki* consciousness, 常識 *jōshiki* common sense; 敷、as in 金敷 *kanashiki* anvil, 屋敷 *yashiki* mansion.

-shimau 終う・仕舞う　接尾語的に　used as a suffix

動詞の連用形+「て」に付いて、多く、残念な気持ちをこめて、動作の完了を表す *Dōshi no ren'yōkei + "-te" ni tsuite, ooku, zannen na kimochi wo komete, dōsa no kanryō wo arawasu* With Base 2 of verbs + *-te,* expresses completion of action; usually implies a sense of regret:

• 財布を落としてしまった。 *Saifu wo otoshite shimatta!* I have (gone and) lost my purse!

• 一気に読んでしまった。 *Ikki ni yonde shimatta.* I read it through in one sitting.

• コーヒーを飲んでしまいなさい。 *Kōhī wo nonde shimai nasai.* Drink up your coffee.

NOTE. Contractions for *-te shimau* are *-chimau, -chau;* for *-de shimau, -jimau, -jau.*

-shimeru しめる 助動詞（古） (classical) auxiliary verb

文語の「しむ」から来た使役の助動詞 *Bungo no "-shimu" kara kita shieki no jodōshi* Causative auxiliary verb derived from classical *shimu.*

動詞の未然形に付く *Dōshi no mizenkei ni tsuku* Added to Base 1 of verbs:

- 私をして言わしめれば、実行は困難ではない。 *Watashi wo shite iwashimereba, jikkō wa konnan de wa nai.* If you ask me, it isn't difficult of execution.
- 悪天候が登頂を中止せしめた。 *Akutenkō ga tōchō wo chūshi seshimeta.* Bad weather caused him to abandon his climb to the summit.
- そういうゆとりを生ぜしめたものは、文明に違いない。 *Sō iu yutori wo shōzeshimeta mono wa, bunmei ni chigai nai.* There is no doubt but that it was civilization that brought about such leisure.

shimo-ichidan 下一段

As applied to verbs, *shimo-ichidan* denotes those ending in *-eru.* A list of the verbs ending in *-eru* but belonging to the *go-dan* category is given in the Introduction (III).

→ *kami-ichidan, go-dan katsuyō*

shi ro しろ 「する」の命令形から Derived from imperative of *suru*

「…にしろ」の形で、「例え…とも」という意味を表す *". . . ni shi ro" no katachi de, "tatoe. . . to mo" to iu imi wo arawasu* In . . . *ni shi ro* form, expresses concession:

- 行くにしろ、そんなに急ぐ必要はない。 *Iku ni shi ro, sonna ni isogu hitsuyō wa nai.* Even if you do go, there is no need to be in such a hurry.
- 行くにしろ、行かないにしろ、ともかく知らせてください。 *Iku ni shi ro, ikanai ni shi ro, to mo kaku shirasete kudasai.* Whether you go or not, please let us know.
- 明日にしろ、明後日にしろ、必ず起こる。 *Asu ni shi ro, asatte ni shi ro, kanarazu okoru.* It may be tomorrow, it may be the day after, but happen it will.

→ *de are, se yo*

shiru 知る 動詞 verb

Since the original meaning of this verb is "come to know", "get to know", it is found almost invariably in the progressive form in positive contexts; however, the simple form will be found in negative contexts:

- 住所を知っていますか。 *Jūsho wo shitte imasu ka?* Do you know the address?
- いいえ、知りません。 *Iie, shirimasen.* No, I don't.

NOTE. The humble form for *shiru* is *zonjiru, zonji-ageru;* the honorific form is *go-zonji desu.*

shita した 動詞 verb
「する」の連用形に、過去の助動詞「た」の連体形で、実際の「時」とは関係なしに、ある物事の実現を表す *"Suru" no ren'yōkei ni, kako no jodōshi "ta" no rentaikei de, jissai no "toki" to wa kankei nashi ni, aru monogoto no jitsugen wo arawasu* Base 2 of the verb *suru* plus Base 4 of past auxiliary *-ta*, denotes realization of a state or condition, irrespective of tense:

1.「こ・そ・あ・ど」ことばを伴って *"Ko・so・a・do" kotoba wo tomonatte* With *ko・so・a・do* words:

- どうしたはずみか失敗した。 *Dō shita hazumi ka shippai shita.* For some reason or other he failed.
- こうした疑念が起こった。 *Kō shita ginen ga okotta.* This kind of doubt arose.

2. 一語の擬声語を伴って *Ichi-go no giseigo wo tomonatte* With a single onomatope:

- あっさりした食べ物 *assari shita tabemono* light food; ぼんやりした顔つきで *bon'yari shita kao-tsuki de* with a vacant look; ちょっとしたこと *chotto shita koto* a trifle; ふっくらした唇 *fukkura shita kuchibiru* full lips; がっちりした男 *gatchiri shita otoko* strongly-built man; はっきりした証拠 *hakkiri shita shōko* clear proof; きっぱりした返事 *kippari shita henji* definite reply; のんびりした田園風景 *nonbiri shita den'en fūkei* quiet country scene; れっきとした事実 *rekki to shita jijitsu* obvious fact; しっかりした人物 *shikkari shita jinbutsu* reliable person; たっぷりした寸法 *tappuri shita sunpō* ample measurements.

3. 畳語の擬声語を伴って *Jōgo no giseigo wo tomonatte* With paired onomatopes:

- でぶでぶした下腹 *debu-debu shita shita-hara* pot belly; ふかふかしたベッド *fuka-fuka shita beddo* soft and comfortable bed; はきはきした少年 *haki-haki shita shōnen* lively youth; こせこせした人 *kose-kose shita hito* fussy person; のびのびした字を書く *nobi-nobi shita ji wo kaku* write in a free and easy style; そわそわした気持ちで *sowa-sowa shita kimochi de* in a nervous frame of mind; つやつやした肌 *tsuya-tsuya shita hada* smooth skin.

shite[1] して 格助詞（文語） case particle (classical)

「す」の連用形に接続助詞「て」が付いて、環境・条件を示す *"Su" no ren'yōkei ni setsuzoku joshi "-te" ga tsuite, kankyō • jōken wo shimesu* Made up of Base 2 of the verb *"su"* (modern *"suru"*) plus the conjunctive particle *-te*, denotes the circumstances of an action:

1. 場所・方法・理由などを表す *Basho • hōhō • riyū nado wo arawasu* Denotes place, method, reason, etc.:

- 弓矢して射られじ。 *Yumi-ya shite irareji.* He is invulnerable to bow and arrow.

2. 使役の対象を示す *Shieki no taishō wo shimesu* Denotes person made or allowed to act:

- 私をして言わしめれば *watashi wo shite iwashimereba* if you ask me.

3. 動作をする人数を示す *Dōsa wo suru ninzū wo shimesu* Denotes the number of persons involved:

- 皆して力を合わせてやれば出来る。 *Mina shite chikara wo awasete yareba dekiru.* If all pull together, it can be done.

→ *de*[3] 6

shite[2] して 接続助詞として （文語的） as a (classical) conjunctive particle

叙述を整えて、次へ続けるに用いる *Jojutsu wo totonoete, tsugi e tsuzukeru ni mochiiru* Adds emphasis to the element of conjunction:

- 御家へ寄り給わずしておはしましたり。 *O-ie e yori-tamawazu shite owashimashitari.* He proceeded without calling at his own house.

shite[3] して 副助詞として as an adverbial particle

格助詞に付いて、語調を整える *Kaku-joshi ni tsuite, go-chō wo totonoeru* Added to case particles, adjusts the tone:

- 休んだことからして許せません。 *Yasunda koto kara shite yurusemasen.* It is unpardonable of him to have taken the day off.

NOTE. This construction carries over into many expressions:

- どうして *dō shite* How? Why?; 得てして *ete shite* liable to; 頑として *gan to shite* stubbornly; ひょっとして *hyotto shite* by chance; 今にして *ima ni shite* at this time; 斯くして *kaku shite* thus; 辛うじて *karōjite* with difficulty; 期せずして *ki sezu shite* by accident; 幸いにして *saiwai ni shite* fortunately; 粛として *shuku to shite* awestricken; そうして *sō shite* and then, in that way; 既にして *sude ni shite* in the meantime; 大して *tai shite* (not) very; 突として *totsu to shite* suddenly; 杳として *yō to shite* dimly, not at all.

-sho[1] 章 接尾語 suffix
文や音楽などの段落を数える語 *Bun ya ongaku nado no danraku wo kazoeru go* Counter for sections of literature, music, and such like:
- マルコによる福音の第三章 *Maruko ni yoru Fukuin no dai san-shō* chapter III of Mark's Gospel.

-shō[2] 升
昔の容量の単位 *Mukashi no yōryō no tan'i* former measure of capacity = c. 1.8 liters

-shō[3] 性 接尾語 suffix
ある性質や傾向を持つことを示す *Aru seishitsu ya keikō wo motsu koto wo shimesu* Indicates presence of a character or tendency:
- 相性 *ai-shō* affinity, congeniality; 飽き性 *aki-shō* fickleness; 悪性 *aku-shō* ill nature, debauchery; 脂性 *abura-shō* greasiness; 荒れ性 *are-shō* susceptibility to chapping; 気性 *ki-shō* disposition; 苦労性 *kurō-shō* nervous disposition; 堪え性 *korae-shō* perseverance; 冷え性 *hie-shō* oversensitivity to cold; 本性 *hon-shō (hon-sei)* one's true nature; 仏性 *hotoke-shō* merciful disposition; 魔性 *ma-shō* devilishness; 水性 *mizu-shō* quality of water; 目性 *me-shō* condition of one's eyes; 手性 *te-shō* skill with the hands.

NOTE. There are also many compounds with the *-jō, -sei* readings of this character.

-shu[1] 首 接尾語 suffix
和歌・漢詩などを数える語 *Waka • Kanshi nado wo kazoeru go* Counter for Japanese and Chinese poems:
- 百人一首 *Hyakunin isshu* Collection of 100 poems by 100 authors. (A game of cards is based on this anthology.)

-shu[2] 株 接尾語 suffix
樹木を数える語 *Jumoku wo kazoeru go* Counter for trees:
- 樹木を十株伐採した。 *Jumoku wo jisshu (to-kabu) bassai shita.* They felled ten trees.

-shū 宗 接尾語 suffix
信仰上の分派の名称に付ける語 *Shinkō-jō no bunpa no meishō ni tsukeru go* Suffix denoting religious sect:
- 浄土真宗のお寺です。 *Jōdo Shinshū no o-tera desu.* It is a temple of the Jodo Shinshu sect.

shū-joshi 終助詞 final particle → *joshi*

shūshikei 終止形 Base 3, final base, in conjugation of verbals. → Introduction (III)

sō[1] そう 副詞 adverb

「そのように」という意味を表す *"Sono yō ni" to iu imi wo arawasu* Means "in that way":

- そうしてください。 *Sō shite kudasai.* Please do (it like) that.
- そうとは限らない。 *Sō to wa kagiranai.* That isn't always the case.
- そうは問屋が卸さない。 *Sō wa ton'ya ga orosanai.* That's expecting too much.

sō[2] そう 感動詞 interjection

1. 相手の言葉を肯定する意を表す *Aite no kotoba wo kōtei suru i wo arawasu* Denotes agreement with words of other party:
   - そう。そのとおりだ。 *Sō. Sono toori da.* Yes, it's just as you say.
2. 相手の言葉に対する驚きや疑問の気持ちを表す *Aite no kotoba ni taisuru odoroki ya gimon no kimochi wo arawasu* Expresses a sense of surprise or doubt in respect of words of other party:
   - そう。 *Sō?* (rising intonation) Really? (You don't say!)
3. 話を切り出す時に使う語 *Hanashi wo kiri-dasu toki ni tsukau go* Word used to preface a remark:
   - そう、それはよくやった。 *Sō, sore wa yoku yatta.* Indeed, you did well.

-sō[1] 艘 接尾語 suffix

小舟を数える語 *Ko-bune wo kazoeru go* Counter for boats. → *-seki*[1]

-sō[2] 荘 接尾語 suffix

人を宿泊させる設備に言う語 *Hito wo shukuhaku saseru setsubi ni iu go* Title for places of lodging:

- 別荘 *bes-sō* villa; 山荘 *san-sō* mountain retreat.

NOTE. This suffix is often used in the names of apartment houses;

- 清風荘 *Seifū-sō;* 緑荘 *Midori-sō.*

-sō[3] 双 接尾語 suffix

二つで一組となるものを数える語 *Futatsu de hito-kumi to naru mono wo kazoeru go* Counter for items that come in pairs:

• 屛風一双 *byōbu issō* one folding-screen; 無双の *mu-sō no* without a peer.

-sobireru そびれる 接尾語 suffix verb
動詞の連用形に付いて、「する機会を失う」「仕損なう」意味を添える *Dōshi no ren'yōkei ni tsuite, "suru kikai wo ushinau", "shi-sokonau" imi wo soeru* With Base 2 of verbs, adds the meaning of "miss the chance to . . .", "fail to . . .":

• 言いそびれる *ii-sobireru* fail to say; 聞きそびれる *kiki-sobireru* fail to hear; 寝そびれる *ne-sobireru* fail to get to sleep.

→ *-sokonau*

sochira そちら 代名詞 pronoun
指示代名詞、他称、中称。方向を示す *Shiji daimeishi, tashō, chūshō; hōkō wo shimesu* Demonstrative pronoun, 3rd. person, mesial; indicates direction.

1. 聞き手に近い所 *Kiki-te ni chikai tokoro* Place close to hearer:

• 昼からそちらに参ります。 *Hiru kara sochira ni mairimasu.* I'll go to your place this afternoon.

2. 聞き手に近い所にあるもの *Kiki-te ni chikai tokoro ni aru mono* Things close to hearer:

• そちらの方を頂きます。 *Sochira no hō wo itadakimasu.* I'll take that one (there near you).

3. 聞き手の側の人 *Kiki-te no gawa no hito* Persons belonging to hearer's group:

• そちらのご意見を聞いてください。 *Sochira no go-iken wo kiite kudasai.* Please ask the opinion of your friends.

NOTE. *Sotchi* is a colloquial form.

→ *achira, dochira, kochira*

-sō da[1] そうだ 助動詞（様態） auxiliary verb (evidential)
動詞の連用形、形容詞・形容動詞・助動詞「ない」「たい」の語幹に付いて、「そういう様子だ」という意味を表す *Dōshi no ren'yōkei, keiyōshi • keiyōdōshi • jodōshi "-nai", "-tai" no gokan ni tsuite, "sō iu yōsu da" to iu imi wo arawasu* Added to Base 2 of verbs, and to stem of adjectives, adjectival nouns and the auxiliaries *-nai* and *-tai*, expresses the idea of seeming to, looking like:

• 火が消えそうになった。 *Hi ga kiesō ni natta.* The fire looked like it was going out.

- 美味しそうなケーキだ。 *Oishisō na kēki da.* It's a delicious-looking cake.
- 涙が出そうなほど辛かった。 *Namida ga desō na hodo tsurakatta.* It hurt so much that he was almost in tears.

NOTE. The adjectives *nai, yoi* take the suffix *-sa* before adding this auxiliary:

- 「だめね」と情けなさそうに言った。 *"Dame ne" to nasake na-sa-sō ni itta.* "You are no good, are you?" she said, heartlessly.
- 生地はよさそうだ。 *Kiji wa yo-sa-sō da.* The material (fabric) seems good.

-sō da² そうだ　助動詞（伝聞） auxiliary verb (quotational)

活用語の終止形に付いて、伝聞を表す *Katsuyō-go no shūshikei ni tsuite, denbun wo arawasu* Added to Base 3 of conjugables, expresses report or hearsay:

- 明日は雨が降るそうです。 *Asu wa ame ga furu sō desu.* The forecast is for rain tomorrow.
- 頭がいいそうだ。 *Atama ga ii sō da.* By all accounts he is clever.
- 今年卒業するそうだ。 *Kotoshi sotsugyō suru sō da.* I hear he will graduate this year.
- 知らない人はないそうだ。 *Shiranai hito wa nai sō da.* It seems there is nobody but knows it.
- もう花が咲き出したそうだ。 *Mō hana ga saki-dashita sō da.* They say the flowers have begun to blossom already.

NOTE. This auxiliary has only Bases 2 (*sō de*) and 3 (*sō da*).

-sodachi 育ち　接尾語 suffix

名詞に付いて、「…で」、「…として」育つこと、または育てられた人 *Meishi ni tsuite, ". . . de", ". . . to shite" sodatsu koto, mata wa, sodaterareta hito* Added to nouns, denotes that one is reared in a certain place, on a certain food, or to a certain status, or the person thus reared:

- 坊ちゃん育ちの *botchan-sodachi no* reared in a sheltered environment; 牛乳育ちの *gyūnyū-sodachi no* reared on milk; 田舎育ちの *inaka-sodachi no* country-reared; 野性育ちの *yasei-sodachi no* ill-mannered; 温室育ちの *onshitsu-sodachi no* reared on a bed of roses; 下町育ち *shitamachi-sodachi* downtowner; 都会育ちの *tokai-sodachi no* city-bred.

soko そこ　代名詞 pronoun

指示代名詞、他称、中称。場所を示す *Shiji-daimeishi, tashō, chūshō.*

Basho wo shimesu Demonstrative pronoun, 3rd. person, mesial; denotes place:

- そこからまだ遠いよ。 *Soko kara mada tooi yo.* From there it is still quite a distance.
- そこまでは聞かなかった。 *Soko made wa kikanakatta.* I didn't go so far in my inquiries.
- そこが彼の特長だ。 *Soko ga kare no tokuchō da.* That is his strong point.

→ *asoko* (*asuko*), *doko, koko*

soko de そこで 接続詞 conjunction

1. 「その時」「それだから」 *"Sono toki", "sore da kara"* "And then", "for that reason":
   - ひどく眠くなっていた。そこですぐに寝てしまった。 *Hidoku nemuku natte ita. Soko de sugu ni nete shimatta.* I was terribly sleepy. For that reason I went to bed straight away.
2. 「さて」 *"Sate"* "Well, then":
   - そこで、何をなさいますか。 *Soko de, nani wo nasaimasu ka?* Well, then, what are you going to do?

-sokonau 損なう 補助動詞 supplementary verb

動詞の連用形に付いて、「その動作に失敗する」という意味を添える *Dōshi no ren'yōkei ni tsuite, "sono dōsa ni shippai suru" to iu imi wo soeru* With Base 2 of verbs, adds the idea of failing or making a mess of:

- 当て損なう *ate-sokonau* guess wrong; 出来損なう *deki-sokonau* turn out badly; 言い損なう *ii-sokonau* fail to say, express poorly; 買い損なう *kai-sokonau* miss a chance to buy; 書き損なう *kaki-sokonau* write incorrectly; 聞き損なう *kiki-sokonau* mis-hear, fail to hear; 見損なう *mi-sokonau* overlook, misjudge; 乗り損なう *nori-sokonau* miss (a bus, train, etc.); 溺れ損なう *obore-sokonau* nearly drown; 仕損なう *shi-sokonau* bungle; 取り損なう *tori-sokonau* fail to take (a prize); 食べ損なう *tabe-sokonau* miss (a meal); 打ち損なう *uchi-sokonau* fail to hit (a ball, etc.), type incorrectly; やり損なう *yari-sokonau* bungle; 読み損なう *yomi-sokonau* mis-read.

NOTE. Both *shini-zokonai* and *umare-zokonai* are found as an extremely pejorative epithets:

- 死に損ない *shini-zokonai:* 長生きして役立たない老人を罵って言う言葉 *naga-iki shite yaku ni tatanai rōjin wo nonoshitte iu kotoba* abusive epithet for an old person who has outlived his or her usefulness.

- 生まれ損ない *umare-zokonai:* 体・性格・能力などが並でないこと・人 *karada • seikaku • nōryoku nado ga nami de nai koto • hito* the fact of being, or the one who is, abnormal in body, character, capacity, and so on.

-soku[1] 足 接尾語 suffix

履物を数える語 *Haki-mono wo kazoeru go* Counter for items of footwear:

- 足袋は五足ぐらいあればいい。 *Tabi wa go-soku gurai areba ii.* Five pairs or so of *tabi* will do.

NOTE. Although the verb *haku* is used for the operation of putting on any item of clothing covering from the waist down, *haki-mono* extends only to footwear.

NOTE. In the phrase *is-soku tobi, -soku* has the meaning of "leap", "bound":

- 初級から一足飛びに三級になった。 *Shokyū kara is-soku tobi ni san-kyū ni natta.* He went from beginners' level to third level in one bound.

-soku[2] 則 接尾語 suffix

列挙した事柄を数える語 *Rekkyo shita kotogara wo kazoeru go* Counter for items on a list:

- 作業心得十則 *sagyō kokoroe jis-soku* ten rules regarding attitude to work

-soku[3] 束 接尾語 suffix

束ねたものを数える語 *Tabaneta mono wo kazoeru go* Counter for bundles:

- 薪を一束準備しておいた。 *Takigi wo is-soku (hito-taba) junbi shite oita.* He prepared a bundle of firewood.

NOTE. Formerly, this counter was used also for reams (200 sheets) of paper and as a unit in the measuring of the length of arrows (one 束 was the width of four fingers).

soku-on 促音

The small っ、ッ that signals doubling of the consonant following.

-someru 初める 接尾語 suffix verb

動詞の連用形に付いて、「…し始める」「初めて…する」という意味を添える *Dōshi no ren'yōkei ni tsuite, ". . . shi-hajimeru", "hajimete. . .*

suru" to iu imi wo soeru With Base 2 of verbs, adds the idea of beginning, or doing for the first time:

- 見初める *mi-someru* see for first time, fall in love at first sight; 馴れ初める *nare-someru* become intimate; 咲き初める *saki-someru* begin to bloom.

NOTE. Originally the verb was 染める、to dye, but it is now written 初める。

→ *hajime, hatsu-, -zome*

sonata そなた 代名詞（文語） pronoun (classical)

指示代名詞、他称、中称。方向を示す *Shiji-daimeishi, tashō, chūshō. Hōkō wo shimesu* Demonstrative pronoun, 3rd. person, mesial; denotes direction.

1. そちらの方 *sochira no hō* that direction.

2. 汝、お前 *nanji, o-mae* you (said to inferiors).

NOTE. Of this group, *anata* and *donata* have carried over into modern Japanese, but *sonata* and *kanata* are considered archaic.

sonna da そんなだ 形容動詞 adjectival noun

「そのような」 *Sono yō na* Such (a):

- そんな時に慌てるのではない。 *Sonna toki ni awateru no de wa nai.* One shouldn't get excited in such cases.
- 何がそんなにおかしいの。 *Nani ga sonna ni okashii no?* What is there to laugh at?

→ *anna da, donna da, konna da*

sono その 連体詞 adnoun

1. 相手に近い事物 *Aite ni chikai jibutsu* Objects close to other party:

- その写真を見せてください。*Sono shashin wo misete kudasai.* Let me have a look at that photo, please.

2. すぐ前に述べたこと *Sugu mae ni nobeta koto* Matter(s) just mentioned:

- その後一週間してまた会った。 *Sono go isshūkan shite mata atta.* We met again a week later.

sore それ 代名詞 pronoun

指示代名詞、他称、中称。事物を示す *Shiji-daimeishi, tashō, chūshō Jibutsu wo shimesu* Demonstrative pronoun, 3rd. person, mesial; denotes things.

1. 事物を指す *Jibutsu wo sasu* Indicates objects:

- これじゃなくてそれにしよう *Kore ja nakute sore ni shiyō.* I'll take that one, not this.

2. 人物を指す *Jinbutsu wo sasu* Indicates persons (only of one's own group, deferentially):

- それが家内です。 *Sore ga kanai desu.* That is my wife.

3. すぐ前に述べた事柄を指す *Sugu mae ni nobeta kotogara wo sasu* Refers to matters just mentioned:

- それを何時聞いたのですか。 *Sore wo itsu kiita no desu ka?* When did you hear that?

4.「その時」を示す *"Sono toki" wo shimesu* Refers to "that time":

- それ以来会っていない。 *Sore irai atte inai.* I haven't met him since.

NOTE. Some idioms with *sore:*

- 今出れば、それだけ早く向こうに着く。 *Ima dereba, sore dake hayaku mukō ni tsuku.* If you leave now, you will get there all the sooner.
- 目が見えない。 それだけに皆に愛される。 *Me ga mienai. Sore dake ni mina ni ai sareru.* He is blind. For that reason he is loved all the more.
- それどころか、食うや食わずのありさまだ。 *Sore-dokoro ka, kuu ya kuwazu no ari-sama da.* On the contrary, it is as much as I can do to make ends meet.
- どうしてそれほど会いたいのか。 *Dōshite sore hodo aitai no ka?* Why are you so anxious to meet him?
- それからそれと用が出来る。 *Sore kara sore to yō ga dekiru.* I'm busy with one thing and another.
- 問題はそれっきりになっている。 *Mondai wa sorekkiri ni natte iru.* The matter remains pending.
- それっきり連絡を取っていない。 *Sorekkiri renraku wo totte inai.* I haven't contacted him since.
- それなりに良いところがある。 *Sore nari ni yoi tokoro ga aru.* It has merits of its own.
- その問題にそれとなく触れた。 *Sono mondai ni sore to naku fureta.* He touched on the matter indirectly.

-soroi 揃い 接尾語 suffix

揃って一組になっているものを数える語 *Sorotte hito-kumi ni natte iru mono wo kazoeru go* Counter for items that come in sets:

- 家具一揃い *kagu hito-soroi* set of furniture; 五冊で一揃いの本 *gosatsu de hito-soroi no hon* set of five volumes.

→ *-zoroi*

-sōtō 相当　接尾語的に　as a suffix

- 二つのものが釣り合っていてふさわしいこと *Futatsu no mono ga tsuri-atte ite fusawashii koto* Denotes equivalence:
  - 子供相当の知恵 *kodomo-sōtō no chie* intelligence-level of a child.
  - 四千円相当の食事 *yonsen'en-sōtō no shokuji* ¥4000 meal.

→ *keiyō-dōshi*

su- 素　接頭語　prefix

1. ありのまま *Ari no mama* Bare, mere:
   - 素足 *su-ashi* bare feet; 素顔 *su-gao* face without make-up, one's true self; 素手 *su-de* empty hand; 素焼き *su-yaki* unglazed pottery.
2. 普通の程度を越える *Futsū no teido wo koeru* Exceeding the norm:
   - 素晴らしい *su-barashii* splendid; 素早い *su-bayai* swift; 素敵 *su-teki* splendour.
3. みすぼらしい *Mi-suborashii* Shabby:
   - 素町人 *su-chōnin* mere townsman; 素浪人 *su-rōnin* mere "ronin".

su す　動詞（文語）　verb (classical)

A carry-over from *bungo, su,* instead of *suru,* is added to single Chinese words; it is conjugated slightly irregularly. Some of the following words will be found also with *suru,* and conjugated regularly:

- 愛す *ai-su* love; 会す *e-su* understand; 付す *fu-su* attach; 服す *fuku-su* submit; 復す *fuku-su* return; 害す *gai-su* harm; 擬す *gi-su* imitate; 議す *gi-su* debate; 拝す *hai-su* worship; 配す *hai-su* arrange; 排す *hai-su* clear away; 廃す *hai-su* abolish; 博す *haku-su* gain; 比す *hi-su* compare; 秘す *hi-su* conceal; 表す *hyō-su* express; 辞す *ji-su* resign; 叙す *jo-su* confer; 序す *jo-su* write a preface; 除す *jo-su* divide, omit; 恕す *jo-su* forgive; 熟す *juku-su* ripen; 会す *kai-su* assemble; 介す *kai-su* have an intermediary, feel concerned; 解す *kai-su* interpret; 供す *kyō-su* supply; 休す *kyū-su* end, rest; 略す *ryaku-su* abbreviate; 制す *sei-su* control; 処す *sho-su* dispose of; 宿す *shuku-su* lodge; 祝す *shuku-su* celebrate; 対す *tai-su* face; 託す *taku-su* entrust; 適す *teki-su* suit; 和す *wa-su* harmonize; 約す *yaku-su* promise; 訳す *yaku-su* translate; 贅す *zei-su* talk idly; 属す *zoku-su* belong.

NOTE. The irregularity consists in this that these verbs are treated as if they were *go-dan* verbs ending in *-su:*

1. Example of a *go-dan* verb, *dasu* (put out):
   - 出そうとする *dasō to suru,* 出さない *dasanai,* 出しません *dashimasen,* 出す *dasu,* 出せば *daseba,* 出せ *dase.*

2. Example of *su* verb, *yaku-su* (to translate):
- 訳そうとする *yakusō to suru,* 訳さない *yakusanai,* 訳しません *yaku-shimasen,* 訳す *yakusu,* 訳せば *yakuseba,* 訳せ *yakuse.*

-sugara すがら 接尾語 suffix
名詞に付いて、副詞的に使われる *Meishi ni tsuite, fukushi-teki ni tsuka-wareru* Added to nouns and used adverbially.
1.「...の間ずっと」"*. . . No aida zutto*" All through (that length of time):
- 終日 *hi(mo)-sugara* all day long; 終夜 *yo(mo)-sugara* all night long.

2.「そのまま」"*Sono mama*" As it is:
- 身すがら *mi-sugara* (i) by oneself; (ii) unencumbered.

3.「...のついでに」"*. . . No tsuide ni*" On one's way:
- 道すがら *michi-sugara* on one's way; 旅すがら *tabi-sugara* while travelling; 行きすがら *yuki-sugara* on one's way.

-sugata 姿 接尾語 suffix
体付き、格好、服装などを表す *Karada-tsuki, kakkō, fukusō nado wo arawasu* Denotes physique, appearance, dress, etc.:
- 艶姿 *ade-sugata* charming appearance; 伊達姿 *date-sugata* smart attire; 道中姿 *dōchū-sugata* travelling attire; 絵姿 *e-sugata* portrait; 晴れ姿 *hare-sugata* dressed in one's best; 夏姿 *natsu-sugata* dressed for summer; 寝姿 *ne-sugata* sleeping posture; 立ち姿 *tachi-sugata* standing posture; 後ろ姿 *ushiro-sugata* back view; 童姿 *warawa-sugata* childlike appearance; 優姿 *yasa-sugata* graceful figure; やつれ姿 *yatsure-sugata* shabby appearance.

NOTE. The word is found also as a prefix:
- 姿絵 *sugata-e* portrait; 姿見 *sugata-mi* full-length mirror; 姿焼き *sugata-yaki* roasting without altering shape; 姿鮨 *sugata-zushi* boned fish on top of rice.

-sugi 過ぎ 接尾語 suffix
1. 時間・年齢を越えていること *Jikan • nenrei wo koete iru koto* Past a certain time or age:
- 到着は八時過ぎになる。 *Tōchaku wa hachiji-sugi ni naru.* It will be after eight when we arrive.
- 五十過ぎの人だった。*Gojū-sugi no hito datta.* He was a man over fifty.

2. 程度が必要以上であること *Teido ga hitsuyō-ijō de aru koto* Degree is excessive:

・食べ過ぎをして腹を壊した。 *Tabe-sugi wo shite hara wo kowashita.* He ate too much and upset his stomach.

-sugiru 過ぎる 接尾語 suffix
動詞の連用形、形容詞・形容動詞の語幹に付いて、「度を過ごす」という意味を添える *Dōshi no ren'yōkei, keiyōshi • keiyōdōshi no gokan ni tsuite, "do wo sugosu" to iu imi wo soeru* With Base 2 of verbs and stem of adjectives and adjectival nouns, adds the idea of going to excess:
・酒を飲み過ぎてはだめです。 *Sake wo nomi-sugite wa dame desu.* You mustn't drink too much.
・十分早く来過ぎた。 *Jippun hayaku ki-sugita.* I came ten minutes too early.
・昇進には若すぎるでしょう。 *Shōshin ni wa waka-sugiru deshō.* He is probably too young for promotion.
・良すぎる *yo-sugiru* be too good.
NOTE. The adjective *nai* adds *-sa* before the suffix:
・なさ過ぎるのは金だ。 *Na-sa-sugiru no wa kane da.* What I lack most is money.

-sugosu 過ごす 補助動詞として as a supplementary verb
動詞の連用形に付く *Dōshi no ren'yōkei ni tsuku* Is attached to Base 2 of verbs.
1. そのままにしておく *Sono mama ni shite oku* Allow to pass:
・聞き過ごす *kiki-sugosu* take no notice of; 見過ごす *mi-sugosu* overlook, fail to notice.
2. 程度を越える *Teido wo koeru* Go to excess:
・言い過ごす *ii-sugosu* say too much; 寝過ごす *ne-sugosu* sleep later than usual (cf. 寝過ぎる *ne-sugiru* do too much sleeping); 乗り過ごす *nori-sugosu* ride past (one's station); やり過ごす *yari-sugosu* let pass, do to excess.

sura すら 副助詞 adverbial particle
極端な例を挙げて、他を類推させる *Kyokutan na rei wo agete, hoka wo ruisui saseru* Cites an extreme case, suggesting that others are similar:
・贅沢品はおろか、日用品すら買えない。 *Zeitaku-hin wa oroka, nichiyō-hin sura kae-nai.* I can't afford the daily necessaries, let alone luxuries.
・あんな弱いチームにすら負けてしまった。 *Anna yowai chīmu ni sura makete shimatta.* We had the misfortune to go down even to such a weak team!

NOTE. This particle may not come between a verb and an auxiliary. → *sae*

suru する　サ行変格活用動詞 special conjugation verb.

The conjugation is: (*kōgo*) 1. *shi, sa, se* 2. *shi* 3. *suru* 4. *suru* 5. *sure* 6. *shiro, seyo;* (*bungo*) 1. *se* 2. *shi* 3. *su* 4. *suru* 5. *sure* 6. —.

NOTE. *Suru* is peculiar because it has three forms of Base 1. The following are some helpful notes about the conjugations:

1. *shi* of Base 1 precedes *-nai, -tai, -yō, -sō da*[1].
2. *sa* of Base 1 precedes *-reru, -seru.*
3. *se* of Base 1 precedes *-ne* of negative conditional (*se-ne-ba*).
4. *se* of *senu, sezu* is Base 1 of the *bungo* verb.
5. *su* of *su-beki,* etc., is Base 3 of the *bungo* verb.

A. 自動詞として *Jidōshi to shite* As an intransitive verb.

1. 感じられる・起こる *Kanjirareru • okoru* Be felt, happen:

- 変な音がする。 *Hen na oto ga suru.* There is a strange noise.
- 嫌な匂いがする。 *Iya na nioi ga suru.* There is a stench.
- 耳鳴りがする。 *Mimi-nari ga suru.* I have a ringing in my ears.

2. ある状態になる *Aru jōtai ni naru* A condition develops:

- じっとしていられなかった。 *Jitto shite irarenakatta.* I was like a hen on a hot griddle.
- 失敗することははっきりしている。 *Shippai suru koto wa hakkiri shite iru.* It is evident that he will fail.

3. 金額を指す語を受けて、「その値段だ」 *Kingaku wo sasu go wo ukete, "sono nedan da"* After an expression denoting a sum of money, states the price:

- 二万円する時計を贈った。 *Niman'en suru tokei wo okutta.* I made (him) a present of a watch worth ¥20,000.

4. 時間を指す語を受けて、「その時間がたつ」 *Jikan wo sasu go wo ukete, "sono jikan ga tatsu"* With time expressions, denotes that so much time elapses:

- 十分ぐらいすると、意識を回復した。 *Jippun gurai suru to, ishiki wo kaifuku shita.* He came to after about ten minutes.

5. 「...うとする」の形で、 *". . . -ō • -yō to suru" no katachi de,* In . . . *-ō/-yō to suru* form,

a. 「実現のために努力する」 *"Jitsugen no tame ni doryoku suru"* Denotes the attempt (sometimes unsuccessful) to do something:

- 逃げようとしたのだが、すぐに捕まった。 *Nigeyō to shita no da ga, sugu ni tsukamatta.* He tried to get away, but was caught immediately.

b. 動作・状態が起こりかけている *Dōsa・jōtai ga okori-kakete iru* Denotes that the action or state is just about to begin:

- 帰ろうとするところへ、雨が降ってきた。 *Kaerō to suru tokoro e, ame ga futte kita.* Just as I was on the point of leaving, it started to rain. (→ *-ō, -yō*)

B. 他動詞として *Tadōshi to shite* As a transitive verb.

1. 行なう・なす *Okonau・nasu* Do, perform (even involuntarily):

- いたずらをするな。 *Itazura wo suru na!* None of your tricks!
- 神田で本屋をしている。 *Kanda de hon'ya wo shite iru.* He runs a bookstore in Kanda.
- 疲れてあくびをしてしまった。 *Tsukarete akubi wo shite shimatta.* I was so tired that I yawned.

2. ある性質や状態を表す *Aru seishitsu ya jōtai wo arawasu* Denotes presence of a certain characteristic or condition:

- 驚いた顔をしていた。 *Odoroita kao wo shite ita.* He had a surprised look.
- 肩まで垂れる髪をしている。 *Kata made tareru kami wo shite iru.* She has shoulder-length hair.
- 熱湯で火傷をしてしまった。 *Nettō de yakedo wo shite shimatta.* I had the misfortune to scald myself with boiling water.
- どんな色をしていた。 *Donna iro wo shite ita?* What color was it?

3. 身に付ける *Mi ni tsukeru* Put on or wear:

- 眼帯をする必要はない。 *Gantai wo suru hitsuyō wa nai.* There is no need of an eye-bandage.
- 覆面をした強盗が入ってきた。 *Fukumen wo shita gōtō ga haitte kita.* A masked burglar entered.

NOTE. *Suru* serves as a substitute for the following verbs:

- *ateru* (affix); *haku* (put on pants, etc.); *hameru* (put on gloves, rings); *kakeru* (put on glasses, etc.); *maku* (wrap); *shimeru* (tie); *tsukeru* (put on mask, watch, etc.).

4. 「…にする」の形で、「…にならせる」という意味を表す *". . . Ni suru" no katachi de, ". . . ni naraseru" to iu imi wo arawasu* In *. . . ni suru* form, expresses "cause to become":

- 息子を医師にしたい。 *Musuko wo ishi ni shitai.* I want to make a doctor of my son.

5. 「…とする」の形で、「…と仮定する」という意味を表す *". . . To suru" no katachi de, ". . . to katei suru" to iu imi wo arawasu* In *. . . to suru* form, expresses a supposition:

- 地震があったとしよう *Jishin ga atta to shiyō.* Let's suppose there has been an earthquake.

6.「お＋動詞の連用形＋する」の形で、へりくだりの意を表す *"O- + dōshi no ren'yōkei + suru" no katachi de, herikudari no i wo arawasu* In *o-* + Base 2 of verbs + *suru* form, expresses a sense of deference:

- お借りした本をお返しします。 *O-kari shita hon wo o-kaeshi shimasu.* I am returning the book I borrowed.

NOTE. The use of *suru* in phrases.

1. With native Japanese words:
   - 暇乞いする *itomagoi suru* take one's leave; 真似する *mane suru* mimic; お供する *o-tomo suru* accompany; 噂する *uwasa suru* gossip.
2. With single Chinese words:
   - 愛する *ai-suru* love; 害する *gai-suru* harm; 決する *kes-suru* decide, collapse; 略する *ryaku-suru* abbreviate, omit; 接する *ses-suru* touch, border on; 訳する *yaku-suru* translate. (→ *su*)

NOTE. With words ending in the *hatsu-on n,* the "s" is voiced:

- 感ずる *kan-zuru* feel; 信ずる（信じる） *shin-zuru* (*shin-jiru*) believe.

3. With compound Chinese words:
   - 安心する *anshin suru* feel relieved; 議論する *giron suru* argue; 成功する *seikō suru* succeed; 運動する *undō suru* take exercise.
4. With adjective-derived words ending in the *hatsuon n:*
   - 甘んずる、甘んじる *aman-zuru, aman-jiru* content oneself; 軽んずる、軽んじる *karon-zuru, karon-jiru* make light of; 重んずる、重んじる *omon-zuru, omon-jiru* make much of; 安んずる、安んじる *yasun-zuru, yasun-jiru* be contented with.
5. With borrowed words:
   - アップする *appu suru* increase; バックする *bakku suru* back; マッチする *matchi suru* match; スケッチする *suketchi suru* sketch.

NOTE. As to whether the case particle *wo* is necessary before *suru* or not, see *wo*.

- 勉強する *benkyō suru* study; 地理の勉強をする *chiri no benkyō wo suru* apply oneself to (the study of) geography.

sūshi 数詞 numeral → Appendix C.

suteru 捨てる 接頭語・接尾語として as a prefix and suffix

Both as prefix (*sute-*) and suffix (*-suteru*), this word has some idiomatic applications:

- 捨て鐘 *sute-gane* three rings before main time-signal (but 捨て金 *sute-gane* wasted money); 捨て石 *sute-ishi* extra rock for effect (in Japanese garden), riprap; 捨て小舟 *sute-obune* (i) deserted boat; (ii) abandoned person; 捨てぜりふ *sute-zerifu* parting shot.

・言い捨てる *ii-suteru* say over one's shoulder; 履き捨てる・着捨てる *haki-suteru* • *ki-suteru* wear out and discard; 聞き捨てる *kiki-suteru* hear but ignore; 切り捨て御免 *kiri-sute go-men* right of *samurai* to slay a commoner; 吐き捨てる *haki-suteru* spit out one's words; 掛け捨てにする *kake-sute ni suru* stop paying instalments; 呼び捨てにする *yobi-sute ni suru* address without using an honorific title; 読み捨てる *yomi-suteru* (i) read and throw away; (ii) read perfunctorily.

T

ta-[1] た 接頭語 prefix

動詞・形容詞の上に付いて、語調を整え、意味を強める語 *Dōshi • keiyōshi no ue ni tsuite, gochō wo totonoe, imi wo tsuyomeru go* Word prefixed to verbs and adjectives, adjusting the tone and strengthening the meaning:

・たばかる *ta-bakaru* cheat, contrive, consult; たなびく *ta-nabiku* hang over; たやすい *ta-yasui* simple.

ta-[2] 手 接頭語 prefix

・手挟む *ta-basamu* carry in hands, wear (a sword) at one's side; 手繰る *ta-guru* reel in; 手向ける *ta-mukeru* offer (flowers); 手折る *ta-oru* pluck; 手弱女 *ta-oyame* • *ta-wayame* graceful woman; 手綱（たづな）*ta-zuna* reins → 目 *ma-*[1]

-ta た 助動詞（特別活用） special conjugation auxiliary verb → *-da*[1]

The conjugation is: 1. *taro* 2. — 3. *ta* 4. *ta* 5. *tara* 6. —.

活用語の連用形に付いて、 *Katsuyō-go no ren'yōkei ni tsuite,* with Base 2 of conjugables,

1. 過去を表す *Kako wo arawasu* Expresses past tense:

・今朝五時に起きた。 *Kesa go-ji ni okita.* I got up at five this morning.

・今年の冬は寒かった。 *Kotoshi no fuyu wa samukatta.* We have had a cold winter.

2. 完了を表す *Kanryō wo arawasu* Expresses completion:

・弟は今起きたところだ。 *Otōto wa ima okita tokoro da.* My brother has just got up.

3. 存続を表す *Sonzoku wo arawasu* Expresses continuance of a state:

・優れた生徒もいる。 *Sugureta seito mo iru.* There are exceptional students, too.

NOTE. This contraction of *-te aru* often translates as an English adjective:

- 似たところ *nita-tokoro* similarities; 異なったところ *kotonatta tokoro* differences; 晴れた日 *hareta hi* fine day; 曇った日 *kumotta hi* cloudy day; 汚れた手 *yogoreta te* dirty hands; 熟した果物 *juku-shita kudamono* ripe fruit; 太った人 *futotta hito* stout person; 痩せた人 *yaseta hito* thin person; にこにこした顔 *niko-niko shita kao* smiling face; 名を知られた作品 *na wo shirareta sakuhin* well-known work.

NOTE. Verbs ending in *-bu, -gu, -mu, -nu* form the past tense in *-da:*

- 飛ぶ *to-bu, ton-da;* 脱ぐ *nu-gu, nui-da;* 読む *yo-mu, yon-da;* 死ぬ *shi-nu, shin-da.*

NOTE. *-Ba* is not added to the conditional *-tara.*

NOTE. Some idiomatic expressions using *-ta:*

- 帰ってきたばかりだ。 *Kaette kita bakari da.* He has just returned.
- 腹を立てたばかりに *hara wo tateta bakari ni* just because he got angry.
- 機会を与えたが最後 *kikai wo ataeta ga saigo* once you give him the chance.
- 寝たきりのお爺さん *neta-kiri no o-jiisan* bed-ridden old man.
- したことがある *shita koto ga aru* have had experience of doing.
- したものだ *shita mono da* used to do, would (often) do.
- した例がない *shita tameshi ga nai* have never had the experience of doing.
- 行ってきたところだ *itte kita tokoro da* have just been there.
- 確かめてみたところが *tashikamete mita tokoro ga* checked and found that . . .
- 鍵を掛けたつもりりだ *kagi wo kaketa tsumori da* I think I locked it.
- 欠陥が明らかになった上は、 *kekkan ga akiraka ni natta ue wa,* since the defect has become apparent.

NOTE. The *-ta* does not always imply the past:

- 謝ったところで *ayamatta tokoro de* even if you apologize (later on)
- 忘れた場合には *wasureta baai ni wa* if I should forget

tabi 度 形式名詞 formal noun

1. 時・折 *Toki • ori* Time, occasion:

- この度はおめでとうございます。 *Kono tabi wa omedetō gozaimasu.* Congratulations on this happy occasion.

2. その時ごと *Sono toki-goto* Every time (that...):

- 会うたびに喧嘩してしまう。 *Au tabi ni kenka shite shimau.* Every time we meet we cross swords.

3. 数詞に付いて、回数を示す *Sūshi ni tsuite, kaisū wo shimesu* With numerals, denotes frequency:

- 幾度やってみても、失敗した。 *Iku-tabi yatte mite mo, shippai shita.* No matter how many times I tried, I always failed.

tachi- 立ち 接頭語 prefix

Besides its literal meaning of "do while standing", this prefix serves also as just an intensifier:

- 立ち食い *tachi-gui* eating while standing; 立ち見 *tachi-mi* viewing while standing; 立ち泳ぎ *tachi-oyogi* treading water; 立ち売り *tachi-uri* street vending, street vendor; 立ち読み *tachi-yomi* stand-up reading.
- 立ち入る *tachi-iru* enter, interfere; 立ち止まる *tachi-domaru* come to a halt; 立ち直る *tachi-naoru* revive; 立ち去る *tachi-saru* depart.

-tachi 達 接尾語 suffix

複数を示す *Fukusū wo shimesu* Indicates plurality:

- 君たちもやりたいの。 *Kimi-tachi mo yaritai no?* Do you want to play, too?

NOTE. This was originally a highly respectful suffix, but it is now found attached to names of animals and even inanimate objects.

NOTE. Added to 友 *tomo,* it does not necessarily imply plurality.

→ *-domo*[1], *-gata*[1], *-ra*

-tagaru たがる 助動詞 auxiliary verb

助動詞「たい」の語幹に、接尾語「がる」からなる助動詞 *Jodōshi "-tai" no gokan ni, setsubigo "-garu" kara naru jodōshi* Auxiliary verb consisting of the auxiliary verb *-tai* plus the suffix verb *-garu.*

The conjugation is: 1. *tagara, tagaro* 2. *tagari, tagatt* (たがっ) 3. *tagaru* 4. *tagaru* 5. *tagare* 6. (*tagare*).

動詞の連用形に付いて、他人が望んでいる気持ちを表す *Dōshi no ren'yōkei ni tsuite, tanin ga nozonde iru kimochi wo arawasu* Added to Base 2 of verbs, conveys the idea that somebody other than oneself desires:

- 誰にも会いたがらない。 *Dare ni mo ai-tagaranai.* He doesn't want to see anybody.
- 見たがれば見せてくれるだろう。 *Mi-tagareba misete kureru darō.* If you want to see it he will show it to you.
- 山に登りたがっている。 *Yama ni nobori-tagatte iru.* They want to go mountain climbing.

- 子供はいつもお菓子を食べたがっている。 *Kodomo wa itsu mo o-kashi wo tabe-tagatte iru.* Children always want to eat sweets.

NOTE. Whereas *-tai* may take either *ga* or *wo, -tagaru* can take only *wo.*

-tai[1] たい（度い） 助動詞 auxiliary verb

The conjugation is: 1. *takaro* 2. *takatt* (たかっ) 3. *tai* 4. *tai* 5. *takere* 6. —.

動詞・助動詞の連用形に付いて、形容詞型活用をし、希望を表す *Dōshi • jodōshi no ren'yōkei ni tsuite, keiyōshi-gata katsuyō wo shi, kibō wo arawasu* Added to Base 2 of verbs and auxiliaries, conjugates like an adjective, and expresses desire:

- 校長先生に会いたいのですが。 *Kōchō-sensei ni aitai no desu ga.* I should like to meet the principal.
- 行ってみたいのですか。 *Itte mitai no desu ka?* Would you like to go?
- 読みたくなければ読まなくてもいい。 *Yomitaku nakereba yomanakute mo ii.* You don't have to read it if you don't want to.
- 誰にも知られたくなかったのだ。 *Dare ni mo shiraretaku nakatta no da.* He didn't want anyone to know it (to recognize him).
- その老人の夢の中で、泳いだり走ったりできる女の子になりたかった。 *Sono rōjin no yume no naka de, oyoidari hashittari dekiru onna no ko ni naritakatta.* She wanted to be, in the old man's dream, a girl that could swim and run.

NOTE. To the stem *-ta-* may be added the suffixes *-ge* and *-sa*, and the auxiliary *-sō da*[1]:

- 何か言いたげな様子だ。 *Nani-ka ii-ta-ge na yōsu da.* He seems to want to say something. (He looks as if he has something to say.)
- 帰りたさに眠れない夜もある。 *Kaerita-sa ni nemurenai yoru mo aru.* There are nights when homesickness keeps me awake.
- 妹も行きたそうにしていた。 *Imōto mo ikita-sō ni shite ita.* My sister, too, seemed to want to go.

-tai[2] たい 接尾語 suffix

名詞・動詞の連用形に付いて、形容詞を作り、「甚だしい」という意味を添える *Meishi • dōshi no ren'yōkei ni tsuite, keiyōshi wo tsukuri, "hanahadashii" to iu imi wo soeru* With nouns and Base 2 of verbs, makes adjectives of them and adds the idea of intensity:

- はばったい *habat-tai* wide, self-important; じれったい *jiret-tai* exasperating; 煙たい・煙ったい *kemu-tai • kemut-tai* smoky, feel uneasy (in a person's presence); くすぐったい *kusugut-tai* tickling; 野暮ったい *yabot-tai* boorish.

-tai[3] 体 接尾語 suffix
神仏の像を数える語 *Shinbutsu no zō wo kazoeru go* Counter for statues:
- 尊像一体 *sonzō it-tai* one Buddhist image.

tame ため 形式名詞 formal noun
名詞＋の、動詞の連体形に付く *Meishi + "no", dōshi no rentaikei ni tsuku* Is added to noun + *no,* or to Base 4 of verbs.
1. 理由・原因を示す *Riyū • gen'in wo shimesu* Denotes reason or cause:
- 病気のために休んでいる。 *Byōki no tame ni yasunde iru.* He is absent because of illness.

2. 目的を示す *Mokuteki wo shimesu* Denotes purpose:
- 通学のために自転車を買った。 *Tsūgaku no tame ni jitensha wo katta.* He bought a bicycle for going to school.
- 念のために尋ねた。 *Nen no tame ni tazuneta.* I asked in order to make sure.
- 生きるために食べるのだ。 *Ikiru tame ni taberu no da.* We eat to live.

-tan 反 接尾語 suffix (no longer used)
1. 反物の長さの単位 *Tan-mono no nagasa no tan'i* Unit of cloth measure. = about 10cm.
2. 土地の面積の単位 *Tochi no menseki no tan'i* Unit of square measure; = about 992 sq. m.
3. 距離の単位 *Kyori no tan'i* Unit of long measure; = about 11m.

-tara[1] たら 助動詞 auxiliary verb
過去の助動詞「た」の仮定形 *Kako no jodōshi "-ta" no kateikei* Base 5 (conditional) of past auxiliary *-ta* (q. v.):
- 行けたらいいな。 *Iketara ii na!* How I wish I could go!
- 降ってきたらどうしよう。 *Futte kitara dō shiyō?* What shall we do if it should rain?
- 本が空いたら貸してくれ。 *Hon ga aitara kashite kure.* Lend me the book as soon as you have done with it.
- 戸を開けてみたら、誰もいなかった。 *To wo akete mitara, dare mo inakatta.* I opened the door, only to find there was nobody there.

NOTE. Idiomatic expressions using *-tara:*
- 暖かいうちに召し上がったら。 *Atatakai uchi ni meshi-agattara.* How about eating it up while it is hot.

- 逃げ出したら逃げ出したで、仕方がない。 *Nige-dashitara nige-dashita de, shikata ga nai.* What if he (the dog) has run away?

-tara² （っ）たら　終助詞　final particle
活用語の終止形や命令形に付いて、非難の気持ちを込めて強く言い切る *Katsuyō-go no shūshikei ya meireikei ni tsuite, hinan no kimochi wo komete tsuyoku ii-kiru* Added to Base 3 or Base 6 of conjugables, ends the sentence abruptly with an air of rebuke:
- いやだったら。止めて。 *Iya dattara. Yamete.* Stop it!
- 早く行けったら。 *Hayaku ikettara!* Off with you, now!

-tara³ （っ）たら　副助詞　adverbial particle
「とやら」の略で、話題として提示し、非難する *"To yara" no ryaku de, wadai to shite teiji shi, hinan suru* A contraction of *to yara,* introduces a topic while attaching an air of censure:
- あの人ったら、とてもけちなのよ。 *Ano hito-ttara, totemo kechi na no yo!* That fellow, he's a real skinflint!
- 朝から開け放しにして、用心が悪いわ、姉さんたら。 *Asa kara ake-hanashi ni shite, yōjin ga warui wa, neesan-tara!* How careless of you (my sister), to leave the window wide open since morning!

taranai 足らない　動詞、非定形　negative verb
A carry-over from classical Japanese, where Base 3 was *taru,* modern *tariru.* The form *tarazu,* Base 1 + *-zu,* has also remained.

-tari¹ たり　接続助詞　conjunctive particle
活用語の連用形に付く *Katsuyō-go no ren'yōkei ni tsuku* Is added to Base 2 of conjugables.

1. 並列を表す *Heiretsu wo arawasu* Denotes listing:
   - 雨が降ったり止んだりする。 *Ame ga futtari yandari suru.* It rains by fits and starts.
   - 飛んだり跳ねたり、大喜びだ。 *Tondari hanetari, oo-yorokobi da.* They are dancing for joy.
   - ああ言ったりこう言ったりしている。 *Ā ittari kō ittari shite iru.* He says now one thing, now another.
   - 暑かったり寒かったりして天候が不順だ。 *Atsukattari samukattari shite tenkō ga fujun da.* The weather is changeable, swinging from hot to cold.
   - 来る人は中国人だったりインド人だったりです。 *Kuru hito wa Chū-*

gokujin dattari Indojin dattari desu. The people who come here are Chinese, Indians, and so on.

2. 概括を示す*Gaikatsu wo shimesu* Denotes generalization:
   - 人の悪口を言ったりするものではない。 *Hito no warukuchi wo ittari suru mono de wa nai.* One shouldn't (do such things as) speak ill of others.
   - 暇な時は読書したりして楽しみます。 *Hima na toki wa dokusho shitari shite tanoshimimasu.* In my free time I enjoy such things as reading.

NOTE. The repetitive construction may mean either that one person does several things by turns, or that several people take turns in doing one or more things.

NOTE. The usual final *suru* is sometimes replaced by some form of *da, desu, de aru.*

NOTE. When the construction involves a verb that excludes the idea of repetition, the meaning will necessarily be that of generalization.

-tari[2] たり　形容動詞の活用（古）conjugation of adjectival noun (classical)

As in the case of *nari*[5], authorities do not agree on the classification of this *tari.* As an auxiliary expressing completion（完了の助動詞）it has only one form for Base 2; as an auxiliary of assertion or description（断定・修飾の助動詞）it has both *tari* and *to.*

The conjugation is: 1. *tara* 2. *tari, to* 3. *tari* 4. *taru* 5. *tare* 6. *tare.*

1. Base 4 is found in such expressions as:
   - 父たるもの　*chichi taru mono* one who is a (real) father.
2. Many adjectival expressions are formed with this Base:
   - 遅々たる　*chi-chi taru* slow; 断固たる *danko taru* resolute; 堂々たる *dō-dō taru* dignified; 炎々たる *en'en taru* blazing; 延々たる *en'en taru* long-drawn-out; 峨々たる *ga-ga taru* rugged; 惨たる *santaru* pitiful; 些々たる *sa-sa taru* trifling; 寂莫たる *seki-baku taru* lonely; 騒然たる *sōzen taru* noisy.
3. Adverbial expressions are formed with the alternative Base 2:
   - 遅々と　*chi-chi to* slowly; 堂々と *dō-dō to* in a dignified manner; 依然として *izen to shite* as before; 悠然と *yūzen to* composedly.

-tarō たろう　助動詞　auxiliary verb

過去の助動詞「た」の未然形に、推量の助動詞「う」、推量を表す *Kako no jodōshi "-ta" no mizenkei ni, suiryō no jodōshi "-u"; suiryō wo arawasu* Base 1 of past tense auxiliary *-ta* plus conjectural auxiliary *-u,* expresses conjecture:

- そのそばに新しい家が出来たろう。 *Sono soba ni atarashii ie ga dekitarō.* A new house has been built near it, am I right?

NOTE. Modern Japanese prefers *-ta darō.*

-tate 立て 接尾語 suffix

動詞の連用形に付いて、「動作が終わって間もない」という意味を添える *Dōshi no ren'yōkei ni tsuite, "dōsa ga owatte ma mo nai" to iu imi wo soeru* With Base 2 of verbs, denotes that action has just ended:

- 洗い立ての *arai-tate no* just washed; 出立ての *de-tate no* newly emerged; 結婚し立ての *kekkon shi-tate no* newly-wed; 汲み立ての *kumi-tate no* freshly-drawn (water); 塗り立ての *nuri-tate no* freshly-painted; 研ぎ立ての *togi-tate no* just sharpened; 生まれ立ての *umare-tate no* newborn.

→ *-date*[1]

tate-[1] 立て 接頭語 prefix

何人かのうちの一番 *Nan-nin ka no uchi no ichi-ban* Chief among several persons:

- 立て行司 *tate-gyōji* chief sumo referee; 立て女形 *tate-oyama* leading female impersonator (*Kabuki*); 立て役者 *tate-yakusha* leading actor, leading man.

tate-[2] 立て・建て 接頭語 prefix

While the ideograph 立 expresses the idea of raising, appointing, and 建 that of constructing, in many compounds either may be used, not always with distinct meanings:

- 建て網・立て網 *tate-ami* set net; 建場・立て場 *tate-ba* stopping-place; 建値・立て値 *tate-ne* market prices; 建具 *tate-gu* furnishings; 建坪 *tate-tsubo* floor space; 立て坪 *tate-tsubo* cubic measure.

-tatte たって（だって） 接続助詞 conjunctive particle (colloquial)

完了の助動詞「た」に、接続助詞「とて」 *Kanryō no jodōshi "-ta" ni, setsuzoku joshi "to te"* Auxiliary of completion *-ta* plus conjunctive particle *to te:*

1.「たとしても」という意味を表す *"-ta to shite mo" to iu imi wo arawasu* Expresses concession:

- どう食べたって、月に百二十ドルはかからなくてよ。 *Dō tabetatte,*

tsuki ni nihyaku-doru wa kakaranakute yo. No matter how you eat, it won't cost $120 a month.

- 世界中捜したって見つかるまいと思われるほど色が白い。 *Sekai-jū sagashitatte mi-tsukarumai to omowareru hodo iro ga shiroi.* She is so fair-skinned that you would think you could scour the world and not find the likes.

2. 「と言っても」という意味を表す *"To itte mo" to iu imi wo arawasu* Expresses the idea "even if you say. . .":

- 子供だったって、このくらいのことは分かるはずだ。 *Kodomo dattatte, kono kurai no koto wa wakaru hazu da.* Even if you say he is only a child, he ought to understand this much.
- 高いったって、一万円ぐらいなら仕方がない。 *Takai-ttatte, ichi-man'en gurai nara shikata ga nai.* "Expensive", you say! But an article like this is bound to cost some ¥10,000.

-te¹ て (で) 接続助詞 conjunctive particle

活用語の連用形に付く *Katsuyōgo no ren'yōkei ni tsuku* Is added to Base 2 of conjugables.

1. 前後の接続を表す *Zengo no setsuzoku wo arawasu* Denotes correlation.

A. 順態接続 *Juntai setsuzoku* Simple correlation:

- 朝六時に起きて食事をした。 *Asa roku-ji ni okite, shokuji wo shita.* I got up at six and had breakfast.

B. 逆態接続 *Gyakutai setsuzoku* Adversative correlation:

- 知っていて、教えてくれない。 *Shitte ite, oshiete kurenai.* He knows, but he won't tell (me).

C. 並列 *Heiretsu* Listing:

- 広くて奇麗な庭だ。 *Hirokute kirei na niwa da.* It is a large and beautiful garden.

D. 原因・理由 *Gen'in・riyū* Cause or reason:

- 病気になって欠席している。 *Byōki ni natte kesseki shite iru.* He is absent because of illness.

E. 手段 *Shudan* Means:

- 手を振って合図した。 *Te wo futte aizu shita.* He signalled by waving his hand.

2. 補助接続を示す *Hojo setsuzoku wo shimesu* Denotes supplementary conjunction:

- 書いてある。 *Kaite aru.* It is written.
- 走っている。 *Hashitte iru.* He is running.

• 放っておいた方がいい。 *Hōtte oita hō ga ii.* Better leave it alone.
• 落としてしまうと困る。 *Otoshite shimau to komaru!* Don't drop it, for heaven's sake!

-te² て（って）　終助詞　final particle (colloquial)

1. 疑問を表す　*Gimon wo arawasu* Expresses a question:
• 毎日遅刻するんですって。 *Mainichi chikoku surun desutte?* You mean to say you arrive late every day?

2. 伝聞を表す　*Denbun wo arawasu* Expresses reported speech:
• 休んだ方がいいんですって。 *Yasunda hō ga iin desutte.* He says you would do well to take a rest.

3. 依頼を表す　*Irai wo arawasu* Expresses a request:
• もっと早く来てね。 *Motto hayaku kite ne.* Please come a little earlier.

4. 意見の主張を表す　*Iken no shuchō wo arawasu* Emphasizes an opinion:
• お願いがあってよ。 *O-negai ga atte yo.* I have a favor to beg of you.

-te³ て（って）

「という」の意味を表す　"T*o iu" no imi wo arawasu.* Expresses the meaning of "*to iu*":
• アメリカって国は広いね。 *Amerika-tte kuni wa hiroi ne.* America is a large country.

NOTE. This *-te* can also be a contraction of *to iu no wa:*
• 人間って、いったい何だ。 *Ningen'tte, ittai nan da?* What on earth is this thing called man?

te- 手　接頭語　prefix

1. 語調を強める　*Go-chō wo tsuyomeru* Strengthens the tone:
• 手荒い　*te-arai* violent; 手強い　*te-gowai* tough; 手酷い　*te-hidoi* harsh; 手緩い　*te-nurui* lenient.

2. 手を使うような　*Te wo tsukau yō na* Requiring use of the hand:
• 手網　*te-ami* scoop net; 手旗　*te-bata* hand-held flag; 手斧　*te-ono* hatchet; 手鏡　*te-kagami* hand mirror; 手仕事　*te-shigoto* handwork.

3. 自分で作った　*Jibun de tsukutta* Home made, handmade:
• 手編み　*te-ami* hand knitting; 手彫り　*te-bori* hand carving; 手製の　*te-sei no* handmade; 手打ちそば　*te-uchi soba* handmade noodles (cf. 手討ちにする slay with one's own hand).

4. 身近（みぢか）な　*Mijika na* Close, familiar;
• 手箱　*te-bako* an etui; 手文庫　*te-bunko* small box for papers; 手帳　*te-chō* notebook; 手回り品　*te-mawarihin* one's effects.

-te aru ～ -te iru

While *-te iru* may be used with both transitive and intransitive verbs, *-te aru* is used only with transitive verbs:

- 戸が閉まっている。 *To ga shimatte iru.* The door is closed.
- 戸を閉めている。 *To wo shimete iru.* The door is closed. They are closing the door.
- 戸が・戸を閉めてある。 *To ga* • *To wo shimete aru.* The door has been closed (and left so).

NOTE. In the negative we get:

- 戸はまだ閉まっていない。 *To wa mada shimatte inai.* The door hasn't been closed yet.
- 戸はまだ閉めていない。 *To wa mada shimete inai.* The door hasn't been closed yet.

-te 手 接尾語 suffix

1. 動詞の連用形に付いて、動作をする人を指す *Dōshi no renyōkei ni tsuite, dōsa wo suru hito wo sasu* Added to Base 2 of verbs, denotes the operator:

- 話し手 *hanashi-te* speaker; 買い手 *kai-te* buyer; 聞き手 *kiki-te* listener; 売り手 *uri-te* seller.

2. 名詞に付いて、その種類・品質を表す *Meishi ni tsuite, sono shurui* • *hinshitsu wo arawasu* With nouns, denotes nature or quality of goods:

- 土手 *do-te* levee, large slice; 派手 *ha-de* gaudiness; 中手 *naka-te* middle-period rice (between 早稲・早生 *wase* early-period rice and 奥手 *oku-te* late rice); 上手 *uwa-te* superior.

3. 形容詞に付いて *Keiyōshi ni tsuite* Added to (stem of) adjectives:

- 浅手 *asa-de* flesh wound; 深手 *fuka-de* deep wound; 厚手 *atsu-de* thick, heavy; 薄手 *usu-de* thin, light; 新手 *ara-te* newcomer; 古手 *furu-te* old-timer.

4. 位置・方向・方面を示す *Ichi* • *hōkō* • *hōmen wo shimesu* Denotes position, location, direction:

- 左手 *hidari-te* left side; 右手 *migi-te* right side; 裏手 *ura-te* back; 横手 *yoko-te* one side; 山手 *yama-te* uptown; 行く手 *yuku-te* destination.

5. 代金を示す *Daikin wo shimesu* Denotes money for . . . :

- 酒手 *saka-te* pourboire.

-teki 的 接尾語 suffix

This suffix, originally meaning "bright"/"target", in Chinese denoted possessive case. From early Meiji times it came to be used as the equivalent of the English adjectival suffix "-tic". It is now attached mostly to abstract nouns or to noun equivalents, forming adjectival noun stems.

傾向・性質・状態などを示す *Keikō • seishitsu • jōtai nado wo shimesu* Denotes such qualities as tendency, nature, state:

補助的な役割を果たす。 *Hojo-teki na yakuwari wo hatasu.* He plays a minor role.

• 人格的な教育を目指している。 *Jinkaku-teki na kyōiku wo mezashite iru.* Their aim is to give a liberal education.

• 徹底的に調べてきた。 *Tettei-teki ni shirabete kita.* He has made a thorough study of it.

NOTE. Base 2, *ni*, is required in the formation of adverbs, except in the case of *hikaku-teki;* the omission of *na* in the case of adjectives renders the construction more literary:

• 月給は比較的高給であった。 *Gekkyū wa hikaku-teki kōkyū de atta.* The salary was relatively high.

• 消極的抵抗の政策を取った。 *Shōkyoku-teki teikō no seisaku wo totta.* They adopted a policy of passive resistance.

NOTE. An idiomatic use of *-teki* is to add it to names, to indicate familiarity, and to words denoting persons, to express contempt:

• 広的 *Hiro-teki* = *Hiro-chan;* 泥的 *doro-teki* (= *doro-bō*) thief.

-te mo ても（でも） 接続助詞 conjunctive particle

活用語の連用形に付く *Katsuyō-go no ren'yōkei ni tsuku* Is added to Base 2 of conjugables.

1. 逆説の仮定条件を表す *Gyakusetsu no katei jōken wo arawasu* Expresses adversative open condition:

• どんなに努力しても、合格しないだろう。 *Donna ni doryoku shite mo, gōkaku shinai darō.* He probably won't pass, no matter how hard he tries.

• 高くても買いたいのだが。 *Takakute mo kaitai no da ga.* I want to buy it even if it is expensive.

2. 逆説の確定条件を表す *Gyakusetsu no kakutei jōken wo arawasu* Expresses adversative condition already fulfilled:

• どんなに食べても太らない。 *Donna ni tabete mo futoranai.* No matter how much he eats, he doesn't put on weight.

• 呼んでも降りてこなかった。 *Yonde mo orite konakatta.* I called him but he didn't come down.

NOTE. Some expressions with *-te mo:*

• 三十分早引けしてもいい。 *Sanjippun haya-bike shite mo ii.* You may go home half an hour early.

- そんなに急がなくてもいい。 *Sonna ni isoganakute mo ii.* There is no need for all that hurry.
- いくらあの子に注意してもだめだ。 *Ikura ano ko ni chūi shite mo dame da.* It's no use warning that child.
- 行かなくても構わない。 *Ikanakute mo kamawanai.* You don't have to go.

-te wa ては 接続助詞 conjunctive particle

活用語の連用形に付く *Katsuyō-go no ren'yōkei ni tsuku* Is added to Base 2 of conjugables.

1. 望ましくない結果が起こる条件を表す *Nozomashiku nai kekka ga okoru jōken wo arawasu* Expresses condition producing an undesirable effect:

- 女房にそばにいられては休めない *Nyōbō ni soba ni irarete wa yasumenai.* I am never at ease, with my wife looking over my shoulder.
- 風が弱くては、凧揚げも出来ない。 *Kaze ga yowakute wa, tako-age mo dekinai.* In such a weak wind it is impossible to fly a kite.

2. 動作や状態が繰り返される条件を表す *Dōsa ya jōtai ga kuri-kaesareru jōken wo arawasu* Expresses a condition in which an action or state is repeated:

- しばしば食事をおごっては彼らを買収した。 *Shiba-shiba shokuji wo ogotte wa, karera wo baishū shita.* He won them over by repeatedly treating them to a meal.
- 頭の中で描いては消し、消しては描いていたスケジュールだ。 *Atama no naka de egaite wa keshi, keshite wa egaite ita sukejūru da.* In his mind he pictured and erased this schedule over and over.
- 札を一枚一枚数えては、一人ニタニタ笑っていた。 *Satsu wo ichi-mai ichi-mai kazoete wa, hitori nita-nita waratte ita.* He counted the money piece by piece, sniggering away to himself.
- 濡れた宗教書を一ページ一ページ開いては乾かしていた。 *Nureta shūkyō-sho wo ichi-pēji ichi-pēji hiraite wa kawakashite ita.* He turned over the pages of the religious book one page at a time and dried them.

NOTE. Some expressions with *-te wa:*

- そんな物を食べてはだめ・食べてはいけない。 *Sonna mono wo tabete wa dame • tabete wa ikenai.* You mustn't eat such things.
- 遅刻してはならない。 *Chikoku shite wa naranai.* We had better not be late.
- とても見てはいられない。 *Totemo mite wa irarenai.* It is too dreadful to watch.

• あの人がいなくては困る。 *Ano hito ga inakute wa komaru.* We are lost without him. (We can't manage without him.)

→ *-de wa*

to[1] と 格助詞 case particle

体言に付く *Taigen ni tsuku* Is added to nominals.

1. 並列を表す *Heiretsu wo arawasu* Denotes listing:

• 朝日と読売を取っている。 *Asahi to Yomiuri wo totte iru.* We take in the Asahi and the Yomiuri.

2. 相伴を表す *Shōban wo arawasu* Denotes accompaniment:

• 友達と映画を見に行った。 *Tomodachi to eiga wo mi ni itta.* I went to see a movie with my friends.

3. 比較の目標を表す *Hikaku no mokuhyō wo arawasu* Denotes target of comparison:

• 無くした時計と違う。 *Naku-shita tokei to chigau.* It isn't the watch I lost.

• これと同じ型のはないでしょうか。 *Kore to onaji kata no wa nai deshō ka?* I wonder if you have one of this same type?

4. 結果や帰着点を表す *Kekka ya kichakuten wo arawasu* Denotes result of change:

• 学生を対象とする。 *Gakusei wo taishō to suru.* It is meant for students.

• 塵も積もれば山となる。 *Chiri mo tsumoreba yama to naru.* Many a little makes a mickle. (→ *naru*)

• 学生と偽って悪事を働く。 *Gakusei to itsuwatte akuji wo hataraku.* Under the guise of a student he does evil things.

• 花は雪と散る。 *Hana wa yuki to chiru.* The blossoms are falling like snowflakes.

• 夜となく昼となく働く。 *Yoru to naku hiru to naku hataraku.* They work morning, noon and night.

5. 動作が行なわれる様子 *Dōsa ga okonawareru yōsu* In adverbial phrases:

• やることだけはちゃんとやる。 *Yaru koto dake wa chan-to yaru.* Whatever he does, he does properly.

• ぐいと飲んでしまった。 *Gui-to nonde shimatta.* He gulped it down.

• 母がにっこりと微笑んだ *Haha ga nikkori-to hohoenda.* My mother broke into a smile. (→ *gitai-go*)

6. 内容・引用を表す *Naiyō・in'yō wo arawasu* Denotes content or quotation:

• 辞書を引いてみたら、「三日月」とあった。 *Jisho wo hiite mitara,*

"mi-ka-zuki" to atta. I looked it up in the dictionary and found *mi-ka-zuki.*

- もう始まったと思っていた。 *Mō hajimatta to omotte ita.* I thought it had already begun.
- 「そんなことはない」と答えた。 *"Sonna koto wa nai" to kotaeta.* "It isn't true," he replied. (→ *-te*[3])

7. 比喩・例えを表す *Hiyu・tatoe wo arawasu* Expresses simile:

- 先祖を神とあがめる。 *Senzo wo kami to agameru.* They worship their ancestors as gods.
- 大黒柱と頼んでいる。 *Daikoku-bashira to tanonde iru.* They depend on him absolutely.

to² と 接続助詞 conjunctive particle

活用語の終止形に付く *Katsuyō-go no shūshikei ni tsuku* Is added to Base 3 of conjugables.

1. 順態仮定条件を表す *Juntai katei-jōken wo arawasu* Expresses correlation:

- しっかりしないと駄目だよ。 *Shikkari shinai to dame da yo!* You must pull yourself together.
- 説明書を読むと分かる。 *Setsumei-sho wo yomu to wakaru.* Read the manual and you will understand.

2. 逆説仮定条件を表す *Gyakusetsu katei-jōken wo arawasu* Expresses adversative condition:

- 人が何と言おうと、僕が行く。 *Hito ga nan to iō to, boku ga iku.* I'm going, no matter what anybody says.
- 雨が降ろうと、風が吹こうと、問題じゃない。 *Ame ga furō to, kaze ga fukō to, mondai ja nai.* Hail, rain or snow, it doesn't matter.

3. 前提接続を表す *Zentei setsuzoku wo arawasu* Expresses a fulfilled condition:

- 家に帰ると、誰もいなかった。 *Ie ni kaeru to, dare mo inakatta.* When I got home, there was nobody there.
- 手紙を読み終わると、笑いだした。 *Tegami wo yomi-owaru to warai-dashita.* He finished reading the letter and burst out laughing.

4. 恒常条件を表す *Kōjō-jōken wo arawasu* Expresses an invariable consequence:

- 秋になると、渡り鳥が現われる。 *Aki ni naru to, wataridori ga arawareru.* Once autumn comes, the migratory birds appear.

to ieba と言えば 連語 phrase

1. 話題を提示する *Wadai wo teiji suru* Introduces a topic of conversation:

- 高橋さんと言えば、もう退院したのですか。 *Takahashi-san to ieba, mō tai-in shita no desu ka?* Speaking of Mr. Takahashi, is he out of hospital already?

2. 譲歩を表す *Jōho wo arawasu* Expresses concession:

- 便利と言えば便利ですが、家賃が高い。 *Benri to ieba benri desu ga, yachin ga takai.* I grant that it is convenient, but the rent is high.

3. 提示された疑問に答える *Teiji sareta gimon ni kotaeru* Proposes a question in order to answer it:

- なぜ欠勤したかと言えば、熱があったからです。 *Naze kekkin shita ka to ieba, netsu ga atta kara desu.* As to why I missed work, it was because I had a fever.

to ii といい 連語 phrase

並列を表す *Heiretsu wo arawasu* Denotes listing:

- 人物といい、学識といい、申し分がない、 *Jinbutsu to ii, gakushiki to ii, mōshibun ga nai.* He is above reproach both as to personality and to learning.

to itta といった 連語 phrase

- これといった特徴のない人だ。 *Kore to itta tokuchō no nai hito da.* He has no outstanding characteristic.
- このように、郵便、鉄道、放送といった機関が *Kono yō ni, yūbin, tetsudō, hōsō to itta kikan ga. . .* In this way the P.O., railways, broadcasting and suchlike organs. . .

to itte といって 連語 phrase

- 読んだからといって、意味が分かった訳ではない。 *Yonda kara to itte, imi ga wakatta wake de wa nai.* My having read it doesn't mean that I understand it.

to iu という 連語 phrase

1. 「**...**と呼ばれる」 "*. . . to yobareru*" "called . . .":

- 松本という人が見えた。 *Matsumoto to iu hito ga mieta.* A man by the name of Matsumoto is here.

2. 「総ての」 "*Subete no*" All without exception:

- 学校という学校はプールがある。 *Gakkō to iu gakkō wa pūru ga aru.* There isn't a school but has a swimming-pool.

3. 「**...**にのぼる」 "*. . . ni noboru*" "as much as. . ."

- 一億という大金を横領した。 *Ichi-oku to iu taikin wo ōryō shita.* He embezzled the sum of a hundred million.

4. 「僅かに」 "*Wazuka ni*" "as little as. . .":

- 五人という小人数ではなにも出来ない。 *Go-nin to iu koninzū de wa nani mo deki-nai.* What can a mere five of us do?

NOTE. Here is a use of *to iu* that can only be explained by supposing an ellipsis:

- 明日大連という夜、船室で眠れなかった。 *Asu Dairen to iu yoru, senshitsu de nemurenakatta.* It was this thought, that tomorrow we would be in Dairen, that gave me a sleepless night in my cabin.

to iu hodo no というほどの 連語 phrase

- 絶望というほどのことではない。 *Zetsubō to iu hodo no koto de wa nai.* The situation is not altogether hopeless.

to iu yō na というような 連語 phrase

- ハムレットというようなものを原文で読んだそうだ。 *Hamuretto to iu yō na mono wo genbun de yonda sō da.* It seems he has read such works as Hamlet in the original.

to ka とか 連語 phrase

1. 並べ挙げる *Narabe-ageru* Enumerates:

- 机とか、椅子とか、全部用意が出来ている。 *Tsukue to ka, isu to ka, zenbu yōi ga dekite iru.* Desks, chairs and so on, everything is ready.

2. 情報が不確かである *Jōhō ga fu-tashika de aru* Information is unreliable:

- あの何とかいう人 *ano nan to ka iu hito* "what's his name."
- 病気とかいうことだ。 *Byōki to ka iu koto da.* They say he is ill.
- 転校するとかいう話だ。 *Tenkō suru to ka iu hanashi da.* There is talk of his changing school.

NOTE. *To ka* is used colloquially by young people in replacement of other particles:

- それから、テレビとか見て、寝ました。 *Sorekara, terebi to ka mite nemashita.* Then I watched television and went to bed.

to kuru to, to kitara → *kuru*

to mo¹ とも 終助詞 final particle

動詞の終止形に付いて、「もちろん」と強く言い切る *Dōshi no shūshikei ni tsuite, "mochiron" to tsuyoku ii-kiru* Added to Base 3 of verbs, ends the sentence with an air of finality:

- 英語が出来ますか。出来ますとも。 *Eigo ga dekimasu ka? Dekimasu to mo!* Can you speak English? Of course I can!

to mo² とも 接続助詞（古） conjunctive particle (classical)

- その時悔ゆとも、甲斐あらむ。 *Sono toki kuyu to mo, kai aramu.* Even if he repents then, it will be of some use.

to shite として 連語 phrase

1. 「...の資格で」 "*. . . No shikaku de*" "In the capacity of . . .":

- 警察官として尋問した。 *Keisatsu-kan to shite jinmon shita.* He questioned him in his capacity of police officer.

2. 「...として置いて」 *". . . To shite oite"* "Leaving aside . . .":

- それはそれとして、次のことに移りましょう。 *Sore wa sore to shite, tsugi no koto ni utsurimashō.* Letting that matter be, let's move on to the next item.
- 冗談は別として、どう思いますか。 *Jōdan wa betsu to shite, dō omoimasu ka?* Joking apart, what do you really think?

3. 「一つとして」「一人として」「一時として」、「例外なく」 *"Hitotsu to shite", "hitori to shite", "ittoki to shite" no katachi de, "reigai naku"* In *hitotsu to shite, hitori to shite, ittoki to shite* forms, "without exception":

- 誰一人として喜ばないものはない。 *Dare hitori to shite yorokobanai mono wa nai.* Every single one of them is delighted.
- 一時としてじっとしていられなかった。 *Ittoki to shite jitto shite irarenakatta.* He was like a hen on a hot griddle.

to³ 斗　　接尾語　suffix

穀物・酒などを量るのに使った語 *Kokumotsu・sake nado wo hakaru no ni tsukatta go* Counter formerly used in measuring grain, *sake* and the like, = about 18 liters. The word also denoted the box-shaped measure for grain, and the ladle for liquids.

-tō¹ 等　　接尾語　suffix

「列挙したもののほかにある」 *"Rekkyo shita mono no hoka ni aru"* Denotes that the listing is not exhaustive:

- 電車やバス等の交通機関が対象となる。 *Densha ya basu-tō no kōtsū-kikan ga taishō to naru.* (The strike) will affect trains, buses and similar means of transport.

NOTE. This is the *-ra* of 彼ら *karera,* 我ら *warera,* etc., and is read *-dō* in 平等 *byōdō.*

NOTE. This *-tō* is the literary form of *nado.*

-tō² 頭　　接尾語　suffix

大きな動物を数える語 *Ookina dōbutsu wo kazoeru go* Counter for large animals:

- 牛を三十頭飼っている。 *Ushi wo sanjittō katte iru.* He keeps 30 head of cattle.

toki 時　　形式名詞として　as a formal noun

活用語の連体形に付く *Katsuyō-go no rentaikei ni tsuku* Is added to Base 4 of conjugables.

1. 動作が行なわれる時刻を示す *Dōsa ga okonawareru jikoku wo shimesu* Denotes timing of an action:

- 今度買い物に行くとき、連れて行こう。 *Kondo kaimono ni iku toki, tsurete ikō*. Next time I go shopping I'll take you with me.

2. 動作が行なわれる場合を示す *Dōsa ga okonawareru baai wo shimesu* Denotes the occasion accompanying an action:

- いざというときには、一肌脱ぎましょう。 *Iza to iu toki ni wa, hito-hada nugimashō*. If the worst comes to the worst, I am ready to stand by you.

toki ni 時に 連語 phrase

1. 特定の「とき」を強めて言う *Tokutei no "toki" wo tsuyomete iu* Emphasizes a particular date:

- 時に大正三年、第一次大戦が始まった。 *Toki ni Taishō sannen, dai-ichiji taisen ga hajimatta*. That year, 1914, World War I broke out.

2. 副詞的に、「時々」 *Fukushi-teki ni, "toki-doki"* Adverbially, "now and then":

- 時に遅刻することもある。 *Toki ni, chikoku suru koto mo aru*. He is late once in a while.

3. 話題を改めたり変えたりする時に *Wadai wo aratametari kaetari suru toki ni* Used to introduce a new topic:

- 時に、今度の成績はどうだった。 *Toki ni, kondo no seiseki wa dō datta?* By the way, how were your marks this time?

toki ni wa 時には 連語 phrase

「たまには」、「場合によると」 *"Tama ni wa", "baai ni yoru to"* From time to time:

- 時には飲み過ぎることもある。 *Toki ni wa, nomi-sugiru koto mo aru*. From time to time he drinks to excess.

tokoro 所・処 形式名詞として as a formal noun

接続助詞的に *Setsuzoku-joshi-teki ni* as a conjunctive particle:

1. 「...てみたところ」の形で、「...た結果」 *"-te mita tokoro" no katachi de, "-ta kekka"* In . . . *te mita tokoro* form, "did something, and this is what happened":

- 聞いてみたところ、やはり、知らないと言った。 *Kiite mita tokoro, yahari, shiranai to itta*. I asked him, but, as I had expected, he said he didn't know.
- 調べてみたところ、僕のものではなかった。 *Shirabete mita tokoro,*

boku no mono de wa nakatta. I examined it and found it wasn't mine.

2. 「**…**たところだ」の形で、「**…**し終えた」 "*. . . -ta tokoro da*" *no katachi de,* "*. . . shi-oeta*" In . . . *-ta tokoro da* form, denotes an action just completed:

- 学校から帰ってきたところだ。 *Gakkō kara kaette kita tokoro da.* He has just got home from school.

3. 「**…**するところだ」の形で、「**…**をしている」「**…**をしはじめる」 "*. . . suru tokoro da*" *no katachi de,* "*. . . wo shite iru*", "*. . . wo shi-hajimeru*" In . . . *suru tokoro da* form, denotes that the action is going on, or about to begin:

- ちょうど食事をするところだ。 *Chōdo shokuji wo suru tokoro da.* He is having a meal just now.
- これから勉強するところだ。 *Kore kara benkyō suru tokoro da.* I am just getting down to study.
- 危うく落ちるところだった。 *Ayauku ochiru tokoro datta.* I came close to falling.

NOTE. Some compounds with *-tokoro* (*-dokoro*):

- 当て所もなくさまよう *ate-do mo naku samayou* wander aimlessly; 出所 *de-dokoro* (*shussho*) source; 踏まえ所 *fumae-dokoro* footing, standpoint; 踏み所 *fumi-dokoro* footing; 行き所 *iki-dokoro* destination; 見所 *mi-dokoro* (1) promise, merit; (2) highlight; (3) seats at Noh; 見せ所 *mise-dokoro* highlight; 狙い所 *nerai-dokoro* objective; 捕え所・摑まえ所のない *torae-dokoro* • *tsukamae-dokoro no nai* slippery, pointless; 摑み所 *tsukami-dokoro* hold, grip; 目の付け所 *me no tsuke-dokoro* aim

tokoro de ところで 連語 phrase

1. 接続詞として *Setsuzokushi to shite* As a conjunction:

- ところで、お加減はいかがですか。 *Tokoro de, o-kagen wa ikaga desu ka?* Well, how are you?

2. 接続助詞として *Setsuzoku-joshi to shite* As a conjunctive particle:

- 今から走ったところで、間に合わない。 *Ima kara hashitta tokoro de, ma ni awanai.* Even if you rush off now, you won't make it.
- どんなに後悔したところで、今更どうしようもない *Donna ni kōkai shita tokoro de, ima sara dō shiyō mo nai.* No matter how sorry he may feel, nothing can be done about it now.

tokoro de wa nai ところではない 連語 phrase

- 僕の関知するところではない。 *Boku no kanchi suru tokoro de wa nai.* It is none of my business.

・泣いているところではない。 *Naite iru tokoro de wa nai.* This is no time for crying.

tokoro e ところへ 連語 phrase

・出かけようとしているところへ、電話がかかった。 *Dekakeyō to shite iru tokoro e, denwa ga kakatta.* I got a phone call just as I was about to go out.

tokoro ga ところが 連語 phrase

1. 接続詞として *Setsuzokushi to shite* As a conjunction:
   ・ところが、だれも知らないらしい。 *Tokoro ga, dare mo shiranai-rashii.* However, nobody seems to know.
   ・試験は難しくはなかった。ところが、失敗した。 *Shiken wa muzukashiku wa nakatta. Tokoro ga, shippai shita.* The exam wasn't difficult. However, I failed it.
2. 接続助詞として *Setsuzoku-joshi to shite* As a conjunctive particle:
   ・調べてみたところが、やはり、本当だった *Shirabete mita tokoro ga, yahari, hontō datta.* I inquired, and found that, sure enough, it was true.
   ・タクシーに乗ったところが、交通渋滞で、列車に乗り遅れてしまった。 *Takushii ni notta tokoro ga, kōtsū-jūtai de, ressha ni nori-okurete shimatta.* I took a taxi, but I missed my train because of a traffic jam.

tokoro no ところの 連語 phrase

A cliché coined to translate the relative construction of western languages:

・今読んでいるところの本は、「坊っちゃん」です。 *Ima yonde iru tokoro no hon wa "Botchan" desu.* The book that I am reading now is *Botchan.*

tokoro wo ところを 連語 phrase

・困っているところを助けてもらった。 *Komatte iru tokoro wo tasukete moratta.* I got help just when I was in trouble.

-tomo 共 接尾語 suffix

1. 全部一緒の状態 *Zenbu issho no jōtai* Collectively:
   ・男女共 *danjo-tomo* both sexes; 英米共 *Ei-Bei-tomo* both England and America; 夫婦共 *fūfu-tomo* both spouses; 両方共 *ryōhō-tomo* both; 両親共 *ryōshin-tomo* both parents; 三人共 *sannin-tomo* all three (persons).
2. 「...も含めて」 "*. . . Mo fukumete*" "Inclusive of. . .":

- 地所共 *jisho-tomo* (house) together with land; ケース共 *kēsu-tomo* including a case; 送料共 *sōryō-tomo* including postage; 税共 *zei-tomo* tax included.

toori 通り 形式名詞として as a formal noun
名詞や動詞の連体形に付いて、「それと同様に」 *Meishi ya dōshi no rentaikei ni tsuite, "sore to dōyō ni"* With nouns and Base 4 of verbs, means "in conformity with":
- 言われた通りにすればよかったのだ。 *Iwareta toori ni sureba yokatta no da.* You should have done as you were told.
- 時間通りに到着した。 *Jikan-doori ni tōchaku shita.* It arrived on time.

-toori 通り 接尾語 suffix
種類を数える語 *Shurui wo kazoeru go* Counter for categories:
- 二通りの品物 *futa-toori no shinamono* two kinds of articles.
- 方法は三通りある。 *Hōhō wa mi-toori aru.* There are three methods.
- 一通りの家具 *hito-toori no kagu* complete set of furniture.

-toosu 通す 補助動詞として as a supplementary verb
1. ずっとし続ける *Zutto shi-tsuzukeru* Continue doing:
- ぶっ通しで *buttooshi de* without a break; 言い通す *ii-toosu* insist on; 着通す *ki-toosu* continue wearing; 眠り通す *nemuri-toosu* sleep through.

2. 終わりまでする *Owari made suru* Carry through:
- 見通す *mi-toosu* (1) see through; (2) foresee; (3) get unobstructed view of (見通し *mi-tooshi* outlook, insight); 立て通す *tate-toosu* remain faithful.

tote[1] とて 連語（古） phrase (classical)
引用の格助詞「と」に、「思って」、「言って」、「して」の「て」 *In'yō no kaku-joshi "to" ni, "omotte", "itte", "shite" no "-te"* Case particle *to* of quotation plus the *-te* of one of these three verbs:
- 景色とて見るだけの価値のある所はない。 *Keshiki tote miru dake no kachi no aru tokoro wa nai.* There is no place (here) really worth seeing.

tote[2] とて 接続助詞 conjunctive particle
1. 「…たとて」の形で、「…したとしても」 *". . . -ta tote" no katachi de, ". . . shita to shite mo"* In . . . *-ta tote* form, means "even though":

- 勝ったとて、別に偉いことはない。 *Katta tote, betsu ni erai koto wa nai.* Don't let this victory go to your head.
- 今からどんなに急いだとて、間に合わない。 *Ima kara donna ni isoida tote, ma ni awanai.* However much you hurry now, you won't make it.

2. 「…からとて」「…こととて」の形で、「…なので」 *". . . kara tote", ". . . koto tote" no katachi de, ". . . na node"* In *. . . kara tote, . . . koto tote* forms, expresses the reason why:

- 時間をかけたからとて、いいものが出来るわけではない。 *Jikan wo kaketa kara tote, ii mono ga dekiru wake de wa nai.* It won't necessarily turn out a success just because you took time over it.
- 如何にベテランだからとて、油断してはならぬ。 *Ika ni beteran da kara tote, yudan shite wa naranu.* For the very reason that you are veterans, you must still be on your guard.
- 慣れぬこととて、どうもうまくいかない。 *Narenu koto tote, dōmo umaku ikanai.* I'm not used to it, so it's not turning out at all well.
- 日曜のこととて、社内はがらんとしていた。 *Nichiyō no koto tote, shanai wa garan to shite ita.* Since it was Sunday, the office was deserted.

-tsu つ　助動詞（古）　auxiliary verb (classical)

動詞の連用形に付いて、完了・強意・並列を表す *Dōshi no ren'yōkei ni tsuite, kanryō・kyō-i・heiretsu wo arawasu* Added to Base 2 of verbs, expresses completion, emphasis and listing:

- 行きつ戻りつする *yuki-tsu modori-tsu suru* go to and fro.
- 追いつ追われつする *oi-tsu oware-tsu suru* chase and be chased.
- 世の中は持ちつ持たれつだ。 *Yo no naka wa mochi-tsu motare-tsu da.* Life is a matter of give and take.

NOTE. Only in this use of listing has this *-tsu* carried over into modern Japanese.

NOTE. An old possessive case particle has remained in a few expressions:

- 天つ神 *ama-tsu kami* heavenly gods; 滝つ瀬 *taki-tsu se* rapids.

-tsui 対　接尾語　suffix

二つ揃って一組となるもの *Futatsu sorotte hito-kumi to naru mono* Things that come in pairs (and counter for such):

- 好一対の夫婦 *kō ittsui no fūfu* a well-matched couple.
- 花瓶二対を手に入れた。 *Kabin ni-tsui wo te ni ireta.* I acquired two pairs of vases.

-tsuke 付け　接尾語　suffix

「それに慣れている」 *"Sore ni narete iru"* What one is used to:

- 行きつけのバー *yuki-tsuke no bā* bar one frequents; 買いつけの店 *kai-tsuke no mise* shop one usually deals with; かかりつけの医者 *kakari-tsuke no isha* one's family doctor.

→ *-zuke*[1]

-tsukeru 付ける　補助動詞　supplementary verb

動詞の連用形に付く *Dōshi no ren'yōkei ni tsuku* Is added to Base 2 of verbs.

1. 「いつも...する」 *"Itsu mo. . . suru"* "Be in habit of doing. . .":

- 飛行機に乗りつけている。 *Hikōki ni nori-tsukete iru.* We are used to travelling by plane.
- 食べつけないものを食べて腹を壊した。 *Tabe-tsukenai mono wo tabete hara wo kowashita.* He ate food he was not used to and it upset his stomach.

2. 「強い勢いで...する」 *"Tsuyoi ikioi de. . . suru"* "Do vigorously":

- 巡査はすぐ現場に駆け付けた。 *Junsa wa sugu genba ni kake-tsuketa.* The policeman rushed to the scene straight away.
- 怒鳴り付ける *donari-tsukeru* roar at; 踏み付ける *fumi-tsukeru* trample; 痛め付ける *itame-tsukeru* torment, rebuke; 決め付ける *kime-tsukeru* make a one-sided conclusion, scold; 殴り付ける *naguri-tsukeru* thrash; 煮付ける *ni-tsukeru* boil with soy sauce thoroughly; にらみ付ける *nirami-tsukeru* glare at; 照り付ける *teri-tsukeru* blaze down.

NOTE. In most other cases, the suffix will have its literal meaning of "apply":

- 引き付ける *hiki-tsukeru* attract; 書き付ける *kaki-tsukeru* write down; 漕ぎ付ける *kogi-tsukeru* row up to; 乗り付ける *nori-tsukeru* ride up to; 縫い付ける *nui-tsukeru* sew on to; 呼び付ける *yobi-tsukeru* summon.

-tsuki 付き　接尾語　suffix

名詞に付く *Meishi ni tsuku* Is added to nouns.

A. 状態を表す *Jōtai wo arawasu* Denotes state:

- 足つき *ashi-tsuki* gait; 顔つき *kao-tsuki* facial expression; 体つき *karada-tsuki* build; 声つき *koe-tsuki* timbre; 腰つき *koshi-tsuki* posture; 口つき *kuchi-tsuki* shape of mouth, manner of speech; 目つき *me-tsuki* look; 手つき *te-tsuki* way of using hands; 生まれつき *umare-tsuki* by nature.

B.「...が付いている」 *". . . ga tsuite iru"* "attached", "included":

- 家付きの土地 *ie-tsuki no tochi* house and lot; 家付きの娘 *ie-tsuki no musume* heiress; 家付きの財産 *ie-tsuki no zaisan* hereditary estate; 保証付きの時計 *hoshō-tsuki no tokei* guaranteed timepiece; 折り紙付きの秀才 *origami-tsuki no shūsai* acknowledged origami expert.

C.「...に付き」の形で *". . . ni tsuki" no katachi de* In *. . . ni tsuki* form,

1.「...のために」 *". . . no tame ni"* "because of . . .":

- 病氣に付き、欠席させていただきます。 *Byōki ni tsuki, kesseki sasete itadakimasu.* Please allow me to absent myself because of illness.
- 改造に付き、休業いたします。 *Kaizō ni tsuki, kyūgyō itashimasu.* Closed for reconstruction.

2.「...ごとに」 *". . . -goto ni"* "a piece":

- 一箱に付き三千円 *hito-hako ni tsuki sanzen'en* ¥3000 a box; 一泊に付き五千円 *ippaku ni tsuki gosen'en* ¥5000 per night's stay.

tsuki 月

For the names of the months, besides the system of prefixing the numerals one to twelve, Japanese has also an alternative system of special names (異名 *i-myō, i-mei*); here is a list of just one each of these names:

- 一月：睦月 *Mutsuki;* 二月：如月 *kisaragi;* 三月：弥生 *yayoi;* 四月：卯月 *uzuki*; 五月：皐月 *satsuki;* 六月：水無月 *minazuki;* 七月：文月 *fu(mi)zuki;* 八月：葉月 *hazuki;* 九月：菊月 *kikuzuki;* 十月：神無月 *kaminazuki;* 十一月：霜月 *shimotsuki;* 十二月：師走 *shiwasu.*

-tsukusu 尽くす 補助動詞として as a supplementary verb

動詞の連用形に付いて、「すっかり...する」 *Dōshi no ren'yōkei ni tsuite, "sukkari. . . suru"* With Base 2 of verbs, means "do exhaustively," "do all sorts of . . .":

- 言い尽くす *ii-tsukusu* leave nothing unsaid; 食い尽くす *kui-tsukusu* eat up, go through; 泣き尽くす *naki-tsukusu* cry one's eyes out; しゃぶり尽くす *shaburi-tsukusu* suck dry; し尽くす *shi-tsukusu* do everything possible; 知り尽くす *shiri-tsukusu* get to know all sorts of things.

-tsutsu つつ 接続助詞（古） conjunctive particle (classical)

動詞の連用形に付く *Dōshi no ren'yōkei ni tsuku* Is attached to Base 2 of verbs.

1. 反復を表す *Hanpuku wo arawasu* Denotes repetition (modern *-te wa*).

2. 継続を表す *Keizoku wo arawasu* Denotes continuation (modern *zutto . . . shite*).
3. 余情を表す *Yojō wo arawasu* Denotes aftertaste (modern *-ta koto*).
4. 同時を表す *Dōji wo arawasu* Denotes simultaneous action (same as *shi-nagara*):

- 酒を飲みつつ語り合った。 *Sake wo nomi-tsutsu katari-atta.* They chatted over a glass of *sake.*
- 悪いと知りつつその日記を読み続けた。 *Warui to shiri-tsutsu sono nikki wo yomi-tsuzuketa.* I went on reading his diary, knowing I was doing wrong.

NOTE. Of the four usages noted above, only the one denoting simultaneous action (**4.**) has carried over into modern Japanese.
NOTE. A modern use of *-tsutsu,* not found in *bungo*, is to express the progressive:

- 今、向かいつつあるのは、少年時代に学んだ小学校であった。 *Ima mukai-tsutsu aru no wa shōnen jidai ni mananda shōgakkō de atta.*
  Where he was heading for now was the elementary school of his childhood.
- いかにも夏子が老いつつある感じであった。 *Ika ni mo Natsuko ga oitsutsu aru kanji de atta.* He got the feeling that Natsuko was aging fast.

NOTE. A sense of concession is expressed by *-tsutsu mo:*

- 嘘だと知りつつも、噂を信じたかった。 *Uso da to shiri-tsutsu mo, uwasa wo shinjitakatta.* I wanted to believe the rumour, even though I knew it was false.

-tsuzukeru 続ける 補助動詞として as a supplementary verb
動詞の連用形に付いて、「ずっと…する」 *Dōshi no ren'yōkei ni tsuite, "zutto . . . suru"* With Base 2 of verbs, means "continue doing":

- 足が痛くても歩き続けた。 *Ashi ga itakute mo, aruki-tsuzuketa.* They kept on walking, despite their sore feet.
- 火を燃やし続けなさい。 *Hi wo moyashi-tsuzuke nasai.* Keep the fire burning.

-tsuzuki 続き 接尾語 suffix
名詞に付いて、「間を置かず存在すること・もの」 *Meishi ni tsuite, "ma wo okazu sonzai suru koto • mono"* Denotes contiguity or contiguous objects:

• 血続き *chi-tsuzuki* consanguinity; 地続き *ji-tsuzuki* adjacent plot; 縁続き *en-tsuzuki* relationship; 不幸続き *fukō-tsuzuki* spell of misfortune; 引き続き *hiki-tsuzuki* continuation, (adv.) without a break; 家続き *ie-tsuzuki* row of houses; 庭続き *niwa-tsuzuki* adjoining gardens; 陸続き *riku-tsuzuki* joined by land; 手続き *te-tsuzuki* procedure(s).

-tsuzuku 続く 補助動詞として as a supplementary verb

As a general rule, supplementary verbs appear in their transitive form, but in some cases, mostly of verbs involuntary in meaning, the intransitive is found:

• 吹き続く *fuki-tsuzuku* continue blowing; 降り続く *furi-tsuzuku* continue falling (of rain, snow, etc.); 引き続いて・引き続き *hiki-tsuzuite* • *hiki-tsuzuki* continuously; 打ち続く *uchi-tsuzuku* continue (cf. 打ち続ける *uchi-tsuzukeru* continue typing, firing, etc.)

-ttara → *-tara*[2], *-tara*[3]

-tte[1] って 終助詞 final particle → *-te*[2]

-tte[2] って 「という」「というのは」の略 abbreviated form of *to iu, to iu no wa.*

→ *-te*[3], *to iu*

-tte[3] って 格助詞（口語） case particle (colloquial)

• すぐ来てくれって言ってきたよ。 *Sugu kite kurette itte kita yo.* He came and said he wanted to see you immediately.

→ *-to*[1] 6

U

-u う 助動詞 auxiliary verb

This auxiliary is treated at length under *-ō, -yō*. The only Bases left are 3 and 4, and this latter is now found only before a few formal nouns *(hazu, koto, mono)*:

• そんなことがあろう筈はない。 *Sonna koto ga arō hazu wa nai.* It is very unlikely that such a thing should happen.

• 水泳などしようものなら、風邪をひくよ。 *Suiei nado shiyō mono nara, kaze wo hiku yo.* If you go swimming or anything like that, you'll catch a cold.

uchi うち　形式名詞として　as a formal noun

活用語の終止形に付いて、一定の時間を示す *Katsuyō-go no shūshikei ni tsuite, ittei no jikan wo shimesu* With Base 3 of conjugables, denotes a definite period:

- 明るいうちに下山しよう。 *Akarui uchi ni gezan (gesan) shiyō.* Let's descend while it is still light.
- ものの一分も経たないうちに、いびきが聞こえた。 *Mono no ippun mo tatanai uchi ni, ibiki ga kikoeta.* Not even a minute had passed before snoring was heard.
- ボーイが注文を聞いているうちに、ホステスが三人席に着いた。 *Bōi ga chūmon wo kiite iru uchi ni, hosutesu ga sannin seki ni tsuita.* While the waiter was taking our order, three hostesses sat down.

NOTE. When this *uchi* accompanies a negative, it is interchangeable with *mae:*

- 暗くならないうちに（ならない前に）帰ろう。 *Kuraku naranai uchi ni (naranai mae ni) kaerō.* Let's go home before it gets dark.

uchi- 打ち　接頭語　prefix

動詞・動詞の体言化したものの上に付く *Dōshi · dōshi no taigen-ka shita mono no ue ni tsuku* Is prefixed to verbs and nominalizations.

1.「すこし」「ちょっと」の意味を添える *"Sukoshi", "chotto" no imi wo soeru* Adds the meaning of "to a slight extent":

- 打ち見る *uchi-miru* cast a glance at;

2.「すっかり」という意味を添える *"Sukkari" to iu imi wo soeru* Adds the meaning of "completely":

- 打ち消す *uchi-kesu* erase, deny; 打ち据える *uchi-sueru* beat to a pulp.

3. 意味を強めたり語調を整えたりする *Imi wo tsuyometari go-chō wo totonoetari suru* Strengthens the meaning and adjusts the tone:

- 打ち勝つ *uchi-katsu* overcome; 打ち寛ぐ *uchi-kutsurogu* relax; うっちゃる *utcharu* throw away, twist down.

-uchi 打ち　接尾語　suffix

1. 刀・銃などで「打つ」こと *Katana · jū nado de "utsu" koto* Hitting or shooting:

- 相打ち *ai-uchi* hitting each other simultaneously; 枝打ち *eda-uchi* lopping of branches; 不意打ち *fui-uchi* surprise attack; 早打ち *haya-uchi* quick shooting; 平手打ち *hirate-uchi* slap; 一打ちに *hito-uchi ni* at one blow; 目打ち *me-uchi* perforating; 盲打ち *mekura-uchi* hitting out blindly; 滅多打ち *metta-uchi* showering blows on; 峰打ち

mine-uchi blow with back of sword; 鞭打ち *muchi-uchi* whipping; 抜き打ち *nuki-uchi* unsheating and striking at once (抜き打ち検査 *nuki-uchi kensa* spot check); 拝み打ち *ogami-uchi* blow on forehead; 太刀打ち *tachi-uchi* sword-fighting; 鳥打ち *tori-uchi* fowling; 釣瓶打ち *tsurube-uchi* volley; 続け打ち *tsuzuke-uchi* rapid fire.

2. 突き砕く、叩くこと *Tsuki-kudaku, tataku koto* Pounding, beating on:

- 蝿打ち *hae-uchi* flyswat; 砧打ち *kinuta-uchi* fulling, fuller; 塊打ち *kure-uchi* clod-crushing; 舌打ち *shita-uchi* tongue-clicking; 田打ち *ta-uchi* tilling of ricefield.

3. 複雑な意味 *Fukuzatsu na imi* Various meanings:

- 頭打ちになる *atama-uchi ni naru* reach the limit; 網打ち *ami-uchi* netting; 博打(打ち) *bakuchi(-uchi)* gambling (gambler); 碁打ち *go-uchi* playing *go, go* player; 火打ち *hi-uchi* flint; 豆打ち *mame-uchi* bean scattering; 面打ち *men-uchi* making of *Noh* masks; 耳打ち *mimi-uchi* whispering into ear; 値打ち *ne-uchi* worth; 乗り打ち *nori-uchi* riding past; 仕打ち *shi-uchi* treatment; 真打ち・心打ち *shin-uchi* star performer; 墨打ち *sumi-uchi* drawing line with ink-pad; 手打ち *te-uchi* (1) slaying with one's sword, (2) being reconciled, (3) closing a deal, (4) handmade (noodles).

uchi-keshi 打ち消し・打消

動作・状態などを否定する文法上の形、助動詞「ない」「ぬ」(文語の「ず」)、推量の助動詞「まい」(文語の「じ」「まじ」)で表す *Dōsa・jōtai nado wo hitei suru bunpō-jō no katachi, jodōshi "-nai", "-nu" (bungo no "-zu"), suiryō no jodōshi "-mai" (bungo no "-ji, "-maji") de arawasu* Grammatical negative; expressed by the auxiliaries *-nai, -nu (-zu* of *bungo)*, and by the conjectural auxiliary *-mai (-ji, -maji* of *bungo)*.

NOTE. Negation is also called *hitei-kei* (否定形).

→ *-nai, -nu, -mai*[1]

-udo 人 接尾語 suffix

A *kun* reading of the ideograph 人、(from *-bito*), found in many compounds:

- 商人 *aki-udo, akindo, akyūdo, shōnin* trader; 掛かり人 *kakari-udo, kakari-bito* dependent; 狩人 *kari-udo, karyūdo* hunter; 方人 *kata-udo* ally; 客人 *marōdo* guest; 召し人 *meshi-udo, meshūdo* court singer; 囚人 *meshi-udo, meshūdo, shūjin* prison inmate; 仲人 *nakōdo* go-between; 落ち人 *ochi-udo, ochūdo* fugitive; 寄り人 *yori-udo, yoryūdo* court singer.

ue 上　形式名詞として　as a formal noun

「体言＋の」や、活用語の終止形に付く *"Taigen + no" ya, katsuyō-go no shūshikei ni tsuku* Is added to "nouns + *no*", or to Base 3 of conjugables.

1. さらに加わる状態を示す *Sara ni kuwawaru jōtai wo shimesu* Denotes an added factor:

- 金持ちの上に、なかなか頭がいい。 *Kanemochi no ue ni, nakanaka atama ga ii.* Not only is he rich, but he has a good head, too.
- 値段が高い上に、品質もよくない。 *Nedan ga takai ue ni, hinshitsu mo yoku nai.* It is not only expensive, but of poor quality as well.
- 道に迷った上に、雨に降られた。 *Michi mi mayotta ue ni, ame ni furareta.* We not only lost our way, but were caught in the rain as well.

2.「…したあと」「…した結果」 *". . . Shita ato", ". . . shita kekka"* Denotes subsequent or consequent action or state:

- 署名捺印の上、書類をお送り下さい。 *Shomei natsuin no ue, shorui wo o-okuri kudasai.* Please send the document after signing and sealing it.
- 欠陥が明らかになった上は、回収致します。 *Kekkan ga akiraka ni natta ue wa, kaishū itashimasu.* Since the defect has become apparent, we are recalling (the cars).

-ue 上　接尾語　suffix

目上の親族の名に添えて、尊敬を表す *Meue no shinzoku no na ni soete, sonkei wo arawasu* Added to names of older relatives, expresses respect:

- 父上様　*chichi-ue sama* (my) father; 母上様 *haha-ue sama* (my) mother; 兄上 *ani-ue* elder brother; 姉上 *ane-ue* elder sister.

→ *uwa-*

ukemi 受け身・受身　passive voice

他から動作を受ける意味を表す *Ta kara dōsa wo ukeru imi wo arawasu* Denotes that the subject is the target of the action.

NOTE. The passive voice is also called *judōtai* (受動態)。

-umare 生まれ　接尾語　suffix

1. 生まれること *Umareru koto* Birth:

- 早生まれ *haya-umare* born between Jan. 1 and Apr. 1.
- 遅生まれ *oso-umare* born between Apr. 2 and Dec. 31.

NOTE. These dates decide year of entry into primary school.

2. 生まれた土地 *Umareta tochi* Place of birth:

- 神田生まれ *Kanda-umare* born in Kanda; スペイン生まれ *Supein-umare* born in Spain.

3. 生まれた年代 *Umareta nendai* Era or time of birth:
   - 明治生まれ *Meiji-umare* born in the Meiji era; 二月生まれ *ni-gatsu-umare* born in February.
4. 家柄 *Ie-gara* Status of family; 素性 *sujō*, lineage:
   - 華族生まれ *kazoku-umare* of noble lineage.

ura- 心 接頭語 prefix

主に形容詞の上に付いて、「何となく」 *Omo ni keiyōshi no ue ni tsuite, "nan to naku"* Prefixed mainly to adjectives, expresses the idea of "somewhat", "slightly":

- うら悲しい *ura-ganashii* somewhat sad; うら恥ずかしい *ura-hazukashii* somewhat ashamed; うら寂しい *ura-sabishii* slightly lonely; うら若い *ura-wakai* youthful.

-uru → *-eru • -uru*

usu- 薄 接頭語 prefix

1. 厚みがない *Atsumi ga nai* Lacking thickness:
   - 薄地 *usu-ji* thin cloth.
2. 程度が少ない・弱い *Teido ga sukunai, yowai* Lacking in intensity:
   - 薄味 *usu-aji* light flavour; 薄明かり *usu-akari* dim light; 薄気味悪い *usu-kimi warui* eerie; 薄目 *usu-me* half-closed eyes; 薄模様 *usu-moyō* light-purple pattern; 薄笑い *usu-warai* faint smile.

-usu 薄 接尾語 suffix

程度が少ない *Teido ga sukunai* Lacking intensity:

- 気乗り薄 *kinori-usu* halfhearted; 望み薄 *nozomi-usu* dim prospects; 品薄 *shina-usu* short of stock.

uwa- 上 接頭語 prefix

1. 場所・順序・値段などが高いこと *Basho • junjo • nedan nado ga takai koto* Position, order, price, etc. is high:
   - 上顎 *uwa-ago* upper jaw; 上葉 *uwa-ba* upper leaves; 上歯 *uwa-ba* upper teeth; 上履き *uwa-baki* indoor slippers; 上っ張り・上張り *uwappari • uwa-bari* overalls; 上側 *uwa-gawa* upper side; 上唇 *uwa-kuchibiru* upper lip; 上回る *uwa-mawaru* exceed; 上値 *uwa-ne* higher price; 上役 *uwa-yaku* superior; 上草履 *uwa-zōri* indoor sandals.

→ *-ue*

2. 表面的であること *Hyōmen-teki de aru koto* Being superficial:
- 上辺 *uwa-be* surface; 上書き *uwa-gaki* address; 上紙 *uwa-gami* outer wrapping; 上着 *uwa-gi* outer garment, coat; 上薬 *uwa-gusuri* glaze; 上前 *uwa-mae* cut, rake-off, outer skirt; 上の空 *uwa-no-sora* absentminded air; 上塗り *uwa-nuri* last coat (of paint, etc.); 上敷 *uwa-shiki* carpet; 上滑り *uwa-suberi* superficiality; 上つく・浮つく *uwa-tsuku* be restless, fickle; 上っ面 *uwattsura* outward appearance; 上っ調子 *uwatchōshi* flippancy; 上背 *uwa-zei* stature; 上擦る *uwa-zuru* sound hollow; 上包み *uwa-zutsumi* wrapping.

W

wa[1] は

もとは係助詞、現代語では副助詞 *Moto wa kakari-joshi (kei-joshi), gen-daigo de wa fuku-joshi* "Bound particle" of *bungo*, now classed as an adverbial particle.

いろいろな語、活用語の連用形に付く *Iro-iro na go, katsuyō-go no ren'yōkei ni tsuku* Is added to various parts of speech, to Base 2 in the case of conjugables.

1. 他と区別して、取り出して言う *Ta to kubetsu shite, tori-dashite iu* Singles out for special attention:
- 私は行きません。 *Watashi wa ikimasen.* I am not going to go.
- 明日は曇りがちの天気です。 *Asu wa kumori-gachi no tenki desu.* Tomorrow will be cloudy.
- 漢字を読みはするが、書きはしない。 *Kanji wo yomi wa suru ga, kaki wa shinai.* I read *kanji* but I don't write them.
- いいえ、危険ではない。 *Iie, kiken de wa nai.* No, it isn't dangerous.
- 君にはあるが、僕にはない。 *Kimi ni wa aru ga, boku ni wa nai.* You have one, but I don't.
- 予想どおりの展開になってはきたが、 *Yosō-doori no tenkai ni natte wa kita ga,* Things have turned out according to expectations, but . . .

2. 「…ては」の形で、動作の繰り返しを示す "*. . . -te wa" no katachi de, dōsa no kurikaeshi wo shimesu* In . . . *-te wa* form, denotes repetition of the action:
- パートの仕事を見つけては働いている。 *Pāto no shigoto wo mitsukete wa hataraite iru.* They work whenever they find a part-time job.
- 小さいくまでを肉に突き刺しては、口に放り込む。 *Chiisai kumade*

wo niku ni tsuki-sashite wa, kuchi ni hōri-komu. They go on sticking little rakes into the meat and heaving it into their mouths.
→ *ga*[2]

wa[2] わ　終助詞　final particle
活用語の終止形に付く *Katsuyō-go no shūshikei ni tsuku* Is added to Base 3 of conjugables.
1. 軽い主張を表す *Karui shuchō wo arawasu* Expresses mild insistence:
• そんなこと出来ませんわ。 *Sonna koto dekimasen wa!* I can't do that!
2. 軽い感動を表す *Karui kandō wo arawasu* Expresses mild emotion:
• 驚いたわ。 *Odoroita wa!* What a fright I got!
NOTE. This particle is used mostly by women; by nature it cannot follow the auxiliaries *-u, -mai.*

waga 我が・吾が　連体詞　adnoun
In *bungo, ga* was a case particle indicating also possession, and this has carried over in some phrases of modern Japanese:
• 吾輩 *waga hai* I, we (the *-hai* of 年輩 *nen-pai,* 先輩 *sen-pai*); 我が意を得る *waga i wo eru* heartily agree; 我が事 *waga koto* one's business; 我が国 *waga kuni* this land of ours; 我が儘 *waga mama* wilfulness; 我が身 *waga mi* oneself; 我が物 *waga mono* one's property; 我が党 *waga tō* one's party.

wakaru 分かる（判る・解る）　自動詞　intransitive verb
Even Japanese students, under the influence of translation, tend to use this as a transitive verb. It will help to consider it as corresponding with Latin *patēre,* to lie open:
• 私には意味が分からない。 *Watashi ni wa imi ga wakaranai.* I don't understand (it).
• 日本語が分かりますか。 *Nihongo ga wakarimasu ka?* Do you understand Japanese?
• 洒落の味が分かる。 *Share no aji ga wakaru.* I appreciate the joke.
• はい、分かりました。 *Hai, wakarimashita.* Yes, I understand.
• 物の分かった人だ *Mono no wakatta hito da.* He is a sensible person.
• 試験の結果がいつ分かりますか。 *Shiken no kekka ga itsu wakarimasu ka?* When will the exam results be known?
NOTE. *Wakaru* is not followed by the auxiliaries *-rareru, -reru, -tai, -uru,* or by the *koto ga dekiru* construction.

wake 訳　形式名詞として　as a formal noun

1.「…わけだ」の形で、断定を和らげる　*"... Wake da" no katachi de, dantei wo yawarageru* In ... *wake da* form, softens the assertion:

- なるほど君がそう考えるわけだ。 *Naruhodo kimi ga sō kangaeru wake da.* You have good reason to think like that.
- その地方の暗さが反映しているわけだろう。 *Sono chiho nō kurasa ga han-ei shite iru wake darō.* Perhaps it's because the gloom of the district is showing through.

2.「…わけにはいかない」の形で、「そう簡単に…出来ない」 *"... wake ni wa ikanai" no katachi de, "sō kantan ni ... dekinai"* In ... *wake ni wa ikanai* form, means "can't very well":

- 手伝わないわけにはいかなかった。 *Tetsudawanai wake ni wa ikanakatta.* I could'nt have done otherwise than lend a hand.
- このままにしておくわけにはいかない。 *Kono mama ni shite oku wake ni wa ikanai.* We can't very well leave it like this.
- 多少の感慨が湧かないわけには行かなかった。 *Tashō no kangai ga wakanai wake ni wa yukanakatta.* She couldn't help being deeply moved.
- 電車に乗せるわけにはいかなかったから、自分の車を使わねばならなかった。 *Densha ni noseru wake ni wa ikanakatta kara, jibun no kuruma wo tsukawaneba naranakatta.* I couldn't very well put him on the train, so I had to use my own car.

3.「…ないわけではないが」の形で、後に言うことの前触れとして、前のことを言い消す　*"... Nai wake de wa nai ga" no katachi de, ato ni iu koto no mae-bure to shite, mae no koto wo ii-kesu* In ... *nai wake de wa nai ga* form, rejects a negation in order to prepare for a subsequent assertion:

- 勉強しないわけではないが、余り勤勉でもない。 *Benkyō shinai wake de wa nai ga, amari kinben de mo nai.* It isn't that he doesn't study, but he is not over-diligent.

-wan 椀・碗・鋺　接尾語　suffix

椀に盛って出す料理を数える語　*Wan ni motte dasu ryōri wo kazoeru go* Counter for bowls of food:

- 一椀の御飯　*ichi-wan no gohan* one bowl of rice.

NOTE. The *hen* of the above three *kanji* denote the material from which the bowl is made.

ware 我・吾　代名詞　pronoun

This classical pronoun has carried over in:

・我頼み *ware-danomi* self-complacency; 我勝ちに *ware-gachi ni* scrambling for first place; 我から *ware-kara* voluntarily, because of one's own deeds: 我ながら *ware-nagara* though I say it myself; 我に帰る *ware ni kaeru* come to one's senses; 我等・我々 *warera* • *ware-ware* we; 我先に *ware-saki ni* fighting to be first; 我知らず *ware-shirazu* unconsciously; 我を忘れる *ware wo wasureru* be beside oneself.

-ware- 割れ　接頭語・接尾語　prefix, suffix

・割れ目 *ware-me* crack; 割れ物 *ware-mono* broken or fragile article; 片割れ *kata-ware* fragment, one of the group; 仲間割れ *nakama-ware* falling out of friends; 割れ鍋に閉じ蓋。*Ware-nabe ni toji-buta.* Every Jack has his Jill.

washi わし　代名詞　pronoun

Formerly women's speech, now used by older men towards juniors:

・わしの言うことを聞け。 *Washi no iu koto wo kike.* Listen to what I (have to) say.

watakushi 私　名詞・代名詞　noun, pronoun

1. 名詞として、「公」の反意語 *Meishi to shite, "ooyake" no han'i-go* As a noun, antonym of "public":

・私事 *watakushi-goto, shiji* private affair; 私立 *watakushi-ritsu, shiritsu* private (cf. 市立 *shi-ritsu* • *ichi-ritsu* municipal); 私小説 *watakushi-shōsetsu* first-person novel; 私する *watakushi suru* turn to private use.

2. 代名詞、人称。自分自身を指す *Daimeishi, ninshō; jibun jishin wo sasu* Pronoun, personal; refers to oneself:

・わたくしとしては、行きたくありません。 *Watakushi to shite wa, yukitaku arimasen.* As for me, I should prefer not to go.

NOTE. Used by both men and women, and rather formal. The form *watashi* is now more common. Non-standard forms are: *washi, atakushi, atashi. Boku* is used by men when speaking to inferiors, and by boys among themselves. *Ore* is still coarser in tone.

wo を　格助詞　case particle

体言または体言に準ずるものに付く *Taigen mata wa taigen ni junzuru mono ni tsuku* Is added to nominals or to nominalized words.

1. 動作の及ぶ対象を示す *Dōsa no oyobu taishō wo shimesu* Denotes grammatical object:

- 手紙を書いてください。 *Tegami wo kaite kudasai.* Please write a letter.
- バスが来るのを待っている。 *Basu ga kuru no wo matte iru.* I am waiting for the bus (to arrive).

2. 動作の経過する場所・時間を示す *Dōsa no keika suru basho • jikan wo shimesu:* Denotes place or time over which an action extends:

- 橋を渡る *hashi wo wataru* cross a bridge; 道を歩く *michi wo aruku* walk along a road; 空を飛ぶ *sora wo tobu* fly through the air; 森の中を通って行く *mori no naka wo tootte iku* pass through the woods; 一学期を遊んで過ごす *ichi-gakki wo asonde sugosu* spend a term idling.

3. 動作の起点を示す *Dōsa no kiten wo shimesu* Denotes starting-point of action:

- 家を出る *ie wo deru* leave home; 席を離れる *seki wo hanareru* leave one's seat; 故郷を後にする *kokyō wo ato ni suru* leave one's home-town.

4. 動作の方向を示す *Dōsa no hōkō wo shimesu* Denotes direction of an action:

- 後ろを振り返ってみる *ushiro wo furi-kaette miru* look behind one.

5. 使役の自動詞の場合、動作を命じられる・許される人・ものを指す *Shieki no jidōshi no baai, dōsa wo meijirareru • yurusareru hito • mono wo sasu* In the case of intransitive causative verbs, indicates the person or thing commanded or allowed to perform the action:

- 菊を咲かせる *kiku wo sakaseru* raise chrysanthemums; 生徒を立たせる *seito wo tataseru* make pupils stand; 子供を隠れさせる *kodomo wo kakure-saseru* let the children hide; 人を暖まらせる *hito wo atatamaraseru* let the people warm themselves.

NOTE. The spelling *wo* has been kept in order to reduce the possibility of confusing this case particle with other words spelt *o*.

NOTE. An idiomatic use of *wo* with the passive voice resembles the retained object in the classical languages:

- ぼくは火炎瓶を投げ付けられる筈がない。 *Boku wa kaenbin wo nage-tsukerareru hazu ga nai.* There is no reason why a Molotov cocktail should be thrown at me.
- 自分の体にメスを入れられる恐怖があった。 *Jibun no karada ni mesu wo irerareru kyōfu ga atta.* I was scared of having a scalpel plunged into my body.
- 重役クラスの椅子を与えられた。 *Jūyaku-kurasu no isu wo ataerareta.* He was given a post equivalent to that of a director.

NOTE. Some cases can be explained only by supposing an ellipsis:

- 今を盛りと咲き乱れる。 *Ima wo sakari to saki-midareru.* They are in full bloom just now.
- その夜を最後に、彼女のことを脳裏から拭い去ってしまう筈であった。 *Sono yoru wo saigo ni, kanojo no koto wo nōri kara nugui-satte shimau hazu de atta.* That was the night when I ought to have washed her out of my mind once and for all.
- 雨の中を、どうも。 *Ame no naka wo, dōmo.* Thanks for going to so much trouble in this rain.

NOTE. In *bungo, wo shite* indicated the agent in the causative construction:

- 私をして言わしめれば . . . *Watakushi wo shite iwashimereba* . . . If you ask me . . .

NOTE. Some further examples of idiomatic uses of *wo:*

- 人を怒鳴る *hito wo donaru* yell at a person; 人を怒る *hito wo okoru* be angry with a person; 人を笑う *hito wo warau* laugh at a person; 道を急ぐ *michi wo isogu* hurry along the street; 角を右へ曲がる *kado wo migi e magaru* turn right at corner; 学校を休む *gakkō wo yasumu* stay home from school; 議長を務める *gichō wo tsutomeru* act as chairman; モスクワを回って帰国する *Mosukuwa wo mawatte kikoku suru* return via Moscow.

NOTE. With verbs in the passive:

- 話を聞かされる *hanashi wo kikasareru* be told a story; 金を取られる *kane wo torareru* be robbed of one's money; 名を知られる *na wo shirareru* be famous; 財布を奪われる *saifu wo ubawareru* be robbed of one's purse.

NOTE. In the case of nouns followed by *suru,* a *wo* may be inserted if one has not already been used:

- 挨拶する *aisatsu suru* greet 朝夕の挨拶をする *asa-yū no aisatsu wo suru* pass the time of day; 中国の地理を勉強する *Chūgoku no chiri wo benkyō suru* study the geography of China.

Y

ya[1] や 格助詞 case particle

体言または体言の資格を作る「の」に付いて、並列を表す *Taigen mata wa taigen no shikaku wo tsukuru "no" ni tsuite, heiretsu wo arawasu* Added to nominals and to nominalizing *no,* expresses listing:

- 青いのや赤いのや様々な色合いだね。 *Aoi no ya akai no ya sama-zama na iroai da ne.* There are all sorts of hues, blue, red, and so on, aren't there?

- あれやこれやですっかり参った。 *Are ya kore ya de sukkari maitta.* With one thing and another, I am dead beat.

NOTE. This particle will be found following *kara* and *hodo:*

- 南からや北からや集まった。 *Minami kara ya kita kara ya atsumatta.* People gathered from both north and south.

NOTE. While *ya . . . ya* is standard, *ya . . . nado, ya . . . soshite* are coming into use.

ya² や 接続助詞 conjunctive particle
活用語の終止形に付いて、「…するとすぐに」 *Katsuyō go no shūshikei ni tsuite, ". . . suru to sugu ni"* With Base 3 of conjugables, means "no sooner. . . than":

- 遺体を見るや泣き出した。 *Itai wo miru ya naki-dashita.* On seeing the corpse, she burst into tears.
- 手紙を読むや家を飛び出した。 *Tegami wo yomu ya, ie wo tobidashita.* Immediately on reading the letter, he dashed out of the house.

→ *ina ya*

ya³ や 間投助詞（古） interjectional particle (classical)
In *bungo,* this particle expressed exclamation; in modern Japanese, it is used to express emphasis and invitation:

- 次郎や、ちょっとおいで。 *Jirō ya, chotto oide.* Jiro, come here a moment.
- 今や宇宙時代となった。 *Ima ya uchū-jidai to natta.* Now we are in the space age.
- もう、止めようや。 *Mō, yameyō ya.* Let's leave off.

NOTE. A frequent use of *ya* is in the form: Base 2 + *ya* + *shinai:*

- 私が面倒を見なければ、だれも面倒を見やしない。 *Watashi ga mendō wo minakereba, dare mo mendō wo mi ya shinai.* If I don't look after him, nobody else will.
- 「結婚」という言葉が出やしない。 *"Kekkon" to iu kotoba ga de ya shinai.* The word "marriage" never crosses her lips.

-yagaru やがる 接尾語（俗） suffix (slang)
動詞の連用形に付いて、憎しみ・軽蔑の気持ちを表す *Dōshi no ren'yō-kei ni tsuite, nikushimi • keibetsu no kimochi wo arawasu* With Base 2 of verbs, expresses a sense of spite or contempt:

- 自由と放縦とをはき違えてやがる。 *Jiyū to hōjū to wo haki-chigaete-yagaru.* (The silly fool,) He is confusing liberty with license.
- シロの馬鹿野郎、主人に恥をかかせやがって、と思った。 *Shiro no*

baka-yarō, shujin ni haji wo kakase-yagatte, to omotta. How stupid of you, Shiro, I thought, to bring disgrace on your master like this!

-yaka やか 接尾語 suffix

形容詞の語幹・擬声語に付いて、形容動詞を作り、「...である様子」の意味を表す *Keiyōshi no gokan • giseigo ni tsuite, keiyōdōshi wo tsukuri, ". . . de aru yōsu" no imi wo arawasu* Added to stem of adjectives and to onomatopoeic words, makes adjectival nouns of them, and expresses the idea of resemblance:

- 艶やか *ade-yaka* charming; 鮮やか *aza-yaka* fresh; 華やか *hana-yaka* gorgeous; 晴れやか *hare-yaka* cheerful; 密やか *hiso-yaka* stealthy; 冷ややか *hiya-yaka* chilly; 軽やか *karo-yaka* airy; きらびやか *kirabi-yaka* gorgeous; 細やか・濃やか *koma-yaka* warm, minute; 真しやか *makotoshi-yaka* plausible; 円やか *maro-yaka* plump, smooth taste; 和やか *nago-yaka* genial; 賑やか *nigi-yaka* bustling; にこやか *niko-yaka* smiling; 伸びやか *nobi-yaka* carefree; 穏やか *oda-yaka* tranquil; 細やか *sasa-yaka* modest; 爽やか *sawa-yaka* bracing; しめやか *shime-yaka* quiet; しなやか *shina-yaka* supple, graceful; 忍びやか *shinobi-yaka* stealthy; 淑やか *shito-yaka* refined; 健やか *suko-yaka* healthy; 速やか *sumi-yaka* swift; たおやか *tao-yaka* svelte; 慎ましやか *tsutsumashi-yaka* modest; 約やか *tsuzuma-yaka* frugal; 緩やか *yuru-yaka* gentle.

→ *-raka*

Yamato-kotoba 大和言葉

1. 日本固有のことば（特に漢語に対して言う） *Nihon koyū no kotoba (toku ni Kan-go ni taishite iu)* Japanese language (particularly, as distinct from Chinese).

2. 雅言、平安時代の古語 *Ga-gen, Heian-jidai no ko-go* The elegant, classical language of the Heian era.

3. 和歌 *Wa-ka* Japanese-style poetry (*Yamato-uta*).

-yameru 止める 接尾語 suffix

The suffix is added to Base 2 of a few verbs; the intransitive form, *-yamu,* will be found with verbs of involuntary action:

- 旅行を取りやめた。 *Ryokō wo tori-yameta.* We've cancelled the trip.
- 雪が降りやんだ。 *Yuki ga furi-yanda.* It has stopped snowing.

yara やら 副助詞 adverbial particle

色々の語、活用語の終止形に付く *Iro-iro no go, katsuyō-go no shūshikei*

ni tsuku Added to various parts of speech, to Base 3 in case of conjugables.

1. 不確かなことを示す（疑問詞に付くことが多い） *Fu-tashika na koto wo shimesu (gimonshi ni tsuku koto ga ooi)* Expresses uncertainty (is often used with question words):

- どうやら授業に間に合った。 *Dō yara jugyō ni ma ni atta.* I managed to be in time for class.
- だれやら来ているようだ。 *Dare yara kite iru yō da.* Somebody seems to have come.
- 何のことやらさっぱり分からない。 *Nan no koto yara sappari wakaranai.* I don't have a clue.

2. 並列を表す *Heiretsu wo arawasu* Denotes listing:

- お菓子やら果物やら色々いただいた。 *O-kashi yara kudamono yara iro-iro itadaita.* I got all sorts of things, candy, fruit, and so on.
- 泣くやら喚くやら大騒ぎだった。 *Naku yara wameku yara oo-sawagi datta.* What with crying and shouting, there was a great hubbub.
- レコードを借りてくるやら、招待状を発送するやら、大活躍であった。 *Rekōdo wo karite kuru yara, shōtaijō wo hassō suru yara, dai-katsuyaku de atta.* He showed tremendous activity, borrowing records, sending invitations, and so on.

yaru 遣る　補助動詞 supplementary verb

動詞の連用形に付く *Dōshi no ren'yōkei ni tsuku* Is added to Base 2 of verbs.

1. 動作が遠くまで及ぶ意味を表す *Dōsa ga tooku made oyobu imi wo arawasu* Denotes that the action extends far and wide:

- 言い遣る *ii-yaru* send word; 見遣る *mi-yaru* glance at, look into distance; 眺めやる *nagame-yaru* gaze into distance; 思いやる *omoi-yaru* sympathize with.

2. 完了の意味を表す *Kanryō no imi wo arawasu* Denotes completion of action:

- 追いやる *oi-yaru* drive away; 押しやる *oshi-yaru* push away; 投げ遣る *nage-yaru* neglect; うっちゃる *utcharu* thrust out (of ring.)

-te yaru てやる

1. 目下の者のためにする *Me-shita no mono no tame ni suru* Do something on behalf of an inferior:

- 貸してやる *kashite yaru* lend; 教えてやる *oshiete yaru* teach, tell how to; 助けてやる *tasukete yaru* lend a hand; 読んでやる *yonde yaru* read to.

2. 「ことさらに…する」 *"Kotosara ni. . . suru"* Do on purpose:

- 怒鳴りつけてやる *donari-tsukete yaru* bawl (a person) out;

殺してやる *koroshite yaru* kill; 死んでやる *shinde yaru* die.
- 今度は一等賞を取ってやる。 *Kon-do wa ittōshō wo totte yaru.* This time I'm going to take first prize (you wait and see)!

→ *-ageru* B

-yasui 易い 接尾語（形容詞） suffix (adjective)

動詞の連用形に付く *Dōshi no ren'yōkei ni tsuku* Is added to Base 2 of verbs.

1.「…しがちだ」 "*. . . shi-gachi da*" Denotes that something is likely to happen, or happens frequently:
- 変わりやすい *kawari-yasui* changeable; 間違いやすい *machigai-yasui* prone to error.

2.「簡単である」 "*Kantan de aru*" Denotes that something is easy to do:
- 書きやすい *kaki-yasui* easy to write (with, on); 覚えやすい *oboe-yasui* easily remembered; 分かりやすい説明 *wakari-yasui setsumei* simple explanation.
- この程度の床なら、踊りやすそうね。 *Kono teido no yuka nara, odori-yasusō ne.* A floor of this standard will be easy to dance on, don't you think?

→ *-gatai, -nikui*

yo よ 終助詞 final particle

体言または活用語の終止形・命令形に付く *Taigen mata wa katsuyō-go no shūshikei・meireikei ni tsuku* Is added to nominals and to Bases 3 and 6 of conjugables.

1. 念を押し、意味を強める *Nen wo oshi, imi wo tsuyomeru* Adds the idea of checking and emphasizing:
- 気を付けるのですよ。 *Ki wo tsukeru no desu yo!* Be sure you take good care!
- あなたの番よ。 *Anata no ban yo!* It's your turn!
- 早く来いよ。 *Hayaku koi yo!* Come quickly!

2. 勧誘を表す *Kan'yū wo arawasu* Expresses enticement:
- 一緒に行こうよ。 *Issho ni ikō yo!* Let's go together!

3. 呼びかけに用いる *Yobi-kake ni mochiiru* Is used as a vocative:
- 太郎よ、しっかりやれ。 *Tarō yo, shikkari yare!* Taro, do your best!

yo-[1] 四（シ、よ、よつ、よん）
- 四月 *shi-gatsu* April; 四方八方 *shi-hō happō* in all directions; 再三再四 *sai-san sai-shi* repeatedly; 四段 *yodan* fourth level; 四隅

yosumi four corners; 四つ足 *yotsu-ashi* quadruped; 四日 *yokka* the fourth; 四方山 *yomoyama* all sorts of; 四人 *yo-nin (yottari)* four people.

yo-² 夜 接頭語 prefix

1. Compounds dealing with human activities:
- 夜遊び *yo-asobi* "flying with the owl"; 夜話 *yo-banashi, ya-wa* night talk; 夜立ち *yo-dachi* departure by night; 夜釣り *yo-zuri* fishing by night.

2. Compounds dealing with atmospherics:
- 夜嵐 *yo-arashi* night storm; 夜風 *yo-kaze* night wind; 夜寒 *yo-samu* cold of night; 夜露 *yo-tsuyu* night dew.

3. Compounds dealing with things that operate or are used at night:
- 夜着 *yo-gi* bedclothes (＝夜具 *ya-gu*); 夜汽車 *yo-gisha* night train; 夜店 *yo-mise* night stall; 夜宮 *yo-miya* vigil; 夜目 *yo-me* night vision (cf. 夜目遠目笠の内 *Yo-me too-me kasa no uchi*. Every woman is beautiful if seen at night, from a distance, or under a bamboo hat.)

4. Adverbs of time:
- 夜通し *yo-dooshi* all night long; 夜毎 *yo-goto* every night (＝毎夜 *mai-yo*); 夜もすがら *yo mo sugara,* よっぴて *yoppite* all night long; 夜中 *yo-naka* midnight; 夜な夜な *yo-na yo-na* night after night

→ *na*⁴

-yo¹ 夜 接尾語 suffix
- 雨夜 *ama-yo* rainy night; 一夜 *hito-yo* (*ichi-ya*) one night; 幾夜 *iku-yo* (how) many nights; 毎夜 *mai-yo* every night; 短夜 *mijika-yo* short (summer) night(s); おぼろ夜 *oboro-yo* night with hazy moon; 小夜曲 *sa-yo-kyoku* serenade; 霜夜 *shimo-yo* frosty night; 常夜 *toko-yo* endless night; 闇夜 *yami-yo* moonless night; 月夜 *tsuki-yo* moonlit night; 夜々 *yo-yo* every night.

-yo² 世 接尾語 suffix
- 御世 *Mi-yo* (Emperor's) reign; 時世 *toki-yo* the times; 常世 *toko-yo* eternity, Hades; 浮世 *uki-yo* (transitory) world; 現し世 *utsushi-yo* this present life.

-yō¹ よう 助動詞 auxiliary verb
- 一人で行けよう筈がない。 *Hitori de ikeyō hazu ga nai.* He can't be expected to go all alone.
- 亭主が家にいようといまいと構わない。 *Teishu ga ie ni iyō to imai*

to kamawanai. It doesn't matter whether her husband is at home or not.

- 幾度彼と別れようと考えたか分からなかった。 *Ikudo kare to wakareyō to kangaeta ka wakaranakatta.* She didn't know how many times she had thought of leaving him.

→ *-ō, -yō*

-yō[2] 様 接尾語 suffix

動詞の連用形に付いて、「...の仕方」という意味を添える *Dōshi no ren'yōkei ni tsuite, ". . . no shikata" to iu imi wo soeru* With Base 2 of verbs, adds the idea of "way of doing. . .":

- ほかになんとも仕様がない。 *Hoka ni nan to mo shi-yō ga nai.* There is no alternative.
- 結婚したかと聞かれると、答え様がない。 *Kekkon shita ka to kikareru to, kotae-yō ga nai.* When asked if I am married, I am stuck for an answer.
- 事情を聞かないでは捜し様がありません。 *Jijō wo kikanaide wa sagashi-yō ga ari-masen.* I have no hope of finding her unless I make some inquiries.

-yō[3] 葉 接尾語 suffix

葉のようなものを数える語 *Ha no yō na mono wo kazoeru go* Counter for (thin,) leaflike objects:

- 白紙三葉 *haku-shi san-yō* three sheets of (blank) paper

→ *-mai*[2]

-yō da ようだ 助動詞 auxiliary verb

The conjugation is: 1. *yō daro* 2. *yō datt* (ようだっ)、*yō de, yō ni* 3. *yō da* 4. *yō na* 5. *yō nara* 6. —.

活用語の連体形・連体詞・助詞「の」に付く *Katsuyo-gō no rentaikei • rentaishi • joshi "no" ni tsuku* Is added to Base 4 of conjugables, to adnouns and to the particle *no.*

1. 不確かな断定を表す *Fu-tashika na dantei wo arawasu* Expresses vague assertion:

- 病気のような顔色だ。 *Byōki no yō na kao-iro da.* He looks sickly.
- 九州では稲がもう実ったようだ。 *Kyūshū de wa ine ga mō minotta yō da.* It seems that in Kyushu the rice is already ripe.

→ *mitai na, rashii*[1,2]

2. 他に例えていう意味を表す *Ta ni tatoete iu imi wo arawasu* Expresses simile:

- 立て板に水を流すように話す。 *Tate-ita ni mizu wo nagasu yō ni hanasu.* He "pours the full tide of eloquence along".
- 東京のような大都会には住みにくい。 *Tōkyō no yō na dai-tokai ni wa sumi-nikui.* A large city like Tokyo is hard to live in.

3. 例を示す *Rei wo shimesu* Furnishes an example:
- 兄さんのように勉強しなさい。 *Nii-san no yō ni benkyō shi nasai.* Study like your brother.
- このようでは、どうも駄目だ。 *Kono yō de wa, dōmo dame da.* This way of doing things just will not do.
- 書き落としが随分あるような気がした。 *Kaki-otoshi ga zuibun aru yō na ki ga shita.* He got the impression that there were a lot of omissions.

4. 「…ように」の形で、目的を示す "*. . . Yō ni" no katachi de, mokuteki wo shimesu* In . . . *yō ni* form, denotes purpose:
- 間に合うように早く起きた。 *Ma ni au yō ni hayaku okita.* I got up early so as to be in time.
- 人が住むように（地を）造られた。 *Hito ga sumu yō ni (chi wo) tsukurareta.* He made it (the earth) to be lived in.

NOTE. The *ni* is sometimes omitted:
- 迷惑を掛けないよう飼い主が注意を払うのだ。 *Meiwaku wo kakenai yō kainushi ga chūi wo harau no da.* The owner must be careful not to cause inconvenience.

5. 「…ように」の形で願望を表す "*. . . Yō ni" no katachi de, ganbō wo arawasu* In . . . *yō ni* form, expresses a wish:
- 明日晴れますように。 *Asu haremasu yō ni!* I hope it's fine tomorrow!
- 体に注意するように。 *Karada ni chūi suru yō ni!* Take good care of your health!

yō ni iu ように言う 連語 phrase
- 本を忘れないように言いました。 *Hon wo wasurenai yō ni iimashita.* I told them not to forget their books.

yō ni kiku · oboeru ように聞く・覚える 連語 phrase
- 帰国したように聞いている。 *Kikoku shita yō ni kiite iru.* I hear he has returned.
- 退職したように覚えている。 *Taishoku shita yō ni oboete iru.* I seem to remember he has retired.

yō ni naru ようになる 連語 phrase
- バスがここを通るようになったのは最近のことだ。 *Basu ga koko wo tooru yō ni natta no wa saikin no koto da.* It is only recently that buses have begun to run here.

• もう、授業中、英語を使わないようになっている。 *Mō, jugyō-chū, Eigo wo tsukawanai yō ni natte iru.* They have reached the stage where they no longer use English during class.

-eru yō ni naru . . . えるようになる 連語 phrase

• 早くから漢字が読めるようになった。 *Hayaku kara kanji ga yomeru yō ni natta.* He acquired the ability to read ideographs at an early stage.

• 赤ん坊はもう歩けるようになっている。 *Akanbō wa mō arukeru yō ni natte iru.* The baby is already able to walk.

yō ni suru ようにする 連語 phrase

• 皆で食事が出来るようにした。 *Mina de shokuji ga dekiru yō ni shita.* They arranged things so that we could all have our meals together.

• こんなミスを繰り返さないようにします。 *Konna misu wo kuri-kae-sanai yō ni shimasu.* I will make sure not to repeat such a blunder.

yōgen 用言 verbals

自立語で、活用があり、それだけで述語になることができ、事物の属性を示す *Jiritsu-go de, katsuyō ga ari, sore dake de jutsu-go ni naru koto ga deki, jibutsu no zoku-sei wo shimesu* Independent, conjugated words that can of themselves become predicates, and denote the attributes of things.

As will be seen in the Introduction (I), in Japanese grammar, verbals include verbs, adjectives and adjectival nouns, but not auxiliaries, which are considered dependent words, and a separate part of speech.

yō-on 拗音

The sound produced by combining *ya, yu, yo* with the *i-dan* of most of the kana syllabary chart, giving *kya, kyu, kyo,* etc.

yori[1] より 格助詞 case particle

体言・準体言に付く *Taigen • jun-taigen ni tsuku* Is added to nominals and to nominalized words.

1. 比較の基準を示す *Hikaku no kijun wo shimesu* Sets standard of comparison:

• 洋食より、和食の方が好き。 *Yōshoku yori, washoku no hō ga suki.* I prefer Japanese cuisine to Western.

• フランスは日本より人口が少ない。 *Furansu wa Nihon yori jinkō ga sukunai.* France has a smaller population than Japan.

• 批判を加えるより、先ず実行だ。 *Hihan wo kuwaeru yori, mazu jikkō da.* What we need is action rather than criticism.

2. 打ち消しを伴って、限定を表す *Uchikeshi wo tomonatte, gentei wo arawasu* With a negative, expresses restriction:

- 譲歩するより、仕方がない。 *Jōho suru yori, shikata ga nai.* There is nothing for it but to make some concession.
- 歩いていくより、ほかはない。 *Aruite iku yori, hoka wa nai.* There is nothing for it but to go on foot.

3. 文語の名残で、「から」の意味を表す *Bungo no nagori de, "kara" no imi wo arawasu* As a carry-over from classical Japanese, is synonymous with *kara:*

- 会議は九時より始まる。 *Kaigi wa ku-ji yori hajimaru.* The meeting begins at 9.
- 街より三キロ以内に *machi yori san-kiro inai ni* within 3 km of town.

yori² 因り・依り 動詞「よる」の連用形 Base 2 of verb *yoru*
「**...**により」の形で *". . . Ni yori" no katachi de* In . . . *ni yori* form.

1. 「**...**に従って」 *". . . ni shitagatte"* "In conformity with. . . ":

- 校長の命令により、 *kōchō no meirei ni yori,* acting on the principal's orders.

2. 「**...**のために」、 *". . . no tame ni"* "Owing to. . . ":

- 濃霧により、列車が延着した。 *Nōmu ni yori, ressha ga enchaku shita.* The train arrived late because of the fog.

→ *-tsuki*

yori³ より 副詞 adverb
A modern coinage used to translate the comparative degree of Western languages:

- より高く、より速く、より強く。 *Yori takaku, yori hayaku, yori tsuyoku.* "Altius, citius, fortius."

yori⁴ 撚り 名詞 noun (from verb *yoru,* twist)
撚ること・撚ったもの *Yoru koto • yotta mono* Torsion, ply:

- 三本撚りの羊毛 *sanbon-yori no yōmō* three-ply wool; 腕に撚りを掛ける *ude ni yori wo kakeru* take the utmost care; 撚りを戻す *yori wo modosu* be reconciled.

yori⁵ 寄り 名詞 noun (used also as a suffix)
「その方に近い」 *"Sono hō ni chikai"* "Approaching", "tending towards":

• 歩み寄り *ayumi-yori* compromise; 耳寄り *mimi-yori* welcome news; 持ち寄りの会 *mochi-yori no kai* "basket party"; 最寄りの *mo-yori ni* nearby, nearest; 身寄り *mi-yori* relative; 泣き寄り *naki-yori* coming together for consolation; 西寄りの風 *nishi-yori no kaze* westerly wind; 似寄りの *ni-yori no* similar; 年寄り *toshi-yori* elderly person; 寄り寄り *yori-yori* occasionally; 存じ寄り *zonji-yori* an acquaintance, (my) humble opinion.

-yuki 行き 接尾語 suffix

場所を示す名詞に付く *Basho wo shimesu meishi ni tsuku* Is added to place-nouns:

1. その場所へ行くこと *Sono basho e iku koto* Act of going to that place:

• 台湾行きはあまり費用がかからない。 *Taiwan-yuki wa amari hiyō ga kakara nai.* Going to Taiwan doesn't cost much.

2. その場所が目的地であること *Sono basho ga mokuteki-chi de aru koto* Denotes the goal of motion:

• 神田行きの電車に乗った。 *Kanda-yuki no densha ni notta.* I boarded a train for Kanda.

3. 複雑な意味を表す *Fukuzatsu na imi wo arawasu* Various applications:

• 桁行き *keta-yuki* length of crossbeam; 心行き *kokoro-yuki* disposition; 雲行き *kumo-yuki* look of sky, course of events; 奥行き *oku-yuki* depth; 先行き *saki-yuki, saki-iki* future (prospects); 売れ行き *ure-yuki* demand; よそ行きを着る *yoso-yuki, yoso-iki wo kiru* dress in one's best.

yutō-yomi 湯桶読み

Reading of a compound with a *kun* reading preceding an *on* reading, as in 赤字 *aka-ji* (deficit), 梅酒 *ume-shu* (apricot wine), as opposed to *jūbako-yomi* 重箱読み as in 団子 *dan-go* (dumpling), 気持ち *ki-mochi* (feeling).

→ Appendix A

yū 言う

This verb has been traditionally written *iu,* without the macron; in *koku-go* dictionaries it will be found as いう、 and in *ko-go* dictionaries as いふ。The verb 結う、do up one's hair, is romanized as *yu-u (yuwa-nai, yui-masu, yutta, yu-eba, yu-e)*.

Z

-zama 様・態 接尾語 suffix
動詞の連用形に付く *Dōshi no ren'yōkei ni tsuku* Is added to Base 2 of verbs.
1. 動作の仕方を表す *Dōsa no shikata wo arawasu* Denotes way of doing. . . :
- 言い様 *ii-zama* way of speaking; 生き様 *iki-zama* life-style; 寝様 *ne-zama* sleeping-posture; 死に様 *shini-zama* manner of facing death.

2.「…するとすぐ」 ". . . *suru to sugu*" "No sooner. . . than. . . ":
- 振り反り様に *furikaeri-zama ni* immediately on looking back; 続け様に *tsuzuke-zama ni* in rapid succession.

-zaru ざる 助動詞「ず」の連体形 Base 4 of the auxiliary *-zu*
- 本当のことを言わざるを得なかった。 *Hōntō no koto wo iwazaru wo enakatta.* I had no choice but to tell the truth.
- 妄想に過ぎなかったと認めざるを得ない。 *Mōsō ni suginakatta to mitomezaru wo enai.* I have to admit that it was only a fantasy.

→ *-zu*

ze ぜ 終助詞 final particle
動詞の終止形に付く *Dōshi no shūshikei ni tsuku* Is added to Base 3 of verbs:
1. 親しみの気持ちを添える *Shitashimi no kimochi wo soeru* Adds an air of familiarity:
- 急がなければバスに遅れるぜ。 *Isoganakereba basu ni okureru ze.* Hurry up or you'll miss the bus.

2. 相手を見下した態度を表す *Aite wo mi-kudashita taido wo arawasu* Reveals an attitude of contempt for other party:
- それはちょっと違いますぜ。 *Sore wa chotto chigaimasu ze.* You have it all wrong.

-zen[1] 然 接尾語 suffix
名詞に付いて、形容詞を作り、「いかにも…のような」という意味を添える *Meishi ni tsuite, keiyōshi wo tsukuri, "ika ni mo. . . no yō na" to iu imi wo soeru* Added to nouns, adjectivalizes them, and adds the idea of "closely resembling. . . ":
- 学者然としている。 *Gakusha-zen to shite iru.* He has a scholarly air.

- 紳士然たる姿だ。 *Shinshi-zen taru sugata da.* He has the bearing of a gentleman.
- 得意然として *tokui-zen to shite* with a triumphant air; 偶然の *gūzen no* casual; 依然として *izen to shite* as . . . as ever; 自然 *shizen* nature; 全然 *zen-zen* (not) at all (The use of this *zen-zen* in a positive context is not recommended.).

-zen[2] 膳 接尾語 suffix

1. 椀に盛った食物を数える語 *Wan ni motta shokumotsu wo kazoeru go* Counter for bowls of food:
   - 御飯を二膳頂いた。 *Gohan wo ni-zen itadaita.* I had two bowls of rice.
2. 箸を一組ずつ数える語 *Hashi wo hito-kumi zutsu kazoeru go* Counter for pairs of chopsticks:
   - 箸を二膳並べておいた。 *Hashi wo ni-zen narabete oita.* She set two pairs of chopsticks.

-zen- 前 接頭語・接尾語 prefix, suffix

- 前後 *zen-go* sequence, thereabouts; 前線 *zen-sen* front line; 午前 *go-zen* morning; 直前に *chokuzen ni* just prior to, just in front of.

zo ぞ 終助詞 final particle

活用語の終止形に付いて、断定を強調する *Katsuyō-go no shūshikei ni tsuite, dantei wo kyōchō suru* Added to Base 3 of conjugables, strengthens force of assertion:

- 酷い目に合うぞ。 *Hidoi me ni au zo!* You'll catch it, I can tell you!

-zoi 沿い 接尾語 suffix

名詞に付いて、「長く続くものの横を進む」 *Meishi ni tsuite, "nagaku tsuzuku mono no yoko wo susumu"* Added to nouns, proceeding along or parallel to:

- 海岸沿いに *kaigan-zoi ni* along the beach; 川沿いに *kawa-zoi ni* along the river; 山沿いの道 *yama-zoi no michi* road running along foot of mountain.

→ *-zutai*

-zome 初め 接尾語 suffix

動詞の連用形に付いて、名詞を作り、「(新年になって) 初めてする」 *Dōshi no ren'yōkei ni tsuite, meishi wo tsukuri, "(shinnen ni natte) hajimete suru*" Added to Base 2 of verbs, nominalizes them, and adds the meaning of doing for the first time (usually at New Year):

- 出初め式 *de-zome shiki* fire-brigade parade; 書き初め *kaki-zome* first piece of calligraphy; 食い初め *kui-zome* weaning ceremony; 渡り染め *watari-zome* first crossing of new bridge.

→ *hajime, hatsu, -someru*

-zoroi 揃い 接尾語 suffix

- 美人揃い *bijin-zoroi* galaxy of beauties; 傑作揃い *kessaku-zoroi* collection of masterpieces 三つ揃いの洋服 *mitsu-zoroi no yōfuku* three piece suit

→ *-soroi*

-zu ず 助動詞（古） auxiliary verb (classical)

The conjugation is: 1. *zu, (na), zara* 2. *zu, (ni), zari* 3. *zu, —, (zari)* 4. —, *nu, zaru* 5. —, *ne, zare* 6. —, —, *zare*.

This list has elements used in successive historical periods; the middle (second) entry has appeared as *-nu*.

活用語の未然形に付いて、打ち消しの意味を表す *Katsuyō-go no mizenkei ni tsuite, uchi-keshi no imi wo arawasu* With Base 1 of conjugables, expresses negation.

1. 副詞を作る *Fukushi wo tsukuru* Makes adverbs:

- 相変わらず *ai-kawarazu* as usual; 必ず *kanarazu* (from *kari-narazu*) for certain; 知らず知らず *shirazu-shirazu* unconsciously; やむを得ず *yamu wo ezu* unavoidably.

2. 「**...**ずじまい」の形で "*. . . -zu-jimai*" *no katachi de* In . . . *-zu-jimai* form:

- 買わずじまいだ。 *Kawazu-jimai da.* They end up not buying it.
- 見ずじまいになった。 *Mizu-jimai ni natta.* We ended up not seeing it.

3. 「**...**ずに」の形で、 "*. . . -zu ni*" *no katachi de* In . . . *-zu ni* form:

- 御飯を食べずに出かけた。 *Gohan wo tabezu ni dekaketa.* He left without having eaten.
- 本屋に寄らずには気が済まない。 *Hon'ya ni yorazu ni wa ki ga sumanai.* I can't bear to pass by a bookshop and not drop in.
- 使わずに置くつもりはない。 *Tsukawazu ni oku tsumori wa nai.* I don't intend to leave it unused.

4. 「**...**ずして」の形で "*. . . -zu shite*" *no katachi de* In . . . *-zu shite* form:

• 期せずして意見が一致した。 *Ki-sezu shite iken ga itchi shita.* Contrary to expectation, our views coincided.

5. 形容詞の場合 *Keiyōshi no baai* With adjectives:

• 暑からず寒からずのいい天候です。 *Atsukarazu samukarazu no ii tenkō desu.* It is good weather, neither too hot nor too cold.

6. 「…ねばならない」の形で "*. . . -Neba naranai" no katachi de* In . . . *-neba naranai* form.

• 土曜日も登校せねばならない。 *Doyōbi mo tōkō seneba naranai.* We have to go to school on Saturdays, too. (Base 5)

7. 「…ざる」の形で "*. . . -zaru" no katachi de* In . . . *-zaru* form:

• ことば慎まざる時は身破る。 *Kotoba tsutsushimazaru toki wa mi yaburu.* Least said soonest mended.

→ *-zaru*

-zuke[1] 付け 接尾語 suffix

1. Compounds dealing with printing and publishing:

• 後づけ *ato-zuke* back matter; 前付け *mae-zuke* front matter; 丁付け *chō-zuke* pagination; 奥付け *oku-zuke* colophon.

2. Compounds dealing with the application of something:

• 餌付け *e-zuke* feeding; 色付け *iro-zuke* coloring; 衣装付け *ishō-zuke* costuming; 肉付け *niku-zuke* fleshing out; 匂い付け *nioi-zuke* perfuming; 糊付け *nori-zuke, nori-tsuke* starching; 名付け *na-zuke* naming; ロウ付け・半田付け *rō-zuke* • *handa-zuke* soldering; 日付 *hi-zuke* date, dating.

3. Compounds dealing with forms of addresses:

• 気付 *ki-zuke* c/o (→ *-kata* 3); 君付け *kun-zuke* speaking down to; さん付け *san-zuke* "mistering"; 脇付け *waki-zuke* term of respect added to name of addressee.

4. Compounds dealing with dates:

• 七月二十日付の手紙 *shichi-gatsu hatsuka-zuke no tegami* letter dated July 20; 四月一日付で採用される *shi-gatsu tsuitachi-zuke de saiyō sareru* be employed as of April 1; 九月十日付で発令する *ku-gatsu tōka-zuke de hatsurei suru* announce on September 10.

-zuke[2] 漬(け) 接尾語 suffix

1. 漬けること *Tsukeru koto* Act of pickling:

• 粕漬け *Kasu-zuke* pickling in *sake* lees

2. 漬けたもの *Tsuketa mono* pickles:

• 一夜漬け *ichiya-zuke* pickles salted overnight, hasty preparation, something hastily prepared; 山葵付け *wasabi-zuke wasabi* pickled in *sake* lees.

-zukuri 造り・作り 接尾語 suffix

Suffix meanings fall into several categories.

1. Types of architecture, some named after famous prototypes:

- 校倉造り *azekura-zukuri;* 武家造り *buke-zukuri;* 権現造り *gongen-zukuri;* 春日造り *Kasuga-zukuri;* 神殿造り *shinden-zukuri;* 書院造り *shoin-zukuri;* 数寄屋造り *sukiya-zukuri;* 住吉造り *Sumiyoshi-zukuri;* 大社造り *Taisha-zukuri.*

2. Format of roofs:

- 合掌造り *gasshō-zukuri;* 波風造り *hafu-zukuri;* 方形造り *hōgyō-zukuri;* 入母屋造り *iri-moya-zukuri;* 切妻造り *kiri-zuma-zukuri;* 流れ造り *nagare-zukuri;* 寄せ棟造り *yose-mune-zukuri.*

3. Use of materials, or the materials used:

- 一木造り *ichi-boku-zukuri* carving statue from one piece of wood; 格子造り *kōshi-zukuri* structure with latticework in the front; 黒造り *kuro-zukuri* making from dark wood; 白木造り *shira-ki-zukuri* making from plain wood; 石造り *ishi-zukuri* stone-made.

4. Various applications:

- 出作り *de-zukuri* farming in distant fields; 土蔵造り *dozō-zukuri* storehouse; 細作り *hoso-zukuri* of slender make; 糸作り *ito-zukuri* kind of *sashimi;* 荷造り *ni-zukuri* packing; 田作り *ta-zukuri* tilling paddy fields; 手作り *te-zukuri* making by hand; 若作り *waka-zukuri* doing oneself up to look younger.

NOTE. In a few cases, several aspects are included; for example:

- 家作り *ie-zukuri (ya-zukuri)* (1) building of house; (2) style of house.
- 宮作り *miya-zukuri* (1) building of shrine; (2) style of shrine; (3) builder of shrine.

-zume 詰め 接尾語 suffix

1. 押しつける意を表す *Oshi-tsukeru i wo arawasu* Compulsion; packing in:

- 瓶詰め *bin-zume* bottled goods; 腸詰め *chō-zume* sausages; ぎゅう詰め *gyū-zume* packed tight; 字詰め *ji-zume* number of letters to a line; 石子詰め *ishiko-zume* burial alive; 重詰め *jū-zume* packed in tiered boxes; 缶詰 *kan-zume* canned goods; 氷詰め *koori-zume* ice-packed; 折り詰め *ori-zume* packed in chip box; 理詰め *ri-zume* force of argument; 雪隠詰め *setchin-zume* driving into a corner; 寿司詰め *sushi-zume* jampacked; 手詰め *te-zume* urging.

2. 一定の所で勤務をすること *Ittei no tokoro de kinmu wo suru koto* Being on duty in a fixed place:

- 江戸詰め *Edo-zume* duty in Edo; 国詰め *kuni-zume* duty in one's own fief; 後詰め *go-zume* rearguard duty; 支局詰め *shikyoku-zume* branch-office duty; 国会詰めの記者 *kokkai-zume no kisha* Diet reporter.

3. 動作の継続を表す *Dōsa no keizoku wo arawasu* Denotes continuity of action:

- 常詰め・定詰め *jō-zume* permanent duty, permanent staff; 立ち詰め *tachi-zume* having to stand a long time.

4. その他 *Sono ta* Other applications:

- 橋詰め *hashi-zume* foot of bridge; 大詰め *oo-zume* dénouement; 差し詰め *sashi-zume* for the moment.

-zurai 辛い 接尾語 suffix

動詞の連用形に付いて、「するのが苦しい」という意味を添える *Dōshi no ren'yōkei ni tsuite, "suru no ga kurushii" to iu imi wo soeru* With Base 2 of verbs, adds the idea that the action is painful or difficult:

- 聞きづらい *kiki-zurai* painful or difficult to hear or listen to; 見づらい *mi-zurai* painful or difficult to see or look at; 別れづらい *wakare-zurai* hard to part from; 行きづらい *yuki-zurai* reluctant to go.

→ *-gatai, -nikui*

-zure[1] 連れ 接尾語 suffix

名詞・代名詞に付く *Meishi・daimeishi ni tsuku* Is added to nouns and pronouns.

1. 伴うという意味を表す *Tomonau to iu imi wo arawasu* Expresses the idea of accompanying:

- 家族連れで *kazoku-zure de* taking the whole family; 子供連れで *kodomo-zure de* taking children with one; 親子連れで *oyako-zure de* parents and children together.

2. 組になっていること *Kumi ni natte iru koto* In a group, in groups:

- 二人連れで *futari-zure de* as a couple; 三人連れで *sannin-zure de* in three.

3. 他人の場合に卑しめを、自分の場合にへりくだりを含める *Tanin no baai ni iyashime wo, jibun no baai ni herikudari wo fukumeru* Entails an air of contempt in the case of others, deference in one's own:

- 町人連れ *chōnin-zure* town rabble; 女連れ *onna-zure* the likes of women.

-zure[2] 擦れ　接尾語　suffix

体言に付く *Taigen ni tsuku* Is added to nominals.

1. 擦れて出来た傷 *Surete dekita kizu* An abrasion:

• 鼻緒擦れ *hanao-zure* thong sore; 鞍擦れ *kura-zure* saddle sore; 靴擦れ *kutsu-zure* shoe sore; 床擦れ *toko-zure* bedsore.

2. 比喩的に *Hiyu-teki ni* Figuratively:

• 人ずれ *hito-zure* sophistication; 世間ずれ *seken-zure* sophistication; 都会ずれした青年 *tokai-zure shita seinen* a citified youth.

HOMONYM. ずれ deviation, gap: 意味のずれ *imi no zure* divergence in meaning; 印刷のずれ *insatsu no zure* not be in register (printing); 時間のずれ *jikan no zure* time lag; 年齢のずれ *nenrei no zure* age gap.

-zutai 伝い（づたい）　接尾語　suffix

地形・建物などを示す名詞に付いて、「それに沿って行く」意味を添える *Chikei • tate-mono nado wo shimesu meishi ni tsuite, "sore ni sotte iku" imi wo soeru* With nouns denoting physical features, buildings, etc., adds the idea of "along. . .":

• 浜伝いに *hama-zutai ni* along beach; 川伝いに *kawa-zutai ni* along a river; 屋根伝いに逃げる *yane-zutai ni nigeru* flee from roof to roof.

→ *-zoi*

-zutsu ずつ　副助詞　adverbial particle

体言・分量、程度の助数詞に付く *Taigen • bunryō, teido no jo-sūshi ni tsuku* Is added to nominals and to counters expressing quantity or degree.

1. 同じ量を割り当てる *Inaji ryō wo wari-ateru* Denotes equal distribution:

• 一人に一本ずつ *hitori ni ippon-zutsu* one apiece; 三人に一個ずつ *sannin ni ikko-zutsu* one to every three persons.

2. 同一の数量を繰り返す *Dōitsu no sūryō wo kuri-kaesu* Repetition of same quantity:

• 写真帳を一枚ずつ繰る *shashin-chō wo ichimai-zutsu kuru* leaf through photo album; 少しずつ *sukoshi-zutsu* gradually; 僅かずつ *wazuka-zutsu* sparingly.

APPENDIXES

APPENDIX A

IDEOGRAPH READINGS

The fact that *kanji* came to Japan in several waves over a long period, and from several parts of China, gives rise to a variety of ways that *kanji* are used in Japanese. The terms used are:

A. 音読 *on-doku,* 音読み *on-yomi*

The imitation, within the limits of the Japanese sound system, of the Chinese-style reading:

1. 呉音 *Go-on*

Imported through Korea from the *Go* region of southeast China before the Nara era, has many Buddhist-related terms:

- 修業 *shugyō* study; 京都 *Kyōto* Kyoto; 経文 *kyōmon* sutra; 灯明 *tōmyō* votive light.

2. 漢音 *Kan-on*

Brought back by envoys and students in the period from Nara to early Heian, from northwest China; it is the most standard:

- 旅行 *ryokō* travel; 京城 *Keijō* Seoul; 経書 *keisho* Chinese classics; 明白 *meihaku* evident.

3. 唐音 *Tō-on*

Brought back by merchants and monks between the Kamakura and Meiji eras, from the time of the Sung dynasty onwards:

- 行脚 *angya* pilgrimage; 南京 *Nankin* Nanjing; 看経 *kankin* reading the sutras.

4. 慣用音 *kan'yō-on*

"Accepted" Japanese readings:

- 攪拌 originally *kōhan,* now *kakuhan* churning; 消耗 originally *shōkō,* now *shōmō* consumption.

B. 訓読 *kun-doku,* 訓読み *kun-yomi*

The Japanese word that gives the meaning of the ideograph:

1. 正訓 *sei-kun*

One Japanese word for one ideograph:

- 水 *mizu* water; 男 *otoko* male; 高い *takai* high; 見る *miru* see.

2. 義訓 *gi-kun*

A Japanese word expressing the meaning of several ideographs:

- 海苔 *nori* seaweed; 老舗 *shinise* old store; 団扇 *uchiwa* fan.

3. 当て字 *ateji*

Kanji used to express sounds, irrespective of their meaning; the term is also applied to the indiscriminate use of ideographs:

- 天晴れ *appare* splendid; 出鱈目 *detarame* nonsense; 愚連隊 *gurentai* hoodlums.

NOTE. Most two-element compounds have either the *on* reading or the *kun* reading for both elements. In the case of a mixture, we get:

1. 重箱読み *jūbako yomi*

In the order of *on-kun:*

- 団子 *dan-go* dumpling; 縁側 *en-gawa* veranda; 気持ち *ki-mochi* feeling; 頭取 *tō-dori* president.

2. 湯桶読み *yutō yomi*

In the order of *kun-on:*

- 赤字 *aka-ji* deficit; 身分 *mi-bun* social status; 梅酒 *ume-shu* apricot liquor; 夕刊 *yū-kan* evening edition.

APPENDIX B

KANA SYLLABARY

あ	か	さ	た	な	は	ま	や	ら	わ	ん
い	き	し	ち	に	ひ	み		り	ゐ	
う	く	す	つ	ぬ	ふ	む	ゆ	る		
え	け	せ	て	ね	へ	め		れ	ゑ	
お	こ	そ	と	の	ほ	も	よ	ろ	を	

Terms concerning the kana syllabary and the above chart are listed below.

- 行 *gyō* vertical column.
- 段 *dan* horizontal line.
- 濁音 *daku-on* voiced sounds, written with *nigori* marks (*ga, za, da, ba*).
- 清音 *sei-on* unvoiced sounds, written without *nigori* marks.
- 半濁音 *han-dakuon* "p" sounds, formed on the *ha* column.
- 拗音 *yō-on* sounds produced when the small *ya, yu*, or *yo* are added to the *i* horizontal line (*kya, shu, cho*).
- 撥音 *hatsu-on* the *n*, pronounced "m" before *b, m*, and *p*.
- 促音 *soku-on* small *tsu* (っ), signalling a double consonant.
- 長音 *chō-on* long vowel sound.

In the case of "*o*", where Japanese has おう (except in the case of Base 3 of verbs), romaji uses ō. However, with words traditionally written おお (formerly おほ), "*oo*" has been kept so as to facilitate the consulting of *kokugo* sources.

頬	*hoo*	cheek
朴	*hoo*	kind of magnolia
氷	*koori*	ice
郡	*koori*	district
凍る	*kooru*	freeze
催す	*moyoosu*	hold (a function)
頁	*oogai*	*tsukuri* of *kanji*
多い	*ooi*	many, much
狼	*ookami*	wolf
大きい	*ookii*	large (+ *oo-* compounds)
概ね	*oomune*	outline
抑せ	*oose*	command
鵬	*ootori*	legendary bird
覆う	*oou*	cover
公	*ooyake*	public
砲	*oozutsu*	cannon
滞る	*todokooru*	stagnate
十	*too*	ten
遠い	*tooi*	distant
通り	*toori*	road; manner
通る	*tooru*	pass
透る	*tooru*	be transparent

APPENDIX C

NUMBERS AND COUNTING

本数詞 *hon-sūshi* in the *on* reading, are *ichi, ni, san,* etc.; in the *kun* reading, they are *hitotsu, futatsu,* etc. While *hyaku* and *sen* usually stand alone in the singular, *man* needs *ichi* before it to represent ten thousand.

助数詞 *jo-sūshi* the counters, like *-chaku, -hon,* and *-mai,* correspond with the English words "head" (of cattle), "dose" (of medicine), "loaf" (of bread), etc. Most of the following counters are listed in the body of this book:

1. ANIMALS
   - 匹 *hiki* for small animals; 頭 *tō* for large animals; 羽 *wa* for birds and rabbits; 尾 *bi* for fish.

2. BOOKS, PAPERS
   - 部 *bu* for copies of same book; 巻 *kan, maki* for volumes in a set; 冊 *satsu* for numbers of various books; 通 *tsū* for letters, written postcards; 葉 *yō,* 枚 *mai* for sheets; 巻 *kan,* 軸 *jiku,* 端 *tan* for scrolls; 括り *kukuri,* 札 *satsu,* 通 *tsū,* 綴り *tsuzuri* for papers; 封 *fū,* 本 *hon,* 札 *satsu,* 通 *tsū* for letters.

3. BUILDINGS, FURNISHINGS
   - 軒 *ken,* 戸 *ko,* 棟 *tō, mune* for houses; 間 *ma,* 室 *shitsu* for rooms; 堂 *dō,* 寺 *ji,* 宇 *u* for Buddhist temples; 社 *sha,* 座 *za* for Shinto shrines; 領 *ryō* for *fusuma;* 畳 *jō,* 枚 *mai* for *tatami;* 脚 *kyaku* for tables, chairs, etc.; 帖 *jō,* 架 *ka,* 双 *sō* for *byōbu;* 面 *men* for mirrors; 張り *hari,* 枚 *mai* for curtains; 張り *hari,* 枚 *mai,* 連 *ren,* 垂れ *tare* for blinds.

4. CULT OBJECTS
   - 躯 *ku,* 座 *za,* 体 *tai,* 頭 *tō* for statues; 基 *ki* for tombstones and *torii*; 柱 *hashira* for mortuary tablets; 体 *tai* for sets of remains; 具 *gu,* 連 *ren* for praying-beads; 柱 *hashira,* 体 *tai,* 座 *za* for deities.

5. ENTERTAINMENTS
   - 曲 *kyoku* for songs, dances; 本 *hon,* 巻 *kan,* 駒 *koma* for films; 番 *ban,* 席 *seki* for theatrical performances; 番 *ban,* 差し *sashi,* 手 *te* for *Noh;* 場 *ba,* 景 *kei,* 幕 *maku* for sections of a play.

6. FOOD AND DRINK
   - 房 *fusa* for grapes; 顆 *ka,* 個 *ko,* 籠 *kago,* 山 *yama* for fruits; 重ね *kasane,* 個 *ko,* 枚 *mai,* 帖 *jō* for *mochi;* 杯 *hai (san-bai),* 本 *hon,* 献 *kon,* 樽 *taru* for beverages; 皿 *sara,* 一人前 *ichi-ninmae* for *sashimi;* 杯 *hai,* 膳 *zen* for meals; 椀・碗 *wan* for helpings of broth; 丁 *chō* for blocks of *tōfu.*

7. GAMES AND CONTESTS
   - 番 *ban,* 局 *kyoku* for *igo, shōgi;* 本 *hon,* 回 *kai,* 戦 *sen,* 節 *setsu,* 勝負 *shōbu* for games, matches; 番 *ban* for *sumō*; 勝 *shō* for wins; 敗 *hai* for losses.

8. HOUSEHOLD APPLIANCES
   - 張り *hari* for paper lanterns; 本 *hon,* 流れ *nagare,* 旒 *ryū* for flags; 具 *gu,* 揃い *soroi,* 対 *tsui* for tongs; 重ね *kasane,* 組 *kumi* for tiered boxes; 口 *kō* for kettles, pots; 本 *hon,* 張り *hari* for umbrellas; 蓋 *gai,* 枚 *mai,* 笠 *ryū* for bamboo hats; 本 *hon,* 対 *tsui* for folding fans.

9. LITERARY COMPOSITIONS
   - 句 *ku* for *haiku, senryū;* 詩 *shi,* 編 *hen,* 什 *jū,* 連 *ren,* 絶 *zetsu* for Chinese poems; 首 *shu* for *tanka,* Chinese poems; 文 *bun,* 編 *hen,* 巻 *kan,* 章 *shō* for novels.

10. MACHINERY
   - 基 *ki,* 台 *dai* for large, fixed machines; 台 *dai* applies generally.

11. MEDICINES
   - 服 *fuku,* 包 *hō,* 錠 *jō* for tablets, 回 *kai* for times taken, 盛り *mori,* 剤 *zai* for measuring amount.

12. MUSICAL INSTRUMENTS
   - 挺 *chō* for stringed instruments like violin; 本 *hon,* 管 *kan* for wind instruments like flute; 張り *hari,* 張 *chō,* 面 *men* for instruments like *koto;* 台 *dai* for instruments like piano.

13. ORNAMENTS
   - 架 *ka,* 面 *men* for framed pictures; 瓶 *bin, hei,* 個 *ko* for vases of flowers, 幅 *fuku,* 枚 *mai* for unframed pictures; 幅 *fuku,* 軸 *jiku* for hanging scrolls, 対 *tsui* for pairs of these.

14. PLANTS
   - 本 *hon,* 輪 *rin* for flowers; 鉢 *hachi,* 瓶 *hei* for potted plants or *ikebana;* 本 *hon,* 樹 *ju,* 株 *kabu* for trees; 枚 *mai,* 葉 *yō* for plant leaves; 片 *hira,* 枚 *mai* for flower petals.

15. TABLEWARE
   - 個 *ko,* 口 *kō,* 組 *kumi* for teacups; 揃い *soroi,* 膳 *zen* for pairs of chopsticks; 口 *kō,* 組 *kumi,* 枚 *mai* for plates; 口 *kō,* 組 *kumi* for bowls; 挺 *chō* for items of cutlery.

16. TEXTILES, CLOTHING
   - 着 *chaku,* 枚 *mai,* 領 *ryō* for most items, 重 *e,* 重ね *kasane* for layers of clothing, 揃い *soroi* for a suit or set; 本 *hon,* 条 *jō,* 筋 *suji* for *obi;* 張り *hari* for mosquito nets.

17. TRANSPORT, VEHICLES
 • 隻 *seki,* 艘 *sō,* 杯 *hai* for boats and ships; 機 *ki* for planes (便 *bin* for flight); 両 *ryō,* 車 *sha* for freight cars; 本 *hon,* 両 *ryō* for trains; 台 *dai* for cars.

18. WEAPONRY
 • 振り *furi,* 剣 *ken,* 口 *kō,* 腰 *koshi,* 刀 *tō* for swords; 門 *mon* for cannon; 挺 *chō* for guns; 本 *hon,* 条 *jō,* 筋 *suji* for arrows; 張り *hari* for bows; 領 *ryō* for suits of armor.

19. VARIOUS ITEMS
 • 台 *dai,* 機 *ki* for telephones; 度 *do,* 本 *hon,* 回 *kai* for telephone calls; 挺 *chō* for most tools; 荷 *ka* 梱 *kori* for items of luggage; 本 *hon* for rail lines; 泊 *haku* for night's lodging; 枚 *mai,* 面 *men* for ricefields.

APPENDIX D

PUNCTUATION MARKS

句読点
kutō-ten

Following is a list of commonly used Japanese punctuation marks:

。	句点，丸	*kuten, maru*	period
、	読点	*tōten*	comma
•	中黒，中点	*naka-guro, naka-ten*	dot used in lists
「 」	かぎ括弧	*kagi-kakko*	single quotation marks
『 』	二重かぎ	*futae-kagi*	double quotation marks
( )	括弧	*kakko*	parentheses
. . .	点線	*tensen*	ellipsis dots

When writing horizontally, the regular comma (,) is often used. The symbols used to signal the repetition of *kanji* and *kana,* 々, ゝ, ゞ are called 踊り字 *odori-ji;* in the past, many more were in use.

Texts for children are often written with spaces between groups of words. This style of writing is called *wakachi-gaki* (分かち書き).
 • でんしゃの なかで せんせいに あいました。
 Densha no naka de sensei ni aimashita.
 I met my teacher on the train.

APPENDIX E

ONOMATOPOEIA

There are four types of onomatopoeic expressions in Japanese:

1. 擬音語 *gion-go* words that mimic natural sounds.
   Ex. *gatapishi, goro-goro, ton-ton*

2. 擬声語 *gisei-go* words that mimic human or animal noises.
   Ex. *kusu-kusu, wan-wan*

3. 擬態語 *gitai-go* words that describe manner of actions.
   Ex. *noro-noro, teki-paki*

4. 擬情語 *gijō-go* words that describe psychological states.
   Ex. *biku-biku, gakkari, ira-ira*

Correct usage of onomatopoeic expressions presupposes knowing: 1. to which part of speech does the expression belong? 2. does it require a *to*? 3. can *suru* be added, and if so, is the expression transitive or intransitive?

For example, *bara-bara* as a *gion-go* functions as an adverb and takes *to*, as shown in this sentence: *Ame ga bara-bara to furu* (Rain patters down). As a *gitai-go*, however, *bara-bara* is an adjectival noun, and is conjugated accordingly: *kikai wo bara-bara ni shita* (They took the machine to pieces).

Chiya-hoya is an expression that is transitive when *suru* is added: *Kodomo wo chiya-hoya suru* (She spoils her children).

A few expressions, such as *gota-gota* are regarded as nouns: *Gota-gota wo kai-ketsu shita* (They calmed the troubled waters).

Here is a key to understanding the symbols used after each entry word.

と *to* is often added to an expression
副 expression is an adverb
する when *suru* is added, forms an intransitive (自) or transitive (他) expression
形動 expression is used as an adjectival noun
名 expression is used also as a noun
音 expression is a *gion-go*
声 expression is a *gisei-go*
態 expression is a *gitai-go*
情 expression is a *gijō-go*

assari と 副 する 自 態
- 〜した食事 *〜shita shokuji* light meal
- 〜した服装 *〜shita fukusō* simple clothes
- 〜した返事 *〜shita henji* brief answer
- 〜とした性格 *〜to shita seikaku* open-hearted disposition
- 問題を〜解く *mondai wo 〜 toku* solve a problem with ease
- 〜と罪を白状する *〜to tsumi wo hakujō suru* confess (sins) frankly
- 〜と負ける *〜to makeru* give in without a struggle
- 〜正体を見破る *〜 shōtai wo mi-yaburu* have no trouble seeing thru

bara-bara と 副 形動 音/態
- 雨が〜と降る *ame ga 〜to furu* rain patters down
- 機械を〜にする *kikai wo 〜ni suru* take a machine apart
- 帰りは〜だった *kaeri wa 〜datta* came home separately
- 群衆が〜に逃げる *gunshū ga 〜ni nigeru* crowd scatters helter-skelter

bata-bata と 副 する 自 音/態
- 羽を〜させる *hane wo 〜saseru* flap wings
- 階段を〜降りる *kaidan wo 〜 oriru* clatter down stairs
- 〜倒れる *〜 taoreru* go down like flies
- 〜倒産する *〜 tōsan suru* go bankrupt one after another
- 問題が〜と片付く *mondai ga 〜to katazuku* problems simply dissolve

battari と 副 態
- 〜友人に出会う *〜 yūjin ni de-au* "run into" a friend
- 〜止まる *〜 tomaru* come to a sudden stop
- 〜倒れる *〜 taoreru* fall with a thud

biku-biku と 副 する 自 情/態
- …について〜する *. . . ni tsuite 〜suru* be nervous about . . .
- 〜しながら *〜shi-nagara* hesitantly
- 〜暮らす *〜 kurasu* live in fear

bon'yari と 副 する 自 名 情/態
- 一日中〜する *ichinichi-jū 〜suru* idle the whole day away
- 景色が〜する *keshiki ga 〜suru* scene is blurred
- 顔の表情が〜している *kao no hyōjō ga 〜shite iru* have a vacant expression
- (名) このぼんやりめ。 *Kono bon'yari-me!* What a day-dreamer!

boro-boro と 副/形動 態
- 涙が〜零れる *namida ga 〜 koboreru* shed big drops of tears
- 垢が〜落ちる *aka ga 〜 ochiru* dirt comes off in lumps
- 〜になった本 *〜ni natta hon* a book in tatters
- 〜の毛布 *〜no mōfu* a ragged blanket
- ケーキが〜になる *kēki ga 〜ni naru* cake crumbles
- 〜になるまで着る *〜ni naru made kiru* wear out (clothing)

botsu-botsu と 副 名 態
- ～出掛けよう ～ *dekakeyō.* Shall we get moving?
- 人が～集まる *hito ga ～ atsumaru* gather by twos and threes
- ～花が咲く ～ *hana ga saku* flowers begin to bloom
- 疣みたいに～がある *ibo mitai ni ～ ga aru* looks wart-covered

buku-buku と 副 する 自 音/態
- 薬缶が～音を立てる *yakan ga ～ oto wo tateru* kettle makes bubbling sound
- ～泡が立つ ～ *awa ga tatsu* (water) becomes foamy
- ～太っている ～ *futotte iru* be plump
- 水で～している *mizu de ～shite iru* be bloated with water

bura-bura と 副 する 自 態
- 足が～揺れる *ashi ga ～ yureru* legs swing (hanging down)
- 風で～する *kaze de ～suru* swing in breeze
- 家で～する *ie de ～suru* remain at home idle
- 街を～歩き回る *machi wo ～ aruki-mawaru* stroll round town
- ぶらりと立ち寄る *burari to tachi-yoru* drop in
- ぶらりと出掛ける *burari to dekakeru* set out aimlessly
- 銀ぶらを楽しむ *Gin-bura wo tanoshimu* enjoy stroll on Ginza

buru-buru と 副 する 自 音/態
- 機械が～と振動する *kikai ga ～to shindō suru* machine vibrates noisily
- 体が～震える *karada ga ～ furueru* shiver (with cold, fear)

chaku-chaku と 副 態
- ～進歩する ～ *shinpo suru* make steady progress
- 準備が～と進む *junbi ga ～to susumu* preparations go smoothly

chan-to 副 する 自 態
- ～座る ～ *suwaru* sit up straight
- ～した服装 ～ *shita fukusō* proper dress
- 時間を～守る *jikan wo ～ mamoru* be punctual
- お金を～払う *o-kane wo ～ harau* pay exact sum
- 部屋を～片付ける *heya wo ～ katazukeru* put room in order

chibi-chibi と 副 態
- ～と酒を飲む *～to sake wo nomu* sip *sake*
- ～と与える *～to ataeru* dole out

chigu-hagu 形動 態
- 言うことが～だ *iu koto ga ～da* talk incoherently
- ～な靴を履く *～na kutsu wo haku* put on odd shoes
- ～なまま分れる *～na mama wakareru* part in disagreement

chira-chira と 副 する 自 態

• 明かりが～する *akari ga ～suru* light flickers
• 雪が～降る *yuki ga ～furu* there is light snow
• 花が～と散っていく *hana ga ～to chitte iku* blossoms flutter down

chira-hora と 副 態
• 明かりが～と見えてくる *akari ga ～to miete kuru* light appears and disappears
• 花が～咲き始める *hana ga ～ saki-hajimeru* blossoms show here and there
• 客が～見え始める *kyaku ga ～ mie-hajimeru* guests show up in twos and threes.

chiya-hoya と 副 する 他 態
• 子供を～する *kodomo wo ～suru* she spoils her children
• ～お世辞を言われる *～ o-seji wo iwareru* be flattered
• 皆に～される *mina ni ～sareru* be fussed over

dabu-dabu と 副 する 自 形動 音/態
• 水が～と音を立てる *mizu ga ～to oto wo tateru* water gurgles
• ～のズボン *～no zubon* baggy trousers
• 私には～だ *watashi ni wa ～da* it is too large for me
• ソースを～かける *sōsu wo ～ kakeru* drown. . . in sauce
• 腹が～する *hara ga ～suru* have an upset stomach
• 尻が～と揺れ動く *shiri ga ～to yure-ugoku* flabby bottom rolls

dara-dara と 副 する 自 態
• ～仕事をする *～ shigoto wo suru* work at leisurely pace
• ～した坂 *～shita saka* gentle slope
• ～した報告 *～shita hōkoku* lengthy report
• 汗が～と流れる *ase ga ～to nagareru* sweat drips off one

doki-doki と 副 する 自 音/態
• 心臓が～する *shinzō ga ～suru* heart pounds
• あがって～する *agatte ～suru* become nervous

don-don 副 音/態
• 太鼓を～叩く *taiko wo ～ tataku* thump on drum
• 人口が～増える *jinkō ga ～ fueru* population increases rapidly
• ～歩く *～ aruku* walk on and on
• 何でも～言う *nan de mo ～ iu* speak out freely

don'yori と 副 する 自 態
• ～した灰色の空 *～shita hai-iro no sora* leaden sky
• 頭が～と重苦しい *atama ga ～to omo-kurushii* head feels like lead
• 目が～と濁っている *me ga ～to nigotte iru* eyes are glassy

fura-fura と 副 する 自 態

- 疲労で〜する　*hirō de* ～*suru*　be tired out
- 頭が〜する　*atama ga* ～*suru*　feel dizzy
- 〜と歩き回る　～*to aruki-mawaru*　wander about in a daze
- 決心がつかずに〜する　*kesshin ga tsukazu ni* ～*suru*　be unable to make up one's mind

fuwa-fuwa　と　副　する　自　形動　態
- 〜した気持ち　～*shita kimochi*　unsettled state of mind
- 〜したクッション　～*shita kusshon*　soft cushion
- 〜のセーター　～*no sētā*　soft sweater
- 〜と積もった雪　～*to tsumotta yuki*　lightly piled snow
- 毎日〜と過ごす　*mainichi* ～*to sugosu*　idle away one's time

gabu-gabu　と　副　形動　音/態
- 〜飲む　～ *nomu*　drink greedily
- 腹が〜だ　*hara ga* ～*da*　stomach is bloated (with liquid)

gakkari　と　副　する　自　情/態
- 〜する　～*suru*　lose heart
- 〜と疲れる　～*to tsukareru*　become exhausted

gakkuri　と　副　する　自　情/態
- 落第して〜と来る　*rakudai shite* ～*to kuru*　become depressed on failing
- 〜首を垂れる　～ *kubi wo tareru*　bow head suddenly
- 〜と膝をつく　～*to hiza wo tsuku*　fall to one's knees

gasshiri (gatchiri)　と　副　する　自　態
- 〜した体格　～*shita taikaku*　robust build
- 〜と結ぶ　～*to musubu*　bind tightly

gatsu-gatsu　副　する　自　他　態
- 〜食べる　～ *taberu*　wolf down
- 食べ物に〜する　*tabemono ni* ～*suru*　crave food

gaya-gaya　副　する　自　音/態
- 〜騒ぐ　～ *sawagu*　raise Cain
- 〜言う声　～ *iu koe*　Babel of voices

giri-giri　と　副　音/態
- 〜と歯ぎしりをする　～*to ha-gishiri wo suru*　gnash teeth
- 〜の値段　～*no nedan*　rock-bottom price
- 時間〜にやってくる　*jikan* ～*ni yatte kuru*　arrive just in time
- 譲歩できる〜の線　*jōho dekiru* ～*no sen*　limit of concessions
- 〜と歯を食いしばる　～*to ha wo kui-shibaru*　clench teeth
- 〜帯を巻き付ける　～ *obi wo maki-tsukeru*　wind *obi* round and round

gisshiri と 副/形動 態
- ～書物の詰まった箱 *～ shomotsu no tsumatta hako* box stuffed with books
- ～細かい字で書き込む *～ komakai ji de kaki-komu* cram full with fine script
- 列車が人で～だ *ressha ga hito de ～da* train is packed

goro-goro 副 する 自 音/態
- ～という雷 *～to iu kaminari* rolling thunder
- 猫が咽を～鳴らす *neko ga nodo wo ～ narasu* cat purrs
- 目にごみが入って～する *me ni gomi ga haitte ～suru* dust gets into eye and irritates it
- 西瓜が～なっている *suika ga ～ natte iru* watermelons are ripe all over the place
- 家で～している *ie de ～shite iru* be at home idle
- 暑いので～している *atsui no de ～shite iru* be prostrated with the heat

gota-gota と 副 する 自/形動/名 態
- 机の中が～している *tsukue no naka ga ～ shite iru* inside of desk is in disorder
- ～と不平を並べる *～to fuhei wo naraberu* pour out jeremiad
- 家庭内の～が絶えない *katei-nai no ～ga taenai* no end to family dissension

gun-gun と 副 態
- ～と押す *～to osu* push hard
- 背が～と伸びる *se ga ～to nobiru* stature shoots up
- 輸出が～と増える *yushutsu ga ～to fueru* exports rise dramatically
- ～とスピードを上げる *～to spiido wo ageru* accelerate furiously
- 病気が～よくなる *byōki ga ～ yoku naru* patient makes rapid recovery

gura-gura と 副 する 自 態
- 地震で家が～揺れた *jishin de ie ga ～ yureta* house rocked in quake
- 机の脚が～する *tsukue no ashi ga ～suru* desk legs are rickety
- 湯が～煮え立つ *yu ga ～nie-tatsu* (hot) water seethes
- 気持ちがまだ～している *kimochi ga mada ～shite iru* he is still vacillating

guru-guru と 副 態
- 独楽が～回る *koma ga ～ mawaru* top spins (round and round)
- 地球が～自転する *chikyū ga ～jiten suru* earth spins (on own axis)
- すだれを～(と) 巻き上げる *sudare wo ～(to) maki-ageru* roll up blind
- 頭に包帯を～巻く *atama ni hōtai wo ～ maku* wind bandage round head

gussuri と 副 態
- ～眠る *～ nemuru* sleep like a log
- ～眠っている *～ nemutte iru* be fast asleep

guttari と 副 する 自 態
- ～(と)疲れてしまう *～(to) tsukarete shimau* be exhausted

- 長椅子で～している *naga-isu de ～shite iru* be sprawled on sofa
- 暑いので～している *atsui no de ～shite iru* be prostrated with the heat

gut-to 副 態
- ～縄を引っ張る ～ *nawa wo hipparu* pull a rope taut
- ビールを～飲みほす *bīru wo ～ nomi-hosu* down a beer at one gulp
- 輸出が～減る *yushutsu ga ～ heru* exports drop dramatically
- 母より～若い人 *haha yori ～ wakai hito* person far younger than Mother
- 胸に～来る *mune ni ～ kuru* feel a pang of emotion
- 言葉に～詰まる *kotoba ni ～ tsumaru* be lost for words

guzu-guzu 副 する 自 形動 音/態
- 鼻が～している *hana ga ～shite iru* have the sniffles
- ～するな。早く起きろ。 *～suru na! Hayaku oki ro!* Stop dilly-dallying and get up at once!
- ～言わないで、はっきり言え。 ～ *iwanaide, hakkiri ie!* Stop your mumbling and speak out!

gyū-gyū と 副 形動 音/態
- 靴が～鳴る *kutsu ga ～ naru* shoes creak
- 鞄に衣類を～詰める *kaban ni irui wo ～ tsumeru* stuff a suitcase full with clothes
- 電車の中が～だ。 *densha no naka ga ～da.* train is jam-packed
- ～の目に合わせる *～no me ni awaseru* make a person beg for mercy
- ～絞られる ～ *shiborareru* be grilled mercilessly

haki-haki と 副 する 自 態
- ～した人 *～shita hito* brisk person
- ～と答える *～to kotaeru* give a prompt, clear reply

hakkiri と 副 する 自 態
- 山が～見える *yama ga ～ mieru* mountains are clearly visible
- ～した区別 *～shita kubetsu* clear distinction
- ～言う ～ *iu* tell frankly
- 天気が～しない *tenki ga ～shinai* weather is unsettled
- 頭が～しない *atama ga ～shinai* be befuddled

hara-hara と 副 する 自 情/態
- ～しながら試合を見る *～shi-nagara shiai wo miru* watch game with breathless interest
- どうなるかと～する *dō naru ka to ～suru* be on edge about outcome
- 花びらが～と散る *hanabira ga ～to chiru* blossoms fall silently
- ～と涙を流す *～to namida wo nagasu* tears stream down cheeks

hat-to 副 する 自 情/態
- …を見て～する *... wo mite ～suru* be startled at sight of...

• 音を聞いて〜する *oto wo kiite ~suru* be startled at sound of...
• 〜気がつく *~ ki ga tsuku* it suddenly strikes one

heto-heto 形動 態
• 朝から働き続けて〜だ *asa kara hataraki tsuzukete ~da* be exhausted after working since morning
• 〜で、もう歩けない *~de, mō arukenai* be too tired to walk further

hira-hira と 副 する 自 態
• 蝶が〜飛んでいる *chō ga ~ tonde iru* butterfly is fluttering about
• 旗が風に〜する *hata ga kaze ni ~suru* flag waves in breeze

hiso-hiso と 副 態
• 〜と話す *~to hanasu* whisper to one another

hot-to 副 する 自 情/態
• 知らせを聞いて〜する *shirase wo kiite ~ suru* feel relieved at news
• 〜溜息をつく *~ tameiki wo tsuku* heave a sigh of relief

hyokkori と 副 態
• 〜顔を出す *~ kao wo dasu* suddenly pop up

ira-ira 副 する 自/名 情/態
• 騒音で〜する *sō-on de ~suru* be irritated by the noise
• 〜が募る *~ga tsunoru* impatience increases
• 咽が〜する *nodo ga ~suru* throat feels prickly

jikkuri と 副 態
• 〜(と) 考える *~(to) kangaeru* think over carefully
• シチュを〜煮込む *shichū wo ~ ni-komu* simmer stew slowly

jime-jime と 副 する 自 態
• 〜した空気 *~shita kūki* damp air
• 〜した土地 *~shita tochi* damp ground

jiri-jiri と 副 する 自 音/情/態
• ベルが〜鳴る *beru ga ~ naru* bell tinkles
• 〜しながら待つ *~shi-nagara matsu* wait impatiently
• 肉を火の上で〜焼く *niku wo hi no ue de ~ yaku* roast meat over fire
• 太陽が〜照り付ける *taiyō ga ~ teri-tsukeru* sun blazes down
• 〜と差を詰める *~to sa wo tsumeru* close in on

jiro-jiro と 副 態
• 人を〜と見てはだめ *hito wo ~to mite wa dame* don't stare at people
• 〜見られるのは困る *~ mirareru no wa komaru* I hate being stared at

kan-kan と 副 形動 音/情/態
- 鐘が～鳴る *kane ga ～ naru* bell clangs
- ～に(なって)怒る *～ni (natte) okoru* fly into a rage
- 太陽が～照る *taiyō ga ～ teru* sun blazes down
- ～におこった炭火 *～ni okotta sumibi* red-hot charcoals

kibi-kibi と 副 する 自 態
- 動きは～している *ugoki wa ～shite iru* move with agility
- ～と仕事を片付ける *～to shigoto wo katazukeru* get the job done briskly

kichin-to 副 する 自 態
- 服装が～している *fukusō ga ～shite iru* be neatly dressed
- 何でも～やる *nan de mo ～ yara* do everything to a nicety

kippari と 副 態
- ～と断る *～to kotowaru* give a flat refusal
- たばこを～と止める *tabako wo ～ to yameru* give up smoking once and for all

kira-kira と 副 する 自 態
- 星が～輝く *hoshi ga ～ kagayaku* stars twinkle
- 目に涙が～光る *me ni namida ga ～ hikaru* tears glisten in one's eyes

koso-koso と 副 する 自 音/態
- ～部屋を出る *～ heya wo deru* slip out of room
- ～と噂する *～to uwasa suru* spread rumors
- ～話し合う *～ hanashi-au* converse in whispers

kossori と 副 態
- ～逃げる *～ nigeru* steal away
- ～会う *～ au* meet in secret

kotsu-kotsu と 副 音/態
- 靴音が～響く *kutsu-oto ga ～ hibiku* sound of footsteps is heard
- 戸を～叩く *to wo ～ tataku* knock on door
- ～働く *～ hataraku* work away steadily
- ～読書する *～ dokusho suru* read assiduously
- ～金を溜める *～ kane wo tameru* save money bit by bit

kowa-gowa 副 情
- 猛犬に～近づく *mōken ni ～ chikazuku* approach fierce dog with apprehension
- ～職員室に入る *～ shokuin-shitsu ni hairu* enter staffroom timidly

kukkiri と 副 する 自 態
- 富士山が～見える *Fuji-san ga ～ mieru* Mt. Fuji stands out clearly

kusu-kusu と 副 声/態
- 〜(と) 笑う *〜(to) warau* titter, giggle

kuyo-kuyo 副 する 自 情/態
- 〜することはない *〜suru koto wa nai* Take it easy!
- 〜して暮らす *〜shite kurasu* fret one's days away

kyoro-kyoro と 副 する 自 態
- 目を〜させて *me wo 〜 sasete* looking around curiously
- 部屋を〜見る *heya wo 〜 miru* stare around room

kyoton-to 副 する 自 情/態
- 〜した顔をする *〜shita kao wo suru* look stupefied
- 見知らぬ人に話し掛けられて〜してしまう *mi-shiranu hito ni hanashi-kakerarete 〜shite shimau* be bewildered on being addressed by a stranger

mago-mago 副 する 自 情/態
- 時間どおりに来ないので〜する *jikan-dōri ni konai no de 〜suru* be at a loss when a person doesn't turn up on time
- 駅で〜している *eki de 〜shite iru* loiter in a station

maza-maza と 副 態
- 〜と思い出す *〜to omoidasu* recall vividly
- 〜と目に浮かぶ *〜to me ni ukabu* visualize clearly

mecha-kucha (目茶苦茶) 形動 名 態
- 部屋は〜だ *heya wa 〜da* room is (in) a mess
- 〜な振る舞い *〜na furumai* reckless conduct
- 〜になる *〜ni naru* be thrown into confusion

mecha-mecha 形動 名 態
- 〜に壊れる *〜ni kowareru* be smashed to pieces

meki-meki と 副 態
- 病気が〜よくなった *byōki ga 〜 yoku natta* he made a rapid recovery
- 〜と売り出す *〜to uri-dasu* suddenly become popular (young idol)

moji-moji と 副 する 自 情/態
- 〜しながら *〜shi-nagara* hesitantly
- 〜せずに言う *〜sezu ni iu* speak frankly

muka-muka と 副 する 自 情/態
- 胸が〜する *mune ga 〜suru* feel nauseated
- 見るたびに〜してくる *miru tabi ni 〜shite kuru* boil up whenever I see him

mura-mura と 副 情/態

- 怒りが〜と沸いてくる *ikari ga ~to waite kuru* anger boils up
- 〜と闘志が湧いてくる *~ to tōshi ga waite kuru* fighting spirit wells up

mut-to 副 する 自 情/態
- 〜して立ち去る *~shite tachi-saru* go off in a huff
- 〜口を閉じる *~ kuchi wo tojiru* clam up sullenly
- 〜した臭いがする *~shita nioi ga suru* there is a stale odor
- 部屋の中が〜する *heya no naka ga ~suru* room is stuffy

neba-neba 副 する 自 態
- キャンデーが〜する *kyandē ga ~suru* candy is sticky
- 納豆は〜して糸を引く *nattō wa ~shite ito wo hiku* natto is tacky and draws out in threads

niko-niko と 副 する 自 態
- 子供を見て〜する *kodomo wo mite ~suru* smile at the child
- 〜しながら、あいさつする *~shi-nagara, aisatsu suru* greet with a smile

niya-niya と 副 する 自 態
- 〜している *~shite iru* have a smirk on one's face

nonbiri と 副 する 自 情/態
- 〜と田舎に住む *~to inaka ni sumu* relax in country
- そんなに〜してはいられない *sonna ni ~shite wa irarenai* can't afford to remain idle like that
- たまには〜したい *tama ni wa ~shitai* I should like to take it easy from time to time

noro-noro と 副 する 自 態
- 〜した亀 *~shita kame* slow tortoise
- 〜運転 *~ unten* driving at snail's pace
- 〜と仕事をする *~to shigoto wo suru* work sluggishly

nuru-nuru と 副 する 自 態
- うなぎは〜する *unagi wa ~ suru* eels are slippery
- 油で〜している *abura de ~shite iru* be oily

pachi-pachi と 副 する 自 音/態
- 〜と算盤をはじく *~to soroban wo hajiku* click abacus beads
- 〜とシャッターを切る *~to shattā wo kiru* snap in rapid succestion
- 〜と火花を散らす *~to hibana wo chirasu* send sparks flying
- 目を〜させる *me wo ~saseru* blink

para-para と 副 形動 音/態
- 雨が〜降り出す *ame ga ~ furi-dasu* rain begins to patter down

- 真珠が〜と飛び散る *shinju ga 〜 to tobi-chiru* pearls scatter with a pattering sound
- 聴衆は〜だ *chōshū wa 〜da* only a few listeners present

pat-to 副 する 自 態
- 明かりが〜つく *akari ga 〜 tsuku* light flashes on
- 噂が〜広がる *uwasa ga 〜 hirogaru* rumor spreads like wildfire
- 〜しない成績 *〜shinai seiseki* unimpressive results

peko-peko 副 する 自 形動 音/態
- 石油缶を〜言わせる *sekiyu-kan wo 〜 iwaseru* make a kerosene can go "clunk"
- 目上に〜する *me-ue ni 〜suru* cringe to one's superiors
- お腹が〜だ *o-naka ga 〜da* I'm famished

pera-pera と 副 する 自 形動 態
- 秘密を〜しゃべる *himitsu wo 〜 shaberu* blurt out secrets
- 英語も〜だ *Eigo mo 〜 da* be fluent in English, too
- ページを〜めくる *pēji wo 〜mekuru* riffle through a book
- 〜の紙 *〜no kami thin paper*
- 〜の手ぬぐい *〜no tenugui* threadbare towel

pika-pika 副 する 自 形動 態
- ダイヤが〜光る *daiya ga 〜 hikaru* diamonds sparkle
- 〜の家具 *〜no kagu* well-polished furniture
- 靴を〜に磨く *kutsu wo 〜ni migaku* polish shoes to a shine

pin-to 副 する 自 音/態
- ギターの糸を〜はじく *gitā no ito wo 〜 hajiku* pluck guitar strings
- 綱を〜張る *tsuna wo 〜 haru* pull a rope taut
- その説は〜来ない *sono setsu wa 〜 konai* that theory doesn't appeal to me
- 危険を〜感じる *kiken wo 〜 kanjiru* sense danger vividly

pittari (pitari) と 副 する 自 態
- 蓋は〜くっついている *futa wa 〜 kuttsuite iru* lid is stuck fast
- 戸を〜閉める *to wo 〜 shimeru* close a door tight
- 〜した挨拶 *〜shita aisatsu* admirably suited greeting
- その帽子は君に〜だ *sono bōshi wa kimi ni 〜da* that hat suits you to a tee
- 〜と止まる *〜to tomaru* stop dead

poka-poka と 副 する 自 音/態
- 〜した春の陽射し *〜shita haru no hi-zashi* warm, spring sunshine
- 頭を〜殴る *atama wo 〜 naguru* rain blows on a person's head

pokkari (pokari) と 副 態

- 雲が～浮かぶ *kumo ga ～ ukabu* clouds float lightly
- ～穴の開いた道路 *～ ana no aita dōro* road having a large pothole

pokkuri と 副 態
- 埴輪の頭が～落ちる *haniwa no atama ga ～ ochiru* head of *haniwa* crumbles
- 倒れて～死ぬ *taorete ～ shinu* suddenly collapse and die
- ～病 *～-byō* disease causing sudden death

pota-pota 副 音/態
- 汗が～落ちる *ase ga ～ ochiru* sweat drips (from forehead)
- 水が～落ちる音がする *mizu ga ～ ochiru oto ga suru* drip of water is heard

potsu-potsu と 副 名 態
- 壁に泥が～付いている *kabe ni doro ga ～ tsuite iru* wall is splotched with mud
- 人家が～立っている *jinka ga ～ tatte iru* there are a few scattered houses
- 雨が～降り出す *ame ga ～ furi-dasu* sprinkle of rain begins

pun-pun と 副 する 自 形動 情/態
- 父は～怒った *chichi wa ～ okotta* Father was furious
- 酒気が～臭う *shuki ga ～ niou* there is a strong smell of liquor

puri-puri と 副 する 自 態
- ～怒る *～ okoru* fly into a rage
- ～太った人 *～ futotta hito* pudgy person

sappari 副 する 自 形動 態
- ～した気性 *～shita kishō* frank disposition
- ～した味の *～shita aji no* lightly seasoned
- ～した服装 *～shita fukusō* neat dress
- 部屋が～している *heya ga ～shite iru* room is neat and tidy
- ～分からない *～ wakaranai* can't make head or tail of
- このごろ～会っていない *kono goro ～ atte inai* haven't seen him recently
- 成績は～だ *seiseki wa ～da* marks are atrocious

sassa-to 副 態
- ～片付ける *～ katazukeru* lose no time in tidying up
- ～食事をする *～ shokuji wo suru* hurry (through) meal
- ～出ていけ。 *～ dete ike!* Get out!

sesse-to 副 態
- ～働く *～ hataraku* work hard
- ～通う *～ kayou* frequent (a place)

shibu-shibu 渋々 と 副 態

- 〜とついてくる *〜to tsuite kuru* follow... reluctantly
- 〜承諾する *〜 shōdaku suru* consent with bad grace

shikkari と 副 する 自 態
- 基盤が〜している *kiban ga 〜shite iru* foundation is firm
- 〜したお嫁さん *〜shita o-yome-san* sterling bride
- 〜働いている *〜 hataraite iru* be working away steadily
- 〜した相場 *〜shita sōba* stable exchange

shiku-shiku と 副 する 自 音/態
- 〜(と)泣く *〜(to) naku* quietly sob
- 腹が〜痛む *hara ga 〜 itamu* have nagging stomach ache

sowa-sowa 副 する 自 情/態
- うれしくて〜している *ureshikute 〜shite iru* be thrilled
- 〜した学生 *〜shita gakusei* restless student

soyo-soyo と 副 態
- 春風が〜と吹いている *haru-kaze ga 〜to fuite iru* there is a gentle spring breeze
- カーテンが風に〜と揺れる *kāten ga kaze ni 〜to yureru* curtain blows gently with the breeze

sugo-sugo と 副 態
- 叱られて〜帰ってくる *shikararete 〜 kaette kuru* come home dejected after being scolded

sukkari 副 態
- 〜人が変わった *〜 hito ga kawatta* be an entirely different person
- 〜白状する *〜 hakujō suru* make a clean breast of...
- 〜破壊される *〜 hakai sareru* be reduced to rubble

sukkiri と 副 する 自 情/態
- 服装が〜している *fukusō ga 〜 shite iru* be neatly dressed
- 問題は〜しない *mondai wa 〜 shinai* matter is unclear
- 〜した文章 *〜shita bunshō* lucid writing
- 頭が〜する *atama ga 〜suru* feel refreshed

sunnari と 副 する 自 態
- 〜した足 *〜shita ashi* slender, shapely legs
- 〜勝ち抜く *〜 kachi-nuku* go on winning comfortably
- 議案が〜と通った *gian ga 〜to tootta* bill passed without dissent

sura-sura と 副 態
- 〜答える *〜 kotaeru* answer without hesitation
- 〜と読む *〜to yomu* read smoothly

sure-sure 名 形動 態
- 地面〜に飛んでいく *jimen 〜ni tonde iku* fly skimming the ground
- 車が〜に通り過ぎる *kuruma ga 〜ni toori-sugiru* cars pass almost touching
- 終電車に〜で間に合う *shū-densha ni 〜de ma ni au* make last train by skin of one's teeth

suya-suya と 副 態
- 〜眠っている *〜 nemutte iru* be sleeping peacefully

taji-taji と 副 形動 態
- 問い詰められて〜となる *toi-tsumerarete 〜to naru* flinch under cross-examination
- 攻撃に〜だ *kōgeki ni 〜da* waver under attack

tappuri と 副 形動 態
- 燃料は〜ある *nenryō wa 〜 aru* have plenty of fuel
- 愛敬〜だ *aikyō 〜da* be full of charm
- 〜一時間はかかる *〜 ichijikan wa kakaru* take a good hour

teki-paki と 副 する 自 態
- 〜した人 *〜shita hito* person of quick decision
- 〜と仕事を片付ける *〜to shigoto wo katazukeru* get a job done briskly

tobo-tobo と 副 態
- 暗い夜道を〜と歩く *kurai yomichi wo 〜to aruku* walk along a dark road at night with faltering steps

ton-ton と 副 形動 音/態
- 〜と戸を叩く *〜to to wo tataku* go "knock-knock" on door
- 話が〜と進む *hanashi ga 〜to susumu* talks make smooth progress
- 損得無しの〜だ *son-toku nashi no 〜da* break even

totto-to と 副 態
- 〜出て行け。 *〜 dete ike!* Get out of my sight!

tsuku-zuku と 副 態
- 〜有り難く思う *〜 arigataku omou* feel deeply indebted
- 〜嫌になる *〜 iya ni naru* be disgusted
- 〜眺める *〜 nagameru* gaze intently at

tsuru-tsuru と 副 形動 音/態
- 〜とうどんをすする *〜to udon wo susuru* slurp *udon*
- 〜に磨く *〜ni migaku* give a high polish to
- 頭が〜に禿る *atama ga 〜ni hageru* go completely bald

uki-uki と 副 する 自 情/態

- 〜と出掛ける *~to dekakeru* set off in high spirits
- 心が〜してくる *kokoro ga ~shite kuru* be elated

ukkari と 副 する 自 情/態
- 〜して駅を乗り越す *~shite eki wo nori-kosu* absent-mindedly ride past one's station
- 〜本を家に忘れてくる *~ hon wo ie ni wasurete kuru* inadvertently leave book at home

unzari と 副 する 自 形動 情/態
- 雨ばかり続いて〜する *ame bakari tsuzuite ~suru* be fed up with the long rain
- 長話に〜する *naga-banashi ni ~suru* be bored with the long talk

uto-uto と 副 する 自 態
- 講演の間〜している *kōen no aida ~shite iru* doze off during a lecture
- 〜と眠ってしまう *~to nemutte shimau* drop off to sleep

uttori と 副 する 自 情/態
- 〜と見つめる *~to mitsumeru* gaze in rapture at
- その美しさに〜する *sono utsukushisa ni ~suru* be fascinated by its beauty

uya-muya 形動 名 態
- 問題を〜にしておく *mondai wo ~ni shite oku* leave a matter unresolved
- 〜のうちに終わる *~no uchi ni owaru* end inconclusively
- 〜な返事をする *~na henji wo suru* be non-committal

waku-waku と 副 する 自 情/態
- 夏休みを〜して待つ *natsu-yasumi wo ~shite matsu* look forward eagerly to summer holidays

yaki-moki 副 する 自 情/態
- 遅れに〜する *okure ni ~suru* be impatient with delay
- 病気が治らないので〜する *byōki ga naoranai no de ~suru* be concerned about not getting better

yochi-yochi と 副 する 自 態
- 赤ん坊が〜歩く *akanbō ga ~ aruku* baby toddles

yota-yota と 副 する 自 態
- 酔っ払いが〜歩く *yopparai ga ~ aruku* drunk walks unsteadily

yukkuri と 副 する 自 態
- 〜話す *~ hanasu* speak slowly; have a good talk
- 〜眠る *~ nemuru* have a good night's rest
- 〜旅をする *~ tabi wo suru* travel by easy stages

• ～してください *～shite kudasai* Make yourself at home

zara-zara と 副 する 自 形動 名 音/態
• 小石が～と落ちる *koishi ga ～to ochiru* pebbles fall with a rattling sound
• 畳が～している *tatami ga ～shite iru* tatami feel rough
• 声が～している *koe ga ～shite iru* is hoarse

zat-to 副 態
• ～言えば *～ ieba* roughly speaking
• ～説明する *～ setsumei suru* explain briefly
• ～目を通す *～ me wo toosu* skim through

zoku-zoku 副 する 自 態
• 寒さで～する *samusa de ～suru* shiver with cold
• 蛇を見て背中が～してくる *hebi wo mite senaka ga ～shite kuru* feel creepy on seeing a snake

zot-to 副 する 自 情/態
• 見ただけで～する *mita dake de ～suru* shudder at mere sight of
• ～させるような話 *～saseru yō na hanashi* blood-curdling story

zuka-zuka と 副 態
• ～と家の中へ入り込む *～to ie no naka e hairi-komu* barge right into house

zuke-zuke と 副 態
• 何でも～言う人 *nan de mo ～ iu hito* one who speaks his mind

zurari と 副 態
• 車が～と並んでいる *kuruma ga ～to narande iru* fleet of cars is lined up